Christian Home Educators'
CURRICULUM MANUAL
JUNIOR/SENIOR HIGH
by Cathy Duffy

Published by
Home Run Enterprises
12531 Aristocrat Avenue
Garden Grove, California 92641

ISBN 0-929320-04-2

Acknowledgements

My thanks to all the home educators who have shared their experience and expertise. I always appreciate hearing about different families' experiences with materials, because the true test of anything is how well it works in practical usage, rather than how good it looks in the brochure. Thus, this book is a reflection of the experience of many, many home educators.

There are a few people who helped substantially beyond sharing their experiences. Valerie Thorpe has contributed in numerous ways to various editions of this book. Bethany Bennett has helped also with substantive editing. Ingeborg Kendall applied the wealth of her professional experience with careers and college entry, along with her experience in home educating her own two children, as she "edited" parts of this book.

My husband has been infinitely patient as I devoted endless hours to research and writing, and my children have provided the encouragement to spend that time because of the growth in Christian character that I see in their lives, which I attribute largely to the privilege that God has given us in home education.

- Cathy Duffy

Table of Contents

Introduction

In our critical thinking class, we discussed an example of how appearances influence our thinking. If we read the local newspaper from Town A, noting that three-fourths of the articles had to do with criminal activity, and compared this to a similar newspaper from Town B, which devoted only one-fourth of its articles to crime, could we rightly conclude that there is much more crime in Town A than Town B? Definitely not! Each newspaper's policy and purposes would need to be examined. We would have to consider how many reporters were assigned to cover crime rather than society, sports, and business news. Numerous other factors could be important.

A nagging concern I have felt all through the writing of this book has been the overall impression which it leaves with the reader. I fear that by devoting so much space to college preparation and traditional educational materials, people will assume that both are always the avenues of first choice.

One of my goals has been to provide the necessary information for whatever approach people choose, while providing some ideas about why we might choose one alternative over another. The description of traditional record keeping and course requirements simply takes up more space than creative alternatives.

In truth, many home educated teens have been educated in very unconventional ways. College entry has not been dependent upon traditional documentation and courses of study.

My concern is that we have some conscious goals rather than that we "do things properly" or follow any particular road to reach those goals.

As I consider all of the information going into this book, I realize that it can easily seem overwhelming. The abundance of information to consider is more than enough to cause us to have second thoughts about this home education venture.

Many of us chose home education for our teens based upon negative reasons such as avoidance of bad situations, school failure, or lack of money for private school. Negative motivation is not enough to carry us through for very long. We need to come up with some positive reasons for going to all this trouble or we are likely to feel resentful and give up easily when the going gets rough.

Here are some positive reasons for home educating teenagers that I have come up with both from our experience and that of others.

Spiritual growth - home educated teens are not constantly weighing their spiritual walk against what is acceptable in the eyes of their peers. There is time and opportunity for spiritual growth.

The ability to stand alone - because they do not have to spend the majority of their time with peers, they are much less concerned about fitting in. (There are exceptions to this among home schooled teens!) They tend to develop their own convictions and stick by them.

Confidence - schools are competitive environments that cause many students to lose confidence in their ability to do anything well. At home we can develop individual strengths and provide encouragement as needed without having to combat the destructive criticism some teens endure in school.

Responsibility - teens at home usually have a significant amount of responsibility. Some help teach and care for younger brothers and sisters. Some help in family businesses. Some are involved with other activities that encourage mature and responsible behavior.

Self-government - most teens are doing much of their work independently. They learn to schedule themselves. Many of them discover that learning is something that they are doing for themselves rather than for someone else, and some of them design their own courses of study based upon their own goals.

Stewardship - they learn that they can make wise and foolish choices in using their time. Most find that they have time to pursue other interests if they wisely use study time.

Pursuit of special interests - home educated teens generally have time to pursue hobbies or sports, develop talents, or work on projects of their own design.

Socialization - most home educated teens are able to interact well with people of different ages since they are not restricted to peer interaction the majority of the time. Most of them can carry on an interesting conversation.

Consideration for special learning needs - teens with learning disabilities can be successful at home because of the one-on-one teaching and use of special resources that fit their needs.

Exposure - teens have opportunities to see more of "real life" than when restricted to classrooms. They are better prepared to make career choices.

Work experience - many home educated teens work for family businesses, other employers, or themselves. They have flexibility in their school schedules that makes working easier.

Family unity - this is one of the most important "by-products" of home education we and others have experienced. Our teens are not ashamed to be part of our families. We are all working together toward common goals. Each of us has a necessary role in the family to support and encourage each other. Instead of trials, our teenagers are blessings!

These are some of the positive goals that we should be focusing on. We realize that home educating some teenagers will be a constant battle. Home education does not automatically change personalities and family relationships. These things take time, energy, and much prayer. There are no guarantees for particular results, but we certainly can influence the situation. When we feel discouraged, tired, and overwhelmed, as we all do from time to time, it helps to examine the fruit of our labors. Is it worth all of the trouble? Definitely yes!

Part One

Planning

Chapter One

First Things First

Why

"Daddy, why do you put gas in the car?"

"Because the car needs gas to make it go."

"But, Daddy, why do you need the car to go?"

"So I can go to work, Sweetheart."

"But why do you need to go to work? Why can't you stay home with us?"

"Because we need the money that I get from working to pay for our food. If I don't go to work, we will need to stop eating."

"Oh."

Conversations with three-year-olds can be very frustrating, but we ought to listen closely to the kinds of questions they ask. A three-year-old is concerned about fundamental reasons for why things are as they are. As we grow older, we still sometimes wonder, but we often cease asking questions, frequently because we are embarrassed that we do not know the answers in the first place. We become accustomed to doing things simply because we see others doing them, and these things then become habit or custom. It is not long before we lose sight of our fundamental reasons for our actions, even if we knew what they were in the beginning.

Our educational plans are easy prey for the forces of custom and habit, partly because it is so rare that anyone dares to do anything radically different educationally. Now, here we are, choosing to educate our teenagers at home—a radical decision. Yet, even having taken that radical step, we still tend either ignorantly or gullibly to accept traditional goals and methods. We accept statements such as, "You can't get into college without a high school diploma," as gospel truth, especially when they come from professionals in the education field. We are just too accustomed to accepting what we read and what we are told (especially by authorities) about education and other topics without asking questions. We also find it more comfortable to do things as we remember them being done in our own educational experience.

Home education is by its nature at least a step or two away from the established trail, so if we have made that initial commitment to home educate a teenager, we have already shown a willingness to consider and choose alternatives. But we need to maintain that questioning attitude. We often get caught up in traps of custom and habit when we choose the methods and materials that we will use. We do not really know what we are getting into, so it usually seems best to rely upon course work laid out by someone who has more educational experience than us. That may not be a bad choice, but, at the same time, it may not be the better choice.

If we are home educating a child who had difficulty with typical school curriculum, more of the same is unlikely to work at home. If we have a child with stronger mechanical skills than academic skills, we should be providing opportunities for development of those mechanical skills rather than concentrating solely on the academic. When honestly evaluating educational choices, how willing are we to choose for ourselves a path that is quite different from everyone else's? Are we willing to ask the fundamental questions, "What should my child learn?; Why should my child learn this?"; and, "How and when will he best learn it?"

We then face questions that take us back to our basic philosophy of life. Why do we do anything? Our thoughts, words, and actions ultimately reflect our basic beliefs—at least they should. Consider the philosophy of some who believe in the theory of evolution. If a person believes that man evolved from animals, then a logical conclusion is that man is essentially of no more worth than an animal. With this belief, it is easy to justify abortion, euthanasia, infanticide, etc. In fact, it makes excellent sense for him to weed out the weak of his species so that the strong have a better chance of survival.

Let us apply this to education. If we believe that man exists to serve the State, then his education should be structured to produce a good servant for the State. The student will learn not to question the authority and wisdom of his master. He will learn the skills deemed useful by the State and look to it for approval for his actions. He will strive to be what the State desires—a productive, uncomplaining, unquestioning servant to further the State's goals. If the State decides that it knows best how to raise young children and mandates state day care centers for all preschool age children, a good citizen will gladly enroll his or her children. If the State decides, as it has done in California, that creation science is false and evolution is true, we are not to question its authority and wisdom.

A more common, although unacknowledged, philosophy that influences education is that of self as the center of one's existence. If we believe that man exists to serve himself ("Looking out for number one!"), then we cannot expect him to do anything beyond that which brings him pleasure and satisfaction. Education may or may not do this. What educational goals are valid for a person who wants to meet only his personal needs? Academic skills are valid only insofar as they serve as a barter item that can be traded for money to spend on personal fulfillment. If those personal desires and needs are already taken care of, what remaining motivation is there for education?

Alternatively, if we believe that man exists to serve God, our allegiance shifts from the State or the self to God. The kind of education given to a servant of the Almighty God should differ drastically from that given to a servant of the State or the self because the purposes are vastly different. A servant of God desires to learn the skills that will help him to serve God's purposes, and he looks to the unchangeable God for wisdom and direction. Meanwhile, a servant of the State wants to do that which pleases other men, and a person who plans to serve only himself, will be asking, "What's in it for me?"

So, before beginning, we need to ask ourselves, "What do we believe—about God, about life, about man's purpose in life?" If we have a strong spiritual foundation, the task is easier. But we need to apply our spiritual beliefs to every area of life, not just those with which we are comfortable. Those beliefs should influence everything we do, including educational choices. We should choose among educational alternatives with God's purposes in mind.

The state you live in may have exceeded its authority in limiting your educational options. It may require that you cover specific course work or that you use specific books or that you have a State certified teacher supervising your work. It has its own purposes in mind. Check carefully before accepting their assertions of authority over you. If they are within the law, try to work with them as much as possible in good conscience without sacrificing the education that your child should receive or the convictions you hold. If necessary, choose as Peter did to obey God rather than man. (Acts 4:19)

How

We should now have at least the beginnings of a philosophical foundation upon which to build. If thinking about the "whys" of life is new to you, you will likely need several years for your ideas to develop. You will probably be adjusting your philosophy periodically as fresh insights find their way into your thinking. We can't wait until we have it all together to begin home education—it will never happen. But at the least, make sure you have a starting perspective, be it even so undeveloped as a new Christian's statement of faith in the saving work of Jesus Christ. Salvation itself brings us into the knowledge that we belong to Him, not to ourselves. This is an important perspective to have when approaching education.

You and I may not be in agreement about our basic philosophy of life, but that is not the point. The point is that we must have a philosophy as a guide to point us in a direction. If we give little or no thought to life or man's purpose here, we have no underpinnings for our educational choices. The State is all too ready to take over the education of our child, filling our purposeless void with its own agenda. Without philosophic direction for our child's education, we might as well relinquish that responsibility to the State.

As we begin to choose how we will proceed to educate our children, our philosophy should be close at hand dictating which choices are appropriate—in fact helping us to form a philosophy of education. That philosophy of education will be the beliefs we have about how education, as we view it, can best be accomplished.

Let us look at three different philosophies of education and some of the outcomes that result.

Public schools, in spite of classes on self-esteem and self-actualization, follow an underlying philosophy that places society above the individual. Their purpose is to produce citizens who will be productive rather than a drain on society, and who will help to support them in perpetuating the public school system. Their purposes have to do with saving welfare costs, providing the business sector with employees of varying capabilities, and producing citizens who are properly socialized—able to interact with others according to accepted custom. Obviously they are having serious trouble meeting these goals. But, based on their philosophical objectives, the public schools have developed an educational philosophy that includes assuming the task of being substitute parents, teaching children about sex, drugs, alcohol, self-esteem, and other subjects that they feel will help to produce adults fitted for our society. Traditional educational courses are still taught, but traditional courses are often overshadowed by these State-mandated courses that go far beyond what many of us feel are appropriate to the role of schools.

Christian Liberty Academy is an education provider with a different educational philosophy. Christian Liberty Academy offers a home education correspondence program. Its goals are overtly religious. It says, "Our educational system is religious in that all education is inescapably religious. It is impossible to train a child in an ideological vacuum that is morally, ethically, and religiously neutral. To attempt to do so is to make the child a practical, if not a professing atheist. Education will either be Christian or it will not be Christian. It will either tend to produce Christians or it will produce the opposite." (Christian Liberty Press Catalog, 1988-89.) Because of its educational philosophy, the Academy stresses the traditional basic subjects, loyalty and patriotism, the free enterprise system, the strength and importance of the family, and the importance of diligence and hard work—the old Puritan work ethic, along with strong Christian course content.

David and Micki Colfax are a non-Christian couple living on a remote ranch in northern California who have gained national recognition home schooling their four sons.[1] Three of their sons have received scholarships to Har-

---

1   You can read about the Colfax family in their book, *Homeschooling for Excellence.*

vard University. The Colfaxes developed their educational philosophy through their experience. They saw that each boy had special interests and talents, so they provided plenty of books, materials, and equipment and let them explore their interests, rather than trying to cover every standard subject. They did believe in and provide a foundation in the basics of math and English, but provided little structure beyond that. Within their educational philosophy is room for developing individual talents and using a wide variety of methods, including some that are very untraditional, to accomplish goals.

These three examples show how diverse philosophies of education and their outcomes can be. The way we proceed with our home education should be an outgrowth of our philosophy.

Diversity in Approach

Just because we are Christians does not mean that we must duplicate Christian Liberty Academy in our approach. All Christians do not have to follow a "party line" when it comes to education. We have to decide what we feel is true about education. Consider questions such as these: Do we feel that children learn best by repetition and memorization or by experience? Should teenagers be allowed to work independently and assume responsibility for either learning or not, or should there be constant enforcement? How much say should teenagers have in choosing which subjects to study? Should vocational subjects be valued as highly as traditional school subjects?

How we approach education should be an individual decision based upon our philosophy or beliefs. If our philosophy is still in the formative stages, we might rely on the example or directions of others as to how to proceed with home education. But, as we develop our philosophy, we will also be developing our own specific ideas about how to best educate our children. In a group of even a small number of veteran home educators, the discussions are sure to get hot and heavy. Each of them has had time to think and work through her (or his) ideas about education. They are bound to have some different and even contradictory ideas.

Since we are talking about teaching teenagers, it is important to remember that these young people are at an age when they too have ideas and opinions and want to understand why they are doing things. If we cannot provide a good rationale, we might find ourselves battling over the validity of daily assignments or else imposing arbitrary authority. Then the issue becomes one of control rather than what is appropriate for study. Enforcement, when not backed up by sound reasons, can lead to serious problems in our relationships with our teenagers.

Be Prepared

Do not casually dismiss the need for personally developing your own ideas about education. At some point you will probably be required to defend your ideas about home education to authorities, relatives, friends, or your children.

What

Our basic philosophy of life tells us WHY we are doing what we are doing. Our educational philosophy takes our philosophy to a deeper, more practical level by telling us HOW we plan to go about accomplishing our goals. By combining the WHY and the HOW we should arrive at the

WHAT—the subjects or courses to study. Sometimes we are bound by the restraints of state requirements and must teach a very specific list of subjects. But, in most states, we have quite a bit of leeway in interpreting requirements. The constriction is more likely to come from our own (parents' and teen's) plans for the future.

One of the primary concerns is college entry. Colleges usually require that high school students complete specific courses to qualify for entry. However, even though colleges list specific requirements, it is good to keep in mind families like the Colfaxes who trusted their own instincts about what was most important for their sons without trying to meet all the specific requirements. Other home schoolers have also been accepted by colleges without the traditional educational background and paperwork. Many colleges are willing to individually evaluate potential students, so the need to plan a course of study to meet college entry requirements is debatable.

Laying aside our old ideas of what high school students need to learn is difficult. We may have done just fine with the courses we had. What worked for us should work for our children. Right? It may work, but it may not be best. And then again, it may not work. Consider: Should all children learn algebra and geometry? Is diagramming essential to a good knowledge of English grammar? Are biology and chemistry the best choices for high school science? If a child already has an excellent foundation in United States history, must he study it again at high school level, or would he do better to specialize in a single area of U.S. history? Does health education need to be taught as a class? Should all high school students write research papers? These are examples of the kinds of questions we must consider when we discuss individual subject areas.

We should each examine carefully our preconceptions and decide what we consider essential and what is open to discussion. Our conclusions will likely be influenced by the weight of state laws, future educational goals, and our accountability to others whether it be a correspondence course, independent study program, or other authority.

Methods and Materials

Most of us are free to choose whatever materials we want to use. At this time no state has a prescribed curriculum for home educators, although there is reason to expect state Departments of Education to try to impose curriculum restrictions in the future. (Fox, Linda P., "Home School Curricula," Home School Researcher, Vol.4, No. 4, Dec, 1988, p. 12.) The limitations on curriculum choices are more likely to come from correspondence courses or independent study programs. Students enrolled in correspondence courses are required to use materials that come with the course. Of course, other materials could be used as supplements, but there is seldom time left for extras. Some independent study programs prescribe a curriculum to be followed, but usually these programs allow home educators to make their own choices.

I expect that most people reading this book will be planning their own curriculum, since those enrolling in correspondence courses are generally provided with the basic information they need within that structure.

I have tried to research a fairly broad range of options since I realize that home educators are an extremely diverse group. Some of us feel that all curricular materials must be

Christian, while others do not. Some of us feel that the spiritual principle of accountability requires that we be enrolled under some authority other than that of our own household. Some of us want to follow a traditional approach to high school education, using typical textbooks, while others of us will want to experiment with more creative, unstructured methods. Many choose a combination of traditional and experimental methods. There are good reasons for choosing any of the above or other options.

A decision does not have to be made as to who is right or wrong in ideas about educational philosophy. Usually each person's philosophy of education grows out of his own personal experience. If our children respond to certain methods, then we will be convinced that those are the best methods, even though those same methods might not work well with other children. Our personality and style of teaching also have a lot to do with our preferences. A warm, gregarious teacher might prefer personal educational methods—discussion, activities, and interaction. An introspective, introverted person might prefer that her children work independently as much as possible. What is right for someone else may not be right for you!

Putting Ideas to Work

After we have dealt with these philosophical issues and come up with our own ideas about what education should be, we must bring all of our conclusions back into the real world and figure out how we can make all of this work with our children in our circumstances—a sometimes uncomfortable encounter with reality.

Chapter Two

Where the Rubber Meets the Road

In this corner—The Home Schooling Parent! In the other corner, Reality! Now shake hands, go to your corners, and come out fighting!

It's fine to read descriptions of correspondence high school programs or browse through A Beka's brochure on their high school video program. They make teaching teenagers at home sound like a breeze. But they are only dealing with a part of the puzzle. We parents are also dealing with a thing called reality. Reality is the younger child who needs to be taught how to read; endless meals that need preparing; medical and dental appointments; chauffeuring to soccer, gymnastics, and little league; pregnancy; ministry; grocery shopping; mounds of laundry; and children who would rather be doing anything but school. If we had nothing else to occupy us besides teaching our children, it would certainly be much easier. But I do not know of any home schooling parent who is free from life's routines, although some do have housecleaning help which I highly recommend.

When we begin to plan how we will teach our teenagers at home, we must first look at our situation. Do we have any experience? Do we have any confidence in our ability to teach our teenagers? How much time do we have available? How many interruptions are we likely to have? Can we expect any support from Dad or from others? Can we survive without support? Are we able to make compromises between our ideal concept of how it should be and reality, then live with those compromises without guilt?

Experience and Confidence

Those of us who have been home educating through elementary school and are making the transition into junior or senior high school will obviously find the task less overwhelming than someone just beginning to home educate with their teenager. Even though there are changes, we have already learned the basics of running a home school—organization, record keeping, purchasing materials, establishing a routine that prevents the house from decaying while school is in session. Those of you who are just beginning might consider enrolling in a correspondence course, independent study program, or other home school service that will help you with these basics so that you can concentrate on the actual schooling. You might want to jump ahead to Chapter Eight to learn more about these options before reading on.

Experience, confidence and finances are probably three of the most important factors to consider when making the choice of whether to enroll in a program or go it alone. Experience and confidence also have much to do with the methods and materials we choose to use. If we have confidence in our ability to tackle new challenges, then we are more likely to fare well working independently. "Going it alone" means we will have to dig for information, take responsibility for keeping our own records, plan course work without help, and rely on ourselves for recognition of a job well done. If you lack confidence, you are with the majority, so do not be discouraged by your doubts. By realizing ahead of time that you need more support, you can make choices with which you will be more comfortable.

Experience goes a long way toward building our confidence. If we have already done some sort of teaching in Sunday school, traditional school, informal classes, or home school, it is not such a mysterious process to us. Educators have tried to create a mystique about the educational process to add prestige to their jobs and, sometimes, to keep parents from interfering. But, once you have taught, you KNOW what is involved. Any positive experience will give you the reassurance that YOU CAN DO IT! You realize that it is often a process of trial and error with each child to find out what produces the desired results.

Most people suffer some doubts before beginning, but just making it through one year of home education will give you a tremendous boost in confidence (unless you make a total mess of it, which rarely happens). But we all have different personalities, some more confident than others, some needing more encouragement. That's all right. Just make sure that you are involved with someone who will provide you with the feedback you need, whether it be a support group, a correspondence school, school service, or an experienced home schooler.

Support groups, as small as two families, are essential for most of us. I have met many, many home educating moms with tremendous doubts about what they have been doing. Ninety percent of the time they are doing a great job and just need to have someone objective tell them so.

At the same time, we do not want to tell someone they are doing a wonderful job if it is not true. We render no one a favor by praising him falsely when he needs someone to confront him with the truth. Some home educators pull their children out of school to protect them from harmful situations or failure but lack any positive goals for accomplishment. They feel that avoiding the negative is sufficient. Yet they harm their children in other ways by not providing for their educational needs. Such people are doing a disservice to their children and to the reputation of all home educators. We need the kind of support that encourages us to do a good job, that holds us accountable, and that urges us to keep on trying when things get discouraging.

Qualifications

When we set out to educate young children at home, our educational background is not a major factor. Most of us had the fundamental knowledge to instruct our children in the basics, and we could easily learn what we did not know already or refresh our knowledge as we went along. Such is not the case when we teach teenagers. Beyond sixth grade, the subject matter becomes increasingly complicated and requires more knowledgeable input from the teacher. This fact does not necessarily mean that we need a strong educational background to educate our teens at home. But we need to know our strengths and weaknesses, and we need to be willing to seek help if necessary.

If our math skills and background are weak, we need to have someone else available on whom we can rely for assistance. Our choice might be Dad, a correspondence course, a tutor, or another home schooling parent. If we did fairly well in high school math, we might do fine just reviewing as our children learn, keeping current on what they are learning so that we can lend a hand as needed.

Writing is an essential part of our teen's education. If we are weak in the area of writing, we have no means of evaluating our child's written work. We need to have someone else available to assess writing assignments and advise us on problem areas.

A correspondence course can be very useful for those of us with poor educational backgrounds, but it is not a total solution. Correspondence courses take time for paper work to travel between teacher and pupil. Quite often, the student needs immediate help which is not available. Sometimes, correspondence teachers are available for telephone consultation, but that can get quite expensive.

Some parents have hired tutors to help with individual classes. Other parents have banded together for mutual benefit, trading skills and talents. (See Chapter Eight for possible options to consider.)

Before you begin, honestly evaluate your capabilities. Make sure that you do not take on more than you can handle. If your child "graduates" from high school without the ability to write a decent paper or solve basic algebraic or geometric problems, his future choices might be seriously limited. At the same time, do not underestimate your potential.

Logistics

Have you ever tried to explain an algebra concept with constant interruptions? It is impossible! I would advise you to think twice about teaching your teen if you already have your hands full trying to educate your younger children. I have often found it frustrating trying to work with two teenagers and just one younger child. My youngest still needs quite a bit of assistance with his work—often just a brief question. But all it takes is one brief question to blow your train of thought when you are explaining a difficult concept. Younger children cannot always tell when you are occupied or when it is the appropriate time to ask questions. And, of course, babies have no concept of proper timing. On the other hand, teenagers generally are able to study much more independently than younger children, so overall you should be spending much less time with them individually. You may be able to time classes so that interruptions are not a problem. Consider saving subjects that cannot be interrupted until evening when Dad can either teach or hold down the fort and run interference for you.

Some families have found it helpful to have older children tutor younger children. This is a great idea since it reinforces the knowledge of the older child while freeing Mom from having to be everything for everyone. However, all older siblings do not make good tutors, and sometimes the friction between older and younger children created in tutorial situations is worse to live with than the pressure of Mom doing it in the first place.

Be realistic in assessing the personalities and relationships in your family for tutoring and working together. Our children do not automatically develop wonderful personality characteristics when we home school. More commonly, they irritate each other from constant togetherness.

Shared Responsibility

Housework is an important topic when we discuss the logistics of home education. It can be very difficult to maintain a home school if the schoolhouse is rotting beneath our feet. Between lesson planning, research, teaching, checking work, field trips, music lessons, Scout activities, sports, and friends, we somehow must find time to maintain the homestead. I am not talking about "House Beautiful" but about keeping the health department from investigating. Some families are fortunate enough to be able to hire someone to come in every week or two to clean. It costs less than visits to the psychiatrist, so consider stretching the budget to cover the cost.

Even better is the situation where home maintenance is every family member's responsibility. Time is set aside for housework. Even the youngest children can help dust or pick up. Older children can mop floors, launder the clothes, prepare meals, wash windows, and mow the lawns.

In our society we have grown used to the idea that children should be involved in "activities" and parents are responsible for providing everything else to allow their children to participate in the activities. We end up shipping our children off elsewhere hoping they will acquire all the skills they need for life. We provide athletics to get them in shape, and then we hire gardeners to do the physical labor in our yards. We sign them up for "culinary arts" while Mom struggles to do all the cooking at home alone. We sign them up for activities to rescue them from boredom and to help them burn up their excess energy while we work ourselves into physical exhaustion.

Home schoolers are making radical changes in educational approaches. It is only right that those changes should extend to the way we view our family life and activities for children. If we have our children take an important role in maintaining the home they will learn far more than by participating in all manner of outside classes. Beyond that, it is important that children realize that the home belongs to the family, not to mom. My family knows not to say, "I cleaned the floor for you, Mom." They clean for the whole family! Every family member wears clothing and can see if the laundry basket is full. Any child older than ten should be able to sort and run a load of laundry with minimal help. Our daughter should never be blaming Mom because her favorite blouse is still in the laundry. Teenagers, especially boys, have a vital interest in food. They are entirely capable of fixing meals, and what better way for them to realize how much work is involved? The point is, to make home education successful, it has to be a joint venture for all family members. One person (Mom) cannot be all things to all people.

Help and Support

Physical help and emotional support are both important to home schooling parents to varying degrees. Interestingly, the two often come together. If another person is heavily involved in helping us teach our children, they are most likely also emotionally involved with us and our children.

In some families, fathers provide both physical and emotional support. However, many families have unrealistic expectations about father's participation. When families first begin home schooling, they often plan on father teaching one or two classes in the evenings along with acting as principal of the school. After Dad has been at work nine or ten hours, he still has his share of home maintenance. Then there are the nights set aside for Bible study, Awana, Scouts, and sports. Dad is lucky if he has a free evening or two a week. Despite good intentions, such plans often do not work out. Even so, some fathers still manage to provide much needed emotional support even though they do not have time to teach classes.

In some cases, unfortunately, fathers may not even be interested in the educational process. Sure, they are concerned that their children are doing well, but they do not want to get into discussions of whether or not John is ready to handle algebra. Count yourself fortunate if your husband is really involved with home education, but, if not, keep in mind that he has other priorities such as providing for his family. Do not try to use guilt to manipulate him into a more active role—it rarely works.

If Dad is not a terrific help when it comes to support or assistance, where do we go? Trading teaching talents with other home schoolers or taking advantage of some of the options discussed in Chapter Eight can help us with physical support in the actual teaching. Emotional support can be more difficult to come by. I have met home educators who have providentially found just the person they need to be a friend and confidante about home schooling, yet I also know of veteran home educators who are still praying that God will supply them with a supportive friend. All it takes is one other person. Emotional support (or lack of it) is a crucial factor for many home schooling mothers deciding whether to stick with it or not. We need another adult with whom we can discuss discipline and motivation problems. We need input from other home schoolers about ideas for methods and materials. And, most of all we need some encouragement that what we are doing is worthwhile.

Many home educating mothers are surrounded with skeptics. At the merest mention of frustration or fatigue, friends and relatives quickly chime in, "Why don't you put them back in school?" Even experienced home educators occasionally consider what it would be like to put their children into school. (Especially on bad days!) Mothers without anyone supportive to turn to do not dare voice such thoughts because the reaction they know they will get is, "Well, it's about time you came to your senses." It can be quite daunting when dealing with self-doubts to have everyone else reinforcing your fears.

Some home schooling moms have sought support from church or Bible study groups. However, it is rare to get the kind of feedback we need from someone who is not home schooling, even though it may be possible. I do know of many supportive grandmothers helping their daughters or daughters-in-law, who wish that they had known about home education when their own children were young. All of us are not fortunate enough to have helpful mothers in the wings. The most practical source of support is usually another home schooling mom—just one person with whom we can compare notes and share frustrations.

It takes time to develop a relationship to the point where we can be honest and open about our experiences. Often these relationships begin with both parties trying to make their home schools sound ideal and afraid to admit their shortcomings, but it does not take long before we are laughing together and commiserating over problems. I realize that this can be difficult if you live in an isolated area. But, even if you can establish a friendship that involves long distance calls, it can be justified like the housekeeping expense. It might be all you need to maintain your sanity and keep on going.

Enrolling in a program or joining a group is great as long as you can afford the time and cost, and if there is something available for you to join. Since many more families are educating teens at home than in the past, there are more possibilities than there used to be. In years past it was a rarity to run into a parent educating a teen at home. Now support groups specifically for home educated teens are springing up across the country.

Independent study programs and school services are better able to advise us about teaching teens as they gather more experience each year. We may find the support we need through such a program, but we need to carefully check a program's knowledge of and experience with teens. It is possible that we may end up paying to be their guinea pig. That in itself may not be bad if they are willing to do the research for us and ensure that we get the service we are paying for.

When We Need Some Part-Time Income

Whatever our family's reasons for home schooling, many home schooling mom's must supplement (or even provide) the family income. This adds a tremendous burden to the already challenging task of home education. However, many moms have discovered opportunities for working from or in their homes enabling them to be available for their children while also earning money.

Certainly, it is easy to let the work take precedence and end up abandoning our children to their own devices, a pitfall that I strongly caution you to guard against.

While some home school moms do work part-time away from home, that situation is even more difficult. I suggest avoiding it if at all possible. For those wondering what they can possibly do at home to earn money, I recommend Barbara Witcher's *Part-Time Jobs for Full-Time Mothers* (Victor Books). Although Witcher is not addressing home schooling moms in particular, she is speaking to Christian moms. She tells us how to find and get work-at-home jobs and also suggests self-employment opportunities. I especially appreciate the way she keeps family needs in the picture rather than simply discussing work.

The Art of compromise

Most of us have our idealized goals for home education. The reality is that we will have to make some compromises between our ideal and what we can physically accomplish in the time we have with the resources available to us.

I love really digging into literature, analyzing plots and characterizations. I wanted to have two days a week for literature discussions, but we were also studying government and economics that year, which absolutely required discussion. There just was not enough time to have literary discussions more often than once every week or two. I could have given up on literature and saved it for the next year, but that would have interfered with important goals for the following year. I could have felt guilty and inadequate, but instead, I compromised. The boys would read the background information provided in the literature texts on their own, and we would have discussions as time allowed. It was not the best approach, but my sons still had the experience of reading many types of literature, and they gleaned some background information on their own.

We can always take the view, "What would they be learning if they were in a traditional school?" Although there are some excellent teachers and classes in schools, there is no guarantee that any child is going to absorb all that wonderful class content listed in the course outline. Often students drift through classes just marking time and completing minimal requirements. We should be able to provide more than the bare minimum even if all we do is choose quality texts and make sure our child reads them.

All this is not to say that just anything will suffice. I believe that we should set high (but realistic) standards and hold our children to them. But we need to be careful of aiming so high that satisfaction is always just out of reach, while guilt and inadequacy stare us in the face.

Blessed are the Flexible for They Shall Not be Broken

Flexibility is a mandatory characteristic of successful home schools. I can guarantee that you will encounter many situations where you will have to alter course, put something on hold, or deal with unanticipated problems. If you are set in your mind that NOTHING is going to interrupt your plan for home education, you are setting yourself up for a nervous breakdown.

We will need to deal with household problems from time to time. If the plumbing is backed up, school will be interrupted for a trip through the yellow pages, several telephone calls, and a visit by the Roto-Rooter man. If mom is sick, we are allowed to declare a school holiday. Planning some "floating holidays" helps alleviate the guilt of taking time off to stay in bed when we have a 103 degree temperature. Flexibility might have to extend to the planned course of study. We may have to change course in midstream if our teen is just not able to learn a certain subject with the materials we bought or needs an extra three or four months to complete Algebra I. If we can bend with these situations, accepting them as normal, we will not find ourselves surrendering in frustration because things are not going the way we planned.

While most of us tend to strive too hard and judge ourselves too harshly, there are those among us who need less flexibility and more accountability and discipline. Some of us drop all planned academic work every time a field trip comes up—whether or not the field trip is worthwhile for our child. Emergencies and sudden changes in schedule are a way of life rather than an occasional occurrence. Priorities shift according to our latest interest. Challenging subjects are easily abandoned and rarely replaced. We justify lack of progress with excuses such as, "We'll make it up later."

Those of us who suffer from too much flexibility might do better under the guidance of an independent study program, correspondence course, or other overseer who will help keep us on track. If it seems like too much trouble to either hold ourselves accountable or work under someone else, perhaps we should put our children back in school.

Living with Our Choices

We begin by deciding what we really wish to accomplish. Next we look hard and long at our situation. Then we decide what we realistically can expect to achieve, while maintaining some flexibility. We must then do what we can to the best of our ability, and trust God to cover our deficiencies.

Chapter Three

Getting Things Done

If we cannot convince our teenager to clean his room, how on earth can we hope to get him to cooperate with his education?

The teen years are sometimes the most trying for parent-child relationships aside from educational issues. We have to realize that we are dealing with young adults, not just larger children. Teenagers are developing (we hope) minds of their own. They want to have more control over themselves and their environment. We should worry if this is <u>not</u> happening. A certain amount of conflict is normal with teenagers since they are trying to become independent from their parents. This situation does not mean that we should expect rebellion from our teenagers! There is a clear distinction between differences of opinion and rebellion. Differences of opinion are normal and should be expected. Rebellion or deliberate disobedience should not be allowed.

Our teenagers will be forming their own opinions about how their lives should be organized and how much freedom or responsibility they should have. Although they are forming their own ideas, it does not mean that they should be able to act upon them at will. As long as teens are living at home under parental authority, parents have the final say. However, parents should increasingly consider the views of their teenagers, gradually allowing more self-government and independence as teens show they deserve it.

Both Gregg Harris, in his seminars on the family and home education, and Dr. James Dobson, the well known Christian child-psychologist and author, paint a balanced picture of carefully shifting privileges and restrictions as teenagers exhibit increased responsibility and maturity or their opposites. If a teen finishes household chores without reminders, takes responsibility for his school work, and is otherwise acting reliably and maturely, then he deserves to have more freedom such as an increase in free time and less parental supervision. If a teen never gets his chores finished and does poorly with his studies, then the reverse should apply—he should have less freedom and more parental supervision.

Unfortunately, it is not quite so simple as it sounds. Friction arises when parents and teen disagree over how much privilege should be allowed and what restrictions are reasonable. The potential parent/teenager problems multiply when home schooling is added to the picture. If our teens were in school, we might not have needed to be involved beyond making sure they completed their homework. Now, we might be contending with them over every aspect of their schooling, especially if the home school choice is the parents' rather than the teenager's. Yet, even though the situation is more complicated, the same principle applies. As teens exhibit responsibility in getting work finished thoroughly and on time, we should give them more freedom in determining their own schedule. As they make wise decisions in choosing courses, we allow them more leeway in those choices. As they show that they do not need to be directed to make wise ethical and moral choices, they can be trusted to make those decisions on their own, and we need to give them opportunities to do so.

We face a challenge in motivating our teenagers to care about education for their own sake. What's in it for them? All they can see is more of the same through high school and possibly for four or more years beyond. Meanwhile, some of them feel that life is passing them by. Some of our teens want to go to "real" schools for the social happenings and sports, but rarely for the educational opportunities there. They want friends, activities, and recognition and often feel deprived of those because of home schooling. Few teens ask to return to school solely for educational reasons. Our entire culture belittles learning. The television/movie/entertainment industry that so heavily influences attitudes, places no value on learning. Instead it advocates concern about appearance, material goods, entertainment, and self-indulgence.

In addition, American teenagers face an identity crisis of sorts. In other cultures and in our country's past history, teens are and were already well along the path of future careers, accepting much adult responsibility that our teenagers often do not have until their mid-twenties.

For American young people, the teen years are often a wasted period, a time of waiting to get on with life. During the teen years, when many are trying to figure out who they are and what they want to do with their lives, society gives them few alternatives. In school, they can aspire to be cheerleaders or sports jocks, nerds or part of the "in" group. At home we can expand their choices some, but legal restrictions limit their options. They are required to be "in school," whether at home or elsewhere. Outside work hours are restricted. Employers rarely hire high school students younger than 16, and most of our families do not rely on the help of our teens for survival. It is no wonder that many teens feel useless and worthless.

Some teenagers will find their self-confidence in their academic work. But others will use their failures in school to convince themselves of their worthlessness. Many parents of teens decide to home educate, hoping to restore their child's self-esteem which has been severely battered by repeated failures. However, to accomplish this, things have to be done differently than they have been in the past.

Many teenagers have never developed good study habits. Whether our children were not taught or refused to learn does not really matter. If our teens do not have the necessary study skills, we end up force feeding school lessons—a very poor way of providing an education.

We have three areas here that we need to address: motivation, learning styles, and study skills. All of these are crucial to successfully teaching our teenagers at home.

Motivation

This issue is probably the one we fear most. We already are aware of difficulties in motivating our teens. Is it worth the hassle to add school to the list of areas of potential conflict? There is an underlying assumption parents make that teenagers would rather avoid school work, and that we will have to force them to do it anyway. Yet, this assumption may or may not be valid.

Whether a teenager has been in a conventional, traditional school or a home school, if he has not developed self-motivation, he has a problem. Some children discover the value of education at an early age, and understand that they are working for themselves more than for teachers or parents. Some children love to learn, and even better, see education as the means of preparing themselves for God's purposes in their lives. That love of learning most often sprouts when a child has been given room to explore areas of learning that interest him in ways that are enjoyable to him. If a child has been regimented through the educational process with little regard for his personal interests and abilities, he is much less likely to develop a love for learning. In fact, many children develop an attitude towards education that asks only, "What am I supposed to do to make the teacher happy?"

Our first task is to enlist our child's interest in learning for his own sake. One important step is to allow our teenagers some say about their course of study. They may have some interests or preferences that can be incorporated into their course of study without any problem. Why arbitrarily force them to take French rather than Spanish? Also, in choosing a course of study, we have a chance to sit down together with our teens, discuss and agree upon goals, examine the requirements, and jointly figure out how best to meet those goals and requirements. Let's not underestimate our teens! Most of them really do care about their futures, but many of our battles originate from their feelings of powerlessness. They have little control over what happens in their lives at a time when they need experience in developing independence. Granted, some of our teenagers may not be very interested or helpful with planning courses. Yet, if they have a voice in the planning, they are likely to take more interest in the outcome.

The average child is going to complain about having to work hard, a normal human reaction to which we can all relate. Yet learning requires work in one form or another. Forcing our teens to work is one solution, but a poor one. If we can shift our teenager's motivation away from performing for us or avoiding punishment, and instead focus it upon performing to meet self-imposed goals, we will have made our job infinitely easier.

Our goal should be to have our child function as a partner in his schooling rather than as a reluctant participant. He should be actively involved in planning course work and in following through to completion. He should be performing for himself, not for us! If we fall into traps like rewarding our children for completing school work, we are sending the message that they are performing for our benefit. Their only benefit is the reward they receive from us—poor motivation to become a life-long learner.

At the same time, if our child is performing for himself, we have to be willing to allow him more room for decision making. Are we willing to allow him five years to finish high school if he wants to spread out his workload? Is there some trade-off agreement we can make? (e.g., He agrees to work at a part time job and contribute financially to the family, since he will be a dependent for a longer time.) Are we willing to allow him the freedom to decide whether or not to prepare for college? Can we set aside our own egos enough to let him choose a future that is not particularly ambitious or promising?

Like many teenagers, our child might feel that school is just something to get through. By about age fifteen, our teenagers are aware of their academic inclination or its lack. If academics are not their strong suit, the specter of two or three years more of the same might seem like torture. We may need to take a radically different approach to learning to arouse their interest. Independent study, self-designed projects, a vocational apprenticeship, part-time school(see Chapter Eight), or another non-traditional approach might provide the turning points in their education. For some teens, a part-time job that convinces them of the need for academic skills, might be necessary before they can make any significant progress.

Programs such as 4-H, Boy Scouts, and Girl Scouts (check your phone book for such organizations in your area) can often provide educational incentive as well as valuable help for parent-teachers. These programs are available to even those who live in isolated rural areas, since members can work either as part of a group or independently.

In 4-H, members work on specific projects of their choosing. Sharing what they have learned is an important part of the process—sometimes through exhibits at state fairs or through individual presentations.

Scouting programs have children work towards merit badges and skill awards with advancement in rank.

A wonderful benefit (and one of the goals) of all of these programs is to expose children to a wide variety of careers. For example, Boy Scouts can work on merit badges in aviation, metalwork, electronics, first aid, cooking, communications, dentistry, home repairs, nature, veterinary science, and many other areas. Scouts can choose whatever topic interests them and pursue it further than the merit badge if they so choose. Counselors are available through the Scout programs to help with the various badges so it is not dependent upon the limited skills of two parents. 4-H leaders serve as teachers in a similar way. In our family, we have used Boy Scout merit badge work as part of our school course work. The added incentive of completing a merit badge does wonders for motivation.

The most difficult type of child to teach will be the one who just does not seem to care about anything. He does not mind if life passes him by. Somehow we need to find what I call "the magic button" that will turn him on.

The magic button might be a specialized study area, athletics, or any one thing in which he can excel. Often the unmotivated teen feels worthless—that everyone does everything better than he. It usually takes persistence and trial-and-error on our part to help him discover a talent or skill that is his special gift, but it is interesting to see how skill in one area translates into increased confidence in other areas.

Responsibility may be the key for others. Some teens have been treated like young children for too long, and have not had opportunity or inclination to develop self-motivation. Granting them more responsibility might encourage them to take charge of themselves.

Others need to be challenged. What does he want to do with himself? If he had to get a job tomorrow, what kind of job would he want? I have heard of a situation where the child was so lacking in motivation that the parents had to literally put him out on his own for survival to arouse any kind of response. A less drastic alternative would be to follow the Biblical injunction of those who don't work don't eat. (Proverbs 19:15) If you have an anorexic child this would be an unwise approach, but for most normal teens, especially boys, it works. For others it may be total social isolation or no money or no new clothes. We hope we will not need to take drastic steps, but if necessary, we are better off taking them sooner rather than later.

Although we might sometimes have to resort to negative motivation such as restricting food, money, clothing, or free time, positive motivation is the preferred choice. Try all the positive ideas you can find before resorting to "takeaways."

Ingeborg U.V. Kendall, a pioneer in the home education movement, offers more positive motivation strategies in her book, *School at Home: Teach Your Own Child.* Kendall's ideas are especially helpful because her goal is not just to get through the schoolwork, but to create a favorable attitude toward learning in the process.

A change in our tactics might also be in order. Instead of ordering our teenager to do things, we should set up "if-then" situations. We tell our child, "If you complete your paper by three o'clock, then you may spend time at your friend's home." Avoid negatively phrased statements such as, "If you do not finish your paper, then you cannot visit your friend." The first sounds more like a privilege, the second more like a threat.

Contractual agreements might also be useful. We are obligated to provide our children with food, clothing, shelter, and love. Everything beyond that is open to negotiation— use of the radio, television, telephone, computer, skateboards, bicycles, cars (even if they paid for them). Such agreements can be difficult to keep track of, so keep this idea for truly challenging situations.

A teen just beginning home school, having spent the rest of his educational years in conventional schools, often relies on external motivation such as that used by schools. Some teens have become apathetic or even rebellious over years of unfulfilling and unproductive schooling. To develop inner motivation and discipline to learn is a long, difficult process of undoing past damage and instilling a fresh perspective. Sometimes a firm, possibly even a heavy hand might be necessary at first (accompanied with heaps of love and encouragement). We might not have enough years of home education available to us to undo the damage! The only solution is prayer that God will intervene and restore a love of learning in our child's heart.

Physical Changes

Another factor that can make home educating teens more challenging is emotional instability. We might feel sometimes that our teenagers are purposely acting irrationally just to bug us. Psychologist James Dobson says of the early adolescent period, "Human chemistry apparently goes haywire for a few years, affecting mind as much as body. ...[U]nderstanding this glandular upheaval makes it easier to tolerate and cope with the emotional reverberations that are occurring. For several years, some kids are not entirely rational! Just as a severely menopausal woman may accuse her innocent and bewildered husband of infi-

delity, a hormonally depressed teenager may not interpret his world accurately, either....He is going through a metamorphosis that has turned everything upside down." (*Parenting Isn't for Cowards*, by Dr. James Dobson, p.144.)

Teenagers often do not know what they really want, and they are often reluctant to communicate their uncertainties to anyone else. This situation seems to be at its worst when teens are going through the greatest physical changes. Their tempers flare for no apparent cause; they are reluctant to get out of bed; they are unable to concentrate on schoolwork; and, they often are easily depressed. A common feeling is one of being overwhelmed—particularly by school work.

The answer is not to remove all pressure by eliminating everything that feels overwhelming, but sometimes a little grace and mercy go a long way in conveying the fact that we are aware they are struggling. If we cut back in just one area temporarily, it might be enough to encourage them to tackle the rest.

After my experience with my sons and observations of many other teenagers, I can see why school officials formed junior high schools. Many kids bottom out when they hit puberty. There is no point pushing some of them ahead academically, when they are barely functioning. A holding pattern is sometimes more appropriate. At the same time, there are a few who breeze through early adolescence and are ready and able to accelerate their school work. Trying to teach to both extremes in one classroom is almost impossible.

Because of the struggles that many junior high teens are undergoing, they can often be difficult to teach. In schools the social atmosphere often brings out the worst in them. However, at home we can deal with the spiritual implications of their actions. Hormonal imbalance is not an excuse to become totally self-centered!

Contrary to common expectations the teen years do not have to be a time of confrontation and rebellion. If we expect our teens to be polite, considerate, and responsible, they are as likely to live up to those expectations as they are to live up to the more common expectations of rebelliousness, laziness, and rudeness. The choice is often ours. In fact, many families with positive expectations feel that the teen years are the best of all. Obviously all home educated teenagers are not paragons, but we have the opportunity to create an atmosphere that will encourage growth in Christian character. We just have to be realistic, reasonable, and optimistic in our expectations.

Socialization

In the elementary grade years we dismiss school socialization as generally more negative than positive. While socialization at junior and senior high levels can be even more negative, teens do have growing needs for social interaction. Teens who feel like they are missing out in the social arena cannot be ignored. Some of them need to interact with other people, stretching themselves in new situations. Some are seeking close friendships. Others are looking for response from others that lets them know that they are "acceptable," while others need to have a chance to excel in one area or another. In schools, the avenues for meeting these needs have been acceptance by cliques, participation in drill team, band, or cheerleading, membership in clubs, sports participation, and academic awards. Since we usually cannot provide all of these opportunities in home schools, many of us jump at any convenient opportunities that come along, good or bad.

We must be conscious of the underlying needs prompting pleas to be allowed to go to school, yet we must recognize that school is not the only place to meet them. If we identify our son or daughter's need, we can better determine what to do.

Besides school, there are other avenues for helping teens develop feelings of competence and self-worth, many of which are mentioned throughout this manual for other purposes.

For friendships, the best place to look is other home schooling teenagers. Church youth groups may or may not have members who would be suitable friends. Having no friend is better than having a friend who is a bad spiritual influence, a difficult fact for many teens to accept. (Refer them to the book of Proverbs if they doubt you.) Friends need not be same-age peers, but might be younger or older.

A sense of purpose and accomplishment might be achieved through volunteer work or a job. Considering that many teens feel unneeded, purposeful accomplishment that helps others seems like one of the best ways of meeting teenagers' needs and motivating them to extend themselves.

With a little imagination we can come up with ideas for academic recognition. Pizza Hut's program of free pizza prizes for book readers comes to mind. Recognition in the local newsletter is another idea.

Sports are a more challenging problem. While there are opportunities through the YMCA, city sport leagues, and private sport organizations, participation on high school teams is the path to college athletic scholarships. This is one area with no easy solutions, and sometimes some hard choices.

We cannot let teenagers pressure us into allowing them to attend school for the wrong reasons, but at the same time we must be sensitive and do our best to provide for legitimate needs.

Learning Styles

I believe that most children prefer to be successful in whatever they attempt, including school work. Unfortunately, many of them have such miserable educational experiences that they abandon all hope of excelling in academics. After a few years of repeated failure and frustration, they balk at each additional opportunity to find out how "dumb" they are. No wonder so many children hate school. But problems rarely have to do with basic intelligence. More often they are related to the way material is presented to the student.

We each perceive information well and process it efficiently in unique ways. Some learn best by interacting with other people; some by studying books in quiet solitude; some by physically handling materials; and, some by working in a typical classroom. Reading books is a treat to one child and a chore to another. Learning by building representational models and other types of hands-on activity stimulates academic learning in one student while it bores another. These individual preferences reflect our different personalities and learning styles.

One of the most important advantages to home education is that we can design our home school program in a way that suits each person's learning style, using methods and materials best for each. We can adjust our methods and materials to suit our child in a way that schools cannot.

I have gone through periods of extreme frustration in our home schooling when I felt like I was simply not communicating at all with one of my sons when it came to school subjects. No matter how much work I put into coming up with great lesson plans, I found it difficult to stimulate his interest and motivate him. Then I read *Learning Patterns and Temperament Styles*, by Dr. Keith Golay. So many things that had been reverberating in my brain fell into place. By examining the situation from a learning styles perspective, I saw that we were communicating on two different wave lengths. What I thought would be an enjoyable way to learn did not coincide with what my son perceived as enjoyable.

I originally made this discovery when my son was about ten years old. Although I had been aware of his need for hands-on work at earlier ages, I assumed that he had outgrown such things. Not so! Like most children, he had changed and matured, yet his underlying learning style was still alive and well and in need of some attention. In high school, I tended to slip back into teaching styles more comfortable to me and again reached a point (although not as serious) where we needed to make adjustments to accommodate his learning style needs. Changing methods to coincide with his learning style has more than once made a significant difference in his attitude and his school work.

Identifying my son's learning style was only part of the puzzle. Another part was my own learning style. Unless we first recognize our own strengths and weaknesses, we cannot know how we are communicating or miscommunicating with others. When we find that our strengths and weaknesses are opposite those of our child, we need to be cautious in our choice of teaching methods. However, since teens should be doing a large percentage of their work independently, our learning style as the teacher is not as crucial as at younger grade levels. It becomes more important to choose texts and materials appropriate for each child, since these will be the primary learning tools.

I have included information, adapted from Dr. Golay's book, to help you identify learning styles for yourself and your teenager. But, before we try to identify learning styles we must add a few cautions. This theory is only one of many that have been used. I feel that this approach is the most workable since it is neither oversimplified nor too complicated.[1]

---

1   For further reading see *One of a Kind* by LaVonne Neff (Multnomah) (Christian perspective); *Please Understand Me: Character and Temperament Types* by David Keirsey and Marilyn Bates (Golay elaborates on some of Keirsey's work. Keirsey discusses sexual and relationship personality characteristics—read it with cautious discernment.); and *People Types and Tiger Stripes: A Practical Guide to Learning Styles* by Gordon D. Lawrence. (Both *Please Understand Me* and

Reflective Educational Perspectives offers another learning style approach in a format that is easy for home schoolers to use. They use a system of five learning styles, four of which correspond to those used in this book (Type A = Performer, Type B = Producer, Type C = Inventor, Type D = Relator). It further breaks each style down by disposition, preferred modality, best study environment, interests, and talents. They have Self-Portrait "tests," more properly called assessment instruments, for identifying learning styles—Level 1 for elementary grades, Level 2 for junior high, and Level 3 for senior high and adults. (The dividing age between Levels 2 and 3 is about age 15.) Instructions and analysis information are included. This method identifies five different learning styles and bears great similarity to the method I use in this book. Their two follow-up/application books I see as particularly useful for home educators. *Home Learning Models* is a seven-page booklet that takes each style and makes suggestions in the areas of curriculum, environment, motivators, time, and areas for growth in working with people of other styles. It also suggests practical schedules that are likely to be comfortable for each style. *Family Portraits* follows a similar format to *Home Learning Models*, substituting tasks for curriculum. It also discusses positive contributions and possible conflicts instead of schedules.

The slant here is on family interaction rather than schooling. Both booklets suggest ways to overcome learning style conflicts in situations where there are significant differences between parent(s) and child(ren). Reflective Educational Perspectives offers other related materials that will help adults in work situations and teachers in classrooms.

Whatever we do with learning styles, we must remember that God did not create people to fit neatly into little boxes. People tend to be untidy mixtures of all kinds of character traits that defy classification more often than not.

Ideally, we like to see a reasonable balance of personality characteristics with no strongly dominant style. A person without extremes usually finds it easier to teach or work with people of all other learning styles.

First, let us look at typical adult characteristics of the four learning styles within the methodology I will be using in this book. We include the technical names for the learning styles on the Adult Learning Styles Chart for those who wish to refer to Dr. Golay's book for further explanation. However, we will be using the terms Type A, Type B, Type C, and Type D for the sake of convenience as we talk about adult learning styles, then give them nicknames when we talk about children.

ADULT LEARNING STYLES

Type A - Actual Spontaneous Learner

- Has trouble organizing and following through
- Would rather play and have fun than work
- Tends to do things impulsively
- Probably did poorly in school (often due to lack of interest or boredom)
- Looks for creative and efficient solutions to tasks
- Dislikes paperwork and record keeping
- Prefers activity over reading books
- Prefers to teach the fine arts, physical education, and activity-oriented classes

Type B - Actual Routine Learner

- Likes everything neatly planned ahead of time
- Likes to follow a schedule
- Is not very good at coming up with creative ideas
- Is comfortable with memorization and drill
- Gets upset easily when children don't cooperate
- Worries about meeting requirements
- Often prefers to work under an umbrella program for home educators
- Prefers to teach with pre-planned curricula
- Is more comfortable with "cut and dry" subjects than those which require exploration with no clear answers

Type C - Conceptual Specific Learner

- Likes to be in control
- Thinks and acts logically
- Likes to understand reasoning and logic behind ideas
- Is a good organizer (at least in selected areas)
- Likes to work alone and be independent
- Is impatient with those who are slow to grasp concepts and those who are disorganized
- Is often uncomfortable in social situations and has trouble understanding others' feelings and emotions
- Tends to avoid difficult social situations
- Likes to make long-term plans
- Usually is organized
- Prefers to teach math, science, and other logic-related subjects rather than language arts and social studies

Type D - Conceptual Global Learner

- Enjoys social interaction
- Likes to belong to groups, especially for activities
- Worries about what other people think
- Tends to be insecure about how well he/she is doing with home education
- Is idealistic about expectations and goals
- May or may not be organized, depending upon accountability
- Is more interested in general concepts than details
- Prefers to teach subjects related to language arts, social studies, and, possibly, the fine arts

People Types and Tiger Stripes are available from the Center for Applications of Psychological Type.) All of the above along with Golay's book are based upon the work of Isabel Briggs Myers. For a different approach read *In Their Own Way* by Thomas Armstrong (Jeremy P. Tarcher, Inc.). All but *One of a Kind* are non-Christian in philosophy.

CHILDREN'S LEARNING STYLES

Type A - WIGGLY WILLY

- Does not like deep thinking or intellectual discussions
- Is impulsive—likes to be free to act spontaneously without restraint; dislikes planning and organizing
- Learns best by doing; a hands-on person
- Carefree—lives for the moment
- Short attention span
- Difficult to motivate
- Can be disruptive in groups
- Often very creative

Type B - PERFECT PAULA

- Responsible/oriented toward duty and "what should be done"
- Likes things to be clearly structured, planned, and organized and is good at those tasks
- Likes to see that everything is done correctly
- Seldom acts spontaneously or creatively, but is more cautious and certain before acting
- Follows the rules, respects authority
- Likes to belong to groups
- Needs approval and affirmation
- Usually works well with typical school curriculum

Type C - COMPETENT CARL

- Likes to be in control of himself and his surroundings
- Likes to analyze things
- Is a problem solver
- Self-motivated
- Likes long-term, independent projects
- Values intelligence and wisdom
- Has poor social skills and difficulty relating to peers
- Enjoys solitary activity (sometimes because it is too uncomfortable or too difficult to understand other people or tends not to think about others)
- Often interested in logical subjects such as math and science

Type D - SOCIABLE SUE

- Social person with warmth and responsiveness
- Wants to understand "Why"
- Interested in people, ideas, principles, and values
- Not a detail or technical person, but more interested in concepts
- Likes to be known, recognized, or acknowledged, and can sometimes be a high (over) achiever because of her desire to please people
- Vulnerable to conflict and criticism
- Dislikes competition, prefers cooperation because of her sensitivity to others
- Gets excited about new projects, but loses enthusiasm once the novelty has worn off

Next, we will see that there are differences between the adult learning style descriptions and the child's. This takes into account the fact that as we grow older, we learn to control our immature tendencies and develop splinter skills (skills for accomplishing specific tasks or acting in certain situations) as needed. You will notice that a Type A child tends to be carefree, living for the moment. Adults might also feel that way, but they are seldom free to act out their lives that way. As we grow older, we learn to adapt to those around us and to act in ways which are socially acceptable. Some of the changes also reflect spiritual growth. For instance, a Type C personality usually has difficulty relating to other people, yet, because of a desire to develop friendships or share the Lord with others, he might stretch to develop the interpersonal skills that were originally lacking.

In the chart on this page which describes learning style characteristics for children, keep in mind that these characteristics are not usually identifiable until around age eight or nine. Then a shift might take place as children hit their teen years. Do not "identify" a child's style and always expect him to respond according to your classification. Use learning styles as indications rather than as definitions. What we like to see is that our child shows characteristics of all learning styles instead of clearly fitting into a single category. If our children do not suffer from the extremes, they can learn from a broader array of methods than can those who exhibit strong characteristics of only one style.

We must remember that people change, and that the teenage years are when a great deal of that change takes place. What may have appeared to be a child's learning

style in earlier years might no longer be valid. We also should be working on Christian character formation which means that we are overcoming personality weaknesses. These changes often appear as shifts in learning style. Some changes are just the true learning style finally becoming apparent. Our middle son, Josh, appeared to have some Perfect Paula (Type B) leanings in the elementary grades, but around age twelve there was a dramatic shift toward Competent Carl (Type C) characteristics. Our oldest son, Chris, seemed to be a classic Wiggly Willy (Type A) in younger years, but exhibits some Sociable Sue (Type D) characteristics as he gets older. So, be wary of mentally and academically "boxing them in" and missing the changes as they mature.

If there are seeming contradictions in learning styles this might indicate that our child has a learning disability, and he is operating in an unnatural (for him) learning style because he is unable to function in his natural style. We most often see learning disabilities appear as Type A, Wiggly Willy, characteristics. The short attention span, inability to concentrate or do paper and pencil tasks, and other problems might be the result of frustration over difficulties with those tasks. Teenagers should be able to adapt to different learning styles with increasing ease. If they have significant difficulty, consider having them tested for learning disabilities.

Learning styles apply directly to the choices we make in course work for our teens. We generally assume that all teenagers should be able to work out of textbooks on their own, but this is not necessarily so. A strong Sociable Sue

SUBJECT PREFERENCES

Type A	Type B	Type C	Type D
music	math	math	writing
arts	history	science	languages
athletics	geography	engineering	literature
drama	grammar	computer technology	philosophy
mechanics	business subjects		performing and fine arts

PREFERRED METHODS

Type A	Type B	Type C	Type D
– variety in methods	– workbooks	– student/teacher discussions and question/answer sessions when he can do a lot of the talking	– small group discussion
– games	– consistent structure		– social interaction
– competition	– routine		– enthusiastic presentation
– audio-visual aids	– lectures following outlines	– logically organized lectures	– creative writing
– short, dynamic presentation	– repetition and memorization	– long-term projects	– role playing
– construction activity	– drill and review	– independent work	– situations where she is personally recognized and valued
– freedom to work independently on projects of his own choosing	– time to prepare for any discussion	– problem solving	– (needs but does not necessarily enjoy) repetition for technical detail
		– debate	
		– brainstorming	

Each learning style also has typical methods that they do not like:

Type A	Type B	Type C	Type D
– long-range goal setting	– creative activities such as role playing, dramatization, and imaginative writing	– listening to peer group discussion	– drill done in a boring manner
– complicated projects		– wasting time on excessive written work or previously mastered material	– competition
– planning	– changes in a planned schedule		– being ignored
– paper and pencil tasks	– constant changes in the curriculum	– repetition	– independent (isolated) work
– workbooks			

(Type D) will suffer from the isolation of working totally independently. She needs more interaction, either with her parents or with other people. Many Wiggly Willys (Type A) in high school still need to work with hands-on materials to help them tackle academic assignments. Many of our high school dropouts are simply Wiggly Willys who were handed materials that suited other learners, although many certainly suffer from learning disabilities.

The way to use learning style information is to identify subjects which pose the most problems for our child. We then look to learning styles to direct us to teaching/learning methods that best reach our child in that subject area.

For instance, a Wiggly Willy might need a math program which has lots of practical application and even some hands-on work in real life situations, or math manipulatives such as *Cuisenaire® Rods* or *Mortensen* materials. (See the Mathematics section for more information.) Perfect Paula (Type B) might need a more clearly structured program with definite objectives that she can achieve. Competent Carl (Type C) might need more independence and control over his studies. He might also need materials

which have less busy work and repetition. Sociable Sue (Type D) might prefer discussion and oral work over workbooks designed for independent study.

We will address learning style needs in each subject area chapter, but, meanwhile, the chart at the top of this page shows general subject and method preferences for each learning style.

Subject area preferences as shown on the chart are very broad generalizations, with many exceptions. They are included to show that different learners are likely to struggle in some subjects, while they excel in others. We need to identify which subjects pose the most challenge for each of our children. Do not assume that the chart will always accurately reflect your child's strengths and weaknesses.

The "Preferred Methods" chart is more helpful. Even though we will certainly find exceptions, the general suggestions for methods should give some starting places when we are searching for alternative teaching methods.

The last chart reflects least preferred learning methods for each type of learner. These are often the weaknesses that we will be working to overcome.

While we can concede that God makes each one of us individually for His purposes, we do not have to submit to the inherent weaknesses of particular personality/temperament styles.

Each style has its weaknesses. Wiggly Willys (Type A) tend to have poor study habits and be irresponsible. They need to learn diligence, and they need to learn that irresponsibility is a selfish character trait that says, "I don't care about anyone except myself!" Perfect Paulas (Type B) have trouble with new situations or new ways of doing things. They are often too rigid. They need to learn that life will not always be neatly organized to keep them safe in their narrow comfort zone. Competent Carls (Type C) often lack social skills, yet they must learn to relate to others to develop relationships and share Christian love and fellowship with others. They also must realize that they will not be allowed to live out their lives in isolation, but that sooner or later they must learn how to work with other people. Sociable Sues (Type D) need to learn how to pay attention to detail and follow through. They also need to recognize that we are not to look to men for approval and direction, but to God. They must let go of their reliance upon what other people think.

Motivation and Learning Styles

Motivating teenagers is difficult, yet understanding learning styles might make the task a bit easier. The key is recognizing that what motivates one person might do nothing for another.

Wiggly Willys tend to live in the here and now. Grades are poor motivators unless there is some immediate effect. With teens, the reward can be a little more delayed than for younger children, yet it must be immediate enough for them to keep it in mind as a realistic possibility. Type A's rarely are concerned with consequences, good or bad, a month or two down the road. Special trips are good motivators, yet they must happen right away. Prizes, time off, and food are more immediate motivators that work well. (Food can be a problem for anorexics and for those who tend to be dependent upon food for satisfaction, so use food as a motivator with care.) We do not want our children to be motivated simply by rewards, but until they reach a point of maturity where they are choosing to do things for worthy reasons on their own, we will probably use some form of rewards to enlist their cooperation.

Perfect Paulas are anxious to follow the rules and do what is right, so motivation is less of a problem. Good grades are often sufficient motivation. We do have to watch that our Perfect Paulas do not become gullible "slaves" to authority—doing whatever is requested of them unquestioningly. This personality type can too easily be manipulated by those with a political agenda or persons in positions of responsibility who mean well but lack wisdom.

Competent Carl likes to be in control. Allowing him to design his own course of study or work under "learning contracts" approved by his parents works well. He can usually be motivated by money since he plans ahead and might have goals, or even business ideas, for which he is saving. Free time to pursue his own interests is another effective motivator. Sometimes Competent Carl's desire to be in control causes him to overstep the boundaries. He has a tendency to want to do things his way, without regard for

the wishes of others. Clear boundaries of authority need to be defined for these learners.

Sociable Sue is motivated by personal recognition and affirmation. A pat on the back goes a long way. They are concerned about what other people think, so they will usually try to please people if they can. There is a danger, though, in whom they decide to please. Type D's easily fall under the influence of their peers in preference to the influence of God and parents. They need to seek approval from God first; next, from their parents; then from others with authority over them; and after that, from their peers.

Perhaps you thought that you were simply covering the school subjects at home. After studying learning styles, you can see that maturity and character training are just as important, perhaps more so, than anything else we hope to accomplish at home.

Study Skills

While all these changes—physical, spiritual, mental, and emotional—are taking place, we sometimes overlook another shift that should have taken place between elementary and high school. Teenagers should be assuming much more responsibility for their own learning. The burden of teaching is shared between parent and teen. Some of us have been spoon feeding our children because it has seemed too large a battle to get them to take personal responsibility for their education. I have seen some parents home schooling their teenagers, providing everything but the air to vocalize answers for their children. They pre-read all texts and explain them to their children. They help them through written assignments. They never hold them accountable for deadlines, independent assignments, or studying on their own. Some of us probably worry that our children might fail if we do not push them along every inch of the way.

This dependency may have been acceptable in early elementary school, but, unless there is a serious learning disability, our teenagers should increasingly be teaching themselves to a great extent. We need to risk letting them fail or fall short! In traditional public and private schools and college, students are expected to take personal responsibility for homework assignments, term papers, etc. No one follows them around with daily reminders. Home schooling parents have a strong tendency (maybe because we have too much opportunity) to nag about assignments. It would be much better to make sure that our child has the assignment and due date recorded in a notebook that is unlikely to be misplaced, then leave it to him to assume responsibility for remembering. We can use the energy we save on nagging to figure out rewards for meeting assignment deadlines and work well done, or appropriate consequences for late or inadequate assignments.

We are assuming that there has been some mutual agreement about goals and deadlines at the beginning. If we want our children to be independent learners, we need to give them a significant voice in setting those goals. However, many teens lack the maturity to follow through to meet those goals without some established schedules and deadlines. For students who need help with scheduling, use the Master Schedule (Chart B) to set up subjects and times allotted. This can be filled out each semester and used as a guideline rather than a rigid schedule. The first Assignment form (Chart C) has boxes for daily assignments. This should be used for students who have difficulty pacing themselves. Self-disciplined learners who know how to set their own priorities and schedules, might be able to work without daily deadlines. You might want to use the Daily Activity Log—Independent Study (Chart I) for these students, by writing out a week's worth of assignments but allowing them to decide how to schedule the work. Another option is to allow self-directed teens to fill out this form as their record of completed work.

I hear repeated reports that home schoolers entering or re-entering the school system in junior or senior high typically have trouble finishing their work on time. They are not used to working under the time restrictions to which other students have become accustomed. Home school schedules are of necessity less rigid than regular school schedules. That is not bad in itself, but we need to teach our teens how to use their time efficiently. Most teens are great at stretching a fifteen-minute assignment out for three hours so that they can complain about being overworked. I know that there are some families demanding too much of their children, but I expect that they are in the minority. More often, we excuse too readily and expect too little. Even in the public schools, teachers are having students do much more work than many home schoolers. Our children have learned how to tug on our heartstrings and elicit sympathy very well by the time they reach high school.

On the other hand, our children may be doing the best that they can. They may simply need practice with such things as math computation and handwriting to acquire speed.

Note Taking

In school, students are expected to know how to take notes from lectures and textbooks and for assignments. They are tested on the information contained in those notes. Many home schooled students are <u>never</u> taking notes! There are many situations in life, other than school, where note taking is essential. There are meetings where we need to take notes about our responsibilities; seminars and church services where we want to record what the speaker is sharing; situations where we want to record information on how to make something; and so on. It is a skill that our teens will need whether or not they go on to college. We can develop the skill little by little. We should not start by reading *War and Peace* and requiring a plot summary. Instead, begin with a paragraph concerning only one topic. Teach them how to summarize in their own words rather than trying to record the paragraph word for word. Help them practice identifying important points.

Alternatively, they might begin with note taking from a textbook. They can outline and take notes from the chapter they are studying in history. This is an excellent way for them to study, in addition to providing practice in note taking. Sunday sermons (if your pastor does not ramble) are also good for practice.

Studying

We will discuss grading and testing later in this book, but we need to realize that children need to know how to study properly before they will be equipped to take tests. Some students retain information well on their first encounter. Others need to go back and review to cement information into their memories. Either way, they need to be able to sort out what they are learning, determining the key points and what is merely interesting background. For some students this is very difficult and requires much practice and maybe some help. Yet, the more they practice, the better they are able to do it.

Do not suddenly introduce studying and tests for every subject at junior or senior high school level when students have been practicing neither. Begin the transition in upper elementary grades. Junior high is a good time to push the transition unless your child is already struggling through this developmental period.

Two resources to help with study skills are *Getting Smarter* and *Efficient Study Skills*. *Getting Smarter* (Fearon Teacher Aids) helps students examine and improve their study habits, set goals and priorities, organize, learn how to study and how to schedule their time, take notes, and take tests. The student book is a reproducible workbook. Students can work independently through most of it, but good teaching suggestions are included in a brief Teacher's Guide. Recommended for grades 6-12.(S)[2]

Efficient Study Skills (Educators Publishing Service) is a workbook for high schoolers that will help them learn to read various kinds of writing for different purposes, develop listening skills, take notes, and concentrate. The Teachers' Edition contains the entire student text with commentary and presentation ideas so you probably need purchase only the Teacher's Edition.(S)

The Skills Bank Home Tutor is a computer program for IBM type machines that includes a module called "Analysis Skills." (See lengthy review of the program under math resources for junior high.) This module covers a number of study skill areas: using dictionaries and books, using references and recording information, using consumer information, and using graphic information. Of particular interest to junior and senior high students should be the sections on using reference materials, taking notes, developing outlines, as well as the consumer information helps such as warranties and guarantees, leases and contracts, and filling out forms.(S)

Research Papers

I am certain that many of you question the value of research papers and will decide that they are not worth the trouble. However, I believe that research papers are useful tools for learning how to integrate writing, thinking, organizing, and research skills with knowledge. Research papers can also be used by teens to investigate topics or subjects that interest them. This will help them become better informed and possibly provide glimpses into future career paths. I personally think that every child of normal ability

---

2   Throughout this book, I use (S) to indicate that a resource is secular in nature rather than Christian.

should complete at least one research paper, and that a goal of one research paper per school year is practical.

Some of us parents have never written a research paper, and the prospect of requiring one from our child is daunting, but it can be relatively simple. Many books are available that break the process down into manageable steps. The process is not overwhelming, just time consuming. Computers are wonderful for saving time on rewriting! Some word processing programs automatically insert footnotes or endnotes in the proper places, a tedious and challenging task on a typewriter.

For a first research paper, it is best to start simply. Have your child use only two or three sources, preferably short books that are easy to read and summarize. Have them take brief notes. Do not hold them accountable to footnote every single statement they make in their paper. Rather than footnotes, they could simply include a bibliography. As they gain experience, require more sources, use of periodicals, interviews, or a wider variety of sources. Hold them increasingly accountable to footnote any information that is not general knowledge. If you feel inadequate evaluating the paper, enlist another parent to help you.

Projects

Projects are not nearly as debatable as research papers. Every teen should complete at least one project (preferably more than one) that requires independent work. It might be for a science fair or assigned school project, but it is even better when the project is designed to fulfill the student's personal interest in a topic. For instance, if a person becomes interested in model railroading he reads books, visits hobby stores, talks to others who have built model railroads, collects and makes his modeling materials, and finally builds the model railroad.

These types of projects are what are more commonly called hobbies. I recently read a newspaper article written by a gentleman (probably a child psychologist) who presented seminars on parenting skills. In his seminars he asked parents how many of them had hobbies when they were growing up. Most of them raised their hands. He next asked, "How many of your children have hobbies?" A very small percentage of the hands went up.

Hobbies were a means for many of us to explore and develop interests and talents as we were growing up, even though we were not aware of it. Today, we schedule our children's time so tightly that they seldom have enough free time to develop hobbies, yet hobbies are often the door to future career interests.

In our home schools I would love to see us allow our children time to develop worthwhile hobbies. However, I doubt that playing Nintendo games or riding skateboards should qualify as hobbies. A hobby should be a learning experience rather than a form of entertainment. In my mind, qualifying hobbies would be such things as animal care, electronic projects, robotics, computer programming, carpentry or woodworking, stamp collecting, cooking, sewing, painting, and playing a musical instrument. Hobbies should not replace more school-like projects, and they should not be turned into mandatory performance subjects, but they certainly do need some space of their own.

Organization

"I couldn't find the paper," is not an acceptable excuse for missing assignments. Some children are extremely disorganized by nature. They "stuff" or "toss" rather than neatly put away. Things disappear into their room, never to be seen again. They are always missing books, papers, pens, and pencils or whatever else is crucial to the task at hand. It makes one wonder whether an attempt to evade schoolwork is in process.

Such habits can create tension and ill feeling. We can waste time arguing about messes and lost items or we can provide some negative reinforcement to improve the situation by requiring that missing assignments be redone from scratch. If a book is missing, give a substitute assignment that is more difficult than the original assignment. If all pencils are missing, charge a premium price and sell him one of yours.

We should expect our children to be at least somewhat organized, and we should provide them with tools to make it easier—shelves for school books, containers for pens and pencils, notebooks for specific purposes.

We also need to set a good example. Are our record books always where they belong? Do we keep our teachers' manuals put away properly? Do we file important papers so we won't lose them? I find it a constant battle to stay organized myself. My desk is always five inches deep with "work in process." It is in a neat stack unless someone brushes the desk. Then disaster strikes. Nevertheless, there is an organizational system of sorts in effect.

What looks like disorganization to some may not be to others. Do not be too hasty in judging by appearance only. As long as our teen can find what he needs in a reasonable amount of time, we should not get too up tight about it, but if he cannot, consider some corrective strategies.

Tools For Success

I would summarize this chapter by saying that motivation, learning styles, and study habits are three tools for success in home education. We need to gain our children's cooperation, address their learning style needs, and help them develop independent learning skills, all of which are important if we wish our teenagers to become life-long learners.

Chapter Four

Goals - Purposeful Planning

In this "Me" generation, the popular philosophy is that everyone deserves whatever they want out of life. We should "go for it" no matter the cost to anyone else. Self-fulfillment has top priority. Sometimes, as Christians, we overreact to the self-centered emptiness of this philosophy by taking the laid-back attitude, "We'll just do whatever the Lord leads." A few years after high school some are still waiting for the Lord to lead them into doing something with their lives. Meanwhile, everything is on hold. Waiting on the Lord has turned into parasitical dependence on others to care for them until something "spiritually meaningful" comes along.

God gives each person talents, abilities, and interests, and I believe that He expects us to develop and use them to the best of our abilities without waiting for special revelation.

We have to discern the difference between selfishness and Godly personal fulfillment. Selfishness is a desire for whatever serves our purposes, without regard to others. Godly personal fulfillment means following a path that brings fulfillment as we follow God's designs for our lives. Personal fulfillment may come through service to others, preparation for a career, or other choices, but the key is our motivation. Is our desire for our own purposes or God's? If we are in tune with God, His purposes usually become the desires of our heart, so the choice to serve God usually means that we will find personal fulfillment, rather than the unhappiness and frustration so many fear.

Sometimes God takes us on circuitous routes in preparing us for His purposes. We may not see the outcome of it all, but that does not give us an excuse to sit back and wait for things to fall into our laps. God uses every experience in our lives, whether it be education, our first job, a service project, or whatever to teach and train us. We need to make ourselves available for all of those experiences, not just the "biggie" at the end. Without each of the little steps, we will never reach the end. Whether or not we see the end goal clearly is not really important. Following God's direction for our lives, as best we understand His will, is the true goal—for ourselves and for our teenagers.

Discovering God's direction is not necessarily easy. Some teens have a close walk with God and are comfortable with following His direction, while others are not. Quite often decisions are in the hands of us parents, and it is up to us to discern God's will. The ideal situation is for parents and teens to pray together for the Lord's leading. No matter who does the praying and deciding, the decisions to be made during the teen years are often very significant and should be bathed in much prayer.

Career Goals

Even though we are boggled by the idea of teaching high school at home, we have to be thinking even further down the line and asking ourselves, "Are we preparing our children to attend college?" There is no right or wrong answer to this question. It all depends upon career and personal goals.

How many teenagers actually know what career lies ahead for them? Certainly, some have strong ideas of what they would like to do, but how many will actually end up in careers they now envision? Ask a group of adults two questions: "What (if any) career did they wish to follow when they were in high school?" and, "Did they end up in that career?" It is amazing to see how few people do find themselves in a career they envisioned for themselves in high school. After all, how many of us planned that we would be home educating our children? How many of us had even heard of the idea?

Even though our teenagers may have no ideas about their future, they can still examine their interests, talents, and abilities for possible choices. If a person likes to be in control with everything well organized, and enjoys tackling difficult tasks and problem solving, he will probably want to pursue a career that includes these challenges, such as business management or entrepreneurship. A person who loves creative activity and solitude for dreaming up ideas should consider careers that allow space and time for creativity, such as freelance art, writing, or a self-created job. A person who loves to tinker with machinery and figure out how to make things work should be looking at careers in mechanical fields.

Academic aptitude is an important factor in career choices. A teenager who hates to read and study is unlikely to want to spend an additional four years or more in college preparing for a career. Whether we like to admit it or not, all home educated children are not cut out for college level work. As with any other cross section of the population, there are those who are below average in their academic ability. Pushing such students toward college for career preparation might be cruel and misdirected.

Vocational training or other options are perfectly legitimate and sometimes better choices. Some teenagers wish to pursue careers that require vocational training that they cannot obtain at a college. College might be a waste of time for them. It makes more sense for them to spend that four years and the college tuition fees to set themselves up in business or learn a trade.

But What If I Don't Want to Go to College?: A Guide to Successful Careers through Alternative Education by Harlow G. Unger (Facts on File) is a useful book for those exploring career possibilities that do not require college. Unger discusses many types of careers in terms of both broad categories and specific jobs. He assesses the demand within the various occupations and likely earning potential. While the careers he discusses do not require college degrees, some do require further education of some kind. Charts in the back of the book compare hundreds of career possibilities (including those requiring college degrees) by the number of workers and average earnings. Checklists entitled "Identification of Essential Employability Skills" help students determine whether they are even ready for the job market or what skills they need to develop. Addresses for career related organizations or alternative education providers are listed throughout the book. Even though I can think of a few promising career options that are not included in the book, there is a great deal of helpful information for those who have no idea what direction they want to go.

For an overview of career possibilities check out *The Occupational Outlook Handbook*, published by the U.S. Department of Labor. It contains information on over 300 occupations within fifteen main groups, including descriptions, occupational outlook (how much demand there is for people trained in each field), training or education required, and sources and reference materials for more occupational information. Order from the U.S. Department of Labor, Washington, D.C., 20212. (Order number S/N 029-001-02941-1, for hardcover or number S/N 029-001-02942-0, for paperback.)

Books such as these need to be updated frequently, so it is often best to look for them in the library rather than invest money in something with limited usefulness.

One older, out-of-print book that I thought very useful in determining the next step after high school is *College Yes or No: The High School Student's Career Decision-Making Handbook*, (by William F. Shanahan, Arco Publishing, Inc., 1980 edition, out of print, but possibly available through your library. The library call number is 650.14.) The author includes helpful tools such as a "self-profile" work sheet to help identify strengths, weaknesses, interests, and personality characteristics. He honestly points out pros and cons of college, vocational training, apprenticeships, enlistment in the armed services, and federal government careers. Unfortunately, he ignores entrepreneurial options, assuming that all high school graduates will end up working for someone else. Mr. Shanahan provides much concrete information that will get students through the fundamentals of the planning process. He also directs them to many other sources for more information on specific areas of interest.

A similar book for those wrestling with the "college or not" decision is *The Question is College: Guiding Our Kids to the Right Choices for the Post-High School Years* by Herbert Kohl (Random House). Although I have not read it, it seems to cover much the same topics. Since it is in print, it will be much easier to obtain.

While doing career research, remember that some of the best career possibilities are never mentioned in books. I recall a gentleman we met who travelled around the world designing rides for theme parks. I never have seen such a career listed in a book, but it sounds intriguing. There is always room for new inventions, new services, and new ideas that are the foundations for new careers. So keep an open mind about possibilities.

Unfortunately, choosing careers is not based solely upon what we would like. It is also based upon what talents and physical abilities God has given us. My son would like to be a pilot, but he has poor eyesight. From what we hear, poor eyesight is one of the factors used to screen the many applicants who want to be commercial pilots. Maybe he can still be a pilot, but he needs to keep other options alive. Many young men would love to play major league sports as a career, but only a fraction of them actually do, and even those who can, frequently find their careers abruptly terminated by injuries. Many young women plan to marry and

remain at home with their children, but what if circumstances force them into the work force? They need to have other possibilities in mind.

Quite naturally, teens first look at career choices from the personal end—what do they most enjoy? However, the world may not respond to their interests by providing jobs that are just what they want. They have to look at career opportunities in their field of interest. How many jobs are available in a specific career? (We cannot have thirty presidents of the United States at one time.) What sorts of prerequisites are there for a career? Are the prerequisites possible for them to attain? (Can they make it through all the years of medical school and internship to be a doctor?) Does the career provide a living wage or would it have to be a hobby? (Many artists have to find another type of job to earn a living while they pursue their art in their spare time.) Is it a dead-end job—one that if terminated would leave a person in the position of starting all over again? (Remember what happened to the buggy whip manufacturers after Henry Ford started producing Model T's on the assembly line?)

No matter how much career planning a person does, it still remains likely that he or she will have more than one career. Career counselors generally agree that the average American adult probably has four or five different careers in his lifetime. So, while career planning is useful in the short run, our teens must also prepare broadly enough to be able to switch careers if necessary.

"Only about ten percent of people end up in occupations they envisioned for themselves as teen-agers," according to George Schenk, a career advisor for colleges and businesses. (*The Register*, Orange County, California, February 9, 1989, p.B2.) He goes on to say that a U.S. Labor Department survey discovered that "forty to seventy percent of all employees are unhappy in their work." From Mr. Schenk's perspective, finding a career that is satisfying is a happy accident that happens too infrequently.

For now we will put aside the spiritual implications of each person choosing his or her career without reliance on God's direction, but we will come back to it later. From a secular viewpoint, the chances of choosing the "right" career can be improved with exposure and testing.

Exposure means letting our teens see, hear, and experience as much as possible of potential careers—the more exposure, the better (assuming that we are excluding unacceptable choices.) Teens who wonder what it would be like to own a restaurant can arrange a behind-the-scenes tour and an interview with a restaurant owner. Potential computer programmers can visit a programmer at work and find out what he really does. Exposure can also mean part-time work at a variety of jobs. In fact, the greater the variety of job experience the better. The more first-hand experience that our teens have with different careers, the more information they will have for making realistic judgments about their future choices. They discover that standing at a cash register for five hours straight can be more physically demanding than it appears. They discover that customers do not always come to the salesperson, but that the salesperson quite often has to travel and search out customers on his own. They learn that veterinarians receive emergency calls at all hours just like family doctors, and that policemen rarely use their guns, but spend a lot of time intervening in family quarrels—not very glamorous. They discover that there are almost always dreary, mundane tasks that go along with any job. While some teens learn which careers to avoid, others are fortunate enough to discover the career of their dreams through such exposure.

Even if our teenagers do not have time to work at many different jobs, interviewing people in different types of careers is an excellent experience both for information gained and for the interview experience itself.

Career Tests

Schools commonly use tests to help identify interests and aptitudes for career planning. While results of such tests are rarely accurate in predicting what career a person will actually pursue, they are useful in helping us examine our strengths and weaknesses, and to cause us to look at various possibilities that we perhaps would not otherwise consider.

Career tests are becoming increasingly available to home educators. One of the most widely used career test publishers is EdITS. They sell a group of tests which anyone can order, and no credentials are required for those administering the tests. The tests are quite simple to use.

The general name for the series is the *Career Occupational Preference System*. There are three types of tests: interests, aptitude, and values. Only one level of each of the aptitude (*Career Ability Placement Survey-CAPS*) and values (*Career Orientation Placement and Evaluation Survey-COPES*) tests is offered. However, there are three levels for interest testing (*Career Occupational Preference System-COPS*): COPS II for grades 6-12 (4th grade reading level); COPS-R for grades 6-12 (6th grade reading level); and, COPS-P for college students and adults. The first two COPS tests are simple and rather fun for junior or senior high students. Mature high schoolers could choose the COPS-P if desired. [The COPS-PIC (COPS Picture Inventory) is now available and is appropriate for non-readers or those with language difficulties.] After scores are tabulated, the student turns to the "career clusters" at the back of the test booklets. Here are listed fourteen major career areas, with many possible specific careers within each area. It also lists suggested courses of study and activities or experiences for further career exploration or preparation. A work sheet instructs students to list skills required for preferred careers, encouraging them to look realistically at their aptitude for careers that interest them. The CAPS test helps students to be realistic in assessing their abilities for careers that interest them by testing such skills as numerical ability, verbal reasoning, mechanical reasoning, and manual speed and dexterity. The COPES test helps to evaluate personality traits and personal values such as practicality, independence, leadership, orderliness, and conformity in terms of careers. (Order specimen sets of the desired tests.)

JIST Works, Inc. is another source for tests as well as for a wide array of books and materials on career planning and job searching. They call themselves "The Job Search People." They offer a number of testing tools. *The Self-Directed Search* (SDS) is written at a low reading level so that virtually anyone can use it. It takes less than an hour and the test-taker can score it himself. Results are used to identify cross-referenced occupations in the accompanying *Occupations Finder* booklet. Results can also be used with *The College Majors Finder* from JIST Works.

The Career Exploration Inventory: A Guide for Exploring Work, Leisure, and Learning (or CEI) (JIST Works) is an easy-to-use assessment instrument which takes into account hobbies, leisure activities, and interests which might not immediately be considered when discussing careers. After results are compiled, the Inventory suggests possible careers which might tie in with activities that people most enjoy. (JIST Works sells an *Assessment Tests Sample Package* which includes CEI, The World of Work and You, The Employability Development Plan, SDS, plus six other assessment instruments.)

Among the many other useful resources from JIST Works is a 32-page workbook entitled *Exploring Careers: The World of Work and You*. Ideal for high school students, it pulls together information, assessment tools, job matching charts, and interpretive assistance all within the one book. For more extensive career descriptions, personal characteristics, training, and education required, they can refer to the 462-page book *Exploring Careers*. An *Instructor's Guide* is available that describes activities and includes some reproducible work sheets. A *Preview Kit* containing all three items is available.

JIST Works sells many other resources useful for career and college planning. Request their free *Youth Materials Catalog* for complete descriptions.

Christian Career Planning

As Christians, our perspective about career planning should be different from non-Christians since we believe that God has a plan for each of our lives. He can lead each of us into the career that He has for us. The catch is that we must be walking in God's will, following His leading, and listening to counsel from those He has put in authority over us. Unfortunately, many of our teenagers do not maintain a close walk with God, and they fall back on their own limited wisdom in making their choices.

A Christian approach to guided career planning is rarely found in career planning guides. However, Alpha Omega has one LifePac in their Social Studies series that focuses on career planning (LifePac number 904.) It stresses God's role in career choices, discusses career selection according to interests and abilities (self-tests included), then concludes with instruction on how to apply for a job.

Accelerated Christian Education also covers career planning throughout various levels of the Social Studies Self-Pacs and PACE's, but concentrates on career planning and the spiritual implications in the Basic Education Self-Pac for social studies, number 138.

Christians who want comprehensive help in career planning will be interested in *Career Pathways*. This is a Christian ministry which has developed from Larry Burkett's financial planning ministry.

Career Pathways uses a variety of assessment instruments to cover the areas of interests, abilities/skills, work priorities, and personality. Those wishing to use the service first fill out an application, which is then used to select the proper testing tools that will be sent to each person. Tests are sent to the test-taker's home in a folder with instructions. After the tests are completed (a three- to four-hour task) they are returned to *Career Pathways* for evaluation. *Career Pathways* analyzes and correlates the results, then mails back to the test-taker the lengthy, computerized (yet personalized) results along with recommendations from a Christian perspective. Personal counseling is also available in some areas. The goal is not job placement, but to identify career areas that are most likely to fit each person, which in turn, helps with placement. I know of no other such career planning or testing service which takes into account the believer's responsibility to and reliance upon God. This service is useful for both teens and adults.

Although we can get assessment instruments to use on our own fairly inexpensively, Career Pathways' in-depth analysis will be worth the extra cost to some.

Career Research

If your teen has narrowed career interests down to a selected range of possibilities, he can conduct further research by talking to people already in those career fields or reading books such as the following:

➡ Career Opportunities for Writers by Rosemary Guiley (Facts on File)(S)[1]

➡ Career Opportunities in Art by Susan H. Haubenstock and David Joselit (Facts on File)(S)

➡ Career Opportunities in the Music Industry by Shelly Field (Facts on File)(S)

➡ Career Opportunities in Television, Cable and Video by Maxine K. Reed and Robert M. Reed (Facts on File)(S)

➡ Careers for.... series (VGM Career Horizons)

Six books in this series will help young people who have identified personality characteristics or avocations, but who have trouble figuring out what career will fit. Titles all begin with *Careers for*. The remainders of the six titles are *For Animal Lovers and Other Zoological Types, For Bookworms and Other Literary Types, For Foreign Language Aficionados and Other Multilingual Types, For Good Samaritans and Other Humanitarian Types, For Travel Buffs and Other Restless Types,* and *For Sports Nuts and Other Athletic Types.*(S)

➡ Careers in.... series (VGM Career Horizons)

This series is advertised as VGM's professional careers series. It includes books on careers in accounting, advertising, business (includes consulting and owning your own business), communications, computers, education, engineering, health care, marketing, and science.(S)

➡ Opportunities in.... series (VGM Career Horizons)

There are well over 100 titles in this series. These books cover all areas. The catalog lists them under groupings: building, industrial, and mechanical services; business and management; office and computer; communication; health care; fitness; art and design; scientific and technical; public and social service; travel and leisure; ecology and environmental; and service occupations. There are about a half dozen books in each category. For instance, Communication includes books about magazine publishing, newspaper publishing, public relations, technical communications, telecommunications, television and video, and writing.(S)

➡ How to Get A Federal Job: A Guide to Finding and Applying for a Job with the United States Government Anywhere in the Country by Krandall Kraus (Facts on File)(S)

Look for titles on other specific careers in the library, secular book stores, or the VGM Career Horizons or JIST Works catalogs.

Vocational/Trade School Preparation

"A craft is described as 'an art or skill,' and a craftsman as 'one who practices some trade or manual occupation.' Contrary to what many believe, the need for qualified craftsmen continues to grow throughout the world....never before have craftsmen been so much in demand." (*College Yes or No*, p.49) Training as a craftsman might start with adult education classes and progress into vocational or trade schools or through apprenticeships. We will deal with apprenticeships separately a little later. Educational institutions for trade or vocational training might be called trade, technical, vocational, or proprietary schools.

Some students might wish to begin vocational training while still in high school. They may be able to do this through work experience or apprenticeship, or they may be able to learn about a trade from a knowledgeable adult. Some school systems offer a combination of both classroom and practical experience, usually structured as a separate vocational arm of the school district. Such programs are often open to home educated teens although usually with a minimum age of sixteen. In California it is called the Regional Occupational Program or ROP. The idea is very practical. However, potential dropouts and underachieving students are often shunted into ROP programs to keep them in school, so the general atmosphere in some classes can be less than ambitious. On the other hand, much of the ROP training is excellent and diligent students graduate with skills that allow them to find immediate employment.

Students without access to vocational classes can study on their own with appropriate textbooks. Macmillan/McGraw-Hill—Glencoe Division has an entire catalog of vocational textbooks under the general headings: automotive and aviation technology; construction, architectural, and civil technology; electricity and electronics; drafting and design; manufacturing technology; mechanical technology; technical physics; and technical writing. Glencoe technical education materials have been incorporated into the Macmillan/McGraw-Hill—Glencoe Division line and include air conditioning/refrigeration; construction/woodworking; graphic arts; industrial materials; metalworking/machine shop; and welding. If students want to study through any of the above texts it would help greatly to have a knowledgeable adult to consult.

One publisher, Education Associates, offers a program called *Project Discovery* which can be used for do-it-yourself ROP type training. The program is packaged in units for specific trades/vocations including such topics as: accounting and bookkeeping, advertising and editorial design, dental care, drafting, electricity, food technology, greenhouse work, masonry, medical records, plumbing, retailing, shorthand, small engine repair, upholstery, and many more (48 kits in all). They are designed to be used as self-contained units. Each includes detailed instructor notes, student instructions, work performance benchmarks, tools, equip-

---

1   Throughout this book, I use (S) to indicate that a resource is secular in nature rather than Christian.

ment and materials needed by student and instructor. These courses do not provide complete training but serve as introductory experience and training appropriate for junior and senior high students. Many of the units were designed for "special needs" students by using high interest/low reading level materials and hands-on work. Prices range from below $200 to over $1000 for each unit. Parents without background should be able to help their teens through some of the units, while others such as plumbing would require a teacher with at least some familiarity with the subject.

For further training after high school, students need to consider various available options. Vocational schools are not all the same in the way they are set up. Different set-ups that are most common are "on campus"[2] study, correspondence, or a combination of both. Courses offered by campus and correspondence schools are similar to each other, however some courses, such as truck driving and diesel mechanics, require at least some time at a "campus" for hands-on instruction. Some courses are set up for the book work to be completed through correspondence, then a residency or "on campus" period arranged for the rest of the instruction. Admission requirements are generally either a high school diploma or an equivalency (GED) certificate.

For some students, it might be too abrupt a change to move from home school to a full-time vocational school far from home. An interim choice might be for teens to take a related course at a local college or through adult education for a semester or two. This transition can help them learn how to function in a classroom environment without the added cost and adjustment of living away from home.

The National Home Study Council, a council of international organizations for adult education, will send you a free brochure listing accredited correspondence schools for vocational training.

Apprenticeships

Apprenticeship programs have been around since Adam began training his sons in farming. Apprenticeships can be formally set up by contract or agreement, or they may be informal situations where an older or more skilled person (mentor)[3] shares his skill or knowledge with another person who acts as an assistant while he is learning. The term mentorships include both apprenticeships and less formal relationships that might be as simple as an older, wiser person providing advice to a younger.

Apprenticeships are most prevalent in the craft trades such as construction work. Usually unions are in control of both craftsmen and apprentices. Sometimes there are long waiting lists for apprentice openings. There are pages of apprenticeship information sources in *College Yes or No* (pages 56-60). A beginning point for more information would be your regional Bureau of Apprenticeship and Training (BAT)

Office. Addresses and states included within each region are listed below:

Region I - JFK Federal Building, Room 1001, Government Center, Boston, MA 02203
Includes: Connecticut, Maine, Massachusetts, New Hampshire, Rhode Island, Vermont
Region II - 1515 Broadway, Room 3731, New York, NY 10036
Includes: New Jersey, New York, Puerto Rico, Virgin Islands
Region III - P.O. Box 8796, Philadelphia, PA 19101
Includes: Delaware, Maryland, Pennsylvania, Virginia, West Virginia
Region IV - 1371 Peachtree Street N.E., Room 700, Atlanta, GA 30309
Includes: Alabama, Florida, Georgia, Kentucky, Mississippi, North Carolina, Tennessee
Region V - 230 South Dearborn Street, Chicago, IL 60604
Includes: Illinois, Indiana, Michigan, Minnesota, Ohio, Wisconsin
Region VI - 555 Griffin Square Building, Room 858, Griffin and Young Streets, Dallas, TX 75202
Includes: Arkansas, Louisiana, New Mexico, Oklahoma, Texas
Region VII - Federal Office Building, Room 1100, 911 Walnut Street, Kansas City, MO 64106
Includes: Iowa, Kansas, Missouri, Nebraska
Region VIII - Federal Building, Room 16440, 1961 Stout Street, Denver, CO 80202
Includes: Colorado, Montana, North Dakota, South Dakota, Utah, Wyoming
Region IX - 450 Golden Gate Avenue, Room 9008, P.O. Box 36017, San Francisco, CA 94102
Includes: Arizona, California, Hawaii, Nevada
Region X - Federal Office Building, Room 8014, 909 First Avenue, Seattle, WA 98174
Includes: Alaska, Idaho, Oregon, Washington

Home schoolers are looking at more innovative approaches to the apprenticeship idea. Bill Gothard of the Institute in Basic Life Principles has been a prime mover in encouraging businessmen, judges, physicians, etc. to offer apprenticeships under Godly men to young people. They have set up a home education program called the Advanced Training Institute of America. Enrollment in that program by the entire family is required for any students interested in any of their apprenticeship opportunities. Applicants for apprenticeships must show individual initiative and diligence in their learning. Faith and character growth are both expected to continue while under apprenticeship. The Institute is preparing a series of *Life Purpose Journals* to lead students through the learning sequence of II Peter 1:5-10 in preparation for apprenticeship assignments.

Rather than advertising a list of apprenticeships to choose from, the Institute relies on the Lord to open up opportunities according to individual needs.

---

2   Campuses may be located near home, in which case, students can live at home while going to school. In many cases, the campus will be at too great a distance for students to remain at home.

3   *The Fine Art of Mentoring* by Ted W. Engstrom (Word Inc., formerly published by Wolgemuth and Hyatt) is a wonderful introduction to Christian mentoring. Although it does not follow through into full apprenticeships, it thoroughly covers relationship aspects of mentoring.

Developing Other Apprenticeship Opportunities

Apprenticeships do not have to be set up through recognized organizations. Anyone can arrange an apprenticeship or mentorship, but we must know if there are legal requirements that might prevent recognition of proficiency. For instance, some states do not require that prospective lawyers graduate from law school but only that they pass the state bar examination.

In the National Homeschool Association's newsletter appeared a discussion of mentorships with some guidelines on mentoring relationships quoted from an article by Sharon B. Bruce in *Nonprofit Times*, September, 1988. Bruce identifies seven steps to follow in making a mentor/mentee selection:

1. Identify what you need from the relationship; carefully spell it out.

2. Identify what you are willing to contribute to the relationship.

3. Be willing to share your needs, expectations, and limits.

4. Identify the qualities you are looking for.

5. Consider several candidates.

6. Make a tentative choice; carefully discuss all aspects of the relationship with your choice.

7. Put everything in writing; agreement will guarantee a good start.

(*National Homeschool Association Newsletter*, Summer, 1989, p.5.)

These guidelines for mentors should be useful in most apprenticeship opportunities. It is important that expectations are clearly understood by both parties.

Sometimes mentoring situations arise on their own; a child meets an adult and forms a relationship that grows into one of mentoring without any plan or decision. While we should be on guard that this does not happen with adults we would not want influencing our children, it is often a blessing and a sign of God's provision for our needs even before we recognize them.

Military

The military services sometimes have different requirements from everyone else. At this time, the military services are categorizing students who either have diplomas from unaccredited schools or have graduated with a GED certificate in a less desirable category of applicants. It does not matter to them that home schooled students who are in the military already function well above the level of average recruits.

This means that young people who want to join a branch of the armed services must plan more carefully. They can do their high school work through an accredited correspondence school or under an accredited Independent Study Program. The other alternative is to attend junior college for one semester (completing 15 units) after completing high school, which will qualify them for a higher category.

We are hoping to see a change in this policy, and the National Center for Home Education is actively pursuing that end as I write.

Meanwhile, it would be wise to consult a military recruiter as soon as we realize that our child is considering entering one of the services.

There are placement tests given by the various armed services, and applicants can prepare with books such as *Practice for Air Force Placement Tests* (Arco).

On the Job Training

Whether or not students are college bound, there is nothing like a dose of reality in the form of a job to help them plan for the future. Work experience helps teens to understand the realities and responsibilities of being an employee, provides them with an income so they can begin to assume responsibility for their own needs, helps them to explore different job opportunities or careers, and helps them learn and develop skills.

When teens are working for someone other than Mom and Dad, they realize that they have to act without waiting for parental reminders. It is now their responsibility to do what they are told or what is needed, or they lose both job and income. The income is often the incentive that prompts teens to seek employment. While we do not want to encourage our teens to earn money to spend foolishly or possibly sinfully, it is good to encourage them to buy their own clothing (especially if they want the expensive fad items), pay for their own entertainment, build a savings account, etc. Teens need some experience managing their own finances, and it is better to gain that experience on a smaller scale while still under their parents' influence than to suddenly have to figure it all out when they get married and move out.

The last two reasons I have listed for gaining work experience—career exploration and development of skills—relate most closely to the purposes of this book. It would be ideal if our teens could all find beginning jobs in the areas of their potential career interest, but, unfortunately, there are many more fast food jobs than engineering jobs available to unskilled teens. Even if that first job is less than ideal, it will help our son or daughter develop basic job skills and possibly alert them to the type of job that they will **not** want. On the other hand they might find themselves in a job which leads to a career. It is often true that we never know whether or not we like something until we try it.

Getting a Job

Some home educated teens have found jobs in their desired career fields simply by making themselves available. One teen helped a veterinarian with animal care, first as a volunteer, later as a hired assistant. Some teens volunteered to help do the "dirty work" on construction jobs, then later went on to more rewarding careers in the construction field. Being willing to fill in for an employer on short notice or at minimum pay, may not be very rewarding at the time, but it often opens doors in the future.

Some teens are fortunate to stumble across a job without having to go through the application process. Maintaining relationships with adults involved in areas of the teenager's own personal interest will help teens to be in the right place at the right time for such jobs.

Actually, it might be better if they have to go through the application process, because it is a good learning experience for the future. A teenager is practicing applying for jobs at a time in his life when his livelihood does not depend upon it. If a teen blows an interview at Jack-In-The-Box, all is not lost, and they have gained valuable experience. Better to undergo the learning process under these conditions, than when he is interviewing with IBM or Bank of America.

Included in the Appendix is a sample job application. It is amazing to read articles about how poorly many job applicants fill out such forms. The application is the first impression a person makes upon his potential employer. Blank spaces, erasures, cross-outs, or inadequate information are certain to hurt an applicant's chances of being hired. Teens should practice filling out this form before they begin job hunting.

Education Associates, Inc. sells many items designed to help job seekers. *Seven Steps to Employment* tells how to develop a resume, find and act upon job openings, fill out applications, interview, and follow up the interview. Individual booklets from Education Associates cover some of that same territory and more. Representative booklet titles are: *Filling Out the Forms, Keeping a Job: Now That You Have It, Face to Face: Making a Good Impression, Your Attitudes Make a Difference, Grooming for Job Success,* and more.

Job seekers with below average reading skills need special help that can be found in *Get That Job!* (Quercus). This book, written at second grade reading level, tells how to complete a social security card application, helps them to understand vocabulary they will encounter on job applications, and discusses the importance of appearance, language, and attitude for a successful interview.

Entrepreneurs

Because they are learning at home, most of our teens have already been exposed to the do-it-yourself approach. Many of them approach the job issue the same way—by creating their own businesses. This approach is certainly more difficult, especially if teens are planning to create a business that will be viable enough to support a family in future years. I have not yet heard of any home educated teen who has grown a business into a life occupation, but some are on their way. One young man we know is writing computer programs and selling them to members of his computer club. Two others provide music and entertainment at parties and other events. *The Teenage Entrepreneur's Guide* (Surrey Books) offers fifty ideas practical for teens who would like to start their own businesses. These ideas go well beyond lemonade stands and lawn mowing. A few examples are auto detailing, house cleaning, bumper stickers, and errand service. For each suggested business venture, the book provides a job description, personal traits required, experience required, materials required, marketing method, expected wages, plus lengthy explanations that will help teens be successful in their ventures.

Some teens intend to form their own businesses in the future, and, meanwhile, they choose to serve apprenticeships to gain knowledge and experience under someone who already "knows the ropes." They use the time to build the foundations for their own future businesses. Those who want to find out what it takes to start their own business need to read books such as *Capitalism for Kids: Growing Up To Be Your Own Boss* and *Homemade Money* (by Barbara Brabec), both available from Bluestocking Press. Another worthwhile resource is The Family Business Workshop Tape Set (Christian Life Workshops). On this set of seven audio cassettes, Gregg Harris covers "...the entire scope of starting and managing a home or family business from a clearly Christian perspective." He outlines ideas such as "stepping stone business ventures" and "family circle financing" which can make it possible for teens to start their own businesses without going into debt.

For more ideas, check out Mary Pride's recommendations in the *Teen and Adult* volume of her *Big Book of Home Learning* series (Crossway) and the Christian Life Workshop catalog, *Our Family Favorites*, which lists more than twenty titles related to business.

Volunteerism

Of equal or greater benefit might be volunteer work. Often the work required by volunteer organizations teaches teens skills that surpass what they might learn in the fast food business or cashiering for a small store. Volunteer organizations tend to hand out job assignments according to what needs to be done rather than according to job descriptions, so teens usually receive much broader training in the volunteer arena. They also have the opportunity to build both personal and professional relationships with adults. Check with your pastor for suggestions, or contact your city hall for a list of volunteer organizations in your area.

Family Life

In our modern society, "liberated" women are free to work full time, raise children, and do the bulk of the housework. We are sure to reap criticism if we offer our young women the option of preparing themselves for careers as homemakers rather than "career-persons." While people say that women who choose to be homemakers are not second-class citizens, the reality is that almost everything in our society (government, taxes, public opinion, and education to name a few) gives us the opposite message.

We cannot rely on our daughters marrying men who will be able to provide sufficient income to allow their wives to remain at home. Yet, it is still possible to live on one income, especially when both husband and wife are willing to make sacrifices. If our daughters wish to be homemakers they will need to know how to budget carefully and make wise use of their resources. We should encourage and help them by providing the skills and knowledge they will need to operate on a limited budget.

Instead of textbooks, life situations can be the teacher. Our daughters can learn to sew, cook, maintain a home, and raise children by practicing those things at home. This is experience that many other young women seldom get since they are not in the home very many hours of the day.

Young women might want to study about child development, learn how to sew, or in other ways develop their skills as a homemaker as part of their high school curriculum. Refer to the home economics recommendations in Chapter 16 for possible resources.

Because of the changes being wrought in our society, our young women may not have the option of choosing to be homemakers to the exclusion of any other employment. They may need to work off and on throughout their lifetimes, or they may need or want to supplement their husbands' incomes with work done from their homes. These are the realities that we must keep in mind. Because of them, we should simultaneously prepare our daughters so they are able to do other things beyond the range of homemaking if required.

Choosing a basic skill to develop for such contingencies is wise. Offering music or dance lessons, providing book-keeping services for small businesses, and typing/word processing services are examples of skills that homemakers can call upon at short notice.

No matter what our young women choose as their desired careers, we cannot know what God has in store for each of them. We cannot neglect academic skills because our daughters wish to be homemakers. They may unexpectedly need to support their families in emergency situations, or they might choose to educate their own children. In either case a lack of academic skills might be a terrific handicap to overcome.

We should not neglect our boys when it comes to instruction in household skills. They should know how to maintain their own household. It is a sad situation when Mom is ill and Dad and the children (girls or boys) cannot figure out how to do a load of laundry. The same goes for meal preparation, grocery shopping, and basic housecleaning. I am not advocating role reversal, but survival skills. Our boys might live on their own. We do not want them to bring home their laundry for us to do every Saturday, or drop in every evening for dinner. We need to think in terms of equipping our sons to survive without mothers, not send them out searching for a wife who will become a substitute mother.

Summary

Whether or not our teens have clear ideas of what they wish to do in the future, we should try to provide them with as broad an education as we reasonably can. We must provide materials and experiences that will enlarge the possibilities for their futures. Meanwhile, we should keep the doors to various possibilities open by providing broad and thorough coverge of academics until it is obvious that goals can and should be narrowed.

We will certainly run into limitations in what we are able to provide for our children, yet that really is not a crucial factor in our success or failure. If we provide the basic tools of learning, our children can apply those in any situation. The ability to acquire knowledge and skill, along with flexibility—the ability to change old or habitual ways of thinking and acting—might be more important than any specialized training that our teens receive in our rapidly changing society.

Chapter Five

A Christian Foundation

Building on a Solid Foundation

We have discussed goals and various ideas which shape them, but before we go on to plan our course of study, we must make sure that we are not "building on sand." Without spiritual foundations our children are gaining knowledge, but without wisdom.

By the time our children reach high school, we hope they will have a solid foundation in Scripture and God's principles.Even more important, but often lacking, is a personal relationship with God. While we have neither the time nor the space to deal with spiritual fundamentals here, do not overlook the priority that should be placed upon them. Because each of us has a free will, some of our teens will not yet have accepted Jesus as their Savior. Even some of those who have, may not be allowing Him to be Lord of their lives. This lack of commitment will definitely hinder our educational efforts. The shared vision of serving God's purposes is missing, and the guidance and strength of the Holy Spirit is missing in each day's activities.

Fortunately, many of our teens have a personal relationship with God and can build upon it. Upon a solid foundation we can build a Christian view of life and the world, including our place in it. There are many, many excellent books and resources which will help teens begin to evaluate themselves and the world around them in light of God's Word. I will recommend a few to you which can be helpful in beginning or building upon a spiritual foundation.

A thought-provoking book for unsaved or questioning/doubting teens to begin with is *How To Be Your Own Selfish Pig*, by Susan Schaeffer Macaulay (David C. Cook). Macaulay speaks to the essential questions without sermonizing. The book has interesting pictures and photographs that help reinforce the ideas presented.

Josh McDowell has also written many books that speak to the thinker who wants to intellectually "see" that Christianity makes sense. *Evidence that Demands a Verdict* (Thomas Nelson, formerly published by Here's Life Publishers) is one of the most well known. Josh set out to debunk Christianity and the Bible and ended up doing the opposite. The evidence he found is presented here. *Don't Check Your Brains at the Door* by Josh McDowell and Bob Hostetler (Word Inc.) presents much of that same evidence but in a version that is great for teens. Chapters are short with more dialogue and stories to make it more interesting. Short "Workouts" end each chapter, taking teens directly to Scripture to learn for themselves. This book actually goes beyond *Evidence* into topics such as the New Age movement, lifestyle choices, sex, televangelists gone astray, and peer pressure. Chapter titles accurately reflect the style of the content. For instance, "The Luke Skywalker God: Exposing the Impersonal Force Myth," "If You're OK, Then I *Must* Be OK: Exposing the God-Will-Grade-on-a-Curve-Myth," and "Stars in Your Eyes: Exposing the Love-at-First-Sight Myth." A four-session, interactive video course, based on the book, is also available. (Recommended for junior or senior high Sunday School classes.) Check your local Christian book store for other titles by McDowell.

A set of six videos from American Portrait Films addresses basic spiritual issues. The series is called *Making a Decision That Lasts Forever: A Traveler's Guide to the Ultimate Destination*. Each video can stand alone, so it is not necessary to purchase the entire set. Videos feature two dynamic speakers, Rice Broocks and Jacob Aranza, each doing three of the videos. Titles are "The Power of a Changed Life" (Broocks), "The Deadliest Three Letter Word" (Aranza), "Repent and Believe" (Broocks), "Sin's Greatest Price" (Aranza), "The Power of the Cross" (Broocks), and "Finishing The Race" (Aranza). The intro (first 5-7 minutes) is very different from the main part of the video. It uses some very flashy, graphic footage that will bother some viewers. You can simply skip that part and start with Broock's presentation if you wish. Both Broocks and Aranza present strong Scriptural messages with lots of humor. They incorporate other video footage that holds your attention. These videos are great for junior high through adult audiences.

Developing a Christian World View

Christians generally interpret the term "world view" to mean looking with God's eyes on all of mankind, and recognizing that all men are in the same sinful, needy state. Developing an understanding of other cultures, often through "missions" education is one of the educational tools we use to implement this idea of world view.

In recent years "world view" has taken on a broader and slightly different meaning. The term is now used to identify the type of philosophical framework through which we interpret all areas of life. Thus, a person might have a secular humanist world view, a Marxist world view, or a biblical Christian world view.

When we discuss world view education for high school, we are generally referring to the second, broader definition, which encompasses the first definition.

For children below the ages of fourteen or fifteen, world view education should be narrower in scope. Providing our children with a strong foundation of Bible knowledge is the most important thing we should do. We can add to that a good foundation in all subject areas which includes the influence of ideas and beliefs, however, with a narrow focus. For example, when we learn about scientists we can study how their religious beliefs influenced their scientific outlook. Missions education also is very appropriate in the foundational years.

Because older students are better able to make connections and relate ideas to one another, world view education should change to the broader definition in the latter years of high school. In those years, students can tie information together, tracing patterns of philosophical thought and their results. We should then encourage them to consider their responsibility as Christians to live a life that reflects a biblical

Christian world view—a suiting culmination to our years of home schooling.

Secular World Views in Action

A 1989 Gallup poll found that "...cheating is rampant in high school and college....about 75% of high school students admit to cheating, while about 50% of college students do."

In 1990, in our neighboring city of Anaheim, California, AIDS activists handed out condoms to eager teens in front of their high school. School officials, observing what was occurring, were only concerned that "activists stayed on the sidewalk and didn't block traffic...." One recipient remarked, "They know we're going to do it anyway, so why not give us some protection?"

Most Christian home educators still find such attitudes shocking or dismaying because they so clearly violate God's law. But there has been such a turnaround in attitudes toward ethics and morality in the United States that basing our judgments on God's law is considered a backwards, ignorant way of looking at things. The Judeo-Christian world view that prevailed in our country two centuries ago has been discarded or perverted so drastically that few even recognize what that world view might be. Unfortunately, many Bible-believing Christians have become so confused because of popular psychology, the media, government, and others with influence that their world views are suffering from distortion and inconsistency. A world view should provide a coherent and consistent foundation for life. From that world view we should be able to develop beliefs, positions, and attitudes about all areas of life.

The Bible provides the guidelines by which we form our world view. It is vital that we study Scripture in relation to ethics, government, science, the arts, and all other areas of life so that we have solid reasoning to back up our biblical Christian world view. Those who reject the Bible use other sources to validate their belief systems. If we want to convince others of the correctness of our position, we will be much more effective if we first understand the world view which is influencing them as well as its sources. In fact, part of developing a Biblical Christian world view should be examination of other possibilities.

We like to think that the truth should be obvious to others, but we overlook the fact that people do not purposely choose to believe something they think is stupid or unbelievable. They have good reasons for what they believe (although those reasons will usually reveal contradictions or faulty reasoning on some level of examination). When we discuss an issue with someone on the other side of the fence, the bottom line is usually not the issue itself, but the world view that informs each of our opinions. For instance many people believe that man is nothing more than a highly developed animal. Each man is answerable only to himself. Since they do not believe in an afterlife, they must do all they can to make their "stay on earth" as enjoyable as possible. So, of course, it makes sense to abort babies who will cramp their lifestyles or interfere with their developing careers or irritate (and possibly scare off) their live-in lovers. The bottom-line issue is the purpose and sanctity of life, while abortion rights and choice are side issues.

What Does This Have To Do with Education?

I believe that ideas result in actions; generally speaking, bad ideas result in bad actions and good ideas produce good actions. The mess facing our society is the natural consequence of belief in and action based upon bad ideas about God, man, man's relationship to God, the family, government and all other areas. For instance, Adolph Hitler believed the Aryan race to be superior to all others. He believed that inferior races and "damaged" Aryans such as the retarded, the ill, and the elderly were a drain on society. It was then his duty to eliminate those problems. His actions were a natural outworking of his belief system. Handing out condoms to teenagers and giving them the message that we know that it is just too difficult for them to restrain themselves is an action based upon the belief that men are no more morally responsible than animals. Cheating follows a slightly different line of logic. The usual excuse is, "It doesn't hurt anyone else, so it's up to me," which denies man's subjection to God's authority and places morality on a relativistic plane.

What ideas do our children truly believe about God and man? Have they begun to develop a biblical Christian world view that will guide them through life? While the media have certainly played a vital role in the advancement of false ideas, schools have had at least as much of a hand in the process. We recognize the obvious distortions such as the idea that homosexuality is merely another, equally valid, lifestyle choice. We have more trouble recognizing the truth twisting behind ideas such as, "All teenagers go through a period of rebellion," and "If we all pay enough taxes, government can solve all of the problems of hunger and homelessness," and "God probably created the world, but he used evolution to accomplish His goal."

While we can and should begin to help our children develop a biblical world view from the time they are young, the teen years are a crucial time for focusing on its importance. This means looking beyond the typical course of study for high school. Most of us have simply adapted the typical course of study which has been followed by most schools for many years. We assume that by using Christian textbooks and including a Bible study course, we will have taken care of any philosophical problems. Unfortunately, if our goal is to help our child develop a biblical world view, it's not enough.

What will our teens face when they complete high school? Some will be able to continue their education at good Christian colleges. Others will continue their education at pagan colleges and universities where they will encounter both obvious and subtle challenges to their faith every day. Still others will be working with people who follow all types of non-Christian belief systems.

Are They Properly Equipped?

We must ask ourselves if we are equipping our children to first of all be able to stand firm in explaining their belief in Jesus Christ as Savior, and, second, to be able to bring the precepts of Christianity back into positions of influence in all areas of life. Unless they understand how those areas of life are dominated by other belief systems, they obviously will not have any idea what changes are needed.

One of our family's goals in home education has been to raise our children to do more than just hang on to their own personal faith. We want them to be used by God. To equip them, an important part of their education is developing a biblical Christian world view, and within that, teaching them how to examine all areas of life.

At the same time, we also teach them how those holding other world views interpret those same areas. Unless they understand the presuppositions that form opinions they are like gardeners trimming branches off a tree that is suffering from root disease.

Defining Your Course

In the early years, providing our children with a strong foundation of Bible knowledge is the most important thing we should do. We can add to that a good foundation in all subject areas which includes the influence of ideas and beliefs. For example, when we learn about scientists we can study how their religious beliefs influenced their scientific outlook. (At older levels, we can tie this information together, tracing patterns of philosophical thought and their results; however, young children are not usually ready to make all of those connections.) Good Christian textbooks along with other resources can be used for this purpose.

While we should be laying the background for world view studies in the elementary grades, our students need to be mature enough to wrestle with challenging ideas before really delving into serious world view studies—usually the upper high school level.

How we choose to approach world view education at high school level will vary from person to person, depending upon our interest in and knowledge of different subject areas. Francis Schaeffer was very interested in the arts, so he developed his discussion of world view based upon historical analysis of the changes in the arts. David Noebel has developed the Summit program with more emphasis on history and political systems, although he addresses many other subject areas. However, history stands out as the common unifying subject for every in-depth study of world views. The flow of events and their results provide obvious evidence with which we can begin our study. From history we can build in any direction we choose—art, literature, philosophy, politics, etc.—going as far as we feel is practical.

How We Did It

We began world view education as a specific study with our two oldest sons (at ages 14 and 16) with a do-it-yourself approach, worked within that framework for a year, then added Summit Ministries' *Understanding the Times* curriculum the second year. Although we had to work from scratch when we began, we are beginning to see materials designed for this purpose such as *Understanding the Times* and will probably see more in the next few years.

I want to share some of what we have done to give you some possibilities to consider. The book that prompted my thinking in this direction and provided the rationale for the course was Francis Schaeffer's *How Should We Then Live?* (Crossway). Although I read the book many years ago, I still use it with my sons after we have studied a time period and the related topics. It serves as an excellent way to review and tie everything together. (Schaeffer presents too many ideas in each chapter for teens to read without preparation. They need background first or else they are overwhelmed with unfamiliar ideas. You might use the book *Turning Point* [see review below] as an easier-to-read alternative.)

Choose A History Text

A good history book which discusses philosophical ideas and their impact on events is crucial. Excellent texts trace those ideas beyond their immediate time period down through following generations. The text that I have found to be most useful is the Bob Jones University Press' *World History for Christian Schools*. It covers art, philosophy, world religions, literature, science, law, and politics (albeit briefly) fairly well. The discussion questions are the outstanding feature. Questions such as, "What motivated European rulers to either support or oppose the Reformation? What influence did Christians have on nineteenth-century Europe? What impact did European society have on Christians?" extend thinking beyond the facts into the realm of belief systems.

Developing Units of Study

Next, I developed unit studies with a world view emphasis, by expanding on content in chapters or units in the history book. I also used a comprehensive time line, *The World History Factfinder*. (A similar book, *The Timetables of History* by Bernard Grun [Simon and Schuster], is more commonly available to home educators.) I looked through the time line for particular people, places, or events that would be helpful in developing world view themes. I was also looking for relationships between ideas and events that are easy to miss in history books. For instance, events on the "religious front" often had dramatic impact upon politics; the French revolution is a good example.

The first year I chose to place varying amounts of emphasis on subject areas according to the time period being studied. For instance, when we began with creation and early history, biology (theories of origins) received more attention than it did in the Middle Ages. I then chose a variety of resources to use for each subject area.

Art

Because of my experience with Schaeffer's book, I incorporated art, music, and architecture. Our primary source for the arts was *History of Art* by H.W. Janson (Prentice-Hall Order Dept.). This very large book is the best resource to use because Janson follows an historical outline, tying in information from other subject areas where appropriate. The abundant illustrations include most paintings, sculptures, and buildings referred to by Schaeffer in *How Should We Then Live?* (A less expensive, slightly abridged version entitled *The History of Art for Young People* is available from Abrams.)

Cornerstone Curriculum Project's *Adventures in Art* can be used for a more thorough study of paintings described by Schaeffer. The first two levels in the *Adventures in Art* series help children to learn to observe art. The third and fourth levels move into world view applications, quoting frequently from Schaeffer and following his line of thought.

Literature

Literature is a wonderful revealer of world views, so I incorporated literature throughout our studies. I chose a few of the influential authors from each historical period and read either excerpts or entire books. The selected readings are not all by Christians. Part of our goal is understanding opposing belief systems, and that can best be done by reading what their proponents have to say for themselves rather than always reading a Christian's interpretation of what they say. Reading an excerpt from Machiavelli's *The Prince* helped us understand the pragmatic attitudes of rulers of the Renaissance and after. (We probably see more pragmatism today than was evident four and five centuries ago!) We discussed Machiavelli's world view and the conclusions he formed because of it. Sir Thomas More's *Utopia*, written twenty years before his conflict with King Henry VIII, described his vision for a perfect world. We watched the movie *A Man for All Seasons* about the later period of More's life and contrasted the evident changes in his philosophy. *Luther on Education* (a translation of two of Martin Luther's educational treatises) provided interesting reading. From his perspective, it seemed a good thing for government to establish state schools to ensure that children learned to read and become industrious. This led into a discussion of government's responsibility to its citizens and imposition of philosophical views through law. Sources for literature were often old editions from thrift stores or library books, but I have found A Beka's *Masterpieces from World Literature* an excellent source for representative reading.

Philosophy

Philosophy certainly is evident within other subject areas, but I chose to spend even more time studying other philosophical/religious systems. While most history books address various religions and their origins, it helped to devote extra study to belief systems that have persisted through the centuries such as Hinduism, Buddhism, and Islam. Many of these ancient religions, particularly Hinduism, are becoming increasingly popular in the United States but go unrecognized under various New Age disguises. The teaching that there are many roads to God, characteristic of some of these religions, provides an important plank of the global, one world government agenda being promoted by our president and others. These philosophical/religious issues are really at the heart of our world view study. By the time we have gone through other subject areas and raised questions that lead back to the origins of beliefs, students are ready to examine such fundamentals of philosophy.

We used a number of resources for these studies. Two examples of the types of books that were very useful are *Roman Mythology* by Stewart Perowne (Peter Bedrick Books) and *A Book of Beliefs* (Lion Publishing).

Understanding the Times

Although we had already been working through our own world view studies the first year, the second year we incorporated the *Understanding the Times* (UTT)curriculum. We continued with history, art, and architecture, and expanded our literature studies, while UTT filled in other areas, saving me much preparation time.

Understanding the Times is a video-based version of the two-week programs offered by Summit Ministries at their Colorado headquarters. The purpose of UTT is to enable Christians to obey two particular Scriptural commands. The first is, "See to it that no one takes you captive through philosophy and empty deception according to the tradition of men, according to the elementary principles of the world, rather than according to Christ." (Colossians 2:8) The second is, "But sanctify Christ as Lord in your hearts, always being ready to make a defense to everyone who asks you to give an account for the hope that is in you, yet with gentleness and reverence." (1 Peter: 3:15)

Understanding the Times divides world views under three headings: secular humanism, Marxism/Leninism, and biblical Christianity. (An appendix addresses New Age world views.) UTT then examines ten areas or topics through each of the three world views. The ten areas are

theology, philosophy, ethics, biology, psychology, sociology, law, politics, economics, and history.

There are over thirty tapes, most having two lessons per tape. Some topics such as creation/evolution and modern history receive much more attention than others.

Students each have a binder containing outlines for the videos which they fill in as they watch. Other supplemental books and readings also come with the course. Discussion of the videos and readings is a vital and exciting part of the course (the best part according to the group I worked with).

Understanding the Times is also the title of a book by Dr. David Noebel of Summit Ministries. The book is designed to be used as part of the course, although it can be used on its own with no problem. The book addresses the same ten subject areas listed above, with an entire chapter addressing each area from each of the three major world views. (This is a very large book!) Unlike the video series, the book balances time spent in each area. The text is very useful in conjunction with the videos. It is written at an adult reading level, and the content is challenging, so it is not a book to assign blindly for teen reading. It is intended to serve as a reference tool to which we can refer when confronted in one of the topical areas. Because of this, there is repetition of content in some chapters, so that we will have all the pertinent information we need within each chapter rather than having to search throughout the book.

[Author's Note: *Understanding the Times* incorporates a number of the books and videos reviewed in this chapter. I have marked those that are used with the course with an asterisk "*".]

Although we began our world view studies with only our family, when we began the UTT course we included five other teenagers. I have seen the effectiveness of the course in meeting its Scriptural goals. In fact, I am so impressed with the course that I think it should be offered to all Christian teens and parents. The catch is the cost, around $800 plus textbook ($15) and notebook ($10) costs for each student. (Notebook pages can be duplicated for class use to save money, but students will definitely need a binder to keep them together.) This can be overcome by forming group classes, a church investing in the videos for their library, or soliciting donations. I strongly recommend using the course with two or more students because of the learning that takes place through discussion and interaction.

Alternative Courses

Those who cannot use UTT for whatever reason can still pursue biblical world view studies. Since I know of nothing other than UTT that is "self-contained" and directed toward high school (and college) students, this means that parents need to design the study themselves.

This is not necessarily a disadvantage since parents can then structure the study to be as comprehensive as they wish. A good place to begin is Francis Schaeffer's book, *How Should We Then Live?* (Crossway). If Schaeffer is too heavy, read *Turning Point* (Crossway) instead.

The second step might be checking out the many, many resources available from the *Christian Worldview Library*. Becky Elder's booklet, *Read for Your Life* (available from the Christian Worldview Library) provides ideas on how to put together such a course of study as well as lists of recommended reading arranged in chronological order. The Christian Worldview Library lends a huge assortment of books, cassettes, and videos on Bible study, American history, world history, economics, business ethics, abortion, current events, home education, plus many more topics. We can select materials to use as either foundations or supplements for world view studies.

Even though I spent a number of years pulling together ideas and materials to use for such a course, everyone need not plan as comprehensive a study as we did. Various aspects of world view studies can be as in-depth as each family wishes.

The following resources are either ones that we have used or ones that others have recommended to me. All of them are useful for some aspect of world view study.

General Resources

➡ American Information Newsletter

This monthly newsletter is a must for those who are interested in balancing the secular news media with all of the important information that they omit or present in slanted fashion because of their anti-Christian and liberal biases.

The newsletter culls reports from conservative and Christian media (and sometimes secular media), summarizing articles in brief paragraphs while providing the original reference. Summaries are often opinionated and include editorial comments.

This newsletter will provide excellent topics for discussion of current events, as well as ammunition for the conservative Christian viewpoint.

➡ The Barna Report, 1992-93 by George Barna (Regal Books)

The Barna Report is an annual survey of life-styles, values, and religious views. It is useful to give us a better understanding of the types of opinions and confused philosophy we are likely to encounter when discussing important issues with others, Christians as well as non-Christians. For instance, while, not surprisingly, 25% of non-Christians believe that "The whole idea of sin is outdated," 11% of born-again Christians also agree with that statement. (That should raise the question, "Why do we need to be born again?") Survey questions vary from year to year, with some overlap, so last year's edition offers some different insights from this year's. Although The Barna Report is not intended to be read like a novel, it offers some eye openers that will keep you turning the pages.

➡ Battle for the Family by Tim LaHaye (Baker Book House, formerly published by Fleming H. Revell Company)

This is one of Tim LaHaye's many thought-provoking books dealing with our secular society, philosophical ideas, and Christianity. LaHaye's books are easier reading than books from authors such as Whitehead, Kilpatrick, or Schaeffer.

➡ Children at Risk* by Dr. James Dobson and Gary Bauer (Word Inc.)

Changing views about families are some of the most visible evidences of world views which have shifted away from a dependence upon Judeo-Christian values. Dr. Dobson and Gary Bauer, president of the Family Research Council, pile up the evidence showing that forces destructive to families are growing in strength. They trace the disintegration through all areas that touch our children—education, families, moral codes, the media, politics, child care, and art. They call for a return to Judeo-Christian values and out-

line a strategy for achieving that goal. While I challenge their recommendation of a voucher system to solve our educational woes, other suggestions are helpful.

➡ Freedom, Justice, and Hope: Toward a Strategy for the Poor and the Oppressed by Olasky, Schlossberg, Berthoud, and Pinnock (Crossway)

This is one of the books in Crossway's Turning Point Christian Worldview Series. It is very broad, encompassing compassion issues, government, economics, Marxist ideology, and many related topics. Each chapter is written by one of the authors, making it easy to read selectively. This means that if we are studying a topic covered within this book, we can pull out one chapter to supplement study of that issue. However, chapters do relate to each other, building a total picture in order to provide a framework for Christian action. Reliance on the Bible as the ultimate source for the answers to society's needs provides solid backing for the ideas presented here.

➡ The Great Evangelical Disaster by Francis Schaeffer (Crossway)

Francis Schaeffer is an author who concentrated on the application of Christianity in our lives. While some of his philosophical works are heavy reading for most high schoolers, some of his books are quite appropriate. An example is his last book, The Great Evangelical Disaster, which I highly recommend.

➡ How Should We Then Live? by Francis Schaeffer (Crossway)

In what is probably his most well-known book, How Should We Then Live?, Francis Schaeffer uses history, religion, philosophy, art, music, literature, and culture as a background for a discussion of society and how we should be living if we are under God's direction. Personally, I would like to see each of our children study this book before they graduate from high school. I recognize that many of them will find the range of information and ideas presented overwhelming, so I would not recommend such a study until junior or senior level. Before then, teens are unlikely to have acquired the educational background (cultural literacy!) necessary to understand ideas Schaeffer speaks about in this book.

Also check out other books by Francis Schaeffer such as The Christian Manifesto.

➡ Jeremiah Films

Jeremiah Films has made a number of films that are useful for studying world views. (The Pagan Invasion series and Gods of the New Age from Jeremiah films are described elsewhere in this section, The Evolution Conspiracy* is described under "Creation Science," and AIDS: What You Haven't Been Told is reviewed under "Sex Education.") They divide their films into four categories: Cult/Occult, New Age/Apologetics, Contemporary Issues/Prophecy, and Pro-Life/Motivational. The films vary in length from 25 to 104 minutes. They have a powerful film on AIDS entitled, AIDS: What You Haven't Been Told*. (They also have a shorter version, "hosted" by a nurse addressing a high school group that is being widely promoted.) One video that targets world views in particular is False Gods of Our Time, a "docu-drama providing Biblical evidence for a Christian world view." Send for a brochure listing all of their titles to choose those appropriate for your studies.

➠ L'Abri Fellowship Foundation

With many branches around the world, the L'Abri Fellowship Foundation offers newsletters on numerous world view related topics, cassettes, seminars, videos, lecture reprints, and referrals for materials. Some L'Abri branches offer opportunities for individuals to come and pursue personally tailored study for up to two or three months, using tapes, books, lectures, and discussions with a tutor's supervision. Older teens especially might be interested in pursuing such an opportunity.

➠ Legacy Communications

Legacy is a Christian ministry, largely reflecting the work of George Grant. They offer Grant's books as well as others, many of which deal with world view issues. RU486, Planned Parenthood, the homosexual movement, politics (Grant's new book is *Perot: The Populist Appeal of Strong-Man Politics*), and history (another new book by Grant is about Columbus) are examples of topics addressed through their book list. The *Legacy* newsletter makes interesting reading; main articles are thought provoking and book reviews are extremely helpful. Write Legacy Communications for information.

➠ National Public-policy Resource Theme-packets by C. Bernard Schriver

Read the complete description under "Current Events." Many of the Theme-packets help to expand study on world view topics. Packets related to the Constitution, separation of Church and State, family issues, education, the free market, elections, and environmentalism would all be useful, as would many others.

➠ The New Millennium by Pat Robertson (Word Inc.)

In this book, subtitled "10 Trends That Will Impact You and Your Family by the Year 2000," Pat Robertson, founder and president of CBN and former presidential candidate, interprets current events in terms of their impact on Christians. He analyzes both world and national scenes in the realms of politics/governmental systems, philosophy/religion, economics, technology, the environment, the family, and education. He is one of the few writers to also address the rise of anti-Semitism throughout the world.

Robertson takes on the risky task of attempting to predict where we will be in each area a decade from now.

While Robertson presents a great deal of factual information, his writing style is interesting and easy to read. Most high school students can handle this book. It covers some of the same topics that David Noebel covers in *Understanding the Times*, but more briefly and at an easier, less scholarly level. It serves well as a source for broad background reading.

See also the review of Robertson's subsequent book, *The New World Order*, which enlarges on some of the themes of *The New Millennium*.

➠ The New World Order by Pat Robertson (Word Inc.)

I found this book to be even more interesting than *The New Millennium*. Robertson presents his case that there is a behind-the-scenes plan for a new world order being enacted by powerful people. He marshals his evidence in lawyer-like fashion, documenting his assertions with facts. Although we might not agree with all of his conclusions, there are enough disquieting and incontrovertible facts to cause us to look beyond information we get from the major media and government. Robertson shows how plans for a new world order will affect our lives in a negative fashion.

Mature teens will have no trouble reading this book and will probably find the writing style engaging because Robertson uses many stories and examples rather than simply presenting information. The world views motivating the drive to achieve a one-world government are discussed. Since the book deals with many areas of life—government, economics, education, family, etc.—it will serve very well as a basic book for world view studies.

➠ Seven Men Who Rule the World from the Grave* by Dave Breese (Moody)

One of the supplemental books for UTT impresses me as being an excellent resource for anyone studying world views. *Seven Men Who Rule from the Grave* provides deeper studies of law, philosophy, and economics. Breese identifies seven key players in recent world history—Marx, Wellhausen, Keynes, Darwin, Dewey, Freud, and Kierkegaard—who have had tremendous impact (often for evil), even though it frequently goes unrecognized. He traces their influence from their lives up through the present.

➠ Symposium on the Christian Worldview [Audio Tapes] (Christian Liberty Academy)

This 1989 conference specifically addressed world views. There are fifteen tapes covering a wide array of world view issues, but with a number of them specifically addressing curriculum. Examples of titles are "Conflicting Worldviews: the Dilemma of Double-Mindedness," "A Christian Worldview of Language," "A Christian Worldview of Mathematics," and "Christian Worldview of the Media."

Other tapes from conferences sponsored by Christian Liberty Academy also relate to world view issues. All are listed in their *Christian Liberty Conference Series Audio Cassette Tape Catalog*.

➠ Turning Point; A Christian Worldview Declaration by Herbert Schlossberg and Marvin Olasky (Crossway)

Turning Point is the introductory book to an entire world view series published by Crossway. It is a foundational book similar to *How Should We Then Live?*, but it is much easier to read. The authors use stories to illustrate world view disagreements which are either confusing Christians or setting Christianity in opposition to conflicting world views. They give us some historical and philosophical background, although they spend much less time in these areas than does Schaeffer. Instead they offer more "connections" between world views and current events. Story illustrations make it easy to read and understand the weighty ideas presented. *Turning Point* strives to motivate Christians to move out of a narrow religious arena to influence the world. Because of this there are a number of topic-specific books in what they call the "Turning Point Christian Worldview Series."

Books in the series cover the topics of the media, international politics, the press, popular culture, national politics, population issues, compassion for the poor, use of resources and scarcity, literature, crisis childbearing, the arts, and education. Series titles reviewed elsewhere in this book are *Reading Between the Lines* (literature), *Recovering the Lost Tools of Learning* (education), *Prospects for Growth* (population issues), *Freedom, Justice, and Hope* (the poor), and *Prosperity and Poverty* (use of resources and scarcity). All of the reviewed books are outstanding, and I assume that the others are similar in quality.

Newspapers and Current Events

Studying the past is helpful in developing a Christian world view, but if we look only at the past and ignore the present, we overlook one of the purposes for even pursuing such study. Current events demonstrate the outworking of world views. Most of us see the results of anti-God world views in the school system, but few of us identify the same elements at work in our judicial or welfare systems. As we study, we begin to identify more cause and effect relationships. The newspaper provides bountiful examples of world views in action in all areas of life. Christian newspapers such as *World* (God's World Publications) are an excellent option for those who cannot or choose not to subscribe to a secular newspaper.

Philosophy, Religion, and Apologetics

➡ **America, The Sorcerer's New Apprentice: The Rise of New Age Shamanism** by Dave Hunt and T.A. McMahon (Harvest House Publishers)

Written in a lively, easy-reading style, this book offers a telling exposè of the New Age movement in America. It documents the rising popularity of the occult, shamanism, satanism, psychotherapy as religious science, sorcery, and other related spiritual pits, that teach man to rely on "the power within himself." The implications are frightening. The authors say, "Many of America's largest and most powerful corporations, with branches in numerous countries, have now joined this unprecedented worldwide missionary effort....The sophistication, advanced degrees, and affluence of these new jet-set missionaries lend a credibility that makes their seductive gospel almost irresistible." (p. 293)

➡ **A Book of Beliefs** (Lion)

What were originally three separate books are combined into one, three-part volume. In "Religions," by Myrtle Langley, the author takes a very objective view of the major religions, summarizing their history and beliefs in an easily readable format. There is a subtle Christian slant throughout the book, yet it does not analyze and criticize the various beliefs as does *Kingdom of the Cults*. The book ends with a strong statement endorsing Christianity. "Cults and New Faiths" by John Butterworth discusses cults such as Jehovah's Witnesses, Scientology, and Baha'i. This book has a much more obvious Christian slant, questioning beliefs as it explains them. Creative layout, plus many illustrations and photographs make this book visually appealing. It is easy for younger teens to read. The third part is "Mysteries," which explores the occult from a Christian viewpoint.

➡ **Comparing World Views** by Roy Hanson

For those who have little understanding of the major philosophies shaping today's society, I recommend *Comparing World Views*. This booklet gives a concise summary of what a Christian "world view" is and compares this with secular humanistic and cosmic humanistic (New Age fits in here) world views in chart form. The implications of how our world views shape our lives are also shown.

➡ **Every Thought Captive: A Study Manual for the Defense of Christian Truth** by Richard L. Pratt, Jr.

Recommended for older teens, this book about apologetics is based upon the methods of the theologian, Cornelius Van Til.

➡ **Gods of the New Age** by Caryl Matrisciana (Harvest House Publishers)

[also available in video from Jeremiah Films]

Author Caryl Matrisciana lived in India for twenty years and speaks from experience when she explores the New Age movement's Hindu roots and the dramatic increase in the numbers of people holding such beliefs. Rather than simply documenting ways that New Age ideas have infiltrated western culture, Caryl shows us through her own personal story including her search for spiritual truth.

However, this is not just her personal story, but a book filled with factual information about topics such as meditation, yoga, chanting, visualization, gurus, as well as tie-ins with the media and globalism.

Caryl's writing style is eye-opening yet not sensationalist. The reading level is easy enough for almost any high school student. This book helps us recognize that New Age ideas, which recognize an anti-God spiritual force, are increasingly replacing or incorporating atheistic Secular Humanist ideas.

➡ **Gods of the New Age** [video] (Jeremiah Films)

See the description of the book above. The film spends more time on the factual information than on Caryl's personal story. Information is presented through interviews and startling film footage. While it is not as comprehensive as the book, it provides plenty of information to expose the growing impact of New Age world views on all of our culture.

➡ **The Islamic Invasion** by Robert Morey (Harvest House Publishers)

Robert Morey is a respected scholar and one of the most well-known figures in the field of apologetics. He has written other "apologetic" books such as *How to Answer a Jehovah's Witness, How to Answer a Mormon, Reincarnation and Christianity*, and *Battle of the Gods*. In The Islamic Invasion, he confronts the teachings of the second largest religion in the world (second only to Christianity). Rather than working, as Geisler does, through the logical fallacies, Morey first presents background and teachings of Islam, then examines all of the problems and contradictions within the belief system. He also shows factual contradictions between the Bible and the Quran (or Koran), although Islam claims that Allah is the same God as the God of the Bible. Morey's writing style in this book is very easy for teens to read. While the table of contents offers general guidelines to the book's content, the lack of an index is an irritation. For information about other books by Morey, write to the Research and Education Foundation of which Morey is the Executive Director.

➡ **The Kingdom of the Cults** by Walter Martin (Bethany House)

This is the classic book on cultic religions. Historical and theological information is included, documenting the origins and teachings of most cult beliefs we will encounter. This is one of the most helpful books available.

➡ **Operation World** by P. J. Johnstone (Multnomah Press)

Operation World is a handbook of information on most countries, including spiritual status. It gives economic and geographical information to help us understand the situations of various peoples, but the emphasis is on religious views and spiritual needs. It tells what percentages of each country's population belong to which religions. Combined with the other background information, this helps us better understand various cultures.

➤The Pagan Invasion video series (Jeremiah Films)

There are thirteen videos in this series, each 48 minutes long. They combine interviews, narration, and location film footage in fast-paced, visually-engaging presentations. Titles of the thirteen tapes are: *Halloween: Trick or Treat* (pagan roots); *Invasion of the Godmen* (eastern mysticism); *Meditation: Pathway to Deception?; The East Seduces the West; Dawning of the New Age; Evolution: Hoax of the Century?; Evolution: From Physics to Metaphysics; Preview of the Anti-Christ; Secrets of Mind Control; The Latter Day Empire* (Mormonism); *Joseph Smith's Temple of Doom; Religion vs. Christianity;* and *Doorways to Satan* (the media).

Many of the titles are helpful for studying new age philosophy, evolution, the occult, and Mormonism. Jeremiah Films uses some of the same footage in these films that appears in some of their others such as *Gods of the New Age.*

➤The Search [video] (Inter-Varsity Christian Fellowship of the U.S.A.)

This 26-minute video is an excellent introduction to New Age beliefs. It clearly contrasts New Age beliefs on key spiritual issues (God, the value of man, the future, definition of truth, and authority) with biblical Christian beliefs. The video comes with a great little discussion guide so that we can develop ideas even further.

➤When Skeptics Ask: A Handbook on Christian Evidences by Norman Geisler and Ron Brooks (Victor Books)

Study of world views almost inevitably leads us into discussions with others about faith issues. This book addresses the common and not so common questions unbelievers raise to challenge our claim that salvation is through faith in the work of Jesus Christ. It begins with questions about God, His existence, and His nature. Examples of questions and challenges addressed: "If God created all things, then how did He create Himself?" and "God is nothing but a psychological crutch, a wish, a projection of what we hope is true." Following chapters deal with other gods, evil, miracles, Jesus Christ, the Bible, Bible difficulties, archeology, science and evolution, the afterlife, truth, and morals.

Geisler and Brooks cover the major issues, although they cannot possibly address every challenge within this one book. They steer us to other sources when necessary. For example, in the chapter on Bible difficulties they recommend Gleason Archer's *Encyclopedia of Bible Difficulties* (Zondervan) for those who want to study further.

I find this book particularly useful because of its topical arrangement and the logical layout. I find it frequently following the common progression of questions into which such discussions fall. This means that it will be more useful than an encyclopedic book where we have to jump around to follow a particular topic.

I also appreciate the fact that opposing arguments are treated with respect rather than ridicule, even while the authors are exposing their fallacies.

While many of Geisler's books are very challenging reading (lots of logic employed to present arguments), this one should be understandable to most high school students, especially if they read it in sections as they confront the various issues.

Look for the follow-up book, *When Critics Ask* (Victor Books), by Norman Geisler and Thomas Howe, which expands the same type of discussion into the beliefs of cults.

➤Worlds Apart by Norman Geisler and William Watkins (Baker Book House)

This is a comparative analysis of seven major world views popular today: theism, atheism, pantheism, panentheism, deism, finite godism, and polytheism. The approach is scholarly relying heavily on logic to refute false belief systems. I appreciate the authors' approach which evaluates both positive and negative points of each belief system while still showing fatal flaws in all but theism. This book is for advanced study or parental reference, not for average teens.

History

Read the section in Chapter Thirteen on "America's Christian History" for many resources that broaden our students' understanding of history beyond textbook content.

➤Modern Times: From the Twenties to the Nineties by Paul Johnson (Harper Collins Publishers)

See the review in Chapter Thirteen under "World History." The theme of this book, that the rejection of moral absolutes results in a decline in societies, makes this an especially apropos book for world view studies.

Science

➤Bible-Science Association

The Mid-Kansas Branch Chapter of the Bible-Science Association operates a lending library for videos, audio tapes, and books on creation and evolution, including some videos reviewed in this book such as *Evolution Conspiracy, The Genesis Solution,* and *Gods of the New Age.* More information about the Bible-Science Association can be found under "Creation Science" in Chapter Fourteen.

➤The Evolution Conspiracy*

Available in either book or video format. See "Science" for a complete description. Either resource is excellent for a study of world views. They both demonstrate how fundamental evolution is in the belief systems of those who reject the God of the Bible.

➤The Genesis Solution (Films for Christ)

See the complete description under "Science." If you have to pick just one film on creation and evolution, the choice might be between this film and *The Evolution Conspiracy.*

➤A Scientist Looks at Creation (American Portrait Films)

See the complete description under "Creation Science." This video offers a simplistic look at world views from a scientific perspective. It concentrates much more on science than on religious implications, but it opens the door for discussions about the evolution/creation debate as well as questions about the age of the earth.

Economics

➤Prospects for Growth by E. Calvin Beisner (Crossway)

The relationship between population growth and economics is a source of great controversy. Non-Christians often see population control as the only way to raise the standard of living. Meanwhile, Christians such as Beisner demonstrate the poor correlation between population control and economic improvement. They also use Biblical principles to suggest other ways of improving the economic situation. This book and *Prosperity and Poverty* provide Biblical alternatives to popular macro economics viewpoints.

➠Prosperity and Poverty by E. Calvin Beisner (Crossway)

Those who want fewer (or no) government entitlement programs are often accused of being callous about the needs of the poor. Beisner analyzes present government economic policies in this regard, and he demonstrates how ineffective they often are. He also recommends alternatives that are in keeping with Scripture.

Psychology

➠Psychoheresy: The Psychological Seduction of Christianity by Martin and Deidre Bobgan (Eastgate Publishers)

The Bobgan's have stirred up a great deal of controversy with their criticism of Christian reliance on psychology. They have not limited their attacks to non-Christians, but have challenged Christian psychologists who "...[treat] problems of living by the use of psychological rather than or in addition to biblical means." They see a dangerously increasing reliance on psychological answers which deters people from seeking Scriptural solutions to their problems. They are basically in line with Kilpatrick, whose book is also reviewed here, but they go further in identifying and criticizing well-known Christian psychologists. Two succeeding books by the Bobgans, *Prophets of Psychoheresy I* and *II*, are more controversial in this way than is *Psychoheresy*.

➠Psychological Seduction: The Failure of Modern Psychology by William Kirk Kilpatrick (Thomas Nelson Publishers)

This is an excellent expose of the failure of man's wisdom. Kilpatrick examines different ideas about the nature of man and how even Christians have come to interpret behavior based on false psychological presuppositions. The reading level is easy enough to make this book one of the few on psychology that is accessible to teens.

Literature/Reading

➠The Great Adventure: A Life-Time Reading Plan for the Great Works of the Western World by Robert D. Linder and Eileen D. Roesler (Mulberry Books)

This booklet is very useful for helping us select books or excerpts from among recognized classics to illustrate world view development. Titles are listed under topics and time periods, making it easy to select those that will supplement a chronologically-based study from the time of the Greeks to the present. Topical areas include literature, history, autobiography/biography, politics and society, and religion and philosophy. A thematic listing at the back offers the alternative of creating unit studies for topics such as "Fantasy and Utopianism," "Good and Evil," "Humor," and "Man and the State."

This book helped me to coordinate readings from A Beka's *Masterpieces from World Literature* with some from other sources into a literature course that both correlated with our history studies and served as a vehicle for studying world views.

Law and government

➠Constitutional Law for Christian Students by Michael P. Farris, Esq. (Home School Legal Defense Association)

This book will help students understand important court decisions that have changed the way our government functions. There are many good examples of world views in action if we closely examine some of these court cases. (See the full review under "Studying the U.S. Constitution and Law.")

➠Does Wrong Become Right If the Majority Approves? [audio or video tape] by Marshall Fritz (Advocates for Self-Government)

Shake up students' basic assumptions about government with this entertaining presentation by libertarian Marshall Fritz. He sets up a scenario, asking under what conditions does taking of a person's goods without his consent become right. This tape will open the door to fruitful discussion about the role of government, taxation, individual rights, and other crucial topics.

➠The Second American Revolution* by John W. Whitehead (Crossway Books)

Constitutional attorney, John Whitehead, has been on the front lines in the battle to defend First Amendment rights for Christians as well as for those of other religious beliefs. In this book, he traces the history of law in the United States from its original theological underpinnings to its present shifting humanistic foundations. He shows how the change in our view of law has resulted in the undermining of our Constitution. This book should shake our faith in the ability of our Constitution to withstand the onslaughts of secular humanists. Instead of leaving us with a dismal outlook, he offers challenging strategies for restoring our nation, which help to answer the question posed by Schaeffer, "How should we then live?"

➠Whatever Happened to Justice? by Richard J. Maybury (Bluestocking Press)

For a very easy-to-understand treatment of law systems, this is the book. It very well depicts the changes that have taken place in our legal system. Highly Recommended. (See complete review under "Studying the U.S. Constitution and Law.")(S)[1]

Social Issues

Abortion

Note: I review a number of different anti-abortion tapes here. Notice that different tapes are more appropriate for different audiences.

➠The Hidden Holocaust [video] (American Portrait Films)

Students who truly want to understand how abortion proponents think will appreciate this video. Jane Chastain interviews key people on both sides of the issue—congressmen, doctors, philosophers, feminists, an ACLU spokeswoman, a priest, etc. We get insight into their logic (or lack of logic, depending upon your viewpoint), which is exactly what we need to see abortion as a world view issue. A sonogram suction abortion and aborted babies are shown, although this is not as graphic a presentation as *The Silent Scream* or *The Massacre of Innocence*. This video is not as emotionally manipulative as others, but instead lines up the ar-

---

1   Throughout this book, I use (S) to indicate that a resource is secular in nature rather than Christian.

guments for consideration while maintaining a pro-life stance. It uses the Bible, particularly at the end, to further strengthen the pro-life position, which limits the potential audience to those who honor Scripture. High school students will benefit from this video more than younger students, since they will recognize more of the names and faces and their influence in the battle.

➠The Massacre of Innocence [video] (American Portrait Films)

This powerful video is for Christian audiences. The first part describes what abortion is, using graphic footage of the process and the results. (Fast forward or skip parts that are too overwhelming.) The next part is unusual among anti-abortion films. It presents the historical context of abortion, its link to pagan worship, and how it fits with modern world views. The Biblical stand is very well presented, tying together all of this information. The second part does not have the graphic footage of the first part, and you might want to use only the second half with viewers who are against abortion but need more background in terms of world views. It also calls on Christians to be active in any number of suggested ways against the American Holocaust.

At the end of the video is a separate segment with host Eric Holmberg who speaks very compassionately from his own experience to those who have had or been involved with an abortion.

➠No Alibis [video] (American Portrait Films)

A pregnant reporter is assigned to write a story on the abortion issue. Part of her research includes a visit to the classroom of a high school teacher with unpopular pro-life views. Within this top-quality drama, there is also a background story about a pregnant girl who has been jilted by her irresponsible boyfriend. The video manages to convey a great deal of factual information about abortion within the story context. It is emotionally charged and engages the audience in the lives of the characters. The lack of graphic abortion footage that we see in many other anti-abortion videos make this video much easier to recommend to groups of all types. Because much of the drama revolves around a high school setting, it is especially appropriate for teens. (It is produced by Pat Boone and stars one of his daughters.)

➠The Silent Scream [video] (American Portrait Films)

Dr. Bernard Nathanson, former abortionist, now a pro-life spokesman, documents the physical reality of what takes place in abortions. He used models and film to show human development. He shows the instruments with which abortions are performed and describes the procedure. The most disturbing parts of this video are footage of an actual abortion and pictures of aborted babies. The abortion is a suction abortion seen via ultrasound images, accompanied by Dr. Nathanson's explanation. Because the video is so graphic, it is not recommended for everyone. I personally would recommend it to those who are considering abortion or who are counseling women who are. There are no emotional arguments, simply a presentation of the truth. The video is so strongly persuasive that I suspect that the numbers of pro-abortionists would drop dramatically if everyone were required to watch it.

➠Who Broke the Baby? [video] (American Portrait Films)

This video is good for teenage girls. It does not contain graphic footage of abortions, although it does describe what is involved. Instead of impressing the audience with the horrors of abortion, it emphasizes the value of life. It addresses the key arguments used in favor of abortion with answers that will reach any audience. There are no religious arguments presented.

Euthanasia

➠The Right to Kill [video] (American Portrait Films)

William F. Buckley, Jr. hosts this educational documentary on euthanasia. Interviews with both advocates and opponents bring out issues on both sides, although arguments are weighted against euthanasia. Some of the most powerful messages are inferred from interviews with Dutch physicians describing the attitudes of doctors in the Netherlands where active euthanasia has become quite common, even without the permission of patients. Interviews with activists in the United States who are promoting liberal euthanasia laws alerts us to the critical nature of the issue. The video ends with a strong message affirming the value of life. The video is suitable for all junior and senior high students as well as adults.

Pornography

➠Fatal Addiction* [video] (Focus on the Family)

Dr. James Dobson's historic interview with convicted murderer Ted Bundy is a powerful message against pornography. Bundy frankly shares how pornography first influenced then drove him to uncontrollable evil. The message is very heavy, but the video is strictly of the interview, so there are no problems with visual content. This is an especially important message to share with teenage boys.

Books in General

Books such as those described above will shape and influence attitudes in a way that textbooks rarely do.

Our teens need access to good libraries that carry books representing all points of view, including that of Christians. Church libraries might be more valuable than public libraries. If libraries cannot provide what you need, Christian bookstores or mail order sources such as those listed in this book (Chapter 19) can certainly help you. An important point to remember is the value of example. If we are reading such books and discussing some of the key issues with our teenagers, later when they are interested in or mature enough to understand more about issues, it is more likely that they will follow our example and read such books on their own.

Serious Consequences

Studying world views certainly involves extra effort, but consider the consequences if we ignore it. Our children will be easy prey for those who can defend their world views. They will lack the knowledge to identify falsehoods and inconsistencies. True Christians are in the minority when it comes to influencing popular opinion in America. We arrived at this state of affairs because almost everything members of our society have learned has been filtered through non-Christian lenses, distorting truth in such a way that we Christians have become unable to even recognize some of the distortions. How can our children turn things around if they cannot identify the problems and their causes?

Ignorance might even be deadly. Growing numbers of people following various New Age gurus are seeking a harmonious convergence of the simultaneous meditations of millions of believers. They believe that this momentous event will usher in a new age in man's spiritual evolution as he grows towards godhood. A major obstacle to man's advancement is the interference from negative vibrations from Christians and other negative thinkers who are impeding the progress of all mankind with their exclusivist and narrow interpretations of truth. The answer? Eliminate the source of negative vibrations (a.k.a. Christians).

A number of non-Christian belief systems battle for dominance in our culture. The Christian belief system right now has the status of an "also ran." It is time for Christians to again make their voices heard, but before we do, we have to make sure those voices understand their own message.

Putting World View Studies on a Transcript

"World view education overlaps many basic high school subjects, sometimes making it a challenge to translate course content onto a standard transcript. What will most likely occur will be that many topics are covered, but it will take two years (or more) of study to accumulate enough study within each area to equal a course in that area.

The end result might even be different than the standard high school course of study. We might list a course in philosophy, ethics, and law—a course unlikely to show up on the typical transcript. However, this should be an asset rather than a liability in terms of college admission.

Even if it means creating a non-traditional course of study, I feel that it is vital that the study of world views be included. As far as I am concerned, developing our sons and daughters into educated Christians who can readily see and explain the validity of their belief in God is at least as important as any other aspect of education.

Stepping Out

Taking this spiritual foundation one step further—that we may be both hearers and doers of the Word—we need to help our teenagers become involved in the world around them through social action and community service.

They can begin by involvement with their church, not just in the youth group fun activities, but in helpful ways such as assisting in Sunday School, visitations, or with jobs related to church upkeep. They can get involved with "adopt a grandparent" programs, meals on wheels, or myriads of other volunteer organizations. There are always hundreds of opportunities for service available to us—as simple as taking cookies to a shut-in, reading to someone who is ill, or helping to collect items for the needy. Everyone can do something!

Short term mission programs are fantastic opportunities for our teenagers. Many organizations train groups of teens and take them to foreign countries to minister with both physical assistance and the gospel. Highly recommended is **Youth With A Mission** (YWAM) with bases for outreach around the world. One of the most popular ministries offering summer missionary opportunities is **Teen Missions**. (Write to Teen Missions Recruitment at the address in the Appendix.) Both YWAM and Teen Missions offer a wide variety of opportunities since they minister in many ways to people in many different countries. A summer spent in volunteer ministry work can be truly life changing.

Obviously, these suggestions for building spiritual foundations are just scratching the surface. Each teenager's spiritual needs will be different. Knowing that God has a plan for each of our children, the most important recommendations that I can give are that we be in constant contact with Him to know what choices He would have us make, and that we encourage our teens to do the same.

Chapter Six

Course of Study

Junior High

The course of study for junior high is fairly easy to deal with. Students should be developing basic study skills and foundational knowledge for the more specialized learning that they will encounter in high school. It is a time for reviewing, consolidating, remediating, and learning according to each student's needs. There is no set list of courses that they must take, although there are generally recognized courses that most junior high students study.

If our teens plan to enroll in a traditional high school, we should make sure that courses typically taught in junior high school have been covered. It will be even more important to make sure that students have the necessary learning skills and work habits to be successful in high school. Read the section on Study Skills in Chapter Three for ideas for improving these areas.

Use the Course of Study form in the Appendix for listing subjects to be studied and resources to be used, or write them out on paper if you wish to include more detail than space permits on the form.

High School

We have talked about philosophies and goals, yet we need still to figure out what subjects our high schooler should study to start him along the road to those goals. These subjects will be the high school course of study.

Before getting into details, we face the personal question of how much confidence we have in defending unusual courses of study or alternative methods of learning. Do we feel safer sticking with a traditional course of study, or are we confident enough to incorporate informal learning situations or unusual subjects? A confident parent can present a unique course of study to a college admissions officer and make it sound like their child has received a fantastic education. An insecure parent is more likely to present such a transcript or portfolio with apologies, implying that it was an inferior education. For our child's sake, we must be honest about our own personalities, because we might be the ones who have to "sell" others on our educational program.

Our confidence in persevering through all of high school is probably even more crucial. Some parents who home educated teenagers for the first year or two of high school, then tried to enroll them in the middle of high school have been told that no credits would be allowed for work done at home. Students would have to begin high school again as freshmen. Schools have the right to refuse to recognize course work from unaccredited schools, and some do. This means that once we begin high school at home, we may have no choice but to continue. If we suffer serious doubts about sticking with it all through high school, we should do one of two things. We can make sure that there is a high school willing to allow credit from home education so that we will have somewhere to turn if things

do not go well. The alternative is to work through an <u>accredited</u> school or correspondence course.

If there is a possibility that our teen will enter a regular high school after his freshman year, we should also take care that his course work parallels that done in the school.

Confidence will definitely influence the choices confronting us. There are many different ways of planning a high school course of study, and the more confident we are, the more freedom we are likely to have in determining how we will proceed.

For both philosophical and practical reasons home educators will have diverse ideas about what they consider essential course content. Let us look at some of the ideas that might shape our course of study.

Cultural Literacy

In his book, *Cultural Literacy, What Every American Needs to Know* (Houghton Mifflin), E.D. Hirsch, Jr. states that people must practice effective communication to function effectively, that effective communication requires shared culture, and that shared culture requires transmission of specific information to children. (Hirsch, p. xvii) That specific information comes primarily from books which have been widely recognized as having had a significant impact upon society's thoughts—books such as the *Bible*, Plato's *Republic*, and other great literary and philosophic works. It also comes from the arts and languages. Hirsch says, "...to understand what somebody is saying, we must understand more than the surface meanings of words; we have to understand the context as well." (p.3) In defining cultural literacy, Hirsch says, "It is the background information, stored in their minds, that enables them to take up a newspaper and read it with an adequate level of comprehension, getting the point, grasping the implications, relating what they read to the unstated context which alone gives meaning to what they read." (Hirsch, p.2) He concludes that general cultural literacy is necessary for people to learn about new ideas, develop new technology, and deal with events and challenges. Hirsch believes that people trained in narrow vocational educational pursuits rather than with broader tools of learning will have difficulty expanding their learning or dealing with new situations. (Hirsch, p.11)

One of the best methods for developing cultural literacy is reading those writings which have been influential in developing men's thoughts and actions. Knowing where to start is a challenge, however, there is a small book written for just that purpose: *The Great Adventure: A Life-Time Reading Plan for the Great Works of the Western World* by Robert D. Linder and Eileen D. Roesler (Mulberry Books). Titles, authors, and dates written are listed under the chapter headings of literature, history, autobiography and biography, politics and society, and religion and philosophy. Within some chapters, books are listed in chronological and geographical order, which is especially helpful for coordinating this reading with history studies. Appendix A lists authors with the dates they lived in chronological order so that we can see when authors lived in relation to one another. A second appendix lists titles under themes, useful for identifying which books are likely to be of greatest interest and also for developing unit studies using great books.

Charlotte Mason

Charlotte Mason a proponent of home education more than sixty-five years ago, promoted ideas similar to those of Hirsch, and her reasoning differed only slightly. Her description of a liberal education is in close accord with what Hirsch promotes—an education that consists largely of reading acknowledged, influential, literary works. She says, "...one of the main purposes of a 'liberal education for all' is to form links between high and low, rich and poor, the classes and the masses, in the strong sympathy of common knowledge." (*The Home Schooling Series: A Philosophy of Education*, p.78 [published by Tyndale House]) Mason further believed that a liberal arts education (as she proposed it be taught) would enhance each person's intellectual ability, attention, and power of recollection—boons to both the intellectual and business worlds. Mason also believed, unlike Hirsch, that education is the "necessary handmaid to religion"—meaning that education provides Bible reading skills and also goes far beyond into shaping moral and character training.

Liberal or Classical Education

In centuries past, education for older levels consisted largely of reading and discussing great books—the liberal (sometimes called classical) education similar to ideas of both Hirsch and Mason. The idea of using workbooks would have seemed ridiculous. Children were expected to have accumulated lots of factual information through study and memorization at younger levels. When children reached their teens, it was time to begin the real thinking and application of knowledge.

Many people in the highest educational circles have been promoting a return to some form of classical education. Proponents would have students concentrate on a liberal arts education in high school and college, learning other skills in college and after graduation, but there is by no means universal agreement about what specifically constitutes a classical education. Generally speaking, it would include literary studies of recognized classical authors from most periods of recorded history. (See *The Great Adventure* described above under "Cultural Literacy.") It would stress writing and communication skills, and probably a foreign language. Study of history, philosophy, world religions, and the fine arts would be incorporated for the light they shed on other subjects. Science and math would receive less emphasis because of time allotted to the other subjects.

In *Recovering the Lost Tools of Learning: An Approach to Distinctively Christian Education* (Crossway), Douglas Wilson discusses various approaches to education, but ultimately promotes a classical form of education based on Dorothy Sayers' *The Lost Tools of Learning*. Sayers divided education into two parts: the Trivium and the Quadrivium. The Trivium consists of three parts: grammar, dialectic and rhetoric. (For easy-to-understand explanations of these terms, I refer you to Wilson's book.) These three areas provide foundational information as well as learning skills for children through high school. The Quadrivium is concentra-

tion on specific subjects (which might begin in high school). The idea is that after children have learned how to think and express themselves, that is the proper time for them to begin in-depth study of particular subjects, particularly for future career or educational goals.

Wilson generally has a favorable attitude toward home education, yet he has difficulty believing that a home school can provide as excellent an education as a good Christian school (which follows Sayers' plan). If we overlook his misgivings, we find that he does a superb job of explaining the need for an education that is both Christian and classical, as well as how to provide it.

Some aspects of a classical education fit very well within a curriculum designed to teach world views. Because of this, you might find yourself (as I have) borrowing some ideas, but not the complete curriculum from the classical camp.

Unschooling

The idea of letting children follow their own inclinations in their education has been called "unschooling." The philosophic ideas behind this approach are most often associated with John Holt, author of numerous books such as *How Children Learn, How Children Fail, Instead of Education*, and *Teach Your Own*. Holt's books are available from libraries and bookstores, especially from Growing Without Schooling, a home-school organization that he began many years ago. Further support for moving away from traditional ideas of schooling ironically comes from New York State Teacher of the Year, John Taylor Gatto. In his book, *Dumbing Us Down* (New Society Publishers), he strikes at the heart of the system, demonstrating how the methods of compulsory state education are doomed to failure.

Many home educators support these philosophic ideas to varying degrees, and have allowed their teens to follow their interests in putting together a course of study to fit their career goals. In general, those following an unschooling approach allow teens to choose what and when and how to study according to their need for knowledge or proficiency in different areas. For instance, a person interested in becoming a veterinarian can work part time with a veterinarian, similar to an apprentice. On his own he can read books related to the subject. If the intent is to go on to college for further training, then the student would study whatever subjects he needs to pass college entrance exams.

In *The Teenage Liberation Handbook: How to Quit School and Get a Real Life and Education*, Grace Llewellyn speaks directly to teens, encouraging them to consider the unschooling option. Philosophically, Llewellyn comes from a very different place than most Christian home schoolers. Because of this foundational divergence, we might find ourselves disagreeing with some of her logic, however, she has exceptional insight into much of the flawed logic of compulsory education and its incarnation in traditional high schools.

Rather than bore us with a recitation of philosophy, Llewellyn writes in a friendly, big sister style, using lots of stories and examples. She does not reject the idea of learning, but suggests better ways to learn than attending school. She even has sections with suggestions for covering basic subject areas for students who either are college bound or want to study those subjects for personal reasons.

She gets into work, apprenticeship, entrepreneurships, and all sorts of other real-life options, all the time encouraging teens that they can do things differently.

Although the book is written to teens (there is an introductory chapter written to parents), because Llewellyn's philosophy is a major part of the book, I would encourage parents to also read the entire book and discuss differences of opinion with their teens. In spite of philosophical conflicts, I recommend this book to challenge and expand our thinking about how we "do" high school.

The unschooling approach advocated by the above authors obviously is dependent upon our teenager being self motivated. It certainly is easier on parents if the student takes responsibility for his own education, but we have to watch that we are not expecting more maturity from our child than is realistic. Even the most independent learner might need a guiding hand or occasional prod to keep him from descending into slothfulness.

Practical

Some home educated teens want to work in construction, farming, plumbing, or another trade that will not require college education. They want a practical course of study that will prepare them to begin work as soon as possible. They do not want to waste time on subjects they never expect to use. Such a narrow course of study has limitations which might present problems in the future if the original career goal does not work out. However, if a teenager has made up his mind that he will learn only what is important to him, we can waste our time and energy trying to force him to go beyond his self-imposed limits. If the original goal has to be scrapped, it is always possible, although it may be difficult, to return to school and learn something else or pursue another career.

The practical approach (or maybe it should be called pragmatic) even appeals to some educators within the school system, although for different reasons. Joe Clark, the notorious principal of Eastside High School in Paterson,

---

SAMPLE STUDENT SCHEDULES/ JAMES MADISON HIGH SCHOOL

Student A

9th Grade	10th Grade	11th Grade	12th Grade
Introduction to Literature	American Literature	British Literature	Introduction to World Literature
Western Civilization	American History	Principles of American	Algebra II and Trig.
Algebra I	Astronomy/Geology	Democracy (1 sem.)	Principles of Technology
P.E./Health	Spanish II	Amer. Democracy and	Art History/Music History
Typing/Word Processing	P.E./Health	the World (1 sem.)	tory
(elective)	Bookkeeping (elective)	Plane/Solid Geometry	Technical Writing (elective)
		Biology	tive)
		P.E./Health (elective)	Graphic Arts (elective)
		Psychology (elective)	

Student B

9th Grade	10th Grade	11th Grade	12th Grade
Introduction to Literature	American Literature	British Literature	Introduction to World Lit.
Western Civilization	American History	Principles of American	Statistics/Probability (1
Algebra I	Plane and Solid Geometry	Democracy (1 sem.)	sem., elective)
Astronomy/Geology	Biology	Amer. Democracy and	Pre-calculus (1 sem., elective)
P.E./Health	P.E./Health	the World (1 sem.)	tive)
Band (elective)		Algebra II and Trig.	Physics (elective)
		Chemistry	French II
		French I	Art and Music History
		Band (elective)	Band (elective)

Student C

9th Grade	10th Grade	11th Grade	12th Grade
Introduction to Literature	American Literature	British Literature	Introduction to World Literature
Western Civilization	American History	Principles of American	Calculus AB (elective)
Plane and Solid Geometry	Algebra II and Trigonometry	Democracy (1 sem.)	Physics (elective)
Astronomy/Geology	etry	Amer. Democracy and	Latin IV (elective)
Latin I	Biology	the World (1 sem.)	Computer Science (elective)
P.E./Health	Latin II	Statistics and Probability	tive)
	P.E./Health	(1 semester)	Painting and Drawing
	Band (elective)	Pre-calculus (1 sem.)	(elective)
		Chemistry	Spanish I
		Latin III (elective)	
		Art and Music History	

New Jersey battled to establish disciplinary standards in his high school so even a minimal amount of education could take place. Despite the improved environment, test scores and other indicators of academic progress remained dismal. Mr. Clark attributed the problem to missing educational foundations. Mr. Clark and others place little hope in making up the void of a worthless elementary education and would rather see these students take a direct leap into the business world. "Clark would urge the present generation to acquire as much wealth (and the power that comes with it) as they can from work, entrepreneurship, and an orientation to the future...."[1] Clark recommends a course of study much more pragmatic than a liberal arts education. Courses in marketing, consumer and business math, and other trade and vocational classes would replace all but the minimal requirements in literature, language, arts, and history studies. In my opinion, this strategy of appealing to the most self-serving motives should be used only in the most drastic cases.

"James Madison High School"

Former Federal Secretary for Education, William Bennett has promoted what he calls "James Madison High School." This is a model for high school courses of study that emphasizes the basic academic subjects while allowing choices that take individual needs into account. Bennett's concern has been the increasing percentage of courses consisting of physical education, health education, work experience, remedial math and English, and personal development which have displaced core academics. Samples of student schedules included in Bennett's recommendations are shown in the chart on the previous page.

Following Bennett's ideas, we would plan a course of study that remains somewhat traditional, yet allows for emphasis on an educational area. For instance, for students interested in one of the scientific fields, the course of study would be weighted towards math and science; communication skills would have next priority; and history, philosophy, and the arts would be covered more superficially.

Traditional

The broad majority of home educators stick with traditional courses of study which include standard courses in math, language arts, history, and science, plus electives. There is more security in conforming to standard expectations, especially when students plan to go on to college. Beyond that, such a course of study does provide a fairly balanced education. The questions home educators raise about the traditional course of study challenge the underlying assumption that "one size fits all." There are thousands of subjects that students could be studying, yet the traditional course of study limits the choices to a small handful. For example, biology and chemistry are the standard science courses, but there is little that makes either inherently better than geology, botany, oceanography, or most any other scientific topic. Algebra is justified for all students because of the logic and thinking skills it uses, yet some people question if there are not more practical ways of teaching those skills.

College Prep

If we choose to follow traditional methods of providing a high school education in preparation for college, the time to begin planning for college is at the beginning of ninth grade. There are important decisions to make in regard to course work that cannot be delayed until later. Maybe your child, like many others, has no idea whether or not he wants to attend college. As long as he appears to have the basic wherewithal to tackle college, plan as if he is going. There is more to be lost by not taking college preparatory courses than there is to be gained in relief by following a student's inclinations to take easier courses.

College preparatory course work does not consist only of those courses which are required for college. Students should also have room in their schedules for electives or outside activities where they have freedom to pursue a wide range of interests. (Outside activities are often an important factor in college admissions, since they demonstrate that the student is well-rounded.) However, if our child desires to attend one of the exclusive institutions such as Yale or Harvard, or a more specialized school such as MIT or Cal Tech, he had better plan his course work carefully and plan to work hard. "The Harvard/Radcliffe and Princeton admissions catalogs specify a [high school] core curriculum upon which many colleges agree:
– four years of English with a continued emphasis on writing
– four years of mathematics, preferably including an introduction to calculus
– two to three years of laboratory science
– two years of history or social science, not only of the United States
– three or more years of a foreign language, with a preference for intensive study of one language, rather than two or more studied only briefly
– one year of course work in the fine arts"
(*Handbook for College Admissions*, Thomas C. Hayden, Peterson's, 1986, p. 117.)

While these requirements are quite stringent, we will find that good colleges across the nation are also tightening up their requirements forcing college-bound high school students to take meatier courses than they have chosen in the past. In 1985, the University of California system issued new preparation requirements that were fully implemented by 1990. These are called the "A through F" requirements. They are:

a. U.S. History/Government - 1 year required - Students entering the University should have a knowledge of U.S. history and government in order to understand the development of American institutions and how our political system functions. High school courses must cover either one year of U.S. history or 1/2 year of U.S. history and 1/2 year of civics or American government.

b. English - 4 years required - Entering students should be able to 1.) comprehend, interpret, evaluate, and use what they read; 2.) write well organized, effective papers; 3.) listen effectively and discuss ideas intelligently; and 4.) know our literary heritage and how it relates to our customs,

---

1   *The American Spectator*, "Eastside Story," by Yale and Rita Kramer, August 1989, p.24.

ideas, ethics, and values. The ability to think critically and to write clearly is crucial to success at the University as well as for advancement in most careers.

c. Mathematics - 3 years required, 4 years recommended - algebra, geometry, and intermediate algebra required. Precalculus is strongly recommended for science and engineering students.

d. Laboratory science - 1 year required, 3 years recommended - biology, chemistry, physics or other acceptable laboratory science. For science or engineering majors, the three listed courses are strongly recommended.

e. Foreign Language - 2 years required, 3 recommended—at least two years of the same language, although a waiver is possible for those who can demonstrate equivalent competency.

f. College Preparatory Electives - 3 years required—selected from English, advanced mathematics, social science, history, laboratory science, foreign language, visual and performing arts, and agriculture.

Not all colleges are so rigorous in their requirements. Bible colleges are often less demanding in prerequisites, although that does not guarantee that the one you choose will be. Most Bible colleges require entrance exams (SAT or ACT), but some do not. Less prestigious colleges cannot afford to be as particular about the students they admit so the standards tend to be lower, corresponding to the prestige of the college. However, prestige and reputation do not guarantee the quality of the education provided, and some small colleges provide a better education than Ivy League institutions.

Assessing Our Options

Old ways are not necessarily better, but our present educational system is obviously missing something important. So much of the material is repeated over and over again from elementary grades through high school. Much time is wasted, and children's talents and gifts that fall outside a narrow academic range are ignored. We need to take a hard look at our course of study in terms of what is best for our child.

Some home educators are using a traditional approach, but are substituting some unusual classes to better suit their students' needs. We can, assuming that we have the legal freedom to do so in our state, approach high school with a very independent attitude, pursuing subjects that are of our choosing and ignoring others. I was encouraged by an interview by television talk show host Phil Donahue with the Colfax family on his program. Their courses of study sounded very flexible and creative. Reed, the second oldest son said that he never read a history textbook, but that he felt that he knew more history than his college classmates. His knowledge came from reading historical novels. The idea that much learning can take place outside textbooks came up repeatedly in the discussion. Following the Colfax's example, we could plan a course of study that includes much informal learning in some subjects along with some textbooks for other subjects. Other such options can be designed to fit your situation.

There is no ethically right or wrong choice to make. Rather it is a choice based upon our best understanding of God's future direction for each of our children. There should be a balance in our curriculum to develop the various faculties of the mind and to explore subjects for which

our teen shows an interest and an aptitude. It is not important that home educators all agree upon the best approach, but it is important that each of us think about the options and make some purposeful decisions in planning a course of study.

A Christian Course of Study

We might choose any of the above or still other ideas for planning courses of study, but I have come to some conclusions of my own about two particular areas we need to address as Christians.

My first concern is that any course of study should help our young people develop their abilities to reason and deal with philosophical issues. Challenges in both areas will arise no matter what occupations they pursue. I want to discuss ethical topics with them while I have my chance to provide input. If I skirt issues now because of their age or immaturity, I may never again have the opportunity to initiate such discussions once my children are out of high school. As our teenagers move on to their separate lives, we often lose opportunities for weighty discussions. Our children become involved in other pursuits that absorb more and more of their time, and rightly so. As young adults they will come under the influence of other adults and peers with strong opinions. If they have not had their ideas and thinking challenged before, how will they be able to defend their beliefs against strongly opinionated adults or friends?

I do not believe that we have to examine every worthless idea or philosophy that comes along, but I want to establish the thinking skills and basic philosophical ideas that will guide my children in confronting unfamiliar ideas. It can be compared to warming up and then practicing weight training for the muscles. Someone who has never done any exercise does not begin by lifting two hundred pound barbells. He begins with small weights and works up as his muscles develop the ability to deal with the increased work. Similarly, we need to warm up our thinking "muscles" and train by using those muscles in the discussion of ideas—what we might term philosophy—with those who are at least somewhat like-minded. Then we will be better prepared to confront those who would seriously challenge our beliefs.

For example, some Christians would avoid any mention of evolution because it is a false teaching. However, if our children do not understand what evolutionists believe, they will not be able to refute evolution or even recognize its influence on what people believe about religion, science, history, philosophy, and so on. (See Chapter Five for further discussion.)

The second point I want to make is based upon my belief that God has gifted each child with special interests and talents for His purposes. I feel that we have an obligation to recognize and develop those interests and talents as much as we can so that we are cooperating with God's plan for our child rather than superimposing our own. I am not talking about fostering purely self-serving interests, but interests which relate to relationships and careers. If a child has a musical interest and ability, God can certainly use that to His glory. If a child has an interest in computers, engineering, and things mathematical, God probably has a plan for him that involves such things. While our culture tends to lopsidedly value academic skills over mechanical, those children with mechanical skills will be the ones that keep all of our vital machinery operating, so we certainly should encourage those with mechanical inclinations. If a girl takes much pleasure in homemaking activities, that too is worth developing in spite of society's bias against such traditional roles.

At the same time, I do not believe that God would have an entire family devote most of its energy to the development of a single talent of one family member at everyone else's expense. We see this happen occasionally with talented athletes who prepare for the Olympics, talented musicians who want to reach the pinnacle of fame or recognition, and even academically talented students who want to attend one of the most exclusive universities. There is a danger of becoming unbalanced in pursuit of recognition or achievement, especially when a child is particularly gifted. We must pray carefully for God's timing and direction in developing such gifts so that they are used for His glory rather than the glory of any one person.

Too Much?

The problem that many of us recognize is that we often are trying to provide too much. We want our children to have a practical education in math and language arts which they will use whatever their futures. We also want them to have a classical education so that they are familiar with ideas and history. We cannot forget spiritual development—an education that influences all other aspects of life. We might also be interested in a vocational education—after all, we need to be practical in equipping our children with marketable skills. We might even want them to have a small business of their own to obtain hands-on experience. They really do need to stay in good physical condition throughout all of this, so we are concerned about physical education and conditioning. If we can squeeze it in, we might also want them to have some training in music or art. Can we really provide all this? Not if we want to do it all well!

Our dilemma is a new one brought on by the industrial and technological revolutions. In past centuries, there was less technologically related knowledge in the math and sciences being taught. There was more time to devote to both the liberal arts and practical education. Today, if a student wants to pursue a technological career, he needs to devote a large portion of his study time to math and science, leaving much less time for the other studies. If a student chooses a business major, he has to sacrifice liberal arts and science study. We face more difficult choices as the body of knowledge continually increases. There are trade-offs that have to be made. The question comes back to goals. What do we wish to accomplish? Even more importantly, what does God wish to accomplish in our child's life?

As parents, we are looking at the total picture in a way that school educators rarely do. We are intimately concerned with the future of our child, so all of these things do matter to us, whereas most teachers deal only with the short term, narrow purposes of the school.

Reality means that we have only twenty-four hours in a day and our children require some rest from our efforts to mold them into ideal human beings. So we cannot do it all.

We (and our children) have to make some choices and recognize what is most important. We must then make conscious decisions about how we allocate our educational energies. I cannot decide for you which things are of highest priority. That will depend upon your personal beliefs and your child's interests and aptitudes.

Writing Down a Course of Study

Once we have determined our priorities and goals, we can begin to formulate a course of study.

A written course of study lists which subjects will be covered, and includes topics within each when subject headings are broad. This list is not as detailed as a scope and sequence which gives detailed goals for subjects in the order that they will be covered. For instance, in our course of study under the subject of Language, we might list as topics a review of grammar and development of expository writing skills. In the scope and sequence we would list details such as review of eight principal parts of speech, learning the steps for writing a research paper, learning to use the computer card catalog at the library, etc. It is wise to first plan a tentative course of study for the high school years as a whole, then break it down into yearly courses of study. This will help us arrange studies so that we can meet educational goals in the time available.

Writing out the course of study is simple, especially if we have already been writing out courses of study for elementary grades.

A course of study should list each subject title, with a brief description of the course content. If you are using a traditional textbook, less description is necessary. We have provided a form for writing out a course of study in the Appendix, but there is room for only brief descriptions there. If you need more space, write it out using some of the examples below. The course of study should be kept on file. In some states this is a legal requirement, while in others it is simply for your benefit. These examples show both brief and more involved descriptions. Use whatever is most comfortable for you.

Sample course descriptions:

➡ Algebra I

Two semester course using Saxon's *Algebra 1* with accompanying test booklet.

➡ Introduction to American Literature

A survey course of modern American Literature using Bob Jones University Press' text *American Literature for Christian Schools: Modern Tradition, 1865 to the Present*. Emphasis will be on analyzing plots, themes, viewpoints, and characterizations, while learning about many genres and authors. Vocabulary work will be derived from reading selections. The novel, *To Kill a Mockingbird* will be used as a supplemental study.

Two semesters

➡ Expository Writing

Skills in expository writing will be developed in a group class through a variety of assignments. Students will also learn how to critique both their own and each others' work for grammar and content. A research paper will be included. The *Basic English Revisited* handbook will be used as a reference tool.

Two semesters

Electives should also be included

➤ Home Economics

Nutrition and cooking will be studied as Mary plans and prepares meals for the family. She will prepare weekly menus, work within a budget, and consider nutritional balance. She will be responsible for preparing dinners three nights a week to practice cooking skills.
One semester

➤ Auto Mechanics

Chris will learn basic engine mechanics as he works with his father to rebuild a car engine. He will refer to repair manuals for information.
One semester

Record Keeping

Planning must move beyond the general course of study to daily or weekly lesson planning. For this purpose, any lesson plan book can be used. Inexpensive plan books are available at teacher supply stores and from Bob Jones University Press or Rod and Staff.

The pages of a lesson plan book or organizer should actually become our records of work accomplished, which then saves the effort of duplicate recording (except the recording of grades onto a transcript).

Family Academy has designed a planning/record keeping book for high school called *High School Your Way*. It is intended for students who are taking charge of their own learning. A student works with an advisor setting goals and planning course objectives. The student and advisor then sign a contract. Periodic evaluations help keep the student on target. Quite a few of these charts are included in the book along with daily lesson plan pages that can be used for recording what actually is accomplished each day. Step-by-step instructions guide both student and advisor as they use this book.

A basic teacher's plan book will suffice for most people, but more extensive organizers are available which help with organizing both home and school. Although organizers are not essential, many home educators have found them very helpful for getting started with record keeping and then also for keeping track of family and school activities that are strongly interrelated.

More comprehensive organizers are available from Christian Life Workshops, The Time Minder, and JL Enterprise. CLW's *Christian Family Complete Household Organizer* includes most planning and record keeping pages that we might need for our home school along with pages for family hospitality and household organization. *The Time Minder*, another useful record keeping organizer, focuses on more basic family functions such as meal planning and phone calls. The forms for school record keeping allow for three different methods of planning/recording, which give us greater flexibility. The distinctive "ruler/marker" helps us quickly locate our place in this organizer. Refills are available, or we have permission to photocopy as needed for personal use. JL Enterprise's organizer is entitled *Complete Homeschool Planner*. While it is particularly suitable for home educators in California, those in other states will probably find it equally useful. Forms included are Purpose of Homeschooling, School Year Calendar (year-at-a-glance without dates), Monthly Calendar, Weekly Lessons,

Monthly Progress, Goals, Attendance, Faculty Qualifications (CA requirement), Course of Study, Quarterly Progress Report, Grades, Field Trip Record, Lending/Borrowing Record, Reading Book List, and Student Assignments. We can purchase these forms either in a binder or as a Master Copy Packet. The Complete Binder includes master copies plus one or more copies of all forms, and a copy of the World Book *Typical Course of Study*. Most families will need to make more copies of some of the sheets. The Master Copy Packet consists of one of each form that we can reproduce. This is an excellent assortment of forms that will suit most families.

There are still other options that allow us to reproduce forms from master copies as needed.

The Home Educator's Lesson Plan Notebook (The Challenge of Raising Cain) has reproducible forms for goals/objectives/evaluations, lesson plans, student weekly assignments, assignment grades, final grades, textbook planning, curriculum recording, scheduling, attendance, health records, library/reading lists, book reports, movie/TV reports, special event reports, and a few other specialized forms.

School Forms for Home and Classroom (Sycamore Tree) has fewer forms, but they are more specialized and might be a useful supplement even to the large organizers. They include reproducible forms for school entry medical examination, curriculum listing, weekly lesson plans, weekly schedule, attendance chart, grade sheet, report cards, work contracts, and achievement and completion certificates. Their separate *Assignment Sheets For Home And School* has twelve different monthly, weekly, and daily assignment forms including charts for chores, extracurricular activities, and practical arts.

Because we sometimes find ourselves using only a few of the forms in the large organizers, it might be more practical to use reproducible masters for those forms, copying them as needed. Of course, this depends upon easy access to reasonably-priced photocopying or it becomes impractical. One other drawback to copying forms ourselves is that low-priced copying generally limits us to copying on one side of each page. Then we end up with twice as much paper as we might have had in the organizer to begin with.

Unit Values

If we choose a non-traditional course of study, applying unit values is useless because the overall course content is not equivalent to what is being done by other schools. However, if we choose to follow traditional methods, assigning unit values makes things look professional.

Unit values are given to completed courses and vary from state to state. California high schools generally assign five units to each semester class. Thus a full year math course would have a value of ten units. However, many states and most colleges assign units differently. Most common in high schools is one unit per year-long course. A one semester course would have a value of one-half unit. Colleges and universities will often look at the total unit value of classes which meet basic requirements, such as math, language, science, and history. For example, the Bob Jones University *Bulletin* reads: "Applicants should have received a high school certificate and have at least 16-18 acceptable units of secondary work. (A unit is defined as five 45-minute periods each week for 36 weeks.)" (1988-89 *Bulletin*, Bob

Jones University, p. 14.) If we list classes completed on a transcript, colleges might or might not infer unit values if we do not provide that information. If we are going to bother creating a transcript, we might as well complete it thoroughly and assign unit values.[2]

Meeting the Requirements

Junior high students do not usually need documentation of their educational history, although I hear that this situation is changing. Some junior highs are assigning unit values to classes and creating transcripts just as for high school. Some private schools request transcripts of junior high work. If you have a transcript (list of classes and grades) for elementary and junior high work, that is fine, but if not, do not worry. Public high schools will generally accept freshman students without transcripts, although they might require testing. Many private high schools require entrance examinations, and they can determine a student's eligibility based upon these test scores alone.

Most of us worry about requirements for high school graduation. Actually, students can "graduate" in a number of ways. We can use GED testing, junior college class completion and other means than the traditional transcript/diploma route. Our concern should be first for what our son or daughter needs to go on to the next step for college or career, since that might well dictate how we choose to "graduate" them from high school.

As we discussed earlier, unless there is an obvious reason for a student to not go to college, we should prepare them for college entry. We need not follow a traditional approach for college preparation, but many of us will choose to do so. Included in the Appendix are Planning Charts G and H for both college bound and non-college bound students, designed for those who prefer following traditional guidelines.

Requirements for college and university entry have been tightening up over the past few years. After the academic laxity of the '60's and '70's produced a generation of college graduates sorely lacking in basic skills, college administrators have resurrected academic guidelines from earlier years. The most obvious of these is the foreign language requirement—two years of the same language. For many years, either one year of foreign language or one year of fine arts had been required by California universities. As we mentioned earlier in discussing a college preparatory course of study, the University of California system is the front runner in the return to more stringent requirements with the "A through F requirements" that are being phased in through the early 1990's.

These requirements are typical of what students will be finding at the better universities over the next few years. However, there are extreme variations in the academic requirements of institutions of higher learning. They range from some Bible colleges who ask for nothing more than a signed statement of faith to schools such as Massachusetts Institute of Technology that have very stringent requirements.

If there is a particular college or university that your child has set his sights upon, it is vital that you check out that institution's requirements as your child begins high school, not during the junior or senior year of high school. If the goal is college, but the choices are many, there is more leeway in meeting preparatory requirements. However, we must also recognize that certain career goals in themselves influence preparatory requirements. If a student plans to be an engineer, he will be required to take many math classes in college. He must have foundational classes completed before college or he will not be able to complete all the classes within the typical four years. An extra semester or two of college may be a costly way to make up for poor high school planning. This situation holds true particularly for scientific fields.

While college preparation should be a primary concern if our teens are college-bound, we may also need to be concerned about state requirements for high school graduation. Some states require home schoolers to meet the same requirements for graduation as public school students. For instance, students in California are required to study economics for one semester. Other states require the study of state history. Also, some students will be working under independent study or school service programs which will set their own requirements for students, incorporating extras such as Bible courses.

If we are the one providing the high school diploma or other evidence of completion, it may be up to us to determine if requirements have been fulfilled. In practice, we only become answerable for units we have granted our child for high school course work when our child applies to a college. If we say that they have taken a particular course, implying competency in that area, we will lose credibility when our child is unable to pass a basic placement examination in that subject.

If our child has acquired equivalent knowledge by creative learning alternatives, we should not be afraid to list it as a completed course, but we must be wary of presenting a false picture of his academic history.

Do not panic because of the courses we are discussing for college preparation. Many of us will not be able to teach all of these subjects at home. Do not lower your sights because of your inadequacies. There are many alternatives available for covering subjects that we are unable to teach ourselves as we will discuss in Chapter Eight. There are also many colleges and universities who will be more concerned with the student's academic potential than with his educational history. The less rigid a student is about which college he wants to attend and how quickly he wants to get through, the more possible solutions there will be for getting into college. Students who do not plan to go on to college need not be overly concerned about meeting requirements other than those needed to "graduate" from high school. That might mean learning what is needed to

---

2   College units differ from high school units. A college unit, also known as a semester or Carnegie unit, is 15 hours in class. However, an hour means 50 minutes. A semester unit is worth more than a quarter unit. Quarter units are converted to semester units by multiplying the number of quarter units by 2/3. In reverse, semester units are converted to quarter units by multiplying the number of semester units by 3/2.

pass the GED test, meeting requirements of a correspondence course or independent study program, or meeting particular requirements imposed by our state.

Testing for High School Completion

The GED is always an alternative for high school completion, although minimum age restrictions make it impractical in some states. (See GED requirements for each state in Appendix B.) Even if we are able to graduate our own son or daughter, some of us are more comfortable with outside affirmation of successful completion of high school through the General Educational Development (GED) or, in California, the Proficiency Examination. These are tests administered by the State. A certificate awarded for passing either test is, by law, equivalent to a high school diploma.

Minimum ages for taking the tests apply in different states. In all but California, only one test, the GED, is offered. Usually a minimum age is set with no maximum age. The minimum age established by the General Educational Development Testing Service is sixteen. However, some states have set the minimum age for testing within those states at older levels, with some allowing no testing option for early graduation from high school before ages eighteen or nineteen. There are also special qualifications in many states. Some states allow testing before the state's specified age, yet will not grant a certificate until the graduation date if the student had progressed with his class!

This situation is a real hindrance to home educators in some states since many of our teens complete high school requirements much earlier than their age mates. Students who wish to go on to college appear to have fewer problems in these situations, since there are several ways of continuing higher education without formal recognition of high school graduation. Some junior colleges will allow students to begin college courses without the GED certificate, but will withhold college credits until they receive a copy of the GED certificate.

While college students might be able to continue their studies before they "graduate" from high school, those who want to enter a career or business field might be refused the right to take the GED test to demonstrate their proficiency in high school subjects until they are eighteen, sometimes blocking them from pursuing jobs and careers. However, some states make exceptions on GED age requirements if an employer requests that a prospective employee be allowed to take the test.

From reading the requirements and exceptions for each state, it seems that exceptions are most commonly made for those entering the military, those who are pregnant, or those in penal institutions! There are a few other possibilities for exceptions, but early graduation is strongly discouraged by GED age requirements in most states. (This situation is an interesting contrast to most European countries which graduate their young people at age sixteen.)

At this time, home educators in at least two states are investigating legal means of changing this situation, either by amendment of existing codes or through a class action lawsuit.

The name given to the GED certificate for each state and minimum age requirements and exceptions are provided in Appendix B of this book. Information about GED requirements may also be found in the educational codes of your state (at the library) or write to GED Testing Service.

Whether or not the local Department of Education looks favorably upon home education has nothing to do with a person's right to take these tests as long as he or she is of legal age and follows proper procedures. When special permission is required from local superintendents, it might be a different matter. Check with your local Department of Education or high school for information pamphlets about these tests. (In California, booklets on the tests are available at most public libraries.)

The GED includes five tested areas: math, writing skills, social studies, science, and interpretation of literature and the arts. The math test covers arithmetic (50%), algebra (30%), and geometry (20%). However, knowing how to apply basic mathematical processes is more important than having in-depth knowledge of algebra and geometry. The writing skills test is in two sections: part one covers sentence structure, usage, and mechanics with multiple choice questions; part two requires applicants to write an essay.

Social studies, science, and literature/arts tests do not rely on particular knowledge from these subject areas, but on the ability to analyze and apply information provided from these subject areas on the test, abstract reasoning and problem solving, and general reading comprehension.

GED test preparation helps are available from many sources. Steck-Vaughn publishes both *Steck-Vaughn Complete GED Preparation* and a six-book GED preparation series, *Steck-Vaughn GED*, that concentrates more fully on each area of the GED test. There are companion exercise books for all six books. Barron's publishes *How to Prepare for the GED*. Look for similar titles in the library, but make sure that they were written since 1988 when the GED tests were revised.

Remedial students wanting to study for the GED should check out the catalog from Contemporary Books, Inc. Contemporary offers GED preparation resources for the complete test or for specific test areas. Their materials are written for older learners or ESL students who have poor educational backgrounds and/or learning difficulties.

The GED tests used in all states are written by the same people to the same specifications, so the test is essentially the same across the country, although there are alternate forms. Each state then sets its own standards on passing scores and age requirements.

Whether students graduate with a transcript or by taking GED or Proficiency tests may or may not matter to colleges or universities. Remember that colleges are seeking bright, capable students, and they might interpret a GED certificate earner as being a low calibre student. At junior or community colleges that are easy to get into, it probably makes no difference whether students come with a traditional transcript and diploma or a GED certificate, although, with the GED schools might still request transcripts of work completed in high school. More selective schools will look twice at GED certificates. Here it is important that SAT or ACT test scores paint a positive picture, and that the reasons for obtaining the GED certificate be fully explained. Sometimes it is possible (and advisable) to rely only upon the SAT or ACT test score and skip the GED.

Some employers also look askance at GED certificates because they know that it is the method that high school dropouts use to go back and graduate from high school.

They often view it as evidence of a second class education. If a student graduated early from high school, and used the GED as the means to do so, that should be explained to employers, letting them know that the student was ahead of schedule in his studies rather than a dropout who took the GED only to graduate. Your teen should let the skeptical employer know that he is getting an eager, bright employee who will be an asset to his business.

For any of these tests mentioned, we need to plan ahead. Tests are administered a certain number of times a year in various locations. Students need to apply well in advance of the testing date to take the tests. They cannot decide to take a test "next week." Check at least six months ahead for dates and locations. Public libraries are a good source for information on schedules and applications.

Grading

Some of us feel that grades are totally irrelevant and useless. If you feel that way, skip ahead to the next chapter. Only those concerned about grading need to read this section.

Grades can be determined either objectively or subjectively. Objective grading means that there are certain standards (usually numerical, such as the percentage of correct answers) against which we measure our student's performance. Our personal interpretation or feelings have little to do with the grades. Subjective grading is the opposite. Grades are determined by our overall evaluation of the student's performance, rather than specific right and wrong answers. We have to use subjective grading for some subjects or assignments such as creative writing, sewing, woodworking, and art. Although there might be some objective criteria involved, most of the grade will be based on our overall impression of competence, skill, or accomplishment. I have tried both types of grading (when we have used grades) and have come to the conclusion that subjective grading can be just as valid in the long run, while it requires a lot less record keeping. By the end of a semester or school year, I have a very good idea of how well my sons know different subjects. I can assign a grade based on an overall evaluation (or gut feeling). Most likely this grade would be identical (as long as I realistically assessed my child's progress) to one figured out objectively by recording grades for lessons and tests. One drawback is that subjective grades are more difficult to validate if someone asks how we assigned them. Schools use objective grading as much as possible, because teachers cannot know each child well enough to evaluate each subject area for each child, and because they need to have documentation to prevent complaints of favoritism or prejudice. Choose whichever method or combination of methods is most comfortable for you unless required by some authority to do otherwise.

There are two aspects of grading to think about. The first is everyday grading of course work. The second is final course grades and transcript preparation.

Course Work

I did not believe in using a grading system when our children were in elementary grades. If they did not complete an assignment properly, I returned it to them for correction or completion. My rationale was that in real life, if we do not do something correctly the first time, we must go back and fix it. We cannot leave things undone, or done in-

correctly. So if it took my children three tries to do schoolwork correctly, they did it three times. The end result was always an "A" paper. I saw no point in giving them straight "A's," so I assigned no grades during the year. However, at the end of the year, I did record a grade that reflected their overall mastery of the subject matter along with their attitude and effort.

I realized the pitfalls of this system after a number of years of home schooling. We had done no multiple choice work up until that time. Answers were mostly sentence writing, oral discussion, or mathematical answers that were either right or wrong. We began that year using a vocabulary workbook that featured multiple choice answers. The first assignments were turned in with several errors. We went over the assignments and reviewed how to use the dictionary to determine correct answers. One of my sons turned in the second assignment with almost 50% wrong. He obviously had not even bothered to look at the dictionary. His attitude had become, "If I don't guess right the first time, I'm down to only one out of three choices for my next try." I caught on to what had happened and immediately changed tactics. From then on, all assignments were graded the first time they were handed in. Then they were handed back for necessary corrections. The grade would not change, but the work would still be done correctly. This approach has worked with the subjects that lend themselves to objective grading.

Grading can be done daily, weekly, or at wider intervals—whatever best fits the type of work being done. Weekly grades should be the most that are necessary to determine an overall grade for course work. With daily grades, grade computation becomes cumbersome, and they are unlikely to provide a more accurate reflection of overall performance.

If we choose to use subjective grading methods, we should make evaluations throughout the semester rather than waiting till the end, so that we do not forget earlier performance levels. Doing well the last few weeks of a semester does not compensate for four months of lackadaisical work.

Final Grades

When we assign grades, we have to be honest. We cannot fall into the trap many schools have of inflating grades in an attempt to make the school (or teacher) look better. High school grades are used to determine a student's grade point average. The grade point average is used in conjunction with SAT or ACT scores by colleges for admissions eligibility. (See page 44.) Because colleges already doubt a parent's ability to objectively grade his or her own child, they are sometimes skeptical of home school grade point averages. However, if they do consider a home schooler's grades, colleges are likely to ask what criteria were used for grading, or how work was objectively evaluated. Do not grade your child on what you know he could do if he just tried a little harder, but upon what he is actually doing. We are not being honest with him if we tell him he is doing well, when he is putting out a minimal effort.

We should have a plan for assigning grades prepared before school begins. For subjective grading, we must have some standards of accomplishment, even though we might not measure achievement numerically. For instance, our teen can be studying math independently, checking his own answers after each lesson, determining where he made errors, and seeking help as needed. We can check occasionally to see if he is making a significant number of errors, and check also to find out how well he is figuring out why errors occurred. Since he is essentially teaching himself, objective grading would be unfair since he may not be aware that he does not understand a concept until after he does the exercises. A student's ability to work independently and correct his own errors should be included in our evaluation. It certainly can be more difficult for us to assign grades in such learning situations, and subjective grading might be most practical.

Objective grading systems are set up before school starts. School teachers write out grading systems for the coming school year, showing the relative value of various assignments and how final grades will be determined. For example, semester examinations might each count for 25% of the final course grade (2 x 25% = 50%), while weekly quizzes are each worth 2% (25 quizzes x 2% = 50%). If everything were done perfectly the student would have 100%. Usually a point system is used. A possible course grading value system might be as follows:

⟹ Government and Economics

chapter reviews -	10 points each (18 reviews)=180
chapter tests -	40 points each (8 tests) =320
newspaper assignments	
	5 points each (4 assignments)=20
semester tests -	40 points each (2 tests) =80

Total possible	600 points

Course grades are based upon the percentage of points earned out of the total possible. For example, if a student earned 450 points out of the 600 possible, his grade for the course would be determined by dividing 450 by 600, which would be .75 or 75%. (Equivalent to a low C on most grade scales.) If you need to provide grades halfway through the year, for the end of the first semester, use the number of points for assignments already completed rather than the total points for the entire year.

A typical grade equivalent scale is as follows:

95-100% =		A
85-94% =		B
75-84% =		C
70-74% =		D
Below 70% =		F

Some courses need to be graded by standards. For instance, a typing course might have a standard to be reached such as being able to type forty words per minute with no more than two errors. A grading system would be set up for standards above and below forty words per minute.

Recording Grades

Report cards are the standard reporting form for recording grades, although they were designed as a tool for reporting to parents more than anything else. Since we, the parents, record the grades in the first place, the only purpose for the report card then is to show the student or an outside party how well the student has performed. If necessary for such a purpose, report card forms are available from Bob Jones University Press (singly or in groups of 25) and Sycamore Tree. Sycamore Tree sells sets of reproducible forms packaged as *School Forms for Home and Classroom*.

Within this set are three different report cards for preschool-kindergarten, grades 1-8, and grades 9-12. The high school form includes a grading system key, space for quarterly and final grades, conduct and attendance grades, and comments. In addition there are forms for lesson plans, medical records, work contracts, completion certificates, curriculum planning, and scheduling.

A more useful form for long range record keeping is the cumulative record. This form, usually printed on heavy card stock, is used for recording yearly grades, attendance totals, standardized test scores, and other such information that might be passed on if a student enters another school. Sometimes it is a file folder in which such information is stored. Usually there are spaces for recording data directly on the file. Even if we create a transcript, we probably also need a cumulative file. The transcript is a more concise form that can be sent to colleges or others to show a student's high school history. The cumulative file will contain more extensive information. Bob Jones University Press sells such a cumulative file form, called Academic Record, either individually or in packages of 25. Shekinah Curriculum Cellar and Sycamore Tree both sell cumulative record forms individually.

Transcripts

A transcript is simply a list of classes taken, grades earned, and unit values. Final course grades are entered on a transcript form such as the one we have included in the Appendix (Chart F) or on a custom designed form such as the one included in the *Personalized School Documents* (Educational Support Foundation). Correspondence schools and independent study programs should provide transcripts for students who have completed high school work under their direction. Otherwise, it is up to us. (See "Creating Transcripts" in Chapter Seven.) A copy of the transcript is required for the admission process at most colleges and universities. The final grade point average should also be shown.

Grade points are determined as follows:
A = 4 points
B = 3 points
C = 2 points

To determine the grade point average, total the grade points earned for required courses (such as those listed under the "A through F California Requirements" discussed earlier), then divide by the number of courses taken (not counting electives.) For example:

Student   Jane Jones

Subject	Grade	Grade Points
Algebra I	B	3
Geometry	A	4
Algebra II	A	4
English I	B	3
English II	C	2
English III	B	3
English IV	B	3
U.S. History	A	4
World History	A	4
Government	B	3

Biology	A	4
Physics	B	3
Spanish I	A	4
Spanish II	A	4
Music	B	3

Total		51

51 divided by 15 courses = 3.4 grade point average

What About Diplomas?

What is a high school graduate? Is it someone with a fancy certificate or is it someone who has completed the standard requirements for high school completion? Sometimes we intimidate ourselves with questions such as, "How can my child graduate from high school without being enrolled in a regular school?" We must recognize that graduation is not the ceremony and recognition but the completion of certain requirements. If we are operating as a private school and are so recognized by the state, we are generally free to recognize such completion ourselves, just as any other school may do. The only exception, according to research from the National Center for Home Education, is Rhode Island, which will not allow anyone outside the recognized school system to issue diplomas. Students in that state can take the GED or work under an accredited program to surmount this difficulty if they truly need a diploma.

In some states, home educators are not allowed to call themselves private schools, and they might run into trouble if they issue their own diplomas. The safest alternative for those who want an acceptable diploma is to enroll the student in a correspondence course such as Pensacola or Christian Liberty Academy (or others listed under correspondence courses) that will issue a diploma upon completion of course work.

The technicalities of issuing a diploma are actually no big deal. The biggest problem I see is getting one of those nice certificates to fill out. That has been solved by a number of sources. Alpha Omega sells blank diplomas. Berg Christian Enterprises has standard certificate forms that they imprint with your school name. Home School Legal Defense Association offers an impressive diploma in a leather case (fill in the information yourself), and the Educational Support Foundation offers a personalized diploma, with all information typeset in calligraphic style, in a padded presentation binder.

In general, I think that we are overly concerned about diplomas. After all, how often does anybody ask to see a diploma? Hardly anyone other than the military services ever asks to see diplomas. They instead ask what level of education has been completed by potential employees, students, etc. Unless a declared high school graduate is quite illiterate, I doubt that an employer would ever ask to see proof of graduation. Colleges never ask to see diplomas, but they do ask if students have graduated from high school and they do ask for transcripts. Even so, some home schoolers have been admitted to colleges without transcripts.

As we mentioned earlier when we discussed goals, we need to consider our son's or daughter's future goals in decisions about graduation methods. If he or she is likely to pursue a career that will require four years of high school, documented by a credible transcript from a recognized school, think carefully before choosing home education. Enrollment in correspondence courses will serve in most cases to provide a credible transcript.

But we do not have to do things as they have always been done in the past. Our transcript does not have to be exactly like one that typical schools would issue. The essential thing when making up our own transcripts and diplomas is to back them up with credible documentation and explanation. We need to be able to explain our process of evaluation in a way that looks like we used some objective standards.

Caps and Gowns?

After figuring out how to "graduate" your child, you might wish to celebrate in a more traditional way. For those who want to provide their graduate with a graduation celebration, a reasonable source for caps and gowns to rent or buy is Collegiate Cap and Gown Company. You can purchase one cap and gown set with no problems. Then create a diploma using one of the sources mentioned above, and the only thing missing is a mob of classmates to share the celebration. The missing "mob celebration" can be replaced by a "coming out" party with relatives and friends of all ages or other creative ideas.

Chapter Seven

Heading for College

"But, if I teach my teenager at home he won't be able to go to college!" This fear confronts many of us facing the decision of whether or not to home educate our high schoolers. Actually, home educated students can and do go to college. Despite our fears, it does not seem to make much difference whether we do everything "properly" or not.

Some of us are very concerned about keeping the proper records, creating an acceptable transcript, completing the set requirements, and so on. There is certainly comfort in knowing that we are giving colleges the paper work that they require in the form to which they are accustomed. While following the rules is more comfortable, it is not the only way to do things.

Many home educated teens are taking the SAT or ACT tests and applying to colleges with little more than the test results. As long as the test scores are good, these students are generally being accepted wherever they apply. The only exception that I know of has been with schools who accept Pell Grants. As I understand the situation, these schools must promise that all enrollees are high school graduates. This means that home educated students must provide some evidence of graduation. The GED will suffice, so this is not a significant problem.

The choice of whether to do things "according to the book" or not depends, as does grading, largely on our confidence. If we feel that we can confidently explain to college authorities why we chose an alternative form of education and rejected traditional forms of grading and documenting, then we should do things in a way that best suits us and forget the busywork. If we lack confidence either in what we are doing or in defending it to others, then perhaps it would be best to stick with traditional ways of planning course work and keeping records.

Of course, our confidence is no guarantee that things will work out as we wish. Although unorthodox approaches have worked in the past, colleges might become concerned about the numbers of home educated students and come up with policies that require specific procedures.

Our freedom to choose how to proceed might well depend also upon our son or daughter's preferences. They may be so intent upon a particular goal, that they are unwilling to take any risks in regard to documentation of their high school course work. We must be sensitive to their feelings since this is their future.

With those thoughts in mind, let us move on to discuss college selection, testing, transcript options, non-traditional alternatives for college, and financial aid.

College Selection

Many books and software computer programs have been written to help with college selection. Some of the most popular resources come from The College Board. *The College Handbook 1993* (updated yearly) is a directory to 3,100 two- and four-year colleges (public and private). It lists admissions requirements, costs, financial aid, majors, student activities, enrollment figures, and more. A guidance section helps with planning and provides checklists and work sheets.

The College Board has many other publications, but it offers a great price on a special package that includes *The College Handbook 1993, Index of Majors and Graduate Degrees 1993,* and *The College Cost Book 1993. Index of Majors and Graduate Degrees 1993* lists over 500 major fields of study showing which are offered at 3,000 colleges and universities. *The College Cost Book 1993* explains costs of various colleges and universities, how to apply for financial aid,

---

The Spiritual Dangers of College

Many of us struggle with the idea of sending our children off to college, where who knows what might happen, after we have invested so much time and energy to educate them in "the way they should go." It is a fact that many Christian young people lose their faith at college. I am certain that this is much more often true at secular colleges, but it does happen even at Christian colleges.

So, do we keep our children inside our homes until they get a job or get married? Some might even say, "That's not a bad idea." (Those who feel this way should look at suggested resources for doing college at home.)

Meanwhile, many of us are willing to let our children venture on to college, yet we still harbor concerns about their spiritual well-being.

My first suggestion is that you make sure that you have spent time with them studying world views (see Chapter Five), discussing challenging faith issues, and ensuring that their spiritual roots are deep.

My second suggestion is that you pray about where they should or should not go, and ask them to pray about this decision.

The third suggestion is to read *Loving God With All Your Mind* by Gene Edward Veith, Jr. (Crossway). The book is subtitled "How to Survive and Prosper as a Christian In the Secular University and Post-Christian Culture." Veith deals with the challenges that college students encounter, particularly on secular campuses. He offers suggestions for meeting those challenges. He also encourages all Christians to pursue the different areas of wisdom and knowledge. He says, "...it is possible for Christians to engage the modern intellectual world without weakening or compromising their faith. Christians in fact need to do so both for the sake of the Church and for the sake of a world that is starving for the truth of the gospel (p. 10)."

If you decide to send your children to college, just make sure they are "armed and ready."

specific data from more than 3,100 institutions, and state-by-state information on grants and student loans. If you prefer the computer approach, The College Board has transferred information from *The College Handbook 1993* to *College Explorer 1993,* a computer program for Apple and IBM computers.

Peterson's publishes many books which help with selecting a college and determining admissions requirements. Some of their titles are: *Guide to Four-Year Colleges 1993* and *Guide to Two-Year Colleges 1993* (both books are updated each year); *Competitive Colleges* (updated every year); seven different regional guides to colleges for the Middle Atlantic States, Midwest, New England, New York, Southeast, Southwest, and West; and *Choose a Christian College.*

Another very useful book for college preparation is *A Student's Guide to College Admissions: Everything Your Guidance Counselor Has No Time to Tell You,* by Harlow G. Unger (Facts on File). Unger lays out step-by-step guidelines and adds advice based upon his experience. The guidelines are available elsewhere, but the advice alone is worth the cost of the book. Unger puts us inside the minds of admissions officers so we can understand what they are looking for and how they evaluate applications. Students who want to go to the most prestigious schools will find this book especially useful since Unger gives them special attention.

Since Christians are often looking for different things than non-Christians when selecting colleges, it is helpful to consult publications which share that Christian perspective. An excellent starting place is *The Christian Parent and Student Guide to Choosing a College* by Dr. Ronald Nash (write directly to Dr. Nash for ordering information. [Listed under Nash in the Appendix]). Dr. Nash goes much further than simply listing so-called Christian colleges. He carefully describes the differences between Christian colleges which have liberal theological foundations (although they operate under Protestant denominations) and evangelical colleges. He discusses the pros and cons of all types of institutions, including secular private and public colleges. He adds chapters on "The Effect of Higher Education on Faith" and "Some Things to Prepare For" which alert potential college students to likely dangers they will face. Dr. Nash believes that evangelical Christian colleges are the best choice for most Christian students, so he includes a descriptive list of sixty such colleges in an appendix.

For more assistance in choosing a Christian source for higher education, *Choose a Christian College* (Peterson's) has information about eighty-four Christian colleges and universities belonging to the Christian College Coalition.

Plan Ahead

You can run into problems with college admission. To avoid problems check with potential colleges as early as possible, so that course work can be planned to meet entrance requirements.

Find out not just their standard requirements, but how willing they are to deal with a student with an unusual educational history.

Many home educators choose to take a very different approach to education—following a child's interests rather than a typical program, skipping testing and grading or constructing educational programs vastly different from those of traditional schools. Some schools will be more willing to deal with this than others. If your teen has his heart set on a particular college, find out ahead of time if they will evaluate an unusual educational history with an open mind.

Some careers may require a traditional education. One family enrolled their student in a public high school, largely because their son wants to go to medical school. They feel that his chances of making it through the highly competitive enrollment process for medical school will improve if he has a traditional education and transcript. However, do not give up on home educating high schoolers just because people say they won't be able to get into college. It just is not true. In fact, small private colleges are begging for students as the number of eligible young people in the traditional college age group is decreasing nationwide.

A few colleges and universities are inviting home educated students to enroll and providing flexible enrollment policies to make it easier. Among those soliciting home educated students are Bob Jones University, Boston University, Houston Baptist University, and Western Baptist College. Houston Baptist is particularly interesting because it offers a premed program seldom found on Christian college campuses as well as double majors. Boston University offers more than 250 fields of major and minor concentration, plus "... the opportunity to seek cross-disciplinary studies that do not fall into conventional departmental divisions."

Time Off Before College?

Before we plunge on, we need to stop and consider whether or not all teens should go directly from high school to college. Many of us are afraid to allow "time off" after high school, probably fearing that our sons or daughters will find other pursuits which will replace their educational ambitions. While this is possible, it can also be a waste of time, money, and energy for a student to attend college if he does not want to be there.

For some young people, it might be better to work for a while, spend some time exploring career possibilities by trying different jobs, or take some lightweight classes while working part-time.

A student who begins college with determination and goals is likely to make much better use of his opportunities than a reluctant student.

SAT, ACT, and Achievement Tests for College

Most colleges and universities require either the SAT (Scholastic Aptitude Test; see College Board ATP for address and phone number) or ACT (American College Testing Program) test for admission. The SAT or ACT score is correlated with a student's grade point average (See Chapter 6 for information about determining grade point averages) to provide a ratio called the Eligibility Index[1], which is then used to determine which students will be accepted. Following is a section of one Eligibility Index. Note that with higher SAT[2] or ACT scores the grade point average needed is lower and vice versa.

Students with G.P.A.'s 3.0 and above qualify with any score. Students with G.P.A.'s below 2.0 do not qualify for regular admission.

Grade Point Average	ACT Score	SAT Score (combined)
2.90	10	480
2.80	12	560
2.65	15	680
2.40	20	880
2.20	24	1040
2.10	26	1120
2.0	28	1200

The SAT test is the most widely used. The ACT test is more commonly used in the Midwest and South than in other parts of the country, and many institutions requesting ACT scores will accept SAT scores instead. Generally, those schools requesting only SAT will accept only SAT. When in doubt, take both tests.

The SAT test is being revised, with new versions scheduled to be used in 1994. New PSAT tests will be implemented in 1993. New versions will have "[l]onger reading passages with reading comprehension questions that measure critical reading skills and knowledge of vocabulary in context." Sentence completions and analogies are retained, but antonyms have been dropped. Math questions will still include multiple choice and quantitative comparisons, but now students will also be required "...to produce their own responses and to enter them on grids...." Calculator use will also be allowed.

Watch out for misinformation! Some of us panic when we see information such as the following: "Before applying [for college], you will need to take a college entrance exam. To take such an exam, you must register through a school." (*Classic Curriculum Newsletter*, Winter 1989, p.8, from Mott Media, Milford, MI.) If we are not registered through a school, does that mean our child cannot get into college? Definitely not! I am sure that the folks at Mott Media intended to say that it would be easier to register for college entrance tests through a school, and this is usually true.

Both the SAT and ACT testing offices say that anyone can take their college entrance tests. No school affiliation is required although an identification card with a photograph is. (ID cards are also required for GED or Proficiency testing so you may need to obtain one for both purposes.) They can be made by the parent. Type information neatly on a wallet size card—school name, city and state, school year, e.g., 1990-91, student's name, student's signature. Take a picture in one of those cheap picture booths or get a passport photo if you do not have one of the appropriate size. Put it together neatly and get it laminated. If you do not want to make your own ID card, they are available from the Department of Motor Vehicles in California and probably in other states. You need only present a certified copy of your birth certificate to get one, but allow a few months for the DMV to process it and mail the card to you.

The tests are offered at various sites—usually high school or adult education campuses, and usually on Saturdays. The tests are given every few months, but students must apply to take the tests well in advance, so again, planning is a must.

Achievement tests are also required by some colleges, and the procedure for taking them is similar to that for SAT and ACT tests. Achievement tests are most commonly required for English, and quite frequently for math. Students entering a scientific or mathematical field at a university such as MIT or Cal Tech will certainly need to take math achievement tests and probably a science test also.

The best way to obtain application forms for these tests is from a local public or private high school, a junior or community college, or the college which the student plans to attend. Or we can write to the College Board ATP.

Changes in the SAT will also affect the Achievement Tests beginning in 1994. These tests will be renamed SAT-II. They will not be part of the basic SAT test but will fulfill essentially the same functions as they have in the past.

Test Preparation

Judy Gelner's book, *College Admissions: A Guide for Homeschoolers* (described further below) will give you details on the various tests. It also discusses test preparation strategies. I highly recommend that students prepare for tests by practicing on sample tests that are included in most test preparation books. The library usually has one or two books for SAT preparation, and others are available from bookstores, directly from publishers, and from some home school sources such as Sycamore Tree. Barron's publishes test preparation books on just about every college related test, so you might wish to send for their catalog to know what is available. Arco (whose books are distributed through Globe Book Company) also publishes preparation aids for the SAT and ACT tests along with helps for the CLEP and Advanced Placement examinations. Educators Publishing Service advertises many test preparation helps (including many College Board publications) for the SAT, aptitude, and achievement tests along with other specialized test preparation review books listed in the EPS catalog. Some of the books and computer programs available include:

For SAT Preparation -
➡ Cliffs SAT Preparation Guide (Cliffs Notes)

This book differs from most of the hefty test preparation books in its diminutive size. It claims to be concise, yet complete. It teaches strategy while also providing some basic information students should master to help improve their scores (e.g., lists of prefixes and suffixes, math formulas). There are two complete practice tests in the book with answer keys and explanations. There are also some helps for analyzing test results. This book is sold on its own but is also packaged with StudyWare for the SAT, a computer program also from Cliffs Notes. The computer program is available for IBM, Apple II, and MacIntosh machines.

---

1   Taken from the admission application for the California State University System entitled *Admission: The California State University* 1989-90, p.1.

2   Average SAT scores are around 910 for combined math and language scores.

➡Preparation for the SAT (Arco)
➡Arco's Cram Course for the SAT (Arco)
➡Simon and Schuster's Computer Study Guide for the SAT [computer program for IBM, Apple or Commodore] (Arco)
➡10 SATS [fourth edition] (The College Board)
>Actual copies of previous versions of SAT tests.
➡SAT-College Entrance Examinations (Barron's)
➡14 Days to Higher SAT Scores (Barron's)
>Basic tips on the SAT and 2 audio cassettes.
➡Computer Study Program for the SAT (Barron's)
>Computer programs available for Apple, Macintosh, and IBM.
➡SAT Success (Peterson's)
>This book offers: three different study plans depending upon how much time students have for test preparation; lots of practice material including two full length mock SATs; test-taking tips; and a light, humorous presentation.

For ACT Preparation -
➡How to Prepare for the American College Testing Program (Barron's)
➡Arco's Cram Course for the ACT (Arco)
➡Computer Study Program for the ACT [Computer programs available for Apple or IBM machines] (Barron's)

For Achievement Test Preparation
➡The College Board Achievement Tests [revised edition] (The College Board)
>Actual copies of achievement tests for English Composition, Literature, American History and Social Studies, European History and World Cultures, Mathematics Level I, Mathematics Level II, French, Italian, German, Hebrew, Latin, Spanish, Biology, Chemistry, and Physics are included in a single book.

Test preparation classes are offered by public and private colleges, and by private businesses. Many of these classes will guarantee a higher test score to their students.

Numerous computer test preparation programs are available. For the most part they duplicate material available less expensively in book form, but if the computer provides the necessary incentive for a student to study well, then the extra expense is defensible.

There are definitely some strategies that test takers can benefit from. Practicing test taking with sample tests available in many of the books and computer programs is probably the single most important thing to do. Learning the extra little tricks shared by some authors will also help, but it is easy to go overboard and spend too much time on test strategies.

I ought to mention another book here as we talk of test preparation. Understanding how the tests are written and how test writers think gives test takers a real advantage. Growing Without Schooling offers *Cracking the System: Revolutionary Techniques for Scoring High on the PSAT and SAT*, by Adam Robinson and John Katzman. This book provides the basics from "The Princeton Review," a highly successful class in test preparation. The authors tell us how test preparers think, and how they try to trip up test takers. They offer practical strategies for eliminating and selecting possible answers. This is a very helpful book, especially for those with test-phobia. There is plenty of review material all through the book, and at the end is one complete test with a computer scorable answer sheet. For an extra fee, we can send in the answer sheet for scoring, analysis, and evaluation.

The authors recommend purchasing a book with more practice tests such as *10 SATS*, to use along with *Cracking the System.*

Creating Transcripts

Colleges usually require a transcript along with test scores, but all private schools make up transcripts for their students. If we consider our home school a private school, we should make up our own. Colleges are not usually very concerned about whether students are coming from accredited schools or not, so we should not be afraid to give our school the same status as other private schools. At the same time, we should not be sneaky about it, trying to hide the fact that this is a home school. There is a transcript form to use in the Appendix of this book (Chart F), or you might be able to obtain a form from a local high school or your support group. We can add additional documentation if we think it will help.(See Chapter Six for more information about completing transcripts.)

Judy Gelner's book, *College Admissions: A Guide for Homeschoolers,* relates their adventures through the application process with their son. They had taken an unschooling approach and lacked the typical transcript, yet he was admitted to every college to which he applied. Gelner's book is encouraging with helpful hints about positive strategies and pitfalls to avoid whether we use an unschooling or a more traditional approach. It also serves as a resource for the type of information students typically get from high school guidance counselors such as what forms they need to fill out and how to get them. (Judy Gelner will relate more experiences and list more resources in the 1993 edition of *College Admissions: A Guide for Homeschoolers.*)

If the format of the typical transcript does not suit your home school history, you might do as the Colfax family did when their sons applied to Harvard. They prepared transcripts listing subject areas rather than classes. They listed books and materials used and included a portfolio of pictures and descriptions of learning projects. The Colfax's approach worked because colleges really want to know what subject matter the student has studied and what level of proficiency he has achieved.

It is a little harder to evaluate unconventional transcripts, and some admissions offices might give us a hard time over such a transcript, but if Harvard could deal with it, other colleges can as well.

In some cases the colleges have not required transcripts from home school students, perhaps assuming that a transcript prepared by a parent will be overly optimistic. Instead they have relied heavily on test scores.

Can We Avoid This Hassle?

Teens may be able to skip all of the diploma, transcript, and testing problems by accumulating college credits without graduating from high school. They can then use those credits as educational history documentation for four-year colleges or universities.

Junior or community colleges are one possible means of doing this. Junior colleges are much less stringent on entry requirements; SAT and ACT tests often are not required until a student applies to a four-year institution. In some states, anyone can attend junior college as long as they can do the work. High school graduation is not necessarily a requirement. Placement tests in basic subjects are usually required to ensure that students will be able to do the work. (Check admission requirements in your state.)

Once a student has completed one to four semesters at junior college (depending on the future college they wish to attend), they can apply to any four-year college. High school transcripts and diplomas are sometimes irrelevant at this point since the student has already demonstrated that he is able to do college work. However, the four-year colleges will look very carefully at junior college records of transfer student applicants. Junior colleges also might help home educated students make the transition from home to the school environment with less pressure because course work is sometimes less demanding than at four-year institutions. [3]

Another alternative for acquiring college credits is college correspondence courses. Teens can remain at home and accumulate college credits by enrolling in college correspondence courses. The University of California Extension Independent Study Program offers courses without any application process, other than filling out a short informational form—no high school graduation requirements. These are available at the same prices to students in any state, and in Canada at only $7 extra. Course prices appear to average about $250-300 each plus the cost of textbooks. Students have one year to complete each course. Many of the courses easily transfer to other colleges.

Some of the well-known schools offering college level correspondence courses include the University of California and the University of Nebraska-Lincoln. [4]

Some students need more assistance than is offered by some of the correspondence courses, and others want to complete their college degree through a single institution. An excellent option for Christian young people is *Liberty University's School of Lifelong Learning*. They offer accredited degrees, almost entirely through home study. Most courses are offered by video cassette. Six to twelve hours (two or four courses) are normally required in residence and that requirement can be fulfilled during summer and selected holiday seasons. Bachelor's degrees are offered in church ministries, business administration, and psychology. The Master's is available in counseling and religion. Faculty are regularly available by telephone via a toll free number. While residential students must have accepted Jesus Christ as their savior, external students are not required to have done so. Liberty's chancelor is Dr. Jerry Falwell.

Testing for Credit

Still another alternative is testing for credit. This is done by obtaining college level textbooks in particular fields of interest (for which tests are available) and studying them thoroughly. Many colleges will allow limited numbers of credits for passing certain standardized tests. In California, the maximum number of units from CLEP testing which can be transferred to an accredited university is forty-four units. It is very important that students check directly with colleges

or universities about their acceptance of such credits. Do not rely on catalog information which can often be inaccurate. The tests are challenging, but students can study for as long as they need before applying to take the tests. This approach allows students to study at their own pace. They can choose which subjects interest them most, and they work under the guidance of their parents (or another adult selected by the parents) rather than under an unknown professor at a distant university.

The two most widely recognized tests used for obtaining college credit are:

➡ **College-Level Examination Program (CLEP)**

CLEP offers testing in five general and thirty specific subject areas. CLEP testing credit is accepted at more than 2000 colleges and universities. Tests are offered at most college campuses by preregistration.

➡ **American College Testing Program Proficiency Examination Program (ACTPEP)**

ACTPEP offers 43 tests with the majority emphasizing occupational subjects such as health and business. They are accepted by over 800 colleges and universities, and are offered at over 160 national test sites.

The College Board, sponsor of the CLEP testing program, has published *The Official Handbook for the CLEP Examinations*. It provides advice on how to determine which colleges will grant CLEP credits, decide which tests to take, prepare for the tests, and interpret test scores. The book also contains complete descriptions of each CLEP examination (general as well as subject exams) with sample questions and answers and recommended resources to help you study for the examination. While sample questions are given, no complete tests are included for practice. Look for other CLEP manuals in bookstores and libraries.

One other source for credit by examination is:

➡ **Ohio University Course Credit by Examination (Ohio University)**

But Can We Get Degrees This Way?

Junior college, correspondence and testing credits can be used to build an educational history to present to four-year institutions, but some might wish to use unconventional methods for all of their college work. Information on other programs is available in books such as:

➡ **College Degrees by Mail** by John Bear, Ph.D. (Ten Speed Press)

Dr. Bear describes different approaches for getting degrees such as correspondence study, credit for life experience, equivalency exams, intensive study, and degree mills. Bear's book is useful for eliminating programs that do not have credibility in the marketplace. Of those remaining, he has selected 100 of the best schools offering degrees entirely through home study.

---

3   Since most of my information comes from California, and things are quite different elsewhere, I would like to hear from families in other states who are using junior colleges either during or after high school. Write directly to me at 12531 Aristocrat Ave., Garden Grove, CA 92641. I will pass on any helpful information I receive.

4   Inge Kendall provides a detailed description of the University of Nebraska-Lincoln's program in *School at Home: Teach Your Own Child* (pages 83-86.)

➡ The Complete Guide to Nontraditional Education: The Newest, Fastest Way to a College Degree by William J. Halterman (Facts on File, Inc.)

➡ Independent Study Catalog: A Guide to Continuing Education through Correspondence Courses (Peterson's)

This volume lists thousands of college correspondence courses from nearly 100 different schools. (This book was developed with the National University Continuing Education Association. It can also be ordered from the University of California.)

Once we begin to read books such as those listed above, we become aware that there are many ways to get a college degree without following the traditional route. To adventurous home schoolers, getting a college degree may just present another challenge to their ingenuity.

At the same time, be aware that when we try using alternative methods for obtaining college credits we can run into trouble. The biggest problem is receiving credit towards a degree. All credits are not transferrable to all institutions. Most institutions will accept only very limited numbers of credits from correspondence, independent study, or CLEP testing.

However, there are several exceptions to this. One program in particular sounds very promising.

➡ The University of the State of New York

Regents College

(Author's note: This type of degree program is often called an external degree program. External degrees are those earned by study and experience outside the classroom.)

This fully accredited university does not offer any actual classes of its own. It evaluates transfer credits, including an unlimited number of correspondence courses, life experience which has been evaluated as college level, standardized tests (again unlimited), learning contracts, and so forth. Their informational brochure and catalog are very informative on all aspects of this approach.

An external degree program is also offered by:

➡ Thomas Edison State College

Thomas Edison State College offers adults the opportunity to complete associate or baccalaureate degrees no matter where they live. Adult learners complete degrees through a combination of methods most convenient to them, including testing, portfolio assessment, learning acquired at work or in the military, Guided Study courses at home, transfer of credit and other options. Thomas Edison's program is fully accredited.

Some external degree programs offer credit for life or work experience. An assumption made by such programs is that the individual has three to five years of life or work experience, thus these programs do not fit most teenagers. However, they might make sense as a long range tool for obtaining a degree through a combination of work and education.

Financial Aid

There are an unbelievable number of sources for financial aid in the form of grants, scholarships, loans, and work/study programs. College financial counselors say that tuition fees may have very little do with the final choice of a college because of the help that is available.

Sixty-seven percent of the students enrolled in college have some sort of financial aid. However, my understanding of the way things operate is this: families fill out a financial aid questionnaire. The questionnaire information is used to determine (according to a formula) what amount the family can be expected to pay towards their child's education. The child is then eligible for help covering any costs beyond that. Unfortunately, what many middle income families I know have been told is that they should be able to pay more than they actually are able. One person summed it up, "They expect you to take out a second mortgage on your home if you have any equity at all."

Special scholarships from parents' employers, organizational affiliations, or clubs seem to be likelier options for assistance to middle income families than general scholarships based on "need."

Books on financial sources must be updated constantly, so I did not spend time personally reviewing books listed below. However, my experience is that publishers of these books generally describe each book's content accurately.

➡ Free Money for College by Laurie Blum (Facts on File)

More than 1,000 grants and scholarships are listed, along with the source's or grant's restrictions, the amount of money given, and application deadlines. Six categories are used for identifying possible special sources of financial aid: state, area of study, grants for women, grants for ethnic students, grants for handicapped students, and miscellaneous.

➡ Paying Less for College 1993 (Peterson's)

This book is updated yearly. Peterson's claims that this is the only complete guide to scholarships, costs, and financial aid at U.S. colleges. It covers scholarships, athletic and merit awards, special aid, tuition plans, and grants, but, as good as it might be, I know there are other books available that you might find equally valuable. (Check out another Peterson's title, *Winning Money for College*.)

More Sources for Financial Assistance

I refer you to the library, local high schools, junior colleges, and the colleges themselves for more resources. Check also with organizations with which you are affiliated, including employers, for special scholarships.

Investing in assistance from a financial aid/scholarship service might be well worth the money for many families. Find out about local services through high school counselors.

FACTS (Financial Aid and College Tuition Scholarship Service is one such service, operated by a home educating father (and state leader). They are able to assist students from all over the country with leads on financial aid available to them. The information is screened to reflect the family's financial situation and special help available for attendance at three different colleges or universities of the student's choice.

National Merit Scholarship Program

One program that home schoolers often miss out on is the National Merit Scholarship Program. The first step by which students enter the competition for Merit Scholarships is taking the PSAT/NMSQT (Preliminary Scholastic Aptitude Test/National Merit Scholarship Qualifying Test). The test is administered by College Board ATP, but offered only through local high schools. You must contact a local high school and make arrangements for your child to be tested along with their students. The test is given in October each year, and a student must take it in the junior year in order to participate in the Merit Program. Some students take it simply for practice for the SAT (it is very similar), while others are trying to qualify for the scholarship competition. If the PSAT/NMSQT was missed, there is a possibility of alternative arrangements for entering the program, but contact with NMSC must be made by March 1, following the October test that was missed.

The SAT test, which is given a number of times each year, is one of the requirements for advancing in the competition.

Test inquiries or requests for the *PSAT/NMSQT Student Bulletin* (information) should be directed to:

PSAT/NMSQT
P.O. Box 24700
Oakland, CA 94623-1700
(609) 683-0449 east coast
(510) 653-5595 west coast

Questions about the *National Merit Scholarship Program* should be directed to:

National Merit Scholarship Corporation
1560 Sherman Avenue, Suite 200
Evanston, Il 60201-4897
(708) 866-5100

PSAT/NMSQT Preparation

Arco publishes a PSAT-NMSQT test preparation book, called simply *PSAT-NMSQT*. It has sample tests which have been constructed to look like the actual tests. The College Board publishes *The College Board Guide to Preparing for the PSAT/NMSQT* which has four actual tests for practice.

Chapter Eight

Options

Now that we have figured out how to get our teens into college, we had better step back and take care of those difficult high school classes. How do we teach our teens a foreign language when we never studied one ourselves? How do we present science lab classes when we don't know a butane burner from a pipette? How do we teach our budding engineer calculus when our math education stopped with survival math? It certainly looks intimidating when we look at college requirements and consider our inadequacies. But we need not stop there. We have lots of help available to us if we just know where to look.

Correspondence Schools

The most obvious place to go for help is a correspondence course that provides books, teaching information, answer keys, and record keeping for us. At high school level, another benefit of enrollment in such a school is that the school has a high school code number which is usually requested on college entrance exams. Using their number saves a little bureaucratic hassle.

The correspondence courses that have consultants available to us are even more helpful.

The cautions with correspondence courses have to do with individual needs. We must check out the textbooks and materials used to see if they are appropriate for our child, judging to the best of our ability. We must look also at the rate at which work must be completed. Might it be more than our child can handle? The rigid requirements are the most common cause of complaints I hear about correspondence courses. We need also be concerned with turnaround time on tests and papers. If it takes a long time to receive feedback on how well a student has mastered a lesson, it can create problems in determining whether or not to move ahead on schedule.

The following correspondence courses are listed for your information, but this does not imply unconditional recommendation. All programs will provide free information upon request.

➡ A Beka Correspondence School

This program uses A Beka texts for pre-kindergarten through 12th grade. It is heavily academic. A Beka prefers that home schoolers enroll in this program rather than buy their books and work independently, but they no longer pressure home schoolers to enroll as they used to. The teaching methods are traditional with little hands-on activity. This is a good program for students who have performed well in traditional schools with high academic standards. It is accredited by the Florida Association of Christian Schools.

➡ A Beka Video Courses

A Beka also offers home school video courses. The videos are of actual school classes with a teacher presenting lessons to the children. The time required is four hours per day for elementary grades and one and a half to two hours per course, per day, for high school. Students use A Beka textbooks and send in work as they would for other correspondence courses. Work is evaluated every six weeks for K-3 and every nine weeks for grades 4-12. Video tapes are shipped back and forth and remain the property of A Beka. Write to A Beka requesting a "Video Home School" brochure for details. I do not generally recommend the video courses for young children because of the lack of interaction and stimulation, but they are useful in special situations, e.g., parent unavailable for interaction and a lack of alternatives, or older students taking a course with which parents are unfamiliar. I have heard mixed reactions from those who have used the video courses—some thought they were great, others thought they were awful—but none of these people were using more than one or two of the video courses a year, and all were working at junior high/high school level. Complete programs are available for kindergarten through high school. Elementary courses come only as complete programs. At junior/senior high level, individual courses can be selected rather than the entire program.

➡ Alpha Omega Institute

This correspondence course is open to students in kindergarten through eighth grade. It uses the Alpha Omega LifePac curriculum. Services included with enrollment include placement and prescription of which levels of LifePacs are needed for each subject, consultation with experienced teachers, academic assistance, report cards, transcripts, permanent records, support to parents, reading remediation program, annual achievement testing, and eighth grade diploma.

➡ American School

This secular, accredited high school correspondence course has been in business since 1897. It provides two main educational services by correspondence study: a diploma program for those young people and adults who do not attend traditional high school and wish to complete their secondary education and earn the American School diploma; and an independent study program for those students who, while remaining regularly enrolled in their local high schools, take classes with American School with the approval of a local school official in order to make up credits, or for enrichment and acceleration. They offer a very wide range of courses, and students may enroll in one or more courses. While the cost is higher for a single year than some of the other correspondence schools listed, the cost drops dramatically for two- three- or four-year enrollments, making the long-term cost much lower than any other correspondence school. Students may also enroll for single courses if they so desire. Payment can be made on a monthly basis if necessary.

➧ Calvert School

Calvert offers academic courses for kindergarten through eighth grades with <u>all</u> materials supplied for each course. Many of the Calvert courses are very good, although a few of the secular textbooks that we get are mediocre. This is not a Christian school and some of the texts contain evolutionary concepts. However, we are welcome to supplement or substitute lessons reflecting our own beliefs and philosophies for the Calvert lessons.

Calvert's strength is in their coverage of geography, history, mythology, poetry, and literature, and in their lesson manuals. Lesson manuals provide clear, concise instruction for the novice teacher which helps us learn how to teach.

Since subject studies are integrated to some extent, mixing of grade levels is not allowed. These courses are, for the most part, pre-packaged curriculum for each grade level, although Calvert allows enrollment in individual subjects at the eighth grade level only. (Recently added courses which are available apart from the entire curriculum are Beginning French, Beginning French Level II, and Algebra.) This arrangement restricts the amount of individualizing that we can do before eighth grade. However, the complete curriculum is a good choice for missionaries or others who have great difficulty rounding up all the necessary materials.

We may enroll our child and work with him or her independently, or we may elect to include the optional Advisory Teaching Service (ATS) for grades one through eight. With the ATS, tests are sent to Calvert for review and grading by a professional teacher/advisor, who also makes comments and suggestions. Only with the ATS will Calvert issue a certificate of completion for courses.

➧ Christian Liberty Academy

Christian Liberty Academy (CLA) offers courses for kindergarten through twelfth grades with a program very similar to Christian schools. They have chosen an assortment of textbooks from various publishers as well as some of their own. The textbooks and program reflect a more traditional approach to education using primarily workbooks and reading. Each course comes with the needed instructions or teacher's manual, and CLA has written their own, simplified teacher's manuals to be used in place of some of the huge volumes offered by many publishers. CLA offers options of either purchasing only books through them, with no record keeping or enrollment (The Family Plan), or full enrollment in the correspondence program. This program is academically sound, but does not meet the needs of learners who require hands-on activity. In the past, people have had trouble with the amount of work required, but the program has been changed slightly—requiring less work and offering more flexibility and discretion to parents. CLA has shown a commendable responsiveness to the needs of home educators. They have done well in their effort to offer good materials at an affordable price.

➧ Covenant Home Curriculum

Covenant offers courses for kindergarten through twelfth grades. They use an assortment of Christian and secular texts, with an option for other curriculum choices tailored to the individual needs of the child (at slightly higher cost). The "tailored course" option makes Covenant a more flexible choice than some other correspondence courses.

The basic texts reflect a traditional approach to education, while optional supplementary books offer a more experiential approach.

Covenant offers two plans for high school. Plan A is the high-intensity four years of solid academics listed in their course inventory catalog. Plan B allows for stretching out science and math courses for students who find these subjects difficult. Both plans are college preparatory. With both plans, "grade-auditing and tutorial" may be purchased so that transcripts will be issued.

Covenant's program has been used successfully by missionaries who needed all of the materials provided through one source, yet who also wanted Christian materials with less emphasis on formal academics than Christian Liberty Academy and A Beka.

➧ North Dakota Division of Independent Study

This school offers complete accredited high school programs with a wide variety of class options to accommodate different learners' abilities and interests. For example, math classes include general mathematics, consumer mathematics, and precalculus as well as the more standard courses. Classes such as child development, etiquette, agriculture, accounting, business law, engines, electricity, aviation, and welding stretch beyond the typical correspondence offerings. The cost is much higher than for Christian Liberty or Covenant, averaging about $100 per course <u>per semester.</u> Students can enroll in as many courses as they choose, but they are required to be under the supervision of a credentialed teacher who receives materials and supervises tests.

➧ Seton Home Study School

Seton Home Study School is accredited by the National Home Study Council. Correspondence courses for elementary through high school are offered for full or partial enrollment. Seton offers a traditional, Catholic education at a reasonable cost. They use an assortment of Catholic and other textbooks to provide a quality education. Because their primary desire is to be of service, Seton offers a wide variety of individual courses (partial enrollment) on subjects ranging from business education and computers through basic academic subjects. At high school level, students might wish to enroll in a complete course or only in Latin, chemistry, higher math, or another specific course. Seton is one of the few private programs which allows single subject enrollment for high school. Of special interest are Catholic religion courses open for partial enrollment also to elementary students (up through eighth grade). Help is available by telephone if necessary.

➧ Summit Christian Academy

Summit offers pre-kindergarten through 12th grade programs. They include testing and placement at appropriate levels in each subject area. They use Alpha Omega for first grade and above, although other materials can be used with their approval. Summit also offers their students credit for a work-study program. The toll free telephone number allows parents to consult with the school when necessary. Summit is an accredited school that will provide a diploma and transcript for graduating high schoolers.

Independent Study through Universities

Some colleges also offer high school correspondence courses known as independent study. The catch is that usually our local school district has to give students permission to enroll, which might present a problem in some areas.

The University of California at Berkeley, the University of Missouri, the University of Alabama, and the University of Nebraska-Lincoln offer courses for high school students unable to complete all of their educational requirements in a regular classroom setting. The Universities of Alabama, California, and Missouri offer courses, but do not award high school diplomas. The home school or another educational institution or school service grants students credit for these courses, and is the diploma grantor. Courses are available to students all over the world.

The University of Nebraska-Lincoln does offer diplomas. The high school course is accredited by the North Central Association of Colleges and Schools and the Nebraska Department of Education. For a list of other colleges and universities offering correspondence courses, we can order *The Independent Study Catalog* from University of California Extension (listed in the appendix).

Correspondence Telecourses

Television can be useful! In some areas of the country school districts and colleges broadcast telecourses on educational channels (UHF or cable). Courses are offered at all different levels, but complete courses are available for college subjects. In our area, about twenty courses are offered each semester. Students enroll by mail, with no high school graduation requirement. They watch the course, read the accompanying textbook, send in the required paper work (usually minimal), then either send in a final test or report to a testing site for the final exam. These courses are for college credit but can also be used without enrollment for high school work. Typical courses are American History, Business, Astronomy, Biology, Freehand Drawing, and Child Development. We used the Biology course to help us with our lower level biology studies. The videos depicted things so well that they were better than most lab work that we could have done. Of course you do have to guard for course content since these courses reflect the secular viewpoint. Check your television guide or write to your educational channel for complete listings.

Independent Study Programs[1]

Independent study programs are offered by both public and private schools and also by school services.

Public School Independent Study Programs

You may be able to enroll your teen in an independent study program through your local public junior or senior high school. Aside from the question of whether or not we should really have anything at all to do with the public school system, in many states we have the right to enroll our child in such programs. Generally, students are required to use the public school texts, although they may be permitted to use Christian texts on their own time at their own expense in addition to their required texts. Such programs are available in many states for elementary grades, but independent study programs at the junior/senior high school level are still quite rare. Enrolling in such a program will make it much easier to get a traditional diploma and transcript, although the trade-off value (being under the authority of the public school system) is debatable.

Private Day School Independent Study Programs

Some private Christian schools are offering independent study programs for junior and senior high. Again these are still rather scarce at the high school level. This option is attractive since we get the assurance of the traditional transcript and diploma, without having to accept non-Christian philosophy, textbooks, and methodology. Participation in selected activities of the school can be a valuable bonus.

Other Independent Study Programs

There are hundreds of independent study programs across the country, which offer services to local home educators. These programs vary tremendously in services offered, requirements, and expertise of the administrators. Check with your local home school group for possibilities.

School Services

School services usually have no campuses. They are similar to correspondence courses in that they serve students all over the country (and beyond our borders), but they allow families to choose materials, usually with their assistance. Often there is quite a bit of choice involved. Depending on the service, they might keep records, evaluate student work, and (usually) provide testing. School services can vary dramatically in what they offer, so check carefully to know what you are paying for.

The following school services provide enrollment throughout the country:

➡Hewitt Research Foundation

This center is a school service originally founded to implement the philosophy of Dr. Raymond Moore, but Dr. Moore is no longer associated with it. Junior high students may enroll in programs and choose services according to their needs. Hewitt provides testing, evaluation, textbook recommendations, and record keeping services. They often include many of their own materials such as *Winston Grammar* in their recommendations, but they also use learning materials and books from many other publishers. Their Limited Program is open to high school students who began the school year in a formal setting, but later chose home education. Enrollment is open between January 1 and March 31 for completion by July 31. A Summer Program is open to junior and senior high students who wish to take one or two classes.

Hewitt is unusual in their ability to assist children with learning difficulties. They can help with assessment and tailoring of a program to suit each child.

---

1   The terms "Independent Study Program" and "School Service" are often used interchangeably and inconsistently. What services are being offered is of more importance to you than how a program identifies itself.

➡ Moore Foundation Curriculum Programs

Dr. and Mrs. Raymond Moore's Moore Foundation now offers membership plus a number of service options.

Moore Foundation Associates (MFA), for families who do not need special services, requires a minimum purchase of materials or donation of $100 and provides an enrollment card which shows that the family is identified with and attached to the Moore Foundation. MFA membership is prerequisite to enrollment in all other programs. MFA members may enroll in any Moore Foundation service programs, as long as there is space.

There are five service options available. Start Up (SU) is for families who want only initial counseling and curriculum planning. Special Assistance Start UP (SASU) is for families with special needs children who still want only initial counseling and curriculum planning. Moore Foundation Independent Study Program (MFISP) offers families ongoing services beyond MFA enrollment. The MFISP provides record keeping, evaluations, and certificate of completion or transcript. Moore Foundation Satellite Students (MFSS) is a limited (in enrollment numbers) plan in which those who need more extensive accountability receive more extensive service which includes maintenance of a cumulative record folder, processing of requests for past school records, customized curricula, telephone or letter counseling, an initial evaluation, two progress evaluations, and certificate of completion or transcript. Moore Foundation Special Assistance Students (MFSAS) is for children who might be "...learning-delayed, learning-different, talented & gifted, handicapped or otherwise in need of special counsel, special materials and perhaps teacher analysis of psychological tests." All programs are available for both elementary and secondary students.

➡ Sycamore Tree

They offer full record keeping, testing, diplomas, transcripts, student body card, educational guidance, and supervision for kindergarten through twelfth grade. They also will grant work experience credit, a feature that should be of interest to many high school students. Enrollment entitles you to a ten percent discount on curriculum and materials ordered through Sycamore Tree. This is an especially good option for isolated families. They recommend materials from a very wide range of publishers, including both traditional and informal learning materials. Students transferring mid-high school into the Sycamore program must have units from an accredited school or from a home school umbrella/independent study program for prior high school work.

➡ Institute in Basic Life Principles/Advanced Training Institute of America

Bill Gothard, founder and president of the Institute, has begun a program for home schooling based upon the Bible, *Wisdom Booklets*, other materials from the Institute, and your own selected textbooks for communicating academic skills. Apprenticeship for older students is another important part of the ATIA program. ATIA is a unique program which requires familiarity with the Institute and its teaching methods and principles. The goal is life training rather than simply academic training. There is a strong emphasis on parental accountability. The entire family is enrolled in the program together, attends a five-day training seminar (offered at one location, only once a year), commits to establishing daily family Scripture reading times led by the father, and agrees to several other guidelines. *Wisdom Booklets* provide the foundation for Scripturally-based unit studies that are excellent. ATIA is not a correspondence course, although the Institute provides forms and booklets to help with scheduling, planning, and record keeping. Write to the Institute for more information.

Part-Time School

Public school

More and more home schoolers are considering part-time school as an option. In some states students may enroll in their local public high school for selected classes. We again face the question of whether or not we want our children to have any involvement with the public school system. However, we may wish to have them take driver's education to avoid having to purchase private lessons. We may also feel that the situation is safe enough to enroll teens in science lab or foreign language classes.

Most schools have not dealt with home schoolers who wish to enroll part-time, so they do not know what to tell you. Before approaching a school, check the law in your state to determine your rights.

In California, according to Education Code number 37113, students must enroll in a minimum of four classes. Exceptions are made for classes in driver's education, occupational training, or science, in which case they may take fewer than four classes. One family enrolled their daughter for two classes that fit the legal requirement for the first year. The second year they again enrolled her, but for two classes outside the legal description. No one seemed to be aware of the law, and things worked out fine. Usually, school personnel do not know the law. It will be up to you to check it out and ask for what you need.

On the other hand, if schools really do not want your part-time student on campus, they can make things so miserable that you do not want to exercise your right to that option. They might also require extras that you might not want. For instance, driver's education is frequently offered as a combination class with health education. The health education class usually is heavy on sex education which most of us would rather handle on our own. Schools have the right to split the class for your convenience or require that your student take both parts.

Private school

Very few private schools have ever had a part-time student, so again we are the guinea pigs. If this option interests you, approach your private school with a positive attitude and a willingness to try it on an experimental basis. The school will make money by enrolling your child, so unless it is disruptive, they should be open to the idea.

Support Group Schools

A new development is the appearance of part-time schools organized by home schoolers for home schoolers. In many states, home schoolers are joining together and hiring teachers to offer classes for the more difficult subjects. Students usually attend school only two or three hours a week per class, then work at home on lesson assignments. The fact that fellow students are also home schooled makes the environment comfortable. Usually there is a tuition fee for such classes. Parents still maintain overall control, yet they have someone to whom they can turn to fill in for their weaknesses in different subject areas. This approach has been very successful, and we should see many more such schools open in the future.

The only problem that has arisen in these types of classes has occurred when students spent most of one or two days together in a school-like atmosphere. Typical peer pressure problems quickly crop up, and teens begin to act much like teens who attend traditional schools. This does not always happen, but it has happened often enough to alert us to potential problems. Keys to preventing problems might be increased adult "participation" (more than one teacher/advisor with a large group of teens) and some relationship and attitude guidelines when students enroll.

Adult Education and ROP

Adult education is sometimes available to older teenagers, whether or not they have graduated from high school. A minimum age of sixteen is common, and teens might have to be accompanied by an adult. Adult education classes range from the basics in reading, writing, and math to vocational and trade subjects. Elective type classes in the arts, foreign languages, computers, cooking, and other subjects are also offered.

ROP, or Regional Occupational Programs are a form of adult education that is open to teens sixteen and older. (Programs might function under different names in different states.) Classes are designed to train students in marketable skills. Accounting, animal care, banking, business machines, cosmetology, electronics, fashion merchandising, legal secretary, photography, and welding are among the typical subjects offered by such programs. Students need permission from school officials to attend these classes since they work closely with the public school system.

Junior College or Community College

Many states have junior or community college systems. Some of these systems are even open to students who have not graduated from high school. In California, any student capable of doing the work (judged by placement tests) is legally able to attend junior college. Some parents are teaching the classes they can handle at home and sending students to the junior college for more difficult classes such as math, science lab, foreign language, and computer. They are not even bothering to try to cover those subjects at home on high school level. This method saves time in the educational process, and credits are accumulated that cost much less at junior college than they would at a four-year college.

There are some cautions here. Junior or community college is not necessarily a good option. Some teens are not able to work at the pace necessary for college classes. The pressure can be very stressful for students who are accustomed to working on loose time schedules and even for disciplined students who are just too young.

Junior college may be no better (or possibly worse) than sending our child to the public high school. Many teenagers, at ages fifteen, sixteen, or seventeen, are too easily influenced by teachers, professors, and other students who hold opposing beliefs. It makes no sense to guard our children at home for many years, then rush them off to a secular junior college to battle ideas on a level too mature for them. Even for the mature student, we should be cautious about the types of classes they take. They are still very impressionable, no matter how strong they are in their faith. Most college campuses are also a culture in themselves, and our son or daughter needs to be mature enough to handle the social environment.

Early Graduation

Some teens are graduating from high school at age sixteen or seventeen (sometimes even earlier) by taking either the General Educational Development (GED) or High School Proficiency Examination. (The Proficiency Examination is available only in California.) They are covering basic courses at home and saving others such as lab classes and foreign language which are not tested by the GED to take at college. However, GED restrictions in many states preclude testing for early graduation. Some states will allow students to take the GED before the minimum age with special permission, but generally that special permission is very difficult to get. (Appendix B describes GED policies for each state.)

Students who can graduate early through testing are then able to enroll in junior or community colleges, or even four-year institutions at younger ages as high school graduates. The same cautions mentioned above apply since diplomas or certificates do not provide spiritual protection.

Compulsory education laws in each state require that students be attending school until a specified age. If they graduate before they have passed the age for compulsory attendance, they will need to continue their education in some manner.

Benefits of Multiple Teachers

Group classes at high school level can be a big help to both teacher and student.

– They experience a variety of teaching styles.
– They respond differently to someone other than a parent and are likely to be more cooperative toward a teacher other than mom or dad.
– Other people are bound to know more than we do about some subjects. Our child can learn more from someone who really knows a subject and is enthusiastic about teaching it.
– In a group, older students often encourage and challenge each other in a positive way that does not happen in a one-on-one setting.
– We can concentrate our teaching energies on fewer subject areas.

Tutors

Hiring a tutor might be a viable option for one or two classes. Even better would be for two or more families to jointly hire a tutor, essentially designing their own private class. We and four other families hired a tutor to help us with Spanish. The tutor came for one hour, one day a week, and we worked with our children on our own throughout the rest of the week. This system worked very well for us, giving us just the amount of help we needed to be successful.

Cross Teaching

This option is free! All of us have different strengths and weaknesses. If we can share our strengths, we can overcome our weaknesses. If one parent is good in science, she or he can teach a science class for a group of students, while another parent whose strength is in writing takes a turn providing writing instruction. The trade-off does not always have to be in teaching skills. One mother might be willing to babysit in exchange for your teaching skills. Another might be willing to trade housework labor. Be creative in drawing upon the talents of other home educators in your area.

Getting a Head Start on College

As mentioned previously, home educated high schoolers can start piling up college credits through junior colleges, telecourses, and college level correspondence courses. Such courses are often challenging, but bright students should be able to handle them. Even though courses are secular, by having students study at home, parents have the opportunity to counter objectionable content with the Christian viewpoint.

Some students may want to take GED or Proficiency Examinations before taking college level correspondence courses partly to eliminate any enrollment problems and partly to give them confidence in their ability to move beyond high school level work. Many more study options are available once students have the GED or high school equivalency certificates and fewer questions arise about a student's educational history.

Summary

Home educators are using all of the above options and creating new ones of their own. The key to overcoming hurdles is to keep an open mind about ways of meeting our goals. Just because something has not been tried before does not mean that we should not try it ourselves. Bureaucratic officials are usually the worst to deal with when we want to do something out of the ordinary, but confidence and a positive, friendly attitude can open many doors and enlist enthusiastic cooperation.

There certainly can be some risk involved when we choose to operate outside traditional channels, but the track record of home educated students already is proving that unconventional methods can produce outstanding results.

Part Two

Recommendations

Under my recommendations, I describe individual items that are worth your attention—some briefly, some more completely. Those with fuller descriptions are usually materials that I have been able to review more thoroughly than others. However, descriptions of materials from the major Christian publishers—A Beka, Bob Jones University Press, Alpha Omega, Christian Liberty Press, ACE School of Tomorrow, and Rod and Staff—are briefer because I have included general information about their materials in the following chapter, "Major Publishers." I suggest that you read through this section before investigating the specific recommendations.

Chapter Nine

Major Publishers

Information about individual items from each publisher is found under subject headings. By including publishers here we are not implying their superiority over others.

A Beka

A Beka offers materials for pre-kindergarten through 12th grade, including supplementary materials. A Beka also offers enrollment in their own A Beka Correspondence School (book or video/book options), but they will sell materials to us without enrollment.

A Beka's philosophy is conservative, Christian, and patriotic. Their approach to education is traditional with an emphasis on drill, repetition, and memorization. All material is written from a Christian perspective. Although this is very evident in the science and history books, it seems to be tacked on in math and some of the language arts. Conservatism and patriotism are most evident in reading/literature and history.

A Beka will sell teacher's guides/curriculum, teacher's editions (answer keys), and texts at retail prices to individuals. Individual subject area curriculum guides lay out lesson plans and offer teaching suggestions, usually most appropriate for the classroom. A Beka is unusual in separating answer keys (teacher's editions) from teaching information (teacher's guides/curriculum).

The organization of teacher material is not the same for all courses which creates some confusion. In some instances we will want both teacher's edition and teacher's guide/curriculum, but teacher's guide/curriculum volumes often are not useful for home educators.

The math and language worktexts include most instruction on new concepts. We need teacher's editions (answer keys) for these when the material gets too difficult to correct without them. The need for teacher's books varies text by text at high school level, so read the information under each subject heading.

A Beka's math and grammar are both challenging. Junior high mathematics worktexts are good in that they constantly review concepts already learned, but they also address topics that are well beyond the typical junior high curriculum. High school math texts should be "taught" rather than used for independent learning.

The grammar goes into great detail, and while it is not exciting, it gives children a thorough knowledge of the subject. Writing needs more attention than is given in the language worktexts alone, so either use ideas from the teacher's guides or use ideas from supplements for composition.

Science books are excellent. However, on junior high levels there is excessive emphasis on detail and memorization, so use tests and assignments with discretion. Junior high texts, *Science: Matter and Motion* and *Science: Order and Reality*, are excellent for general science background. The high school *Biology* text is well-written and practical for home educators. *Chemistry* and *Physics* are much more difficult to use.

History books are very good at junior/senior high levels, although A Beka's history books are a bit more extreme than others in stressing the patriotic viewpoint. A Beka's biggest weakness here is a lopsided emphasis on detail recall. It is easy enough to challenge our students with only the appropriate questions, so this does not present a major problem. Good supplementary materials are offered.

We can use history and some science books without Teacher's Guides unless we want answers to text exercises which are found in the Guides.

Many A Beka books are paperback, and while they are sometimes less expensive, they might not last a long time. Worktexts used in many subjects are definitely not reusable.

A Beka materials can be ordered directly from A Beka, by writing for a catalog and order form. We might be able to save a little money by ordering A Beka materials from Great Christian Books at discounted prices. They carry most of the A Beka texts, but not the teacher's books. Used A Beka texts (selected titles) are available from Rainbow Resource Center at terrific discounts.

A Beka also has courses on video cassette. See the description under "Correspondence Courses."

Bob Jones University Press (BJUP)

Bob Jones University Press is newer to the Christian school publishing field than A Beka. They try to be very helpful to home educators, both in providing information over their toll free phone lines and in selling to home schoolers at wholesale cost (same prices charged to other schools).

Their philosophy is conservative and Christian. Educationally, they seem to have balanced their curriculum with teaching methods that suit most learning styles, although much of the necessary information to properly teach to all the learning styles is contained in the teacher's editions, not in student books.

BJUP offers mostly hardbound student texts with the separate teacher's editions bound in three-ring binders. New teacher's editions are in a revised format—spiral binding with a hardback cover. The pages will not rip out of these as they might from the binders, plus they have rigidity for easier handling because of the hardback cover. Teacher's editions are quite expensive (as are just about all publishers' teacher's editions) but contain material that often is essential to proper use of the texts. Check my descriptions of individual courses to determine when they are essential. Sometimes the teacher's editions contain the student text without answers so that a separate text is unnecessary. Check with the publisher about each teacher's edition—this information is also included in the home school ordering form.

Material is colorful and well presented. It also has strong Biblical material incorporated throughout in a very effective manner.

The Bible curriculum for junior and senior high school is well written, purposeful, and easy to use, even without the teacher's editions.

The math program is not as advanced as A Beka's through junior high, but is similar in difficulty at high school level. BJUP math encourages children to think and analyze through well designed word problems, but requires more one-on-one presentation than do many other math programs. At high school level, the teacher's familiarity with math topics is assumed, making BJUP higher math difficult for many home educating parents to teach without lengthier explanations.

Upper level history texts are outstanding. They are well-written, Christian in content, and have worthwhile discussion and assignment questions.

Junior high science (*Life* and *Earth Science*) and ninth grade *Basic Science* are good texts that will work well in the home school. Higher level texts assume the classroom environment for lab work and are increasingly difficult to use.

Cost may be higher than other publishers if we purchase teacher's editions for all subjects. Quality and durability are good.

Families with only one or two grade levels to teach generally find that they can make use of BJUP texts and teacher's editions more easily than families with more grade levels to teach. Because it takes so much time to wade through the enormous amounts of material in the teacher's editions, families sometimes use only the texts or workbooks, thereby eliminating essential parts of many courses. Check under individual subject headings whether the teacher's edition is essential or not, then determine if you have time to use the material properly.

New from BJUP is the *Ask It* test generation software for IBM or Macintosh computers. *Ask It* helps us create and edit test questions, setting them up in a database. Or, if we do not want to write questions ourselves, we can purchase the computerized test banks designed specifically to accompany various BJUP textbooks. (Book form test banks are already available for a number of textbooks.) We can easily select test questions, then print out tests and answer keys. For multiple choice and true-false questions we can even set it up so students take their test on the computer, which also scores the test. The *Ask It* program serves as the master program, and we then purchase the computer data disks as needed. Data disks presently are available for *Family Living*, *Heritage Studies* (history), *Literature* for grades 7-9, *Life Science*, and *Biology*.

Used BJUP materials are also available from Rainbow Re-Source Center at discounted prices.

Rod and Staff

Rod and Staff is a Mennonite publishing company that is very cooperative with home schoolers. Their curriculum relies heavily on Biblical material in all subjects. Among the distinctives of the Mennonite philosophy is nonresistance and separation, including the belief that the church should not involve itself in government, and this is reflected in their texts.

The Mennonite philosophy is also one that emphasizes hard work and diligence, and this is very evident throughout the material.

There is much busywork and extra material in Rod and Staff textbooks since they were designed for classroom use, so we should not be using everything in every book. If we know our goals and use curriculum as a tool, we can use Rod and Staff effectively by choosing how much of the material to have our child use.

Rod and Staff has few texts for junior and senior high at this time. They offer Reading for 7 (8th grade book will soon be available), English for 7 and 8, Math for 7 and 8, History for 7, Music for 7, and Science for 7-9.

The *Building Christian English* series is excellent for 7th and 8th grades. Science books are also excellent.

Christian Liberty Press

Christian Liberty Academy was one of the pioneers in home education. They have offered educational assistance through their home education program at extremely low cost because they view their role as one of ministry. To keep the cost of home education as affordable as possible, they have begun publishing many of their own books. Some of these books are reprints from the last century, but many are newly written. The quality of these reprints used to vary considerably, but in the last few years CLP has improved print and page size as well as rewritten most of those which were poorer in quality. All CLP books are very inexpensive. Some of them are tremendous bargains.

The *Eclectic Reader* series (for grades K-10) are reprints with the flavor of the original *McGuffey Readers*. CLP has put together a very inexpensive reading kit for remedial instruction that incorporates their books along with others.

The *Spelling* series books (for grades 7-9) are reprints that look much like the readers in format. Unlike most spelling books today, students do not write in these.

History books are an eclectic assortment of reprints and newly written books that can be used at various levels from second through eighth or ninth grade. Some supplementary books are also offered including: biographies of Robert E. Lee, Stonewall Jackson, and George Washington; two good books on the Pilgrims; and, an interesting little book entitled *Training Children in Godliness*. All history/civics textbooks come with teacher's manuals written by CLP staff at no extra cost. They are very brief, containing answer keys and teaching suggestions. If you are not satisfied with CLP books, they may be returned within thirty days of shipment; however, you will be charged a ten percent restocking charge.

See also the description of Christian Liberty Academy's correspondence school, which uses a mixture of CLP books with those from other publishers.

Alpha Omega

Alpha Omega materials are unlike typical school textbooks in several ways. Children are placed at the appropriate starting point in each subject area in the program, and they work sequentially through a number of workbooks, called LifePacs, as they master the material in each. These small workbooks contain instruction, information, questions (with blanks), and tests. Alpha Omega includes a variety of questions to encourage deeper thinking rather than simple recall of factual information. Children take tests as they complete each section of a workbook before proceeding to the next. Tests check on student mastery of current subject matter and also review previously mastered material.

Students can work at their proper levels in all subjects rather than being regimented into a single grade level for all subjects.

Alpha Omega offers full curriculum for grades 1-12, including Bible. LifePacs consist of ten booklets for each subject each year. Subject areas are: Bible, Math, Language Arts (English), Science, and Social Studies for the elementary grades, with typical high school courses and electives offered for high school.

Only five of the LifePacs require the use of supplementary books to complete the courses. Biblical perspectives are incorporated throughout the material.

Unlike A.C.E., Alpha Omega emphasizes that this material should not be used by a child working totally independently, but that parents need to be involved, supplementing with activities and other interactive ideas from the teachers' manuals to ensure an effective program. Even though the LifePacs enable children to work more independently than most curricula designed for classroom use, parental involvement is essential for providing the complete learning experience intended by the publisher. Unfortunately, there is a tendency among home educators to ignore the teachers' manuals and allow children to use the material completely on their own. Because this happens so frequently, I recommend that LifePacs be used with older learners (junior and senior high) who are independent, self-motivated, and need less hands-on experience to learn well. However, if parents plan to use the material as designed by the publisher, then it will work with learners who need more parental interaction.

The LifePac approach can be a real boon to parents with many children, widely spaced in age, or to parents who feel inadequate to help their children in particular subjects. (Caution: High school math is not one of Alpha Omega's strengths, so if parents are also weak in this area, it might be wiser to choose a different math program.)

Materials are available through correspondence courses, through home school suppliers, or by direct order.

Direct ordering: You may order directly from the publisher. A Starter Kit is available to help you, which includes diagnostic testing materials, placement and ordering information.

Diagnostic tests are also available separately for use in placing your child correctly in this material. The diagnostic tests might be useful as a general testing tool for others as explained in the section of this book about testing.

Christian Light

Christian Light publishes a Mennonite version (reflecting Anabaptist doctrine) of Alpha Omega's materials. There are five strands of workbooks (called *Lightunits*): Bible, language arts, math, science, and social studies. There are ten *Lightunits* in each strand at each grade level.

Christian Light has its own hardcover text with matching *Lightunits* for high school literature, as well as for a number of elementary subjects and grade levels.

Christian Light incorporates materials from other publishers at the upper levels. These are primarily for high school electives, which include typing, bookkeeping, home economics, Spanish, consumer math, Greek, carpentry, small engines, automobiles, woodworking, and art.

Canadian social studies is covered in a set of four special *Lightunits* used typically at seventh grade level. Also available is a broad line of supplementary books and resources, including science kits.

Three ordering/service options are offered: Option 1, send $20 for basic information for procedures and ordering; Option 2, receive a one-week parent training program by mail for $75; or, Option 3, for $100 receive parent training, plus one year of CLE assistance and record keeping that can lead to a CLE diploma. To maintain Option 3, the fee is $50 for each subsequent year. (An option is <u>required</u> only for purchasing language arts, math, science, and social studies *Lightunits*, achievement tests, and CLE diplomas.)

ACE School of Tomorrow (A.C.E. and Basic Education materials)

This publisher offers two different but similar lines of material. There are numerous differences between the two lines, but they are similar in methodology. Materials are designed for children to work independently. For the most part, minimal lesson preparation or presentation by the parent is necessary, although parents should use preparation time to develop activities that correlate with lessons to help children stretch beyond the limits of the curriculum. High school level materials require increased parent presentation and interaction.

The A.C.E. line has math, English, social studies, science, and word building for grades 1-9.

Children work through individual workbooks, called PACES (12 per course, per year) which look similar to the LifePacs from Alpha Omega (although PACES were the first to use this format). Children are placed at the appropriate place in each subject area by using the publisher's diagnostic tests. Children then work sequentially through the workbooks as they master the material in each. These small workbooks contain instruction, information, questions (with blanks), and tests. Children take tests as they complete each section of a workbook before proceeding to the next. Tests generally cover only what has recently been studied. Students might be working at different levels in different subjects according to their individual abilities and needs.

Students are directed to Basic Education for subjects unavailable in A.C.E. materials or as supplements if they need more challenging material at any level.

Word building reinforces phonics, then works on vocabulary and etymology at upper levels. A.C.E. Social Studies is big on the "social" end (the first half of the seventh grade level is entirely devoted to careers) along with church and Bible history, but lacking in coverage of world history. United States history and geography are covered in eighth and ninth grade levels respectively, offering better coverage of both topics. (Basic Education material provides much more coverage of world history.) A.C.E. uses fewer supplementary books than Basic Education, although both use good literature books along with English studies from fourth grade up.

The Basic Education line has materials for grades K-12, printed in black (or another dark color) and white. Subjects are covered under general headings of Math, Language Arts (English), Science, and Social Studies, and Spelling. Many electives are available at high school level. The workbooks are available in two formats, individual small workbooks (Self-Pacs), or a large workbook equivalent to a year's worth of Basic Education Self-Pacs (called a Self-Text). Lessons within Self-Texts are essentially the same as Self-Pacs with a few differences. Self-Texts have more closely monitored vocabulary so that new/unfamiliar words are always defined for students. The scope and sequence varies some; for example, seventh grade social studies Self-Pacs cover both government and state history, while the seventh grade Self-Text covers only government. Midterm and final exams are found in the Self-Texts, but not in the Self-Pacs.

The most obvious difference we see in A.C.E. material when compared to Basic Education is that it is printed in full color. The less obvious difference is that the A.C.E. materials were designed to better assist below average to average students, because they teach in small increments with much review. As noted above, there are also differences in which subjects are available in A.C.E. material. A.C.E. is an easier curriculum than Basic Education at the primary levels. The material is purposely designed to move very slowly, using a mastery approach to insure that the student actually masters the material before moving on. For instance, there is no multiplication until fourth grade. The difficulty curve rises quickly at upper elementary and junior high levels.

At elementary levels, both Basic Education and A.C.E. use questions that rely upon simple recall of information word for word. Students can scan for the correct answer (which should be discouraged by parents) without having to really think about the material. There is little in either program to encourage deeper thinking. However, thinking skills are better developed at upper levels as students are required to analyze and respond to material they are studying.

A.C.E. has also developed a new *Videophonics* reading program that is excellent for teaching reading to older children and adults.

I believe that young children benefit from an interactive learning environment, so I generally do not recommend either Self-Pacs or PACES for children in early elementary grades. This approach to learning better suits the older child who has developed independent learning skills. However, this curriculum is particularly useful for the slow learner and learning-disabled child.

Some of the most exciting developments in the A.C.E. curriculum have been in the field of computer technology. Computer-integrated programs now teach keyboard skills. A.C.E. is developing their vision for integrating the use of computer software throughout their curriculum. They have chosen a variety of software that they sell along with their materials for reinforcement and enhanced learning. Most of the software is for drill purposes, but at upper levels they have set up programs for students to work on databases and word processing. A.C.E. claims that a student who spends the last five years of his schooling in the A.C.E. School of Tomorrow program can graduate with computer literacy skills and application program skills.

The School of Tomorrow now also offers programs utilizing the latest CVI (computer-video interactive) technology. Videos and software based courses for Algebra I, Physical Science, and Biology are now available, and other courses are in the works.

Chapter Ten

Bible Resources for Junior and Senior High

We hope that by this time, our children are very familiar with the Bible. They should understand basic doctrine and be ready to investigate the Bible more deeply. Rather than choosing a curriculum we could use any of the many Bible study materials from our local Christian book store. Choose particular books of the Bible each year or choose a topical approach. There are hundreds of study aids for the individual books of the Bible. Topical studies can be done with a few tools such as a Concordance and an Expository Dictionary. A commentary set is also very useful. (Most single volume commentaries will frustrate you, so look for a good buy on a more comprehensive set.)

You can purchase all of these very reasonably from Great Christian Books, Christian Book Distributors (CBD), T & D Christian Sales, or your local Christian bookstore. If you need help, almost all distributors will answer questions and help you find resources which support your theological perspective or address a particular issue or topic.

Home educating families tend to be even more strong minded about their religious beliefs than they are about their educational beliefs. It is impossible to recommend Bible study materials that are in total agreement with all of our readers' convictions. Those included in this chapter agree on the divine inspiration of the Bible, salvation through Jesus Christ, as well as many other doctrinal areas.

Bible curriculum or study material should never be a substitute for individual Bible reading.[1] God speaks to each of us through Scripture according to our present spiritual condition and need. No curriculum can even pretend to provide such individually tailored lessons, although it can still be helpful.

The *Life Application Bible for Students* (Tyndale) stands out as being especially good for teens since it is directed toward that age group with the goals of helping them understand and apply God's Word. It is a study Bible, but different than adult study Bibles. It includes charts, summaries of themes, personality profiles of Bible characters, character trait examples from Scripture, overviews of books of the Bible, maps, memory verses, real-life case studies of moral dilemmas faced by teens, stories based upon interviews with teens about situations in their lives where they applied God's Word, plus sections on current issues such as AIDS and rival belief systems such as New Age religions. Questions following each book can be used for private study or discussion. With all of these features, it might be rather difficult to find what you are looking for. They solve that problem by including a number of specialized indexes. Among them are the Life Changer Index (references to topics such as goals, gossip, homosexuality, sin, and thankful-

ness), Index to the Charts, Index to the Personality Profiles (Abel, Abraham, Absalom, etc.), and "Where to Find It" Index (Bible stories such as Elijah on Mt. Carmel, teaching parables, gospel parables, miracles, etc.). The text is Living Bible version. I like the *Life Application Bible for Students* because it directs teens to Scripture for the answers to life questions rather than revolving around a curriculum or another book.

Bible Curriculum

➡A Beka High School Bible Curriculum

Although I list the high school level titles here, I have found the A Beka Bible curriculum too classroom oriented for use in most home schools.

Joshua and Judges - Teacher's Kit IV [8th grade level]

Includes Teacher's Guide, Student Study Outline and Review Questions.

Kings of Israel: Israel's United Kingdom - Teacher's Edition Kit [9th grade level]

Includes Teacher's Guide, Student Study Outline, and Review Questions.

Israel's Divided Kingdom [9th grade level]

Purchase Student Study Outline and Questions and separate Teacher's Edition.

Old Testament Survey - Teacher's Kit [Grades 11-12]

Includes Student Worktext and Teacher's Guide.

New Testament Survey - Teacher's Kit [Grades 11-12]

Includes Student Worktext and Teacher's Guide.

Bible Doctrines for Today 1 and *2* [10th grade level]

Two separate student books with one teacher's guide covering both books.

➡Bob Jones University Press' Secondary Level Bible Study Curriculum [for grades 7 through 12]

Worktext format. Start at the first book in the series, regardless of age, because of the sequence of the study. All levels are a revised second edition. The second edition is much better than the old, first edition that is still available through BJUP and some other suppliers. These books are excellent and can be used either with or without Teacher's Editions. Teacher's Editions are helpful, but there is plenty to work with without them. Most lessons open with a story to illustrate the theme, then study the Scripture from which the lesson is drawn. Memory work is included.

Level A: New Testament, Learning from the Life of Christ
Level B: Old Testament, Portraits from the Old Testament
Level C: New Testament, Lessons from the Early Church
Level D: Old Testament, Themes from the Old Testament
Level E: New Testament, Directions for Early Christians

---

1   International Bible Society is dedicated to spreading God's Word, so they sell Bibles at extremely low prices. Items purchased from IBS are not to be resold but are only for outreach and evangelism. IBS carries Bibles in NIV, NKJ, NAS, and Spanish versions, along with audio cassettes of the entire Bible in the NIV version.

Level F: Patterns for Christian Living
➡️ Precept Upon Precept (Precept Ministries)

These are a series of Bible study workbooks which are "...designed to teach people of any background or educational level the inductive method of study which gives people the skills and, thus, the ability to go straight to the Word of God." Books are available in two formats for most titles: *Precept Upon Precept* books should take about five hours of study per week; *In & Out* should take only one to two hours per week and is an easier course. Both books were written for use along with a weekly, hour-long presentation in a class setting. Sets of either audio or video tapes are offered for sale or rental to be used with the books if no class is available. The set of audio tapes rent for a very reasonable price, and one or another of these presentation tools seems necessary to fully benefit from the courses. Titles in the series are *Genesis (Parts 1 and 2), Judges, Daniel, Habakkuk, John (Part 1 and 2), Romans (Parts 1-4), Philippians, Colossians, I Thessalonians, II Thessalonians, James, I John, II Timothy, Hebrews (Parts 1 and 2), I Peter, II Peter, Sermon on the Mount, Spiritual Gifts, Covenant,* and *Marriage without Regrets.* There are a few studies directed specifically to teens: *Daniels for the 1990's* and *The Mask of Hypocrisy Melts in the Flames of Suffering* (study in I Peter). Younger level materials (for ages 9-12 and for ages 7-8) are also available on a few of the above topics, but in different formats more appropriate for younger learners. These books are called *Line Upon Line* and include the titles *The Book of Genesis, The Gospel of John,* and *The Book of Philippians.* Using these will help to include younger students in family study of these books of the Bible.

A companion is also available which teaches the basics of the *Precept Upon Precept* study methods. This book, *How to Study Your Bible Precept Upon Precept,* should be used to learn how to use the Precept materials.

All teaching is non-denominational, following a basic Christian statement of faith.

➡️ Pro Series Bible Curriculum

Although this curriculum is written for the classroom, almost everything is easily adaptable for the home school. This is a "meaty" Bible-based curriculum with a strong emphasis on character development.

Since the teaching comes primarily from the teacher's manual, this is not an independent study curriculum, but one that requires teacher/parent involvement. However, a minimal amount of lesson preparation is required because the teacher's manuals are well-designed.

An important feature of the curriculum is that it recognizes various levels of thinking skills and goes beyond simple recall of facts to develop understanding and application of knowledge. It also recognizes that teens are at different levels of spiritual growth. This fact has prompted Positive Action to offer a number of choices for the junior high level so that we can select that which best fits our teen's need. The original junior high material assumes a more mature Christian walk. Since those materials are similar in format and challenge level to those for grades 9-12, I will discuss them first.

High school level books (grades 7-12) are challenging studies for students who are interested in spiritual growth. *The Christian Life and Witness* (suggested for seventh grade) is the foundation for the remaining levels. (Start here if in doubt.) It covers salvation, the Bible, prayer, witnessing, and Christian living. Eighth grade students come to know the person of Jesus Christ at a deeper level through a study of the book of John called *The Life of Christ.* The Inner Man (ninth grade) confronts students with the need to develop inner character rather than rely on the outward appearances of Christianity. *The Christian Adventure* (tenth grade), based on *Pilgrim's Progress,* is an exciting study of the application of the classic allegory in our lives. *Behold Your God* (eleventh grade) is designed to help students develop depth in their personal relationship with God. Twelfth graders study the principles of life as laid out in the book of Proverbs in a study called *Proverbs.* These studies, like the elementary level, are dependent upon presentation from the teacher's manuals. A separate student book contains study questions plus reading material (e.g., the text of *Pilgrim's Progress* is contained in the student book, *The Christian Adventure.*) Student books are designed to be written in, so they are not reusable. The "high school" level studies should even be useful on an adult level. These are not simple, fill-in-the-blanks materials, but challenging, growth-provoking studies.

The new options for grades 7-8 are *Wise Up!* and *Route 66.* Some preparation time is needed to read the teacher's supplement (2-3 pages) each week, but it is essential to each course. Both the teacher's manual and student book are required for each study.

Content in these courses assumes a lower level of spiritual maturity (probably a more realistic viewpoint) than the above courses. They assume that the teenager is struggling with typical issues—salvation, friends, obedience to parents, self-control, decision making, etc. The student books have written exercises, but most of them direct the student to Scripture rather than provide entertaining busy work. *Wise Up!* is subtitled "Wisdom in Proverbs." Scripture study here ranges far beyond Proverbs, but it centers around "getting wisdom" in all areas of life. *Route 66* (of which I have only seen a preview) looks like a Bible survey course with an emphasis on understanding God's relationship with man throughout history. It moves chronologically from Genesis to Revelation, even covering the minor prophets. Either of these courses is easier than those described above, yet they are still spiritually challenging.

➡️ The Story of God and His People Series (Christian Schools International)

This is a new Bible curriculum for preschool through eighth grade. Of all the Bible curricula designed for schools, this series appears to come closest to what I believe they should be. The underlying and guiding theme throughout the series is the Bible and the story of God and His relationship with man. It deals with the Bible as a total picture rather than isolating Bible stories and incidents. Teachers are encouraged to use visual aids and activities to help children better understand what they are studying.

The Teacher's Guides are essential for all levels. While the thematic approach is the same throughout the series, there are different authors for the different levels, so the levels vary in lesson presentation and format. While there are student texts for sixth through eighth grades, a significant part of the teaching originates in the Teacher's Guides. Lesson plans are clearly laid out and very easy to use. Some supplemental materials are needed for lesson presentation.

For sixth through eighth grades there are both a student text and student workbook. Both are not necessary. The student text provides reading material and questions. There is not enough room in the text for written answers, so they would need to be done in a separate notebook, or students can use the student workbook which has the identical questions with space for answers. The student text is reprinted in the Teacher's Guide, so it would also be possible for us to read and present the lesson from the Teacher's Guide, then have our child work in the student workbook on his own. Alternatively, students could do most of their work independently from the student text with only a short discussion of essential material from the Teacher's Guide. Bible reading and memory work (NIV or KJV) are both important parts of the curriculum.

Because a chronological approach has been used to keep the Biblical story in context, it is important to choose the proper level for our children according to topic rather than grade level. Sixth grade reviews the Old Testament through Ecclesiastes. Seventh grade overlaps sixth grade by beginning with First Samuel, then going up through the gospels. Eighth grade reviews the gospels and covers through Revelation.

The curriculum authors recognize that there are different purposes for Bible courses in church and in school. The authors have defined their purpose in writing Bible curriculum for schools, as that of imparting knowledge and equipping students for lives of service in the world, in contrast to the church's tasks of proclaiming the good news of salvation and calling people to faith, worship, and service. Thus we have a curriculum that assumes that children have already heard the gospel message, and that the school's task is to help equip these children for a Christian life.

Other Resources for Bible Study and Spiritual Growth

➡ Basic Bible Studies by Francis Schaeffer (Tyndale House)
A foundational book for adult or mature teen Bible study. (Published in 1972.)

➡ Bible Mapbook by Simon Jenkins (Lion)
Here is a colorful little book that illustrates events of the Bible with maps. The combination of maps and commentary gives a much clearer view of scriptural events. Good for elementary through adult levels.

➡ Christian Ethics for YOUth: A Study of Wisdom from the Book of Proverbs by Wilmer Bechtels (Speedy Spanish)
I received a review copy of Christian Ethics for YOUth in the final weeks of updating this book, so I have not had time to give it a thorough review. I would have just skipped it for now, but it really caught my interest. This book is written directly to teens. The author has designed the book so that teens can do about one lesson per day. (They might choose to take longer, especially if they do the companion workbook exercises.) Each lesson hits a topic addressed in Proverbs by interweaving the point of the lesson with a story illustration. It might seem too "preachy" to some teens, but this will depend very much on their spiritual status and background. The few lessons that I had time to read were very effective; the stories evoke an emotional reaction (effective for conveying a message), and the instruction is solidly based on Scripture. At the back of the book is a section entitled "Topical Proverbs," which, as you might guess, lists individual proverbs under topical headings.

The companion workbook has two pages per lesson with vocabulary work and questions (e.g., true-false, sentence-response, short essay) that often lead students to the Bible for answers.

The content seems appropriate for mature junior high students as well as those in high school.

➡ Christian Life Series (Putting God First, Making Your Life Count, Living Your Life...As God Intended, Giving Yourself to God), Christian Growth Series (Commitment to Growth, Congratulations! You Are Gifted, Getting It Together, Building Relationships...With God and Others), and Life of Christ Series (The Incredible Christ, Getting Your Priorities Straight, The Greatest Stories Ever Told, Radical for the King) by Jim Burns (some also have a second author) (Harvest House Publishers)
The Christian Life Series is for teens just beginning their walk with God. The Christian Growth Series takes them further into Bible study, the gifts of the Holy Spirit, and life-application of Biblical teaching. Teens who need to be challenged to a deeper spiritual walk will benefit from the Life of Christ series. There are four student workbooks in each series, but each can be used alone. A single leader's guide covers all four books in each series, but it is not essential. since teens can work independently in the workbooks. The books become progressively more difficult, with more text and more pages at each level. These books reflect author Jim Burns' recognized talent for communicating with teens. Choose level and topic according to the needs of your teenager.

➡ Devotional Tools (MEMLOK)
How do we move our teens beyond head knowledge into deep relationship with God? I personally think that meaningful prayer and worship play a major role. But focusing those activities and investing them with meaning can be a challenge. Devotional Tools provides practical strategies for developing that deep relationship. Devotional Tools is not a heavy-duty curriculum, but more of an idea resource that should be used with all of the teens and adults in your family. It works sort of like story starters that some of us use to encourage younger children to start writing. The seven tools are presented with brief explanation and helpful activity suggestions (some mental, some active, some written). The tools can be summarized as examining our hearts, focusing our worship, supporting our brothers, stating our desires, writing our thoughts, using our minds, and building our bridges. For example, there is a reproducible Daily Journal sheet to encourage us to focus more clearly on a Scripture passage, what it says to us, and what our response should be. (We fit seven days on one page, so we're not talking about lengthy writing here.) Other reproducible sheets are for intercessory prayer schedules, personal prayer diary, meditation on Scripture, and "Ambassador Praying" (some intriguing ideas here!). An extra sheet is included which describes fifty ministry ideas and discussion questions for using Devotional Tools in group settings. The set of devotional tools is quite inexpensive, but might turn out to be one of your most fruitful investments.

➡ Every Thought Captive by Richard L. Pratt, Jr.
This is a concise statement of the tenets of Christianity (based upon the teaching of Cornelius Van Til) that is written in simple, straightforward language, rather than in theological vocabulary. The second half of the book is a foundation in apologetics—defending the faith. The author takes issue with apologetic approaches commonly used by Campus Crusade for Christ and other organizations that

rely on rational persuasion and presents what he feels is a more Biblical approach based upon recognition of the truth of the Bible and man's spiritual need. The other basic approach is presented in *Know Why You Believe*, described below. Our teens should have some knowledge of how to defend their belief, and they may not pick this up anywhere else.

➡ Family Walk or Youthwalk (Walk Thru the Bible Ministries, Inc.)

These excellent little monthly magazines are divided into weekly topics. Each topic is presented in segments that include stories, Scripture search, and practical application. Some topics in *Family Walk* (marriage, dating) are appropriate for teens or adults, but most are appropriate for the entire family. *Youthwalk* is written expressly for the teenage audience. *Youthwalk* is also available through Focus on the Family, Colorado Springs, CO.

➡ Know Why You Believe by Paul Little (Inter Varsity Press)

This is one of the most popular books about apologetics. It uses a rational approach to deal with questions and arguments. It is concise and easy to understand.

➡ Reading and Understanding the Bible (Vic Lockman)

Cartoon illustrations are used to present topics such as the canon, types of revelation, figurative language in the Bible, symbolism and typology, which are usually taught in adult classes or at Bible college. The cartoon format makes these seemingly difficult topics fairly easy to understand. What we have in this book is essentially an introduction to hermeneutics (the science of interpretation) that demystifies the subject. However, those who want to do deeper study and practice that goes beyond definitions and examples should look elsewhere.

Lockman's theological outlook is fundamentalist, although in this book he tries to stay on common ground rather than get into doctrinal differences among Christians. Four quizzes and a final exam are included in the book (as well as answers).

➡ What the Bible Is All About for Young Explorers by Frances Blankenbaker (Regal Books)

Here is an overview of the Bible geared for upper elementary and junior high, but interesting still to adults. Maps, charts, plenty of illustrations, background information, chapter summaries, and archeological information provide an excellent introduction for Bible study.

Bible Memory

Since there are a limited number of resources for Bible memory, I include all those I am aware of that are practical for the home school. Bible memory courses choose verses from the thousands of possibilities, to work toward a predetermined goal. Thus there is inevitably doctrinal bias in any program. The following recommendations have tried to maintain a non-denominational appeal in their verse choices, by addressing topics of common belief.

➡ Bible Memory Association (BMA)

BMA has been around a long time and has a proven track record for having helped many thousands of Christians to memorize tremendous amounts of Scripture (King James Version). *BMA* offers courses for preschoolers through adults using memory books that contain both verses and a bit of instruction about their meaning. Memory plans cover the basics of salvation, Christian living, and essential doctrine from a conservative viewpoint. Courses

begin three times a year. Enroll at least six weeks to two months ahead for courses beginning in January, May, and September. (Enrollment closer to the final deadlines listed in the *BMA* brochure is allowed but at increasing cost.) Rewards are given for completed courses—coloring books, puzzles, Christian books, etc. Successful completion of a course may also qualify you to attend one of a number of *BMA*, week-long camps at reduced cost. Memory books are available for all ages and at differing levels of difficulty. A supervisor is chosen who may be someone at a local church or mom or dad. A schedule is already preplanned so that you know how many verses are required to be memorized and how often. Courses are very inexpensive. BMA has prepared an information packet especially for home educators that describes their programs plus a special home school option. Request either the free brochure or information on how to use a BMA program as a supplement to your home school curriculum.

➡ MEMLOK Bible Memory System

This new memory program uses visual cues. It comes in the New International, King James, and New American Standard versions of the Bible. There are a few things that set this apart from other programs.

We are given visual clues on memory verse cards that illustrate beginning or key words of verses to act as memory cues. Some of the clues are silly, some stretch for the connection, some are great, but the overall idea is that by establishing a visual connection for each verse, the verses (with references) are recalled much more easily. Verses are arranged under 48 topics, with over 700 verses on 550 cards (the size of a business card) included. We learn the verses under whichever topic we choose. The verses are stored in the clear, plastic, binder cardholders for review. Summary cards are provided for verses about each topic. An optional pocket cardholder is also available.

The visual clues are all incorporated onto one summary card, providing another memory device to recall related verses. The entire family can share one *MEMLOK* book (an 8 1/2" X 11", three-ring binder) by having each member choose a different topic to work on or by keeping memory verse cards in a central location in the home. The program should take only five to ten minutes a day, and long term retention of verses should be greater than with other programs because of the review system. Accountability is stressed. There is a Completion Record sheet to be initialed by whoever hears us recite the verses, but we must make our own arrangements for that person to check on our progress.

➡ Scripture Memory Fellowship International (SMFI)

This organization, with many, many years of experience, offers Scripture memory programs for preschoolers through adults, along with awards to be earned as memory students progress. They provide each "student" with a memory book which the memorizer selects according to grade level or previous experience in memorizing God's Word. For the most part, verses are in King James Version and are all arranged topically. You are enrolled as a family, one person, a church class, or a neighborhood group. You also select your supervisor who encourages you and helps keep track of progress. You may either purchase the memory books outright or enroll with rewards which you select from their list contained in the *SMF Digest*. These incentives (rewards) are primarily Christian books—selections for all ages and a variety of interests. There are memory books for memorizers at all levels, including easier adult programs for those new to Scripture memorization. They suggest that Fall is the best time to enroll but enrollments are welcomed at any time of the year. Each September a new list of rewards is available. The enrollment fee is kept to a minimum and represents about one-third of their actual cost; the remainder is subsidized by supporters of the ministry. No one is turned away.

➡ Well-Versed Kids (NavPress)

This is a dynamite little package! We get a brightly colored box with 108 memory cards, a *Parent-Teacher Manual*, and a handy *Verse Pack* for carrying the memory cards we are studying, all for a very reasonable price. Cards are color coded under six topics: Understanding Salvation, Knowing God, Growing as a Christian, Enjoying God, Building Character, and Great Bible Truths. Within each topic, verses are arranged in three levels of difficulty with different subtopics covered. For instance, under Growing as a Christian, Level One has two subtopics, Listening to God and Talking to God, with three verse cards for each subtopic. Children learn the name (subtopic), address (reference), and the verse. The *Parent-Teacher Manual* lays out the program and gives helpful teaching hints for each verse. Each concept is explained with ideas for how to communicate the concept to our child so that he does not merely memorize but understands what he is learning. The *Verse Pack* is a simple plastic envelope contraption with one clear window so the verse being learned is visible. The other cards for the same topic on a single level can be kept in the Pack for review, or an entire level of cards will fit if so desired. Verses are written in the New King James version on one side, New International on the other. Some of us will appreciate finally having a memory program available that corresponds to the Bibles that our children own. Although this is not a "fun and games" program, the easy-to-use layout and colorful appeal should make it a very effective tool for Scripture memory.

It should be particularly helpful for slow learners or those who have difficulty with memorization since the selected verses are either short or partial verses.

Church History

Church history is a sadly neglected area of education. Some history textbooks incorporate church history, but most simply ignore it. However, there are some interesting books available on the topic. The best way to find good resources is to check your church library or local Christian bookstore. The following suggestions are simply a few that I have encountered, rather than a selection of "the best."

➡ The Church in History by B.K. Kuiper (Christian Schools International)

This is a soft cover, 412-page book that covers the history of the Church from its beginnings to recent times. The author appears to be writing from a Reformed Christian perspective, but he takes a very even-handed approach to differences between denominations. Even Catholicism is treated fairly, although changes within the Catholic Church over the past few decades are not dealt with adequately. The original edition of this book was written in 1951, and it has been updated periodically, but there are occasional areas that need further updating. Questions are posed at the end of each chapter. Also available from CSI is a *Guide*

for Teaching Church History by Dale Cooper and John Vander Lugt. This *Guide* was not written specifically for *The Church in History* although it is cross referenced to that book throughout. It is actually an outline with commentary that can form the foundation for study of church history on its own or with other resource books. It succinctly outlines events and provides commentary and references from other books. Suggestions for student discussion and activities are included. Both books should be used in the last years of high school. The *Guide* actually seems more appropriate for college level study. *The Church in History* may be used without the *Guide for Teaching Church History*. (There is no answer key to text questions in the *Guide*.) The *Guide* is most appropriate for those studying Church history in a group setting.

➡ From Jerusalem to Irian Jaya by Ruth A. Tucker (Zondervan Publishing House/Academie Books)

Here are the stories of Christian missionaries in historical and geographical order. This book makes a wonderful supplement to world history studies. Use it for the complete historical picture of what God was doing in different countries throughout history. Instead of concentrating on the ecclesiastical (organized religion) side of church history, it tells us about the personal impact of those who shared the Gospel. Teens can read excerpts from this book on their own, but it makes interesting read-together material.

➡ A History of Christianity in the United States and Canada by Mark A. Noll (Wm. B. Eerdmans Publishing Co.)

While this book is not intended to be a typical church history book, it certainly covers the topic. Read the complete description under "American History" in Chapter Thirteen.

➡ Kids for the World: A Guidebook to Children's Mission Resources by Gerry Dueck (United States Center for World Mission)

For resource ideas for learning about church history through the study of missionaries, get *Kids for the World: A Guidebook to Children's Mission Resources*. Resources are keyed according to age groups (pre-school through adult). The majority of the resources listed are for younger children, but there are still many for older students. Two very beneficial supplements to the book are now available—one dated March, 1991; the other dated April, 1992.

➡ Perspectives on the World Christian Movement edited by Ralph D. Winter and Steven D. Hawthorne (William Carey Library)

This is a collection of scholarly articles about Christianity through history. One article of special interest is a mini history course of God's movement through history, somewhat similar to the Old Testament story told through the Bible. This book is for parents to digest and pass on to children. It provides information lacking even in church history texts. (An updated and expanded 1992 edition is now available.)

➡ 30 Days to Understanding Church History by Max E. Anders and Judith A. Lunsford (Word Inc., formerly Wolgemuth and Hyatt)

Church history is presented in a simplified manner, perfect for students or adults who have little knowledge of the subject. The authors set up a simplified framework, breaking church history into three eras: ancient, medieval, and modern. Each of those eras is broken down into two eras: infant and adolescent church eras, Roman and Reformation eras, and denominational and global eras. Key people and events are related to the different eras.

Following this, the book is divided into sections for the three main eras. Each era then has chapters on geography, the "story line," headlines (news, money, sports, life), concepts, foes, key figures, writers and writings, and trends.

All of this is presented with charts and illustrations throughout the text. Each chapter includes fill-in-the-blanks summary questions, a self-test, charts to be completed, maps, and other learning reinforcement activities. An interesting writing style which includes anecdotal stories, biographies, and "news" articles from history keep the reading lively.

The book is over 300 pages long, so, although the format is simplified, the content is fairly comprehensive for introductory study. Most high school students should be able to use this book on their own.

Comparative Religions

I want to teach my children about other religions and their teachings myself. I do not want them introduced to false doctrines by a teacher who believes that all theologies have equal validity. Yet most of us are not familiar with all religions and belief systems. We can find many helpful resources at our local Christian bookstores and from mail order sources. Also see Chapter Five, "Philosophy, Religion, and Apologetics" for reviews of some helpful resources.

Chapter Eleven

Mathematics

High school math poses the biggest hurdle for many home educators both because it is required and because it is many a parent's weakest subject. Some of us never studied algebra or geometry. How can we possibly teach these subjects to our children? Admittedly, the task is challenging, but there is more help available than we realize.

Broadening Our Horizons

Our first instinct frequently is to turn to correspondence courses, but they do have their drawbacks. The biggest problem is the time lag between sending back completed assignments and receiving the corrected work. It is wasteful for students to keep working ahead without knowing if they have completed last week's lessons correctly, since repeating mistakes just reinforces them. Some correspondence courses do allow us to get in touch with a teacher right away if we encounter difficulties, but I think that many times students do not realize that they have a problem with a mathematical concept until they receive their corrected paper with their errors indicated. Some correspondence courses have parents check daily work and send in only tests for grading. This might be a more practical way of operating for higher level math courses.

The real need is for immediate feedback and help. Tutoring services can be a worthwhile investment, especially if we can work out a deal where we use the tutor on a consultation basis as needed. A "mathematically minded" friend who is supportive of our home education endeavors might be willing to tutor at no charge. A high school student already proficient in algebra or geometry might also be willing to provide tutorial help. If no tutor is available, it's up to us parents. However, teaching high school math does not have to be formidable for inexperienced parents because of the helpful resources available to us.

The Saxon math series (some of which are co-authored by John Saxon and Stephen Hake) has been overwhelmingly popular with home educators because it is easy for both parents and students to use and understand. New topics come in small doses with plenty of explanation (most of the time). Students can work fairly independently. Parents can study up on new concepts without having to wade through too much material. Some other math programs are equally easy to use.

Computer Programs

For junior high students check out *The Skills Bank Home Tutor* computer program's math module.

Other computer programs might provide just the help we need for more difficult math topics. I have seen various math programs available in the public domain at minimal cost. *Algebra* from Professor Weissman's Software is an example of such programs. For a few dollars check out some of these for yourself from any catalog of public domain software or from a bulletin board service. (See computer sources.) Other, more thoroughly tested programs are available from major software companies such as Davis and

Broderbund, and lesser known companies such as Stone & Associates (*Algebra Plus*). (See reviews below.)

Also, check *Pride's Guide to Educational Software* (Crossway) for lengthy reviews and comparison information on math software for all levels.

Video Helps

Video can be a helpful alternative for some of us. A Beka offers complete classes on video, with students working in textbooks on the side. We can rely on the experienced video instructor to present the information, and we just have to oversee our child's understanding and completion of his assignments. All A Beka textbooks are now available as video courses.

Other video options such as the complete course from Keyboard Enterprises and the supplementary Video Tutor are well worth investigating. (See reviews.)

Individual Needs

It is also important to recognize our child's learning style, aptitude, maturity, and potential before plunging into math courses. If he has a horrible experience with his first introduction to algebra, he might decide that math is something he cannot grasp, which in turn might limit his future educational choices. The problem might lie with the textbook, his preparation in earlier math courses, or his maturity rather than with his potential. Some home educators have found that waiting until age fifteen to study algebra instead of the traditional freshman age of fourteen made the difference between success and failure.

Learning Styles

By the teen years, most teens have overcome the most serious limitations of their learning styles as they apply to math. Type A's, who cringed at the sight of pages of math problems to be worked, might still not enjoy using workbooks, but are now able to work in them when necessary. Type B learners need to still be on guard against their tendency to learn by rote without thinking through the reasons for doing things. Type C learners will usually find math one of their favorite subjects. Type D learners will probably continue to struggle through the principles, rules, and theorems of math that need to be mastered.

Math programs for junior and senior high do not allow for the great variations in learning styles evident in elementary math programs. We have to look further to find materials to meet special learning style needs. Most programs assume that teens can think abstractly, and that they no longer need work with concrete materials, which is not always true.

Type A learners (Wiggly Willys) are most likely to need concrete experiences to learn math. Their entire curriculum cannot be concrete work. There must be some paper and pencil activity accompanying any hands-on work. These learners work best with a text that uses real-life situations and practical application of math concepts. Abstract texts that deal only with math theory are more difficult for them to understand. Wiggly Willys often do better with geometry (but not with the formal proofs) than with algebra, yet they need some foundation in algebra to be able to solve geometry problems. Keeping in mind occupational and educational goals, consider using practical math texts such as the business, consumer, and career texts listed below. *Career Math* (Houghton Mifflin) is especially good.*Discovering Geometry* and the *Key to Geometry* series (both from Key Curriculum Press) should appeal to Type A learners more than other geometry texts. Cornerstone's new *Principles from Patterns: Algebra I* builds in manipulative activity throughout the program, making it uniquely helpful for hands-on learners. *AIMS* activities are also great supplements for these learners. In addition, their need for drill and review of basic math skills can often best be met by using games.

Type B learners (Perfect Paulas) need texts such as the Saxon series, that teach concepts from several different angles to ensure understanding. Look for good word and application problems in whatever you choose.

Type C learners (Competent Carls) might be able to move ahead into college level texts such as *Developmental Mathematics* from D.C. Heath. (Do not confuse this with the elementary math series of the same title.) Consider using Harold R. Jacobs' *Geometry* (W.H. Freeman), which has a heavy emphasis on thinking skills and logic rather than hands-on learning. Also, look for texts that have solution keys to help students work independently.

Type D learners (Sociable Sues) will need to understand how math concepts will be used in life situations before they continue into higher math. The Barron's books *Algebra the Easy Way* and *Calculus the Easy Way* use an approach that appeals to these learners, although neither book is as comprehensive as a basic textbook. Also consider using the same materials recommended for Wiggly Willys.

Maturity

Abstract thinking skills are slower to develop in some students (particularly boys) than in others. This does not have anything to do with their long-range potential in math, but it has much to do with how quickly they move into abstract math topics. Some students need to wait until they are fifteen or sixteen to take algebra. They can take introductory courses in algebra and geometry, business or consumer math, or pursue more interesting books about mathematics such as Harold Jacob's *Mathematics, a Human Endeavor* (Freeman). Jacob's book can be "browsed" through rather than used as a text. This is an inviting way to let teens explore math without killing their interest. (Initial chapters of Jacob's book are much easier than later chapters, so caution students to choose something they can understand.)

Math Options for Those Not College Bound

If a child is definitely not bound for college, there are still worthwhile math courses available. He can tackle alge-

bra and geometry, of course, but he can also take consumer math, business math, or career math depending on his areas of interest. Some of these courses are as challenging as algebra and geometry, but apply directly to work skills that these students might use as soon as they graduate from high school. The choice is not necessarily between "dumbbell math" and "real math," although there are business and consumer math texts for students who are working below level. (See specific recommendations later in this chapter.)

Tighter College Requirements

Colleges are tightening their requirements. Where algebra and geometry used to be the standard requirements, some colleges are now requesting a third year of advanced math. Colleges specializing in math and science fields are requesting four years of college preparatory math. The reason for this is that there is so much more math to be taken in college that there is not enough time to make up high school courses, take college level courses, and finish within the standard time.

Goals and Recommendations for Junior High

Goals

Junior high is a time for consolidating basic math skills and knowledge before progressing on to the more difficult subjects of algebra and geometry. There are not as many new concepts covered at these levels as there were earlier. Below is a typical scope and sequence covering seventh and eighth grades.

- Review of all previous material
- Read and convert exponents
- Define and find "mean," "median," and "mode"
- Use distance formula
- Calculate volume of given geometric solids
- Construct and interpret graphs
- Convert numbers from one system of measurement to another
- Read and write numbers written in expanded notation and/or scientific notation form
- Solve basic equations using any of the four basic operations
- Define and calculate the square root of given numbers
- Understand and apply the Pythagorean theorem
- Learn properties of positive and negative numbers
- Begin learning about algebraic equations

Seventh Grade Recommendations

➠Algebra 1/2 (Saxon)

This hardbound text is recommended as an eighth grade text, but consists heavily of review for those who have been through A Beka, BJUP, or any other good math program. Use after completing *Math 76, Math 87*[1] or an-

---

1   There is typically a great deal of review in most junior high level math texts. Saxon effectively eliminated much wasted time in their original math series, allowing students to actually skip a year. However, some schools needed a text for that "extra year," so Saxon wrote Math 87. It is not necessary to use that book, although it can be useful for those needing more review.

other good sixth or seventh grade program. The Saxon series provides leeway so that we can stretch out math lessons if our child is struggling, or advance them into *Algebra 1* even though they are working at eighth grade level in other subjects. Plenty of review, a steady, spiralling[2] learning process, thought-provoking word problems, and clear instruction make this one of the top recommendations. As is typical of the Saxon books, the level of difficulty rises sharply towards the end of the text. Saxon sells home educators a package containing a student edition, answer key, and tests. This is the 1990 revised edition of this book. The content has been slightly expanded with the addition of geometry fundamentals and application problems working with percents and ratios. Flaws in the older edition are minor, so if you can find a used copy, go ahead and get it.(S)[3]

➡ Basic Mathematics 1 (A Beka)

This worktext follows A Beka's traditional approach like the books for younger levels. You need to buy the student worktext and the Teacher's Edition (this is your answer key). The method is similar to that of younger levels with introduction of new concepts using explanation, examples, and practice followed by review of previously learned material. There are more word and application problems in this text than in those for younger grades, but the format is not as colorful and print is small. Topics include review of previous math concepts, metric measurements and conversions, consumer math topics such as checkbook maintenance and computation of interest, a significant amount of both plane and solid geometry, an introduction to trigonometry plus assorted topics such as recording bowling scores and meter reading and analysis. This text is unusual in that it covers consumer math and practical topics that are often neglected in basic texts (unless students cover them in high school consumer math courses). It also goes far beyond typical seventh grade level with the geometry and trigonometry. I do find this book useful to broaden math application understanding rather than only review as happens in too many seventh grade level math books. Choose which topics to cover according to each child's needs.

➡ Math for Christian Schools 7 (BJUP)

This hardbound text covers integers, exponential notation, mathematical sentences and functions, and reviews basic computational skills. Word problems and application exercises are well written and help to develop higher level thinking skills. Purchase both student and teacher editions.

➡ Math 76 (Saxon)

This hardbound math text is advertised as being appropriate for bright sixth graders or average seventh graders, but many seventh graders will be ready for *Algebra 1/2*. It reviews all math concepts that have been learned in a spiralling method of constant review. Progression is on the slow side. Children who have been working in A Beka or Bob Jones University Press math programs should be ready for

this in sixth grade. Topics covered include decimal numbers and money; fractions; measurements including area, perimeter, and volume; place value; types of numbers; solids; percents; ratios; unit conversions; probabilities; angles; and coordinate points. Saxon sells a homeschool packet of *Math 76* with a student edition of the text, an answer key, and tests.(S)

➡ Math 87 (Saxon)

If students move through the Saxon series at an average pace, they are ready to move on to *Algebra 1* in eighth grade. Some students are ready to do so, while others are not. Saxon has created a text to fit that in-between period for those who need it. It reviews much of the same material that is in *Math 76* and *Algebra 1/2*, adding very little new material. If students skip this book, they will not be lacking any topics that are necessary before going on to algebra or other high school math courses. The format is the same as other Saxon texts.(S)

➡ Moving with Math, Level D for grades 7-8 (Math Teachers Press - MTP)

This program incorporates hands-on activity into a complete math curriculum. It is the only such program that I know of for students who still need extensive manipulative (hands-on) work at this level. There are three essential components to this program: *Skill Builders, Moving with Math* workbooks, and *Math Capsules. Capsules* is the diagnostic tool that will help determine which concepts your child needs to learn. The program is set up as a diagnostic/prescriptive approach, so after you determine the need, you then assign appropriate exercises. There are five *Moving with Math* workbooks covering numeration and problem solving with whole numbers; problem solving with fractions and decimals; problem solving with percent; geometry and measurement; and pre-algebra. *Skill Builders* is one large book containing instructions for manipulative activities and reproducible work sheets that rely more on use of manipulatives than do exercises in the workbooks. Reproducible review work sheets are included in *Math Capsules* to ensure that students continually review previously learned concepts. Optional Teacher's Guides are now available for each book, which lay out daily lesson plans integrating *Skill Builders* with the workbooks. The program can be taught without the Teacher's Guides by determining from the diagnostic tools and the objectives which concepts your child needs to learn in what order. MTP recommends purchasing the program first, then determining whether or not you need the Teacher's Guides. Teacher's Guides remove the need for determining the order and number of lessons to use. However, the trade-off is that we are then no longer individualizing the program. The inexpensive answer keys for each workbook are needed, unless you buy the Teacher's Guides which contain the answer keys. Manipulatives you will need: either *Base 10 Blocks* (the expensive 1000's cube is unnecessary) or *Cuisenaire® Rods* (cut squares 10 cm. by 10 cm. from poster board to use in place of 100's

---

2   The spiralling method means that small amounts of new material are taught in each lesson while constantly reviewing previous material. There is a constant building process, but a simultaneous strengthening of the foundation.

3   Throughout this book, I use (S) to indicate that a resource is secular in nature rather than Christian. (SE) indicates that it is secular and also might require some caution or "editing" for objectionable or untrue content.

squares that come with Base 10 sets); fraction bars; and a geoboard (easily made with a twelve inch square piece of wood, with nails arranged a few inches apart in five rows of five nails). Manipulatives are available from MTP, Creative Teaching Associates, Creative Publications, Builder Books, Shekinah, and other sources. MTP also offers an *Intermediate Introductory Calculator Kit* for grades 5-9. The kit includes a calculator and instruction manual. This Texas Instrument calculator performs computations with fractions. Calculator activities which emphasize estimation, checking answers, and looking for patterns are integrated throughout the Level D Teacher Guides.(S)

➠Principles from Patterns: Algebra I (Cornerstone Curriculum Project)

This program is designed to follow immediately after Cornerstone's Level 6 of *Making Math Meaningful*. Even though it teaches algebra topics, because it uses manipulatives (*Unifix Cubes* and heavy graph paper cut into shapes resembling *Base Ten* or *Mortensen* materials), teens who are not mature enough in their abstract thinking for other *Algebra 1* texts should be successful with this course. It also covers pre-algebra topics. See description under "Algebra."

Eighth Grade Recommendations

➠Algebra 1/2 (Saxon)
     see above
➠Algebra 1 (Saxon)

This is the most widely used algebra text among home educators. The spiralling method of presentation and constant review help students to work fairly independently. A few of the explanations are more complicated than they need be, but overall, the book is fairly easy for students to work with independently. If students have used *Math 76* and *Algebra 1/2*, they might be ready for this book in eighth grade. Very bright children might even feel that the progression is too slow.

Although many eighth grade students would have no problem with this book, there are many who will not be developmentally mature enough to begin algebra for another year or two. If you feel that your child is not ready for *Algebra 1* at eighth grade level, either academically or developmentally, alternatives might be to use Saxon's new *Math 87*, a consumer math program such as A Beka's *Consumer Mathematics* or Barron's *Survival Math*, or a specialized topic study such as one or more of the *Key to...* series at eighth grade level, before continuing with algebra. Or you might have your child begin *Algebra 1* in eighth grade, but move at a slower pace, taking a year and a half or two to complete it. You can give credit for high school algebra for this course, even if it is taken early. The 1990 revised edition that is now being sold, has more geometry included than does the previous edition. Working through the Saxon series, students do not take a separate geometry course, but learn geometry through the algebra series. However, because the geometry has been added to the original book, we find sporadic doses of geometry. It is not introduced incrementally as are algebra topics. Explanation of geometry topics is fairly brief, and does not begin to compare with the quality of presentation in such texts as *Discovering Geometry*. (Some home educators are considering skipping the geometry in Saxon and substituting a separate geometry course.) Saxon sells home educators a package containing a student edition, answer key, and tests.(S)

➠Basic Mathematics II (A Beka)

This is a traditional textbook in worktext format. It reviews basic math, and covers introduction to algebra, scientific notation, geometry, statistics, and trigonometry. Many of these topics are usually taught in high school level texts, so be cautious about overwhelming students with work that is too advanced. Purchase the student worktext and the Teacher's Edition (your answer key).

➠Math for Christian Schools 8 (BJUP)

This hardbound text covers negative exponents, logical reasoning, equation solving, probability, and statistical measures. Word problems and application exercises are interestingly written and help students develop understanding of concepts. Purchase both student and Teacher Editions.

Extras and Supplements

Games such as *Monopoly, Pinochle, Mastermind*, and many others make excellent supplements for developing mathematical thinking and proficiency. Some math games such as *Operations*, described below, can be used with younger children also, but work well at higher levels.

➠AIMS Education Foundation

The *AIMS Education Foundation* publishes a number of books for upper elementary and junior high levels that mix math and science in fun learning activities. Choose books by topics: food, aerodynamics, the human body, floating and sinking, geology, and other science areas. Mathematical and scientific thinking are developed through activities, and math is applied to help arrive at conclusions. Activities are time consuming so plan to use these no more than one day a week. Most activities lend themselves to groups better than individuals, although they can be used either way.(S)

➠Math Practice Books (Essential Learning Products)

These half-size books are handy for reviewing some of the tougher concepts in pre-algebra courses. Book 1—*Tables, Graphs, Statistics, Probability*—offers help with using previously learned math skills in applications. Book 2—*Exponents, Squares, and Square Roots*—takes students a step or two further into these topics than do most junior high level texts. These topics are stumbling blocks to many algebra students, so using this book to be well prepared for algebra is good preventive medicine. Book 3—*Signed Numbers*—needs some revision, so skip it for now.(S)

➠O! Euclid (Ampersand Press)

Introduce geometry to junior high and high school students with *O! Euclid* and they will be ahead on definitions and characteristics of many geometric shapes before they get into a serious geometry course. Instructions for four different versions of the game are included, but the first two are probably the ones that home schoolers will play. The first version leaves cards with pictures of fourteen geometric shapes visible while players try to construct those shapes from partial pieces shown on the remaining cards. The second variation is more challenging. Players have to recognize pieces belonging to the shapes as well as the name. To win, they also have to answer a question about the shape. (Questions vary in difficulty, so we can choose one appropriate for each player.) Knowing some basic geometry terms such as "congruence" and "vertex" help when playing the second variation. (We found ourselves devising a few rule clarifications while playing the second version, so the rules can use a little more fine tuning.)(S)

The thing that makes this game effective is that it requires players to make either intuitive or rational judgments about which shapes each card belongs to. For instance, if a player has the bottom half of a triangle, he must identify what type of angle will be necessary to complete the top half. Other shapes such as the pentagon, octagon and trapezoid also help develop this sort of mathematical insight.

➡ Operations (Behavior Development Products)

This double-size card deck comes with a small, 46-page booklet describing 15 different games that can be played with the cards. The deck includes cards for numbers 0-12, the four basic functions, fraction and decimal cards, and wild cards (x, y, and z). Different cards are used for the various games, with choices sometimes made to adjust the level of difficulty. Just about all ages can play these games at one level or another. Most of the games help develop thinking/logic skills as well as review math facts.(S)

➡ The Skills Bank Home Tutor (Skills Bank Corporation)

The Skills Bank Home Tutor (for IBM type and Apple II machines) has five modules, including one on mathematics. This software mimics the design of very expensive classroom programs which provide tutoring, testing, evaluation, and progress recording. However, it is much less expensive. The total cost for all five modules at this writing is $399 plus shipping (or $87.50 per module). Student access disks are necessary for each person who will be using the program. Five such disks come with the purchase of all five modules. (Only one with each individual module; we get two student disks if we buy two modules, and so on.) Each student disk allows <u>five</u> students to use any of the modules. That means that 25 students will have access when all five modules are purchased. It still sounds like a lot of money, but families might share the five lesson disks/modules. ("You take language arts this month, while I take math.")

The programs themselves are easy to use, uncluttered, but also unexciting. The documentation could use a little work, but it is fairly easy to figure out. Students can begin work wherever they need to. Programs cover all basic concepts within the selected subject areas for the elementary grades up through junior high and some high school.

The math program covers computation, concepts, word problems, and an introduction to geometry and algebra. I take issue with the way they teach the order of operations at the top level, but other than that, instruction seems sound and worthwhile. This is a great tool for junior highers to make sure their skills are sharp before going on to high school math. (See descriptions of other modules under subject headings.)(S)

➡ Stock Exchange (Creative Teaching Associates)

Junior high students practice fraction/decimal conversions, applying those skills to buying and selling stocks. The game is a very good simulation of the stock market, with students reading and interpeting stock information just as it appears in newspapers. Play money, share cards, and a game board are used as students learn about appreciation and depreciation of stocks, dividends, and market fluctuations. While *Stock Exchange* is my favorite for junior

high level, you might also want to check out *Big Deal, Bank Account, Budget*, and *Discount*.

High School Level

Most states require two years of high school mathematics, but requirements are being raised by both colleges and local school districts. For college-bound students three or four years of math are recommended, including algebra, geometry, and other courses in higher math. Students aiming for careers in engineering or some science fields are strongly urged to take precalculus and/or calculus in high school so they will have time to take the math needed in college. Students who are certain that they will not go to college can satisfy the requirement with practical math, pre-algebra, and other general math courses. If high school students do not get the math they need in high school, they might be able to make it up at a junior college, but it might set back their college graduation a semester or two.

In states that allow students to attend junior college while still in high school, students might be able to take algebra, geometry, or other courses that parents are not capable of overseeing at junior colleges. However, students are expected to be able to handle college level studies, so this is not an option for all students.

Sequence of Math Courses

One problem that seems to arise frequently with home educators has to do with the sequence of math courses. The Saxon series is the primary cause. Because Saxon has integrated geometry with algebra across a span of three years/textbooks, students who wish to use Saxon are obligated to take three years of algebra to cover the required geometry course work. Those students who prefer to only take two years of high school math need to switch midstream if they want to cover geometry. (In my opinion, geometry seems to be far more useful than advanced algebra in terms of general life applications, making it a more vital course than a second year of algebra.)

Saxon's *Algebra 1* (or *Algebra 1* and *2*) can be used, followed by a geometry text from another publisher. We might wish to skip geometry content in Saxon if we will be covering it from another text.

Some people choose to substitute another geometry course for the geometry content in Saxon simply because geometry is the weakest link in Saxon's books. This can be accomplished by skipping geometry within the Saxon books, and speeding up the course work to compensate. A different geometry text can be used between books or, in some cases, simultaneously.

Of course, choosing another publisher for both algebra and geometry is another possibility, and many such options are listed below.

New Approaches to Teaching High School Math

The new directions in math education are likely to greatly change our traditional high school math scope and sequence over the next decade. The new mathematics framework[4] in California (a leader and model in educa-

4   Frameworks are plans that teachers write that outline which concepts should be taught at what levels and suggest

tional changes) is encouraging integration of algebra, geometry, trigonometry, statistics, probability, and discrete mathematics. Another recommendation is that calculators and other technology be used to perform complicated arithmetical calculations as an essential part of any program, freeing students to develop better thinking and application skills. Inductive skills (discovery learning methods) are also being emphasized as a means of developing thinking skills and understanding concepts. This means that in the future we might no longer have courses labeled with the familiar titles of algebra, geometry, etc. Instead, we will have courses with "generic" names which will include all areas of mathematics instruction, at increasing levels of difficulty each year. We already see some of this in the Saxon math series. Geometry is integrated in *Algebra 1 and 2* and in *Advanced Mathematics*. Trigonometry is included in *Algebra 2* and *Advanced Mathematics*. (However, the Saxon series is not a purposeful attempt to meet the framework standards, as we see reflected in the choice of topics covered and the methodology.) Colleges and universities will accept these generic math courses in lieu of traditional courses as long as the students have learned the necessary algebra and geometry.

Three publishers (Wadsworth, Houghton Mifflin, and McDougal Littell) already have series of high school textbooks that are designed to fit the new California framework. However, the present series mostly seem to be cut-and-paste efforts from traditional textbooks and fall short in end results. Typically, they jump from major topic to major topic too often, without providing integration of learning from one area to another, as should be happening in the ideal situation. I also question the usefulness of including in-depth study of logic, probability and statistics for the average student.

There are other texts, generally written to address a single topic that do a better job of both implementing the new standards and teaching the subject matter. Recommended texts that reflect these changes are:

➡ **Career Mathematics** (Houghton Mifflin)

See review under "Consumer, Business, and Career Mathematics." While this book is not a typical course purposely designed to meet the new standards, it actually does a better job than most texts that were so designed.(S)

➡ **Discovering Geometry** (Key Curriculum Press)

See review under geometry recommendations. There is strong integration of algebra, hands-on activity, and thinking skills—excellent implementation of the new standards.

➡ **For All Practical Purposes: Introduction to Contemporary Mathematics** (W.H. Freeman and Co.)

This college level text, designed to meet the new standards, might be used by home schoolers either in conjunction with or following a second-year algebra course. See the review under "Consumer, Business, and Career Mathematics."(S)

➡ **Intermediate Algebra, Sixth Edition** by Miller, Lial, and Hornsby (Harper Collins)

See review under algebra recommendations. This is sold as a college-level text, but it can be used for high school.

Tuning in to Mathematical Thinking

➡ **Mathematics, a Human Endeavor** by Harold Jacobs (W.H. Freeman and Co.)

This is not a complete math program. Instead it is a book about math that introduces a variety of topics in interesting contexts. Learn about inductive reasoning, deductive reasoning, functions and graphs, logarithms, polygons, mathematical curves, permutations, probability, statistics, and more with billiard balls, optical illusions, satellites, and other interesting applications. Cartoons, mathematical history tidbits, and a friendly writing style make this book inviting to read. Students can choose whatever topics they wish to explore rather than going through chapters in order.(S)

➡ **How to Lie with Statistics** by Darrell Huff (W.W. Norton and Company)

See the review in Chapter Seventeen under "Thinking Skills." It is important to get a realistic view of how statistics are actually used before deciding to devote much study time to the topic. This book very entertainingly exposes the misuses of statistics. Watch for some objectionable subject matter.(SE)

Algebra

Algebra does not have to be a fearsome undertaking. Algebra is actually an easy way of performing mathematical problem solving, once we learn the "shorthand." Some students are intimidated if they begin algebra too soon, that is, before they are able to mentally manipulate a number of abstract concepts simultaneously.

Sometimes students are overwhelmed by the number of strange concepts they encounter in algebra, especially when they are not given any explanation as to why or how they can use these things in real life. Watch out for algebra programs that provide no examples or applications of its usefulness. If you can and will provide such information yourself, choose whatever program you want to use. If not, make sure the program provides that information.

An excellent supplement to use for any higher math topics is *When Are We Ever Gonna Have to Use This?* (Dale Seymour). Author Hal Saunders interviewed people from 100 different occupations, then came up with application word problems that these people encountered all the time. Problems are arranged by occupation and math content so that we can identify problems to fit current math topics being studied. The book is written for grades 7-12, and there are three levels of difficulty so that we can choose appropriate problems. An answer key is included as well as a useful poster showing in chart form the 100 occupations and 71 kinds of math required. Parents should choose problems from the book as needed rather than expecting a child to use the book independently.(S)

Also consider *Career Mathematics* (Houghton Mifflin) as another source for practical application of algebra, geometry, and trigonometry.

The biggest differences in algebra programs are in the methods of presentation. Some books break concepts down into small bites (increments), while others provide a "meal"

methods to be used. Textbooks are then written to match these frameworks.

at a sitting. Also, explanations in some books are clearer than others.

I have found that explanations in most first-year algebra books are sufficient on their own, but the same is not true for second-year algebra. It is very helpful to pick up a second textbook, possibly from a used book or thrift store, simply to have for an alternative explanation of a concept that is hard to understand. Perhaps an even more practical way to tackle second-year algebra is to select one of the intermediate algebra texts written for college students, since they are designed for use by students who do much of their work independently.

Algebra Resource Recommendations

(Arranged in approximate order of increasing difficulty)
➠Basic Algebra (Educational Design, Inc.)

This is a very basic, introductory algebra worktext that covers the bare essentials. This book is for those who need a more gradual introduction to Algebra (perhaps a step in between Saxon's *Algebra 1/2* and *Algebra 1* for review and reinforcement). This book will take only a few months to complete, so it will not be a full year's math course. There is no practical application included; you simply follow instructions and learn the mechanics. Large print and few problems per page reduce the intimidation level tremendously.(S)
➠Algebra: An Introductory Course (Amsco)

This course is written for the student who struggles with abstract math concepts. Algebra content is simplified and includes review of arithmetical skills and incorporation of some easy geometry. Instruction is followed by examples, then practice problems. Word problems and examples of life applications are included. The course comes in two choices of format: worktext or textbook. The worktext format consists of two volumes that are self-contained except for answer keys (inexpensive). Because the worktexts allow space for student work, there is less print per page, and the overall impact is less threatening than "heavier" looking books. The textbook format (either hard or softbound) does not allow space for problem solving within the book, but otherwise has the same content. Either format works well for independent study. This course will satisfy high school graduation requirements, but is probably not a good choice for college-bound students.(S)
➠Key to Algebra (Key Curriculum Press)

This series has been expanded from seven to ten workbooks. Where previously it was considered sufficient only as an introductory course, it now is equivalent to a complete first year algebra course, although it is less difficult than most. Titles of each book indicate topics covered: *Operations on Integers; Variables, Terms and Expressions; Equations; Polynomials; Rational Numbers; Multiplying and Dividing Rational Expressions; Adding and Subtracting Rational Expressions; Graphs; Systems of Equations;* and, *Square Roots and Quadratic Equations.*

The worktext format provides instruction, examples, and room for problem solving all within each workbook. Word problems help students understand life applications for algebra. As in the *Key to Geometry* series, much of the time students "discover" mathematical principles through problem solving activities with presentation of the rules following. This is in contrast to most algebra programs which teach rules first, with application practice following. Re-

view takes place at the end of each book. Reproducible tests are available for Books 1-7. Answers and Notes come in three separate books: one covering Books 1-4, one for Books 5-7, and one for Books 8-10. Like the other *Key* series, the books are black and white, consumable workbooks. They have large print and fewer exercises per page than most standard textbooks, so they are unintimidating.

Because they are easy to use and understand, these books are especially good for both students and parents who are weak in math. While *Key to Algebra* can be a full first year algebra course, it can also be used for review or as a gentle introduction, possibly using only the first seven books before a student begins a rigorous algebra course.(S)
➠Algebra Essentials (Merrill) [ISBN# 0675054915]

This is a less drastic alternative than Educational Design's *Basic Algebra*. This text covers most, but not all, of the content of a typical algebra course, yet it moves more slowly and does not require as much work. Print on the pages is larger and less overwhelming than in most algebra texts, yet it has the appearance of a standard text.(S)
➠Algebra I [Computer Video Interactive course] (ACE School of Tomorrow)

The videos are the the essential part of this course. Although videos are integrated with computerized course, the videos can actually be used without the computer, by using A.C.E. PACES with the videos (one video for each of twelve paces). However, the computer version provides an intriguing option. To go the computer route, we need to purchase the special all-in-one computer/video player (called AcceleTUTOR II) from A.C.E., as well as the software and videos. Software consists of twelve disks, which are essentially computerized versions of the PACES. However, the software also acts as the master controller to transform the videos and software into an integrated course. The software and video are inserted into the AcceleTUTOR. A simple command starts the software, which signals the computer to change to video mode at appropriate moments, at which time the video runs for the allotted time. There are switches back and forth throughout the course, all of which happen automatically. The software also provides feedback on student responses, on-line help, lesson summary, tracking of student progress, computerized testing, scoring, and reporting. It will also take a student back through material which has not been mastered. The videos are the most expensive part of the program (aside from the AcceleTUTOR), but they can be reused by many students. The software is much less expensive, but can be used by only one student because the interaction overwrites the data stored on the disks.

Using the Algebra PACES alone can present problems. They occasionally introduce concepts without laying a proper foundation with concepts or definitions that are necessary for understanding. I am told that those problems have been corrected with the video presentation. This means that using either the PACES or the computer version along with the videos should provide a good algebra course which students can use with little parental assistance.
➠Algebra by Smith, et al. (Addison-Wesley)

This first-year algebra course for average students is easier than Addison-Wesley's *Algebra I* by Foerster. Exercises have three levels of difficulty: practice, extension, and challenge. Mixed review follows every lesson to enhance retention. A student text and the Solution's Manual are required. *Instructional Software for Algebra I* is available (but optional) to use with the course. The software is available only for Apple II series machines and allows students to practice linear equations, factoring and polynomials, fractional expressions, equation systems, and radicals.(S)

⮕ **Algebra 1 and Algebra 2** (Saxon)

This is an excellent series. (Saxon also offers *Algebra 1/2*, a pre-algebra course which could be used for remedial review work before taking algebra.) *Algebra 1* and *Algebra 2* are designed to be used sequentially, a different approach than commonly found in high schools. Most high schools teach one course in algebra, then geometry, then return to algebra. The Saxon series teaches geometry within all algebra courses. A student planning to take only one year each of algebra and geometry could use Saxon's *Algebra 1* (possibly skipping over geometry instruction and problems), then switch to another publisher for geometry.

The geometry content within these texts is the weakest part of Saxon's approach. Originally very little geometry was found in the first two books. *Advanced Mathematics* provided the bulk of the coverage, which was insufficient. Geometry was then added to *Algebra 1* and *2*, but it is scattered and presented very briefly in both books. Because of this problem, you might consider using a different geometry text and skipping geometry exercises and instruction within Saxon. This can be done after *Algebra 1* or *2*, as well as after *Advanced Mathematics* (a less recommended option); or geometry might also be studied simultaneously.

Algebra 2 covers standard second year algebra topics, although the inclusion of a significant amount of trigonometry is unusual. Right triangle trigonometry basics are introduced and practiced in many lessons. It also contains a significant portion of the geometry instruction which takes place throughout the Saxon series.

These books continually review concepts, requiring thinking and understanding by the student, yet they allow students to work independently most of the time. Lessons introduce bite size concepts that are fairly easy to deal with. Explanation is included with each lesson, although a few of the explanations seem to make things sound more difficult than they really are. Saxon sells home educators a package containing a Teacher's Edition (identical to the student text, but with an answer key in the back) and tests with an answer key. These texts can be used independently by good math students, although many students will need occasional help as they progress beyond the first few chapters. Parents can review or learn along with the students, or they can find someone capable of tutoring when necessary. These texts are the easiest that I have found for independent work.(S)

⮕ **Algebra I by Isidore Dressler** (Amsco)

This book is written for the average student and can be used for independent learning. Instruction is fairly brief, followed by model problems, then exercises. This is a solid algebra course in topic coverage, in fact, it includes a good bit of geometry and trigonometry in addition to advanced algebra concepts. However, it was designed to be used as a supplement or review book, so instruction is a little more cursory than we find in some texts. (My impression is that the model problems are sufficient to help students grasp concepts without more extensive instruction.) The book is available in hardbound or paperback editions (each more than 580 pages), and a separate, inexpensive answer key is

available. Seven different versions of a final exam are also included in the book, although there are no chapter tests.

If students enjoy Dressler's presentations, they should consider continuing with one or more of his other math books: *Modern Algebra Two*, *Algebra Two and Trigonometry*, and *Trigonometry*. Advanced students can jump to the *Algebra Two and Trigonometry* course, but others should probably tackle *Modern Algebra Two* as the continuation.(S)

⮕ **Algebra 1 and Algebra 2** (BJUP)

BJUP recommends these texts only to those parents who have an excellent knowledge of algebra themselves. Bright students can work with these books, although they really need someone to confer with if they encounter problems or feel there is not enough explanation. As with most textbooks, *Algebra 1* appears easier to use than *Algebra 2*. Each lesson covers a larger chunk of material than in the Saxon books. *Algebra 1* is planned for ninth grade level. We can use only the first ten chapters and still provide a solid course. The last three chapters can be covered by bright students, however, the topics in these chapters are covered again in *Algebra 2*. *Algebra 2* is suggested for eleventh grade level, and geometry is a prerequisite. Standard topics are covered, as well as trigonometry, matrices and determinants, and probability, although these latter chapters can be skipped if necessary. Purchase both student and Teacher's Editions. The Teacher's Editions contain a copy of the student text with answers as well as lesson presentation information. A TestBank is available for *Algebra 1*.

⮕ **Algebra I and Algebra II** (A Beka)

Similar to BJUP in that they are recommended only to parents with strong math background. These are designed to be used for ninth and tenth grades. For the new editions of *Algebra I* and *Algebra II* which are now available, you will need to order a student text and the Solution Key. The Teacher's Edition is not necessary; the minimal amount of instructional information there is simply a restatement of information already in the student text. The Solution Key contains the answers and demonstrates how to reach them. Each lesson introduces a goodly amount of information—more than Saxon, but with less explanation. Instruction is fairly easy to follow for those with a strong math background. The Solution Keys are a big help, since we can always check the process followed to solve the problem.

⮕ **Algebra I or Algebra II Video Courses** (A Beka)

A Beka has tried to improve on the correspondence course with their video correspondence course. The videos are of actual classrooms. They are not edited, but include everything that occurs in the classroom. Our students learn by watching the teacher instruct the class, and by listening to interaction between students and teacher. Students work in the A Beka *Algebra I* and *II* texts at home and send in work as they would for any correspondence course. Even though the videos are rented rather than purchased, the cost is significant, and the time required is the same as in a traditional day school. Despite these drawbacks, this might be a practical alternative for some.

⮕ **The Basics of Algebra on Video Tape by Leonard Firebaugh** (Keyboard Enterprises)

This set of eighteen videos with accompanying work sheets and answer keys comprises a complete first year algebra course. Presentation is not exciting, but it moves along at a steady pace without wasting time. Firebaugh uses a white board to demonstrate problem solving, explaining concepts clearly as he goes. (Although Firebaugh appears very stiff and forbidding at the very beginning, he soon loosens up and appears more natural.)

Each video lesson presentation (145 in all) takes about fifteen minutes, then students practice on work sheets for about 30-45 minutes. Answer keys showing full solutions are included as well as tests. About 800 pages of work sheets, solutions, and tests comes with the course.

I see this as a more time- and money-effective solution than A Beka's video course. We keep the videos rather than returning them. The cost varies according to different quality options—choices of professionally or manually reproduced tapes, or reproduction on six-hour tapes versus two-hour tapes. Even the most expensive choice is only about the same as A Beka's cost for rental of their course. Other options are much less expensive. We do not have to watch all of the classroom interaction that is part of the A Beka course, which saves time, even though some of that interaction can be helpful to students.

Another option of interest to those who want only introductory algebra is to purchase the Part One course, which includes 49 lessons, or about one-third of the course. This option also includes work sheets, tests, and answer keys.(S)

➡ **Elementary Algebra** by Harold Jacobs (W.H. Freeman)

This is an atypical algebra text. It invites students to explore algebra concepts in a friendlier environment than other texts. Cartoons, interesting and creative applications, puzzles, and even poetry capture the interest of students who struggle with abstract mathematics. Jacobs always provides reasons for learning and using what is taught in each lesson. Students can jump around in this text to some extent, since all lessons do not build one upon the other. Four exercise sets are at the end of each lesson, with problems ranging from simple computation, through word and application problems, to challenging thought problems. By assigning appropriate problems, the text can be used with students of varying capabilities. Answers to questions from one of the sets from each lesson are in the back of the student text, so that students can see if they are getting the correct answers. The inexpensive teacher's guide is the source for the rest of the answers.(S)

➡ **Algebra and Trigonometry** by Smith et al. (Addison-Wesley)

This text covers second year algebra and an introduction to trigonometry. As with the first book by the same authors, exercises are at three levels of difficulty, and review and application are included. The student text and the Solutions Manual are required. Addison-Wesley offers the additional option of *Instructional Software for Algebra* 2 for Apple II computers covering inequalities, coordinate geometry, complex numbers, quadratics, and more.(S)

➡ **Developmental Mathematics** by David Novak (D.C. Heath)

Although this is sold as a college level text, it covers the same material as typical first-year algebra courses. The format lends itself to home education since it was designed to be used either in classrooms or for independent study. The book's layout is also a bit unusual. The book is softbound—over 900 pages. Each page contains instruction with examples, then exercise problems are set up in wide margins along each page and may be worked in the book. Bold print within the text, directs students when to do which problems. Answers to margin problems are at the end of each

section. A review "test" is at the end of each section. Answers to review tests are in a separate *Answer Key*. Of great help to parents weak in math will be the *Student Guide to Margin Exercises for Developmental Mathematics*, a solution manual to the daily problems. The *Instructor's Guide with Tests for Developmental Mathematics* is not absolutely necessary. It contains extra word problems although there are plenty in the basic text. While the review "tests" at the end of each section in the text might be sufficient, some might want to use the tests provided in the *Instructor's Guide*. Test answers are in the *Instructor's Guide*. *Algebra* (Professor Weissman's Software) computer software, listed below, coordinates easily with this text.(S)

➡ **Algebra I: Expressions, Equations, and Applications** by P. Foerster (Addison-Wesley)

This course is designed for average or better students. A hardback student text and either the Teacher's Edition or the Solutions Manual are necessary. Life applications in problems help students to understand how to apply algebra. An introduction to BASIC programming is included. The parent/teacher should have a solid algebra background and be prepared to work with their teen in this text. It is challenging, yet it is one of the most highly rated. It is frequently used for honors courses in schools.(S)

➡ **Algebra and Trigonometry: Functions and Applications** by P. Foerster (Addison-Wesley)

This book continues where the author's *Algebra I* text leaves off. Application of concepts is again an important emphasis of the course. Special classes of functions are introduced early and used continuously throughout. BASIC programming is reviewed and computer applications of algebra are integrated into exercises in an appendix. A hardback student text and the Solution's Manual are required. An Instructor's Commentary provides a flowchart diagram of topics and subtopics so that you can plan what to cover and what to skip according to available time.(S)

➡ **Algebra the Easy Way** by Douglas Downing (Barron's)

This is a <u>really</u> different approach to algebra. It is written as an adventure novel! The characters learn about algebra, why it is used and how it works as the story unfolds. Part of the rationale is that algebra is simply a shorthand way of writing mathematical situations; we should all appreciate short cuts and know how to use them. Rules are simply stated with technical terms pointed out but not emphasized. In 289 pages, the author covers concepts from both algebra I and II, so coverage is rather hurried. Concepts are presented in a different order than in most algebra programs, which makes it difficult to switch to another algebra II course. Exercises for practice are included. I love the approach for its creativity. I am afraid that it might move too quickly for those who have difficulty with math, and it might also be too incomplete for those who need a thorough math foundation to go on to higher math. It should be useful for students who would benefit from the more "user friendly" approach, and should certainly satisfy the high school algebra requirement. There is a sequel from the same author, *Calculus the Easy Way*, covered below. Other books in the "Made Easy" series are by different authors and lack the creativity of Downing's books.(S)

➡ **Intermediate Algebra, Sixth Edition** by Miller, Lial, and Hornsby (Harper Collins)

My frustration with the quality of high school texts for the second year of algebra has led me to look at some college textbooks as options. This text looks like a practical alternative to high school texts. Instructions for independent study are included. Key definitions and rules are conveniently placed for reference.

It is designed to cover the content of second-year high school algebra courses, as preparation for college math. While it does not include trigonometry, it covers all typical topics covered in second year algebra. This newest edition as been updated to try to adhere to the NCTM guidelines, which means that they have added more concept development, writing activity, and algebra integrated with some geometry applications. Instructions for the use of scientific calculators is very helpful.

I find the introductions to new concepts easier to understand in this text than in most others. Practical applications are clearly explained at the beginning, and concept presentations are written in understandable language. Bright yellow boxes caution students about common errors to avoid. Answers to selected exercises (usually all odd numbered problems) are at the back of the student text. I recommend purchasing the *Student's Solutions Manual*.(S)

➠Intermediate Algebra for College Students by Thurman S. Peterson and Charles R. Hobby (HarperCollins)

This book is well-designed for students doing much of their work independently as opposed to the typical high school book which assumes that the student does most of his learning in a classroom. It is probably a little more difficult than the *Intermediate Algebra* by Lial, Miller, and Hornsby.

The HarperCollins catalog accurately describes it. "For students with one year or less of secondary-school algebra, this carefully-paced and heavily practice-oriented textbook explains the basics of algebra from operations with real numbers to sequences and series. Individual sections within chapters are short and emphasize one idea or type of problem, and are organized by a consistent, step-by-step framework that helps students teach themselves. Each section describes a particular type of problem, presents a rule or procedure for solving it, and illustrates the solution with numerous examples." Topics covered, in addition to those mentioned above, are factoring, fractions and equations, exponents, roots, radicals, graphical methods, systems of linear equations and linear inequalities, quadratic equations and inequalities, the quadratic formula, systems involving quadratic equations, exponentials and logarithms, tables of squares and square roots, and mantissas. Trigonometry is not included.

Answers to odd-numbered problems are in the book. An inexpensive answer key is also available.(S)

➠Principles from Patterns: Algebra I (Cornerstone Curriculum Project)

This program is designed to follow immediately after Cornerstone's Level 6 of *Making Math Meaningful*. However, students working in other publishers' math series can use this course for a high school algebra course. It also covers pre-algebra topics (positive and negative numbers, radicals, exponents, order of operations, etc.) as well as all topics covered in most first-year algebra courses.

It comes in a three-ring binder, and we are given permission to copy reproducible work/activity pages for all children in our family. An answer key is included in the binder.

Principles from Patterns incorporates the use of manipulatives (*Unifix Cubes* and heavy graph paper cut into shapes

resembling *Base Ten* or *Mortensen* materials) which make it much easier to grasp some of the abstract concepts. Some unique techniques are used as well as the rectangle building technique featured by *Mortensen*. *Unifix Cubes* (sold separately by Cornerstone) are used in conjunction with grid paper included within the binder. However, *Lego* bricks can be substituted if we draw new grid paper to fit. The heavy graph paper, included in the binder, works well as a manipulative, but you might want to substitute Nasco's *Algebra Models* which function the same way and are easier to handle. Teens who need concrete learning experiences will particularly benefit from the teaching methods used here. Those who function well on an abstract level should also benefit with better understanding of concepts, although they might be able to shortcut through some of the hands-on activities.

Inductive teaching methods are frequently used, which lead learners to discover concepts themselves rather than just memorize rules and study examples.

Topics are covered in a progressive fashion, working toward mastery of each concept, rather than the scattered approach we encounter in the Saxon texts. At the end of each unit is a review lesson to ensure retention and understanding of previously learned concepts. Many word problems within each unit help students understand the practical application of concepts.

Unlike the previous *Making Math Meaningful* courses, this one does not offer a script ("Say this," "Do this"), but speaks directly to the learner. Because of this, many students will be able to work independently.

Algebra Supplements

➠Algebra (Professor Weissman's Software)

Professor Weissman has developed an excellent series of computer programs for algebra. A good sampler disk (titled *Algebrax*) is available from Professor Weissman or through the public domain for IBM compatible machines at minimal cost. The sampler will help with many topics from typical first-year algebra courses. When you are ready for more, there are disks 1 through 6—order one or more according to your need. Content of each (version 2) disk is as follows: 1.) Absolutes; inequalities; signed numbers; exponents; order of operations; combining like terms; substitution; GCF distributive law; solving linear equations; word problems. 2.) solving inequalities; word problems; equations with fractions/decimals; multiplying binomials; graphing lines. 3.) reducing, combining, multiplying, and dividing algebra fractions; exponent rules including negative exponents; scientific notation. 4.) polynomials; special products; difference of squares; trinomial squares; common factors; factoring trinomials. 5.) fraction equations; systems of equations; word problems; quadratic equations. 6.) simplifying radicals; all operations with radicals; evaluating radicals. *Algebra* is designed for practice and review, not initial instruction. However, it does help students understand where they went wrong when they miss a problem. It also records the student's performance and progress. It should be useful with any algebra (I and II) programs covering the above topics, but has been keyed to Addison-Wesley's books by Keedy and Bittinger, *Introductory Algebra, Fifth Edition* and *Intermediate Algebra, Fifth Edition* and to D.C. Heath's *Developmental Math* by David Novak by special agreement with those publishers. (Note: the aforementioned texts are listed in college catalogs, rather than high school catalogs, but the content is essentially the same as in high school texts.) The program runs on IBM compatibles with 384 K and a CGA or Hercules card. The disks are normally $30 each, but Professor Weissman will sell them at $20 each if you tell him that you are a home educator ordering from *Christian Home Educators' Curriculum Manual*. For the best bargain, purchase *Introductory Algebra* (Keedy and Bittinger). In the book is a coupon for the entire six disk set for only $95.

Trigonometry and pre-calculus software will be available in January of 1993. Write for details.(S)

➡ **Algebra Plus, Volume One [Apple, Amiga, Tandy 1000, and IBM] and Volume Two [IBM and Tandy 1000 only]** (Stone & Associates)

Each level of this computer program comes with two disks, one has problems and tutorials, the other has tests and a glossary of mathematical terms. Because these programs are not designed to be the primary teaching tools, students should have already learned the concepts, then use these programs for review and testing. Level One actually begins with pre-algebra, reviewing number operations and simple equations. It then moves on to linear equations, graphing, solving inequalities, general properties of polynomials, and factoring polynomials. Level Two works with both monomials and polynomials (progressing through addition, subtraction, and multiplication of polynomials), covers logarithms and exponents, and reviews solving quadratic equations. Short tutorials precede problems on each topic. If students encounter difficulties in trying to solve problems, they can pull up help screens to walk them through the solution process; however, the program does not fully explain every step. Both volumes feature numeric and word problems. Each test program tracks right and wrong answers to score each student's performance.

Both programs make good supplements to any algebra program, and a helpful "substitute teacher" for parents who cannot help their children with algebra concepts they do not understand. Both volumes should be used in conjunction with first-year algebra, however students in second-year algebra courses will be reviewing then applying many of these same concepts and can benefit from the practice.(S)

➡ **Algebra Video Math Tape** (Bly Academy)

The widely advertised videos from Bly Academy each cover a single subject area in approximately six hours. Obviously this is not enough time for complete coverage of a subject, so consider these as supplemental help.

These videos do help with teaching, however, the presentations move very, very slowly, and the quality is rather poor—colors on visual aids vibrate, and sometimes lettering is difficult to read.(S)

➡ **Laugh with Math** by Professor Martin Weissman and Keith Monse (Laugh and Learn)

The advertisement for *Laugh with Math* poses the riddle, "What do you get when you cross *Mad Magazine* with an Algebra textbook?" The answer is Professor Weissman's *Laugh with Math*. The underlying idea was to create an alternative to the "made easy" books which make numerous digressions to maintain their story line. There are still digressions in *Laugh with Math*, but they are most often one-liner jokes. The book reads sort of like a television situation comedy with a purpose. The characters are there to be funny, while the Professor teaches the basics of algebra. He covers signed numbers (values, addition, subtraction, multiplication, and

division), inequality symbols, absolute value, basic operations, rounding numbers, laws of exponents, the use of a scientific calculator, and scientific notation. These are the key concepts necessary for success in algebra. There are hundreds of problems for practice, as well as an answer/solution key in the back. While the publisher recommends it for all types of learners from gifted elementary students on up, I feel that it is more appropriate for older learners who need to review algebra basics in an entertaining, non-threatening way. (Younger students tend to be silly without reinforcement.) By sending in our proof of purchase, we can also get a free copy of Weissman's *Algebrax* software.(SE)

➡ **Math Motivators: Investigations in Algebra** by Alfred S. Posamentier (Addison-Wesley)

This book offers intriguing exercises in number theory, equations, probability and statistics, problem solving, recreational math, logic, and linear proportions for the math whiz (Type C). This is challenging application for students willing to work at math in interesting settings.(S)

➡ **Video Tutor, Algebra I** (Video Tutor, Inc.)

This set of six videos is designed to supplement a first-year algebra course or as a refresher course. The videos vary in length from 30 to 103 minutes. They cover all first-year algebra topics including variables, equations, radicals, square roots, graphing lines, and solving quadratic equations by both factoring and using the quadratic formula.

Explanations are brief, assuming that the student has encountered instruction elsewhere. However, John Hall, the video instructor offers problem-solving tips which he has gleaned from his years of actual teaching experience. Hall does the teaching from a white board as does Firebaugh in *The Basics of Algebra on Video Tape*. However, Hall is more expressive and lively and, consequently, more engaging to watch. (Keep in mind that Firebaugh's course is complete, while this course is for supplement or review.)

Small booklets with some practice problems (and answer keys) accompany each tape.

(Cost is about $30 per tape or $150 for the set of six.)

Video Tutor also has videos for other junior and senior high math topics with presentations similar to those in the *Algebra I* series. Titles are *Percents, Decimals, Fractions, Pre-Algebra, Basic Word Problems, Basic Number Concepts* (pre-algebra level), and *Basic Geometry*.(S)

Hands-On Help for Algebra

Many teens still need experience with concrete materials to understand mathematical concepts. Concrete materials used for math, such as *Cuisenaire® Rods, Base Ten Blocks, Mortensen* materials, and others are called manipulatives. Teens rarely need an entire program built around the use of manipulatives, yet they often benefit from introduction of new concepts with them. For instance, factoring polynomials is much simpler when first experienced with manipulatives.

Algebra

Mortensen Math has an entire strand of workbooks on algebra to use with their manipulatives. (There are five different strands in the total program: arithmetic, problem solving, measurement, algebra, and calculus.) *Mortensen* uses good visual/hands-on techniques for understanding algebra, which are based on building rectangles. However, this is a supplement, not a complete program. *Mortensen* is great on techniques which are explained well in their *Manuals*. However, the Mortensen workbooks are uneven in quality and content.

Other tools that work on the same principle are available. Both Nasco's *Algebra Models* and Teacher Designed Products *Xactor* are much less expensive than Mortensen products, although neither is as comprehensive.

Algebra Models includes an instruction booklet with manipulatives that can be used to demonstrate algebraic concepts with both positive and negative numbers. In addition, a teacher presentation package is available which includes 14 blackline masters with problems, a 15-page teacher introduction, and answer key. A video introduction to *Algebra Models* is also available at no cost if we return it within 30 days. (Otherwise, it sells for $19.95.)

Xactor covers the same territory with a larger instructional book and a very simple cardboard manipulative device. The *Xactor* would serve well for those simply needing a visual aid rather than manipulatives to demonstrate factoring and division of expressions, square roots, and algebraic work with negative numbers.

Algebra Models provide more hands-on activity than *Xactor*.

Cuisenaire® Rods and *Base Ten Blocks* can be used for upper level math concepts, but most books explaining how to use them concentrate on elementary grades. Either product could be used with Mortensen instruction manuals or ideas from *Algebra Models* or *Xactor*. *Cuisenaire®* does not include hundreds squares found in other products, although they are necessary for working with large numbers and algebra. You can make your own hundreds squares by cutting 10 cm. x 10 cm. squares from poster or mat board.

Geometry

We have three basic directions to go with geometry. We can provide an introduction to geometry and leave it at that. We can offer a college preparatory geometry course that includes formal proofs. Or, we can choose a course that does not include formal proofs, but that still provides adequate preparation for college math.

Secular publishers have recognized that formal proofs (proofs written in two columns of mathematical language) are the downfall of many a geometry student and have come up with alternatives that disguise proofs by asking questions that require plain English answers rather than mathematically stated proofs. While proofs themselves are helpful in logical thinking, there is no evidence that formal writing of proofs is essential to understanding and applying geometrical knowledge. The alternative—informal proofs—is becoming increasingly popular in textbooks. Generally, students who are mathematically minded will prefer the conciseness of formal proofs, while students who are more language oriented will find informal proofs more comfortable.

Geometry Resource Recommendations

(Arranged in approximate order of increasing difficulty)
➡ Key to Geometry (Key Curriculum Press)

No prerequisite knowledge of algebra is required. The series of eight booklets provides a basic introduction to geometry. It is not equivalent to a typical high school geometry course. It might be used as a substitute for a non-college bound student or as an introductory course for a student

who needs to mature before getting into geometry. One booklet looks manageable to a student who would be overwhelmed by a two-inch-thick hardback text. Multiply this booklet eight times and there is still a decent amount of learning taking place.

Construction with compass and straight edge, combined with inductive reasoning, are the primary learning tools. Proofs and theorems are lacking, but students can build a beginning foundation without them. The publisher is very conscientious about stating clearly that this is not a full geometry course, but schools are using them with students who need a simpler course. Home schoolers should be able to do the same. Just be cautious about putting it on a college transcript.

The books have large print, so students go through these very quickly (ten pages a day is reasonable). They are largely self-instructional. Books one through six have only 55 pages each, while book seven has 154 and book eight has 138. The entire course should take about twelve weeks, so you will need to do something else the rest of the year.(S)

➡ Informal Geometry (Addison-Wesley)

Prerequisite: Algebra I. This text is easier than many others reviewed here since it does not use formal proofs. Instead, it uses language such as, "How can we know?" (informal proofs). It is similar to Houghton Mifflin's *Basic Geometry* in that it uses larger print and less work on a page (593 pages altogether), but it uses more real life applications than the Houghton Mifflin text. Purchase both the *Student Edition* and the *Teacher's Edition*.(S)

➡ Basic Geometry (Houghton Mifflin)

Prerequisite: Algebra I. This text is a step down from traditional geometry texts since it does not place as much emphasis on proofs as do traditional texts. Theorems and proofs are covered but they are not as intimidating here. Even though the book has 558 pages, the print is larger than many other texts, with less work on a page—two more factors that make this text easier. You need to buy a student textbook and the *Solution Key*.(S)

➡ Informal Geometry (Merrill)

Prerequisite: Pre-algebra. While similar to Addison-Wesley's *Informal Geometry*, this text focuses on reaching a wider range of students. It also takes more of a discovery approach to learning. Constructions are used throughout the text as tools for discovering geometric concepts. Calculator and computer (Logo) problems are integrated throughout the text. Short chapters prevent students from feeling overwhelmed. All concepts usually taught in traditional geometry courses, except formal proofs, are included. Buy the student book and the *Teacher Annotated Edition*. (ISBN# 0675058546)(S)

➡ Geometry (Broderbund) [computer progam]

Computer program. This program is certainly complete! (It has so much data that you really need a hard disk drive, otherwise you are constantly switching the two disks.) Geometric forms can be manipulated on the computer which certainly makes things interesting. Instructions on all the basic concepts appear to be covered including theorems and proofs. You can choose whether or not to bother with the proofs since they are on separate screens that you either click on or not as you prefer. Hints, solutions, and tutorials are all on screen menus. Without actually using the program I cannot say for certain that this would suffice alone as a geometry course, but it looks like it should. The quality is up to Broderbund's typical high standards. IBM owners will be disappointed to know that the program is only available for the Macintosh and Apple IIGS. (Check out Learning Services for a discounted price.)(S)

➠ Discovering Geometry (Key Curriculum Press)

Here is a truly different approach to teaching geometry. This is a complete, college-preparatory course, but it is more interesting and inviting than any other text. The first thing students encounter in the book is art—geometric art. The art leads students into their first investigations about lines and shapes. Investigations by students helps them discover postulates and theorems by inductive reasoning. Many investigations involve students in activities, including making and working with models. Word problems are imaginative. Real life applications are more true to life than in other texts. Formal proofs are taught only in the last three chapters after students have mastered concepts and understand relationships between theorems. (However, students are applying deductive reasoning and working with informal proofs much earlier.) The only negatives with this book are in the word problems—constant role reversal and a few others that refer to wizards and dragons. (These word problems are presented in a comical rather than serious way.) You need the hardback student text and the *Teacher's Guide and Answer Key*. The Teacher's Guide includes a section that will help you plan which chapters of the text to use, tailoring the course to be more academic or less, according to the needs of each student. Extra geometry investigations are included for ambitious students.(SE)

➠ Geometry for Decision Making (South-Western)

I see this text as being similar to Discovering Geometry in topical content, yet it uses different methodology. It too combines inductive and deductive reasoning, but it relies much less on discovery learning through construction activities. Construction work with a compass begins in chapter six, and is used less extensively throughout the book. Discovery activities are included in each chapter, and often full explanation is provided with the activity. (*Discovering Geometry* does not always immediately restate discovered concepts as does this text.) This text teaches formal proofs earlier, although it also teaches informal proofs. Trigonometry is introduced at the end of the book. There is a similar amount of real life application problems. Plentiful illustrations make concepts fairly easy to understand. The format is uncluttered, but has variety and color. This is actually a fairly traditional geometry course, enhanced with more activities, life application, and an easy-to-use format.

The student text contains answers to the odd-numbered problems, plus chapter tests and a cumulative review that might serve as a final test. The Teacher's Edition has answers overprinted on pages identical to the student text, as well as lots of extra teaching helps.(S)

➠ Geometry [second edition] by Harold R. Jacobs (W.H. Freeman)

Jacobs has managed to write a user-friendly geometry text that is heavy on logic, deductive reasoning, and proofs. He uses entertaining illustrations (including cartoons) as well as practical application explanations and engaging word problems.

He spends the entire first unit (nine chapters) on logic. Many people cite the value of geometry as being the development of logical thinking skills. Jacobs takes this idea seriously so that students are truly tuned in to logical thinking

before tackling geometry topics. Given the foundation in logic, students then immediately begin work with proofs which continues throughout the text. Topic arrangement is different than I have seen in most texts. For instance, work with circles follows introductory lessons on trigonometry. (The trigonometry is introduced as a natural progression in the study of triangles, so this is not really an outlandish arrangement.) Even if the arrangement is unusual, there is a clear continuity to topics, building one upon another.

Construction activities (using straight edge and compass) are very minimal. Because of this and the emphasis on logic, I recommend this text for abstract thinkers rather than hands-on learners. A very reasonably priced Teachers'Guide and Test Masters are also available.(S)

➠ Advanced Mathematics (former title Geometry, Trigonometry, Algebra III) (Saxon)

This highly recommended text is one of the easiest to work with, as are other Saxon math books. This is designed to be a one-year course, although it could easily be spread out longer if desired. Saxon sells to home educators a package containing a Teacher's Edition (identical to student text, but with the answer key in the back) and tests. A Solutions Manual is also available. The 1989 revised edition of this text appears to be identical to the previous edition, with the exception of introductory information and the title. Geometric proofs are taught, along with trigonometry, logarithms, infinite series, conic sections, matrices, and determinants. This text moves even more into the theoretical math realm than earlier Saxon texts. By the time students complete Saxon's *Advanced Mathematics*, they are on a par with students who have completed pre-calculus work.(SE)

➠ Geometry (BJUP)

This text is recommended by BJUP only for students whose parents have an excellent knowledge of geometry. This text has a traditional presentation of formal proofs, with strong emphasis on development of deductive thinking skills and logic which continues throughout the text. Constructions are taught beginning in chapter four, and are used frequently throughout the lessons. Purchase both student and Teacher's Editions. The Teacher's Edition contains lesson presentation ideas and student pages with some answers overprinted. Lengthy answers are contained elsewhere in the Teacher's Edition. There is also a section called "Lab Experiments" describing rather involved hands-on activities that we can use if desired.

➠ Plane Geometry and Analytical Geometry (A Beka)

A Beka offers two geometry texts. *Plane* is a one-year course with a new edition now available. *Plane Geometry* uses traditional methods including the use of formal proofs. The emphasis is on logical, systematic thinking skills. The course is primarily theoretical rather than practical. (An example of a more practical course would be *Discovering Geometry*.) Order the student text and the *Solution Key*, which demonstrates solutions to problems. A *Student Test Booklet* and *Student Quiz Booklet* are also available. This text is equivalent to the typical high school geometry course.

Analytical Geometry can be either a semester or one-year course. The latter book is recommended only for parents with good math knowledge and students who plan to major in math-related fields. (A Beka recommends using *Analytical Geometry* one semester and their *Trigonometry with Tables* the other semester.) It appears that it is necessary to purchase the Teacher Guide/Curriculum for *Analytical*

Geometry to obtain a complete answer key. A Solution Key for selected problems is available as well as a Student Test/Quiz Booklet.

Geometry Supplements

➠Geometric Constructions by Daniel, Sarah, and Kathleen Julicher (Castle Heights Press)

This inexpensive little book can supplement any geometry course after students have learned some construction techniques. Techniques required are all demonstrated at the front of the book, but the presentations there are designed to be "memory joggers" rather than complete explanations. There are eight story problems which are quite lengthy—about a page each plus an accompanying map on which the student works through the various constructions to solve the problem. For example, in problem 3, "You are the captain of the USS Swift Shark, a submarine. While en route to the secret submarine base, your ship's computer fails and deletes the secret location of the base. You must get there with critical information before the enemy destroys Rockcliff Harbor. The only way there is by following a set of coded instructions sent from the base..." By constructing an angle bisector, perpendiculars, a circle, and a tangent we locate the secret base on the map. Only a straight edge and compass are required. Art work is not professional, yet it should appeal to most teens. An answer key is included.

➠Geometry Video Math Tape (Bly Academy)

See description under algebra supplements above.

➠Investigations in Geometry by A.S. Posamentier and G. Sheridan (Addison-Wesley Publishing Co.)

This supplement is much more challenging than *Geometric Constructions*. Lots of algebra is incorporated into problem solving, and investigations purposely explore avenues for application that stretch beyond those found in the typical geometry textbook. Activities are keyed for slower, average, and above-average students. However, all activities are best used as presentations/demonstrations (parent/teacher shows how to work through the investigation) or cooperative tasks (student works with parent or another student). There are 33 investigations (reproducible student pages), each accompanied by "teacher's notes" that give thorough explanations with the answers. Valuable background information is provided at the front of the book as well as suggestions for selecting which investigations to use. Sample topics: trisecting a circle, constructing a pentagon, taxicab geometry (Cartesian coordinates), the Golden Triangle, mathematics on a billiard table, the nine-point circle, Napoleon's Theorem, and projective geometry.(S)

Hands-On Help for Geometry

Drawing tools such as protractors and compasses incorporate hands-on work into most geometry courses. Because of this, many hands-on learners prefer geometry over algebra and other math courses. Take advantage of this natural preference to use drawing as a learning tool.

Some students will appreciate three-dimensional, visualization tools such as the *D-Stix* sets from Nasco or Dale Seymour Publications. *Tensegritoy* (from Nasco Math Catalog or Dale Seymour Publications), another model building set, incorporates tensile forces.

Mira is an interesting tool that acts somewhat like a mirror. It can be used for introduction of geometric concepts or for higher level study with the supplementary books *Mira*

Math Activities for Elementary Schools (for grades 3-8) or *Mira Math Activities for High School*. Still more advanced activities using the *Mira* are in *Geometry: Constructions and Transformations* by Iris M. Dayoub and Johnny W. Lott. (The *Mira* tool and books are available from Nasco and Dale Seymour Publications.)

Trigonometry and Higher Math Recommendations

(Arranged in approximate order of increasing difficulty)

➠Trigonometry with Tables (A Beka)

This book is a one-semester course that can be combined with A Beka's *Analytical Geometry* for a full-year math course. A Solution Key (for selected problems), Answer Key, Test/Quiz Booklet, and Teacher Guide/Curriculum are available. Recommended only for parents with an excellent knowledge of trigonometry.

➠Advanced Math (BJUP)

Covers trigonometry, advanced algebra, and pre-calculus. This text should be used after a second year algebra course. As with other BJUP math texts, this is designed for classroom use by a teacher familiar with math concepts.

➠Advanced Mathematical Concepts (Merrill)

This is a topical course rather than a sequential one. It is organized into five units: 1) Relations, Functions, and Graphs; 2) Trigonometry; 3) Advanced Functions and Graphing; 4) Discrete Mathematics; and 5) Introduction to Calculus. It also has up-to-date instruction in the use of calculators. Purchase the student edition and the *Teacher's Guide and Solutions Manual*.(S)

➠Advanced Mathematics (Saxon)

See description under Geometry above.

➠Advanced Mathematics: A Precalculus Course (Houghton Mifflin)

This text covers precalculus plus some probability and statistics topics usually covered in calculus. Use of the calculator and computer are strongly recommended. Purchase the student's edition and the *Teacher's Manual* that contains solutions.(S)

➠Functions/Trigonometry (Alpha Omega)

This LifePac course was designed for independent work. While I have not reviewed this course, I have heard from a number of home educators that LifePac high school math courses are sometimes difficult to understand. I suggest purchasing one LifePac to try before buying the entire course.

➠Pre-Calculus Mathematics (Merrill)

This is Merrill's more challenging precalculus course. The publisher says that the sequence is very similar to that of college calculus courses. It covers advanced algebra and trigonometry, second-degree relations, transcendental functions, vectors, matrices, analytic geometry, and an introduction to limits, derivatives, and integrals. Applications are included so the course is not just theory. Purchase the student edition and the *Teacher Guide and Solutions Manual*. (ISBN# 0675049784)(S)

➠Calculus (Saxon)

Following the incremental method used in previous books, many students can learn calculus on their own. A *Calculus Solution Manual* is available if they get stumped. The student text and answer key are packaged together for home educators, but it is more practical to buy a student text by itself rather than in the package, then also purchase the *Solution Manual*. A *Testmaster* is also available for preparing tests, but it is designed for the classroom (it has two versions of each test) and is too expensive for most home educators.(S)

⇒ **Calculus The Easy Way** (Barron's)

Calculus is taught through a fantasy story—a unique and engaging approach. All math should be this fun! Practice exercises, tests, and answers are included in one book. This is not as comprehensive as other calculus books, but any high school student who gets this far is already ahead. Highly recommended.(S)

Supplements for Advanced Math

⇒ **Trigonometry Video and Calculus Video Math Tapes** (Bly Academy)

See description under supplements for algebra above.

Consumer, Business, and Career Math

Some students are not going to study algebra or geometry at home. Whether it is because they do not plan to attend college or other reasons is not important. Consumer or survival math has been the only alternative until recently.

Concerned educators have recognized that many high school students take consumer math since it is often the only alternative to algebra offered to them, even though they are interested in business and trade careers. To correct this situation, we now have some specialized alternative textbooks from which to choose in place of consumer math.

Consumer Math

⇒ **Applications of Mathematics** (Merrill)

High school students who have a shaky math background would do better to use this text than to jump into algebra. This text is similar to consumer math texts in that it covers many basic math applications such as interpreting transit system schedules and tax tables, applying percentage to sales, and using measurements. Most of the book would be repetitious for students who learned seventh and eighth grade math. It begins to stretch to new concepts in some of the geometry lessons, some of the work with graphs, probability, statistics (depending upon which curriculum has been used), patterns, and functions (very simple), and plotting on the coordinate plane. Algebra is introduced as solving open sentences—most pre-algebra students will have already covered this material. This is definitely remedial level.

Students who need concrete applications for understanding will find plenty of real-life situations used as the foundations for each lesson. Each new topic is introduced with an application situation. Examples and instruction follow, then students do the exercises. Exercises include computation, word, and mental math problems. Both chapter and cumulative reviews are included at the end of each chapter along with a chapter test. (Answers are in the Teacher Annotated Edition.) A Basic Skills Appendix, forty-one pages long, explains and provides review exercises for skills that should have been mastered such as place value, estimation, division, decimal operations, factoring, and fractions. Students who have not learned these concepts must do so before they can go on. After completing the book, stu-

dents might be able to go on to algebra. Some students will need to pursue a more practical math education by using texts such as *Career Mathematics* (published by Houghton Mifflin) or one of the many business or practical math texts from other publishers.

The Teacher Annotated Edition contains answer keys, teaching information, and a copy of the student text with answers. (ISBN # 0675057175)(S)

⇒ **Applied Mathematics** (A Beka)

This new A Beka math text is a little more challenging than A Beka's Consumer Mathematics. It covers personal finances, bookkeeping and accounting, business formulas, investments, taxes, and banking. Concepts from arithmetic, algebra, and geometry are incorporated into problem solving strategies, although not at a deep level. The student edition and Solution Key are the most useful components, although a Teacher's Edition and test booklet are also available. The text can be used as either a one-semester or full-year course. Recommended for grades 10-12. (A Beka recommends their *Using the Personal Computer* text as a second-semester course.)

⇒ **Consumer Math** (BJUP)

Listed as an alternative to Algebra at ninth grade level, this text provides a general review of math and basic algebra (learned in pre-algebra courses) in addition to practical life applications of mathematics. Purchase both student and Teacher Editions.

⇒ **Consumer Mathematics** (A Beka)

This text is recommended for non-college-bound students. Purchase student and Teacher Editions. A Skill Workbook is also available. This is a very practical text, appropriate for any level. It covers topics similar to *Survival Mathematics* above.

⇒ **Survival Mathematics** by Edward Williams (Barron's Educational Services)

Students learn practical application of skills such as sales tax computation, following recipes, figuring area, purchasing, payrolls, banking, and checkbook balancing. This is the minimal level of competence that our children should have before graduating from high school. Even better than using such a textbook would be real life training such as having our teenagers handle the family budget for a month or two.(S)

Business and Career Math

⇒ **Career Mathematics** (Houghton Mifflin)

Prerequisite: Algebra I or introductory algebra. This is a challenging text based entirely on applications. Part one reviews measurements, fractions, decimals, and percent. Part two applies algebra to such topics as ratios and proportions, electrical and horsepower formulas, and begins working with geometry, while teaching about machines, mechanical advantage, gears and pulleys, car transmissions, etc. Part three covers plane and solid geometry in construction, machinery, and manufacturing operations. Part four provides study through occupational simulations of building a house and publishing a book. Part five gets into trigonometry and statistics through topics such as navigation, data analysis and graphing. A parent using this text should have some familiarity with geometry since the instruction provided is rather scanty. It would not hurt for a student to take geometry first (perhaps an introductory course such as *Key to Geometry*).

Students interested in a career in the business world might do well with one of the following business math textbooks. (S)

➡ **Contemporary Business Mathematics** by Ignacio Bello (D.C. Heath and Company)

In this text, students study business applications of mathematics.(S)

➡ **Essentials of Mathematics: Consumer/Career Skills Applications** [1987 edition] (Harcourt Brace Jovanovich)

This text offers more career application math than typical survival or consumer math programs.(S)

➡ **For All Practical Purposes: Introduction to Contemporary Mathematics** [Second Edition] (W.H. Freeman and Co.)

This college level text, designed to meet the new standards, might be used by home schoolers either in conjunction with or following a second-year algebra course. The emphasis throughout is the practical usage of math, but at higher levels than is covered in other books reviewed here such as *Career Mathematics*. Algebra and geometry topics are developed through applications—e.g., historical anecdotes, examples, and real world problems. Answers to odd-numbered problems are in the back of the book. The Instructor's Guide contains teaching strategies and other teaching helps as well as answers to even-numbered problems.(S)

➡ **Mathematics for Trade and Industrial Occupations** (Dale Seymour Publications)

For students with mechanical inclinations, this text looks outstanding. This is serious math designed to prepare future machinists and tradesmen, not a watered-down course. It includes practical trigonometry, geometry, and algebra as used in various trades.(S)

➡ **Mathematics and Your Career** by Geier and Lamm (Amsco)

This text covers basic math skills by application to simulated life situations. The books incorporates information and lessons that also help teenagers explore career possibilities. Each unit is based upon one of six job clusters described by the U.S. Department of Labor and features exercises with on-the-job math, descriptions of job qualifications, salary expectations, and career opportunities with suggested information sources. That glamorous career may look less appealing when our teen discovers how much math is involved.(S)

Remedial Math

There are a number of options for remediating poor math skills. We can always choose a lower level text and have our child review areas of weakness, speeding through until they are up to level. However, some students either are far behind or simply unable to complete typical high school level math, so we need to consider other solutions. Programs such as *Mastering Mathematics* or *Developmental Mathematics* (reviewed in the *Elementary* volume of this book) can be used to cover basic math topics from the elementary grades without grade level stigma attached to the books. The *Key to...* series of books on fractions, decimals, percents, geometry and algebra also can be very useful. The *Key to...* books use large print and an uncluttered format, incorporating drawing and visual helps for the learner who has trouble with abstract presentations. The geometry course is strictly introductory, and remedial students might be able to use only part of the algebra series, but both are

options used by other schools for students who cannot complete standard courses.

Other options have been designed expressly for adult learners or teens who are lacking functional math skills.

➡ **Number Sense** (Contemporary Books, Inc.)

For grades 4 and up. This is a series of ten, sixty-four page workbooks designed for remedial, special, and adult education. (Parents lacking the basics can go back and learn through these books.) Instruction is brief and clear, and lessons are presented in a highly visual format. When a more thorough introduction, alternative presentation, or manipulative activity is needed, the *Teacher's Resource Guide* (covering all books) is very useful. Topics covered include whole numbers (addition, subtraction, multiplication, division), decimals, fractions, and ratios/proportions/percents. Relevant life-skills applications are presented in each lesson. This is not a complete program like A Beka or BJUP that would be used to begin instructing younger children. Some concepts are not taught directly—I cannot find where measurement or money are ever taught specifically (see *Real Numbers* books for help with these topics), although both are incorporated into word problems. This series could work well with children who have delayed beginning formal academics until they are older or with children who have a poor math background and need to review. They can move very quickly through these books, covering most of the basic topics that are learned in first through sixth grades. Diagnostic placement and mastery tests are available as well as a separate answer key. Students can work independently unless they need further instruction on a concept.(S)

➡ **Real Numbers: Developing Thinking Skills in Math** (Contemporary Books, Inc.)

This series has six titles: *Estimation 1: Whole Numbers and Decimals; Estimation 2: Fractions and Percents; Tables, Graphs and Data Interpretation; Measurement; Algebra Basics;* and *Geometry Basics*. These eighty-page books cover topics quickly, but they use illustrations and drawing activities throughout to aid the visual and kinesthetic learners who struggle with the abstract presentations of most math textbooks. Life applications are also abundant so that learners understand the purpose of learning the concepts. What is lacking are explanations of mathematical logic. For instance, formulas for solid geometry volume are given, but explanations of why those formulas work are not. This is not to be taken as a negative comment. Because many remedial students just do not have the time and energy to work through the logic, it might be a good choice to present information in this way. These books also lack the depth of typical course content in all areas. I can see these books being most useful for the student who has been removed from school in the middle of high school and who has been failing math courses for a few years. They will help that student become mathematically literate, but will not equip him for college. Answers are in the back of the book and there is no teacher's guide since they are designed for independent work.(S)

➡ **Number Power** (Contemporary Books, Inc.)

This series of eight books designed for older learners moves beyond the level of *Real Numbers*, with the goal of equipping students to pass the GED examination. The first and second books cover addition, subtraction, multiplication, division, fractions, decimals, and percents. The third and fourth books cover algebra and geometry respectively.

Book five teaches graphs, tables, schedules, and maps. Book six concentrates on word problems, applying all previously learned math skills. Book seven is entitled *Problem Solving and Test-Taking Strategies*. The last book assumes that these students will probably be weak in calculation skills, so it teaches the use of calculators. Each workbook is self-contained including both instruction and practice, with answers in the back.(S)

Chapter Twelve

Language Arts

By junior high, we hope that our children are reading well and have already mastered basic composition and grammar skills. Unfortunately, these are areas in which our students sometimes fall short, either because of learning difficulties, lack of cooperation on the part of our children, or neglect on our part. It really is necessary that reading and writing skills be at least at grade level before students advance to high school work, otherwise they are not equipped with the tools of learning necessary for further progress. If any of these areas pose problems at junior high level, NOW is the time to correct them.

Remedial Reading

For several reasons, junior high students might still read poorly. Many of us are in situations where we have hoped that our child would outgrow his problems as he matured. Sometimes, the problems persist, and both we and our child have become very discouraged. If our child still has reading problems at junior high level, we need a professional evaluation. There may be a vision problem, a learning disability, or an emotional problem. Whatever the reason, it needs to be identified and dealt with.

Some students have simply never deciphered the phonics code. They probably learned to read by sight at younger levels and have relied on sight method crutches which become very inadequate at older levels. Many people unconsciously figure out phonics principles on their own as they read, whether or not they have actually been taught phonics; but many do not. For those who need a phonics foundation, use a remedial program rather than one designed for young children. These students already feel "dumb" and giving them childish materials validates their feelings.

Professor Phonics has a simple-to-use remedial program in a single book, *Sound Track to Reading*. This is a good resource for those with minor problems who need to review or solidify phonetic concepts.

For those who need basic phonics instruction, the people who originally published *Sing, Spell, Read, and Write* (CBN Publishing) have put together a program for older students called *Winning*. The content is very similar to the younger level program, but everything has been rewritten to appeal to pre-teens through adults. The program uses multi-sensory learning methods. There are six cassette tapes, four consumable student workbooks, two card games, four instructor's manuals, and a carrying case. Instead of the cute little songs of *Sing, Spell, Read, and Write*, we now have catchy rap, blues, country, and swing style songs to teach phonetic concepts. Games and workbooks provide reinforcement and writing practice. Art work and stories both reflect the interests of teens and adults.

Discover Intensive Phonics is a complete phonics program that can be used with all ages. There are no readers or other content that is age specific. Much of the learning takes place in one-on-one instruction at a chalkboard (or whiteboard,

etc.) This is a serious, no frills approach, but it works well for students who want to learn to read and spell quickly.(S)

Some students understand and use phonics, but read so slowly that their comprehension is limited. Unless there is a vision problem or learning disability, students need to spend more time practicing reading to increase their speed. Comprehension also may be poor simply because students have never learned to think about what they read. Comprehension activity workbooks are easily available from teacher supply stores and sources such as Builder Books and Shekinah Curriculum Cellar listed in the Appendix.

The Amsco Language Arts Catalog lists a number of resources that will be useful for developing comprehension skills. *High Marks: Stories That Make Good Reading* (Amsco) features twenty-two short stories from authors such as Leo Tolstoy, O. Henry, H.G. Wells, and Nathaniel Hawthorne as well as some from less well-known authors. While some of these are similar or even identical to stories found in anthologies, because they are printed in a large type style in a smaller book, the reading seems less intimidating. Stories are also short enough to keep the interest of reluctant readers. Each story is followed by questions covering main idea, fact recall, word meanings, plus a variety of other reading skills.(S)

Amsco also publishes a series of three books in the same type of format entitled, *The Reader as Detective*. Book I has a readability level of grades 5-7; Book II, grades 6-8; and Book III, grades 7-9. Reading selections are "high-interest and suspenseful," again, to involve the reluctant reader. Stories are interrupted sometimes once, sometimes more frequently, to challenge the reader to analyze the clues in the story thus far and answer some questions. The denouement of each story follows a challenge to the reader to figure it out for himself. The idea works something like the Encyclopedia Brown books (popular with younger readers), but at a more advanced level. Questions with each story have to do with factual recall, inferences, and understanding word meanings. Examples of stories are "The Adventure of the Red-Headed League" (Doyle), "A Retrieved Reformation" (O. Henry), "The Disappearing Man" (Asimov), and "The Tiger's Heart" (Kjelgaard). All of the Amsco books have inexpensive answer keys available. Check their catalog for other titles.(S)

Even if you use one of the resources mentioned above, one of the most effective ways to increase comprehension is to have the student read a selection of his choice out loud, and at the conclusion ask him questions about both details and meaning.

Reading skills are so vital to all other academic studies that it might be better to spend a few months on nothing other than reading to bring those skills up to a satisfactory level. Students can catch up in other subjects later, since their improved reading skills will enable them to work more quickly and with more retention than before.

What Should Our Children Read?

Not everything in print is worth reading. Some of it is even harmful. Unfortunately, this is true of much of what passes for "teen literature" today.

➠ **What Are Your Kids Reading?: The Alarming Trend in Today's Teen Literature** by Jill Carlson (Word Inc., formerly Wolgemuth and Hyatt)

Those of us who are alarmed at tales of horror and the occult, sexual perversion, and dysfunctional families that dominate teen literature are told that such "realistic" themes are used because they appeal to today's teens.

Jill Carlson became concerned about the abundance of such books and the extremely limited availability of morally uplifting alternatives, particularly in public libraries and school libraries. She wrote *What Are Your Kids Reading?* to alert parents to the danger of the current pro-reading philosophy that says, "It doesn't matter what kids read, just so they read."

Seemingly, no standards other than "will the kids read them" are applied in library literature selection. Unfortunately, libraries are not usually considering the increasingly well-written literature from Christian publishers. There seems to be a blindness to the fact that some of these books, such as *This Present Darkness*, are selling hundreds of thousands of copies and deserve a place in our public libraries.

Carlson outlines strategies for influencing book purchases at your local schools and libraries. She relates the stories of successful activists in a number of communities. Usually their strategies concentrated on adding good literature rather than challenging what was already there (although some of the so-called literature can be challenged under pornography laws).

While Carlson's book is not written for home educators, it is written for people who use libraries. Our children tend to read lots of books. Most of us can't afford to buy every book our children read, so we depend heavily upon libraries. When our children are young, it is fairly easy to screen books for content. Older children are choosing lengthier books, making it increasingly difficult for us to find time to preview them. Yet, according to the study done by Carlson and her assistants on teen literature, it certainly is not a good idea to encourage our children to read most of what is offered at the library. They studied a random sampling of forty-five popular titles for many content areas such as life views, sexual attitudes, the role of God in lives of characters, problem solving strategies, and faithfulness in marriage. The data from the study is supplied in the back of the book. Summaries of the story lines of the "studied" books are provided, so that we can get an idea of themes addressed. We cannot help but conclude that today's teen literature has serious problems.

Carlson offers summaries of fourteen "good books." Many, but not all, are from Christian publishers. We can recommend these titles to our local libraries, or purchase and donate them to help our librarians see that there are many, many worthy books available that do not appear in their review magazines and journals.

I recommend *What Are Your Kids Reading?* for two reasons. First, we need to use discernment in what we encourage our children to read, recognizing that so-called teen books are often filled with spiritually deadly content. The second reason is that someone has to help our libraries improve the contents of their shelves. Why not home educating families who have to be among the most frequent of library patrons? This book will provide you with data and strategies for improving the situation.

Many of us have recognized problems in popular literature and have set restrictive guidelines. Yet, often our hold on those guidelines is shaky. *Reading Between the Lines* will help.

➠ **Reading Between the Lines: A Christian Guide to Literature** by Gene Edward Veith, Jr. (Crossway Books)

Do you have trouble figuring out what types of books your children should or should not read? I have been told by many home educators that they allow their children to read only books that are true. But we overlook an important aspect of literature when we do this. When an author writes a biography about a person who lived a century or more in the past, and there is little first hand information about him or her (such as diaries, eye-witness reports, letters to friends, etc.), we must ask ourselves how much of that biography will be true and how much is manufactured to fill in the blanks of the author's knowledge. Do such biographies constitute truth any more than do stories that are written about fictional characters but based upon real-life events? The only written work that is wholly true is the Bible. Everything else has the possibility of containing untruth. If we do not want to restrict our children's reading to only the Bible, we must wrestle with the issue of what is acceptable.

Reading Between the Lines helps us to sort through the different factors relating to our Christian faith, literary value, and enjoyment when choosing reading material. Veith, a university instructor, loves literature, and because of this he promotes guidelines that some of us might feel are too liberal. However, as you read this book, you will probably do some rethinking about your view of literature. Even with the area of fantasy, which seems to be one of the biggest problem areas, he does an excellent job of explaining how to differentiate between that which is worthwhile and that which is not.

For those of us with a poor literary background, this book provides an excellent mini-course in literature. Veith piques our interest by quoting from various authors, and whetting our appetites for "the whole story." You are likely to find yourself making a list of books that you need to read. Some of us might find ourselves overwhelmed if we try to read this entire book straight through. I recommend taking a leisurely approach, reading those sections that are most pertinent to our concerns first and others as we find the time or need.

Remediating Handwriting and Spelling

If our teenagers still have abominable handwriting, it is tempting to just let them use the computer and give up on efforts to improve handwriting. However, there are going to be times when they will need to be able to take notes or communicate without the aid of a computer or typewriter. If they cannot write important information quickly and legibly, they are going to be handicapped. Spelling presents the same sort of problem. Poor spellers are in the same boat as sloppy writers since they have trouble deciphering what they have written.

Often, the two deficiencies go hand in hand. Putting these students into typical texts where they practice more of the same, in the same ways, is not very helpful. One resource written particularly for these students is *Writing Skills for the Adolescent* by Diana King (Educators Publishing Service). The author covers handwriting, grammar, spelling, typing, and composition instruction methods for dyslexic and dysgraphic students. She offers strategies that work from her experience with many struggling students.(S)

Cursive Writing Skills (also by Diana King from Educators Publishing Service), in editions for right-handers and left-handers, should be used along with *Writing Skills for the Adolescent*.(S)

Remediating Composition Skills

Some students are still unable to write a coherent paragraph by junior high. This sometimes occurs because of learning disabilities that, like reading problems, need to be professionally diagnosed. More often this occurs because students have not been taught and have not practiced writing. The process is dependent to a large degree upon the teacher, and many of us doubt our ability to teach our children to write since our own writing skills are poor. We must overcome our inadequacies and establish a writing discipline for our students. There are resources (see below) that will help with the first part, but the discipline is up to us. We must have our children writing frequently. However, lengthy writing assignments are discouraging to poor writers, so it is much better to have many small assignments rather than a few lengthy ones.

A crucial factor in stimulating writing skills is our reaction. If students write papers that we simply check off and toss in the trash, we communicate to them that their writing is worthless. If we discuss their writing, with both praise and constructive criticism, have them rewrite to improve it, then "publish" their final result by passing it around for others to see, we send the message that their writing is of value and interest to others. It is obvious which message will stimulate them to writing excellence. This is the kind of approach that can never come from a textbook.

If language arts skills are up to par we can then move on to more challenging goals.

Language Arts Goals

Approximately 6th through 8th grade levels

- Read widely at challenging levels with comprehension
- Develop a love for reading
- Use plural possessives and contractions
- Recognize and write compound sentences
- Identify and write topic sentences
- Write outlines
- Apply proper word usage in writing and speech
- Write using correct punctuation including quotation marks, indentation, colon, and semicolons
- Write compositions, dialogue, simple poetry, short research papers, book reports
- Write business and friendly letters
- Write with unity and coherence
- Proofread and edit their own work
- Use dictionary to locate word origins, dictionary spellings (pronunciations), usages
- Recognize and diagram basic parts of speech: subject, verb, adjectives, adverbs, prepositions, conjunctions*
- Recognize prepositional phrases
- Recognize appositives and direct address
- Recognize helping and linking verbs
- Identify predicate adjective and predicate nominative/noun
- Diagram predicate adjective and predicate nominative*
- Diagram more complicated sentences*
- Understand use of italics
- Recognize and use simple similes and metaphors
- Use a thesaurus or the *Synonym Finder*
- Take notes from printed and oral material
- Use card catalog, or the modern computer equivalent, and other reference materials
- Organize information from reference materials for reports
- Write research paper including bibliography (7th-8th grade)
- Give oral reports
- Participate in discussions
- Give oral presentations in front of a group, with attention given to body movements, voice, enunciation, speed, eye contact, and effectiveness of presentation

* or use Winston Grammar or other methods for identifying parts of speech

High School Goals

Model Curriculum Standards, Grades Nine through Twelve, first edition (California Department of Education)[5], sums up what they call the <u>prerequisites</u> for high school language arts work with the following:

Students who are most likely to succeed in this [high school] curriculum are: (1) those who have acquired a core of knowledge about people, ideas, and literature which equips

5   Language Arts goals have been slightly modified in the new *English Language Arts, Model Curriculum Standards, Grades Nine through Twelve*. The new edition presents "...an elaboration of each standard together with a few detailed representative activities." Activities are classroom oriented, but many are useful for home education.

them to take on more sophisticated materials; (2) those who have learned to listen and speak in a variety of situations and are thus able to engage in discussions of central literary issues; (3) those who have written about topics that have meaning to them and are thus prepared to express their convictions with greater clarity; and (4) those who have acquired basic reading and study skills.

The first area has to do with the idea of cultural literacy that was discussed in the first part of this book. This comes primarily from reading. There is simply no adequate substitute. Students who have read widely have a foundation upon which to build additional knowledge. Those with a limited foundation read and discuss with limited understanding. A good example that comes to mind is a column that runs in our county newspaper once a week. A reporter stations himself at some public location and asks passersby a current events or opinion question such as: "Should the United States help to support Israel financially?" The answers usually reflect total ignorance of the background of the situation. Typical answers sound like, "The people are poor so we should share with those who have less than we do." Or, "The countries that are closer to Israel should be helping them." The scary thing is that answers rarely sound any more well informed than this! To help our children become culturally literate, our language arts curricula should include extensive reading over a broad range of subject areas.

The second area—listening and speaking—also is not covered by a textbook. Instead we must interact with our children. Then they must interact with other people. They need to practice listening with care to what someone is saying. They need to practice clearly expressing their own thoughts both one-on-one and in front of a group. We need to see that they have opportunity to practice speaking beyond specifying their daily needs. (That also means we have to practice being good listeners.) Public speaking opportunities must be arranged whether in front of a small group of home schoolers, our family and friends, or a more varied group. Public speaking only becomes easier with plenty of experience. If we provide the opportunities for experience in less threatening situations at younger ages, public speaking will come more easily later on.

The third area is the ability to express oneself in written form. This includes both the proper use of the English language (grammar, spelling, and vocabulary) and composition skills.

Many students (and parents) have trouble comprehending a reason for learning grammar and parts of speech. It is generally acknowledged that a knowledge of grammar does not clearly correlate to excellence in writing, so learning grammar to write well should not be your only rationale for grammar instruction.

What has been recognized is that students who read a great deal usually write well. This is because they are familiar with how written language should sound. Students who do not read much, usually do not write well. So, if we wish to improve our child's writing skills, one of the most important things we should do is encourage them to read from a broad selection of well-written books.

While there is no direct correlation between grammar knowledge and good writing, grammar provides the common vocabulary for discussing writing. We can encourage our child to write more colorful sentences by using descriptive adjectives and adverbs if he understands what adjectives and adverbs are and which words they describe. We can also do this by asking questions such as, "How did the boy run?," but grammar vocabulary provides a much more efficient way of doing this. Additionally, grammatical knowledge will help to "fine tune" writing for those who go on to do much writing later in life.

We have also found that knowledge of English grammar is essential for learning a foreign language beyond a conversational level. We need a common vocabulary of grammatical definitions to learn corresponding parts of speech in the new language. The application of grammar concepts in a foreign language also provides both a reinforcement of and incentive for further learning of English. As an extra bonus, knowledge of a foreign language often results in improved English vocabulary.

Spelling and vocabulary can be combined as one subject, included in other language arts activities, or dealt with individually. The majority of students profit most from vocabulary work at high school level. Spelling of common words should be mastered by high school level, and dictionary skills should be adequate for looking up the more difficult words. For students who need some spelling review, a list of the most commonly misspelled words is included in this manual. (See "Most Commonly Misspelled Words" in the Appendix.) If a student spells well, let him concentrate on vocabulary rather than spelling.

Composition skills can be divided into creative, experiential, and expository writing, although dividing lines are not always clear. Creative writing consists of all of those "fun ideas"—imaginary newspapers, "The Day I Turned into a Piece of Chewing Gum," and other nonsense—along with short stories, poetry, and other fiction writing. Students write about about and from their own experiences in experiential writing. Expository writing includes reports, essays, themes, and research papers—the types of writing that most of us find least enjoyable. Most basic textbooks deal with all these types of writing, and many supplementary books specialize in particular areas.

The fourth area of prerequisites deals with reading and study skills. Study skills have already been discussed in Chapter Three. Reading skills should be good enough that we need not devote school time to reading instruction. The study of literature is different than reading instruction and should begin in junior high. Students will spend time studying literature in depth, becoming familiar with renowned authors of both past and present.

What we have just discussed are the areas that *Model Curriculum Standards'* authors say are prerequisite to high school level work, yet most of our students are working on developing some of these skills as they enter high school, so do not be alarmed if your child has not mastered all of these goals before high school—he is probably about where most other students are. However, if he is weak in a number of language arts areas, these should receive attention before other subjects since language art skills are necessary for success in other areas of study.

A Summary of Goals

To sum up our goals at high school level—for the majority of students, the most important goal is improvement in writing and communication skills. Grammar, spelling, and vocabulary may be learned or reviewed depending upon prior knowledge. Literature should be studied. All of these aspects of language arts should be balanced to complete the English requirement. Three years of English are required by many states for graduation, while many colleges and universities require four. While English courses may concentrate on one area or another from year to year, over the high school years all of the above areas need to be addressed.

Language Art Tools

No matter what else students use, they need a few basics.

Dictionary: Do not buy a children's dictionary unless it is because of a problem such as learning disabilities. An unabridged dictionary is essential to avoid the frustration of being unable to locate a word simply because it has not been included.

The facsimile reprints of Webster's original *American Dictionary of the English Language* (Foundation for American Christian Education) are useful for looking up definitions of archaic words or some words that we encounter in British Literature.

Grammar Handbook: There are lots of choices, and it does not matter much which we choose. The *Write Source/Basic English Revisited* versions, *Composition Handbook* (Longman Publishing), BJUP Handbook, or others will all do the job. The object is to have an easy-to-use reference for grammatical details rather than trying to sort through a textbook.

Thesaurus: Stretching to find just the right word is a hallmark of a good writer. It is expected that writers will consult a thesaurus rather than have all of the possibilities on the tips of their tongues. I particularly like the *Synonym*

THE COMPUTER AND LANGUAGE ARTS

Language Arts subjects are probably the best excuse for purchasing a computer for your home school. Most of the drill exercises that are available for other subjects can be duplicated with workbooks, but nothing other than an actual word processor can compete with the computer's value as a word processor.

If we truly want to have our teenagers writing prolifically and working through the writing process—planning, organizing, writing, and revising—the best encouragement we can give them is a tool that eliminates the busy work. When students use the computer, they can make corrections without rewriting the whole paper. Some of us can remember retyping term papers in the good old typewriter days. One rewrite was probably the most we could manage. With a computer, all that is needed to rewrite is to plug in a few corrections and make another printout.

A word processing program is essential. It does not have to be expensive. *Bank Street Writer, Apple Works,* and similar programs will get kids started. I understand that some public domain word processors are quite good, so you could experiment with one or two of those at minimal cost. If you can afford it, I strongly recommend getting a good word processing program such as *Microsoft Word* or *Word Perfect.*

Finder by J.I. Rodale (Warner Books) and other thesauruses that include figures of speech and slang expressions.

Grammar and Composition Resources for 7th and 8th Grades

Basic texts

➠Building Christian English 7 and 8 (Rod and Staff)

Building Securely is the subtitle for the seventh grade book. This is a hardback student text with a heavy emphasis on grammar. Godly character receives strong emphasis in the content. Rod and Staff covers grammatical concepts by eighth grade that other publishers spread out through high school, so this text is more difficult than others for seventh grade. It is too detailed for the needs of some students and has extra busywork that should be used only as needed. Using the exercises selectively helps overcome any problems this presents.

Preparing for Usefulness, the subtitle for the eighth grade book, accurately reflects the shift from grammar to application at this level. Remaining elements of grammar are covered, but, more importantly, students work with many forms of written communication. Then, an entire unit concentrates on speaking and listening. Research techniques are also taught. This book requires the use of the *Rod and Staff English Handbook.*

Teacher's manuals and test booklets are available for both seventh and eighth grade texts.

I appreciate the fact that Rod and Staff is one of the rare publishers who recognizes that grammar skills can be mastered in much less than twelve years.

➠English 7 and 8 (McDougal, Littell, and Co.)[1988 edition]

Student books are hardback texts, and workbooks and teacher's editions are available but not necessary. These are excellent texts that do a good job of helping students find reasons to want to write. Grammar is comprehensive with an emphasis on application, but there is a very minimal amount of diagramming. The writing part of the program is outstanding with lots of creativity. The text is set up such that we can use the composition lessons or grammar lessons according to our needs.(S) (1990 edition is available)

➠Grammar and Composition 1 and 2 (A Beka)

In these worktexts for seventh and eighth grades the emphasis is more on grammar than writing. If students have been using A Beka until seventh grade, they have had a lot of grammar already. We might choose to use only one of these books or switch to BJUP or another publisher to put less emphasis on grammar. (If they are really having problems with grammar, consider *Winston Grammar.*) When using these texts, be sure to have students do extra composition work. The Teacher's Edition is the student worktext with answers (your answer key). The Teacher's *Curriculum Guide for English 7* gives daily lesson plans correlating grammar, literature, vocabulary and spelling from A Beka books.

➠Harvey's Revised English Grammar (Mott Media)

While this book can be used in junior high, it is a comprehensive grammar text which can also be used through high school. It is a revised edition of a nineteenth century text, which is evident in some of the subject matter and vocabulary as well as the style of presentation. The book is divided into four parts: orthography (study of letters, syllables, sounds, and spelling), etymology (meaning parts of speech, tense, number, mode, and other attributes of words as they are used in sentences), syntax (study of punctuation plus the study of sentences, their elements, and the relationships of parts), and prosody (study of accent, quality and tone of language as well as technical aspects of poetry). Harvey's goes beyond any grammar texts commonly used today, particularly in the fourth section. An answer key is available.

➠ **Learning Language Arts through Literature** (Family Learning Center)

Gray Book

The *Gray Book* (for 7th-9th grades) has twenty-five lessons. Because of variations in time needed for each lesson, each book has enough material for one school year. This language arts curriculum is based upon ideas from Ruth Beechick's books. Literary passages from books such as the *Bible, The Black Arrow, A Little Princess, A Tale of Two Cities, Moby Dick,* and *White Fang* are the foundation for study each week. Students practice taking the passages by dictation. Using the passage as a springboard, they study and apply grammar, spelling, vocabulary, and writing skills. The method is "whole language" in that all language skills are taught in relationship to one another. Lessons are also keyed to *Learning Grammar through Writing* for those who wish to use that book as a grammar reference/text, although other grammar books can be used instead. Large-print copies of the literary passages, called Student Editing Models, are also included in the back of each book to make it easier for students to either copy or correct their work.

A section at the beginning of each book provides specific teaching methods for each of the language arts areas, plus suggestions for including younger children and for multi-level teaching.

The bibliography at the end of the book can also serve as a reading list.

Some students might need more in-depth work in particular language arts areas than is provided within these books, so you might use other materials to round out your curriculum. Even though this curriculum lacks the review and repetition we find in most others, the effectiveness of the methods used here should help children to learn better without frequent repetition. The scope and sequence is a little unusual, but the Skill Index at the back of the book lists the goals of each lesson so that we can identify each skill area covered. All of the concepts covered in typical language arts programs for junior high receive attention, and writing skills are well developed. In addition to instruction in mechanics and composition, the lessons are also designed to provoke an interest in good literature that will take children beyond the small literary excerpts included in the lessons.

Lessons are presented by the teacher, and students maintain their work in a notebook. There are no extra costs for student workbooks, and the book itself is non-consumable.

The books are written by Christian home educators and reflect Christian attitudes, although religious perspectives are not dealt with in studying every literary selection. For instance, a selection from *White Fang* by Jack London does not deal with London's atheistic philosophy. However excerpts such as those from the Bible and the work of Francis Schaeffer do provide Scriptural lessons.

➠ **Macmillan English 7 and 8**
(Macmillan/McGraw-Hill—School Division)

This 1987 series looks better than others from secular publishers. It appears to be similar to McDougal, Littell's series. Composition instruction uses creative ideas while covering basics of the writing process. There is strong emphasis on grammar and usage, and the format is eye-catching and colorful. Strands for composition and grammar are intermixed rather than separated as in McDougal, Littell's *English*.(S)

➠ **Macmillan English: Thinking and Writing Processes 7 and 8** (Macmillan/McGraw-Hill—School Division)

This series is very similar to *Macmillan English* above, but formatted like McDougal, Littell, with grammar and composition strands separated. It is not quite as colorful as *Macmillan English*. The Teacher's Edition is easy to use and has practical guidelines for evaluating student's written work, an aid many home educators will find useful.(S)

➠ **Understanding Writing** by Susan Bradrick

subtitle: A Christ-centered, Mastery-oriented English Language and Composition Curriculum for Grades 1-12

In *Understanding Writing* Susan Bradrick has successfully combined the teaching of language and composition skills in a format that adapts easily to multi-level teaching and is totally Christ-centered in philosophy. This is an approach to writing that places equal emphasis on development of skills and development of godly character.

Although it is quite comprehensive, literature is not included. Two supplemental resources, *Easy Grammar* and *Easy Writing,* are incorporated into the program at junior high level to improve skills in those areas. Also, the author recommends that we have a grammar handbook available for reference for all levels.

This one-inch-thick book is divided into three parts: "Part I, 'Rethinking Writing' deals with the theory behind an effective approach for studying English composition; Part II, 'Understanding the Basic Elements of Writing', discusses the elements of content, style, and mechanics essential for effective writing and gives examples of each; Part III, 'Teaching the Basic Elements of Writing',...provides detailed lessons for teaching your child to master the content, style, and mechanical skills of effective, God-honoring written communication."

Although Part III is divided into twelve levels, they need not necessarily correlate to grade levels. Instead, we should use the Diagnostic Check List in the Appendix to identify which goals have been accomplished within each level, then determine from there a starting point for each child. Children of varying skill levels can easily be instructed at the same time upon a new concept, then work at their ability level in their individual writing time. (The Bradricks have used this method successfully with their nine children.) Each child maintains an "English notebook" (folder or three-ring binder containing drafts of written work rather than copied exercises), so there is no need to purchase student books other than dictionaries or thesauruses.

Students working in Levels 7-12 should be able to do much of their work independently. A well-motivated student who begins *Understanding Writing* in grades 9-12 should be able to read through the curriculum on his own, doing necessary exercises (identified by the Diagnostic

Check List) as he encounters them, thus learning at his own pace the concepts he has not yet mastered.

For students working under a parent/teacher, lessons are structured in units with daily assignments which include a balance of discussion and writing time that varies according to a child's level. While most lessons require no parent preparation time, the few that do state this clearly at the beginning of the lesson.

Children write about personal experiences and observations rather than fiction until the high school level where they branch out into creative and expository writing. Suggested topics are included in the Appendix. Because the thrust of this curriculum is mastery of God-honoring communication, most composition assignments are to be written for a specific reader. They are also to be actually delivered (usually in letter form) to that individual so that a habit of skillful, genuine communication is the result of the student's writing study.

A reproducible "Composition Planning and Evaluation Sheet" is used to help students think through their composition before they begin, then provide key areas for parents to address in their evaluations. (These sheets are also available from the publisher in pads of fifty, three-hole-punched sheets.)

Understanding Writing is well-structured with clear goals yet it retains flexibility enough for multi-level teaching.

➡ Warriner's English Composition and Grammar (Harcourt Brace Jovanovich) First Course (Grade 7) and Second Course (Grade 8)

These are the highly regarded Warriner series English books which have appeared in a number of editions. The current edition, renamed *Elements of Writing* (described below), reflects significant changes from these earlier editions. These books are complete and well written, reflecting traditional teaching methods. The writing process and composition assignments are excellent. As with any school-designed texts, repetition from year to year is heavy. You might choose to use one text more slowly over a few years or else concentrate grammar and composition study into a shorter time span, then work on application in composition and speech for the next few years. Teacher's Editions are helpful, especially for the inexperienced parent, although they are quite expensive. The answer key for grammar exercises is found in the Teacher's Edition, which alone may be reason enough for its purchase. If you are strong in grammar and can correct work without an answer key, then the student text alone can suffice.

Following the merging of Harcourt Brace Jovanovich with Holt, Rinehart and Winston has come a revision of the Warriner series. The new series is entitled *Elements of Writing*. It is co-authored by Dr. James L. Kinneavy, who strengthens the composition aspects of the series. It emphasizes composition instruction, with grammatical instruction presented within that context. Literary models are included within each text as learning tools. This helps students learn both grammar and composition skills within the context of actual usage, which helps with motivation and retention of information. Writing assignments are defined more by process than topic, which gives students much more room to individualize their writing than do assignments found in some other texts.

Grammar is also presented separately in the second part of the book. It can serve as a handbook (particularly when used in conjunction with exercises in the first part of the book), and it also has exercises, diagnostic tests, review/posttests, and writing assignments.

Following the grammar section are chapters on speaking, listening, library/media, dictionary, vocabulary, letters and forms, and studying and test taking. An appendix covers diagramming.

There is quite a bit of overlap in content from year to year in each, although some new topics are presented in each text. Various types of writing activities would be the most prominent difference between the First and Second Course texts. Consider using a single text over a two-year period rather than buying separate ones for each year, since there is plenty of material in any one book. (The Second Course book is 972 pages!)

The look has been updated with color and illustrations. As with the original series, The First Course and Second Course are for seventh and eighth grades respectively. Student books are about $30 and the Annotated Teacher's Editions run around $50. (Order from Holt, Rinehart and Winston.)(S)

➡ Wordsmith: A Creative Writing Course for Young People by Janie B. Cheaney

Junior high tends to be a transition time for many students, particularly in the area of language arts. However, most curricula for this level simply repeats what has already been taught, instead of stretching students in new directions.

Wordsmith skillfully fills the gap between elementary and high school learning. It can be used with children as young as ten or eleven, and with high school students whose writing skills are undeveloped.

Wordsmith assumes that the student knows basic grammar. It moves on from there to work with grammar through written applications. For example, one assignment has them come up with vivid action verbs to replace weak verbs accompanied by adverbs. The goal is to sharpen writing skills by choosing words carefully for the best effect.

After working on grammar, they tackle sentence construction, again with the goal of writing more interesting yet concise sentences. Once grammar and sentence structure are under control, they can apply those skills to composition writing.

Although *Wordsmith* does not teach all the different forms of writing such as reports, research papers, etc., it covers techniques that can be applied in almost any writing situation. Lessons work on skills such as describing people, narrowing the topic, and writing dialogue. At the end, students write their own short story.

Helps on proofreading and editing are included.

The student book may be written in, or used as a reusable text by doing the brief activities in a notebook. Lesson organization is clear and well-designed. Some teaching, primarily in the form of discussion and evaluation, is required, although students will do much of the work on their own. The author's humorous touches scattered throughout the book add special appeal.

A bright, motivated student might be able to work through the book in a semester or less, although most students should need a year or more.

Parents who lack confidence in their ability to teach students how to write will appreciate the inexpensive Teacher's Guide. It includes answers, lesson plans, teaching suggestions, and ideas for expanding lessons. Parents with strong writing skills will probably be able to manage without it.

Other books attempt to meet the same goals, but the presentation here is better than anything similar at this level.

➧Writing and Grammar 7 and 8 (BJUP)

Seventh and eighth grade BJUP language courses should be used as parts one and two of a series. The Teacher's Editions are essential for a complete program. The student workbooks serve as practice and reinforcement rather than as the primary source of instruction. There is a good balance of grammar and composition, but lessons do seem to jump from topic to topic, sometimes with insufficient coverage. However, these books are much stronger than A Beka's *Language* in writing instruction. Christian themes flow through each course, helping to provide a rationale to students for learning language skills.

Extras or Alternatives for Junior High Level

Grammar

➧Amsco School Publications (Amsco)

Amsco has a Language Arts catalog listing many resources appropriate for junior high through adult learners. Their books work well for home education because they are designed for independent learning, generally in a worktext format. They are inexpensively priced, and, instead of costly teacher's editions, they sell very low priced answer keys. Available titles cover a wide range of topics. Examples: *Essentials of English, Laugh Your Way through Grammar* (lower, upper, or remedial levels), and *English Alive.*(S)

➧Basic Language Principles with Latin Background (Educators Publishing Service)

With this book, students review basic English grammar with beginning instruction in Latin. It jumps around too much to be used as a basic Latin course, but serves as a thorough introduction. It helps students to see how knowledge of grammar is used in learning foreign languages.(S)

➧Caught'ya!: Grammar with a Giggle by Jane Bell Kiester (Maupin House Publishing)

Grammar review can be truly customized using Jane Kiester's ideas from *Caught'ya!* The teacher uses a story (already written by someone else or invented) as the primary vehicle for review. It helps if the story is funny or takes unexpected twists and turns. Each day the teacher writes a few sentences on the board, leaving out all capitalization and punctuation. Students copy the sentences, putting in proper capitalization and punctuation. Vocabulary words can be incorporated. Stories/sentences can be adapted to review whatever grammatical skills students need. *Caught'ya* outlines the methodology and includes three sample stories—one each for grades 3-5, grades 6-8, and grades 9-11. Since the book is not written for Christian audiences, you might want to find or make up your own stories rather than use these. (I suggest using stories with which your children are not familiar to maintain their interest in "What happens next?") However, the stories will give you excellent models with which to work.

This method is truly fun, and it works well across fairly wide age spans at junior/senior high levels. We used this method very successfully for one year with our boys when they ranged from ages 11-16.

A sequel with more stories, *Caught'ya Again!* should be available by the time this manual is printed.(SE)

➧Easy Grammar (ISHA Enterprises)

This is one very large book of bare bones instruction on grammar with exercise pages. Answer key and reproducible student pages are both included in one big book, or we can buy the big book and separate books of student pages if photocopying is a problem. One key difference from other approaches is the presentation of prepositions and prepositional phrases first to eliminate confusion in identifying subjects, objects, indirect objects, and objects of prepositions. We tried this idea with our youngest, and it worked well. It gets a bit boring to do nothing but *Easy Grammar* work sheets, so we use these as a supplement to other things. It is not age graded, so it can be used for many years and grade levels.(S)

➧Exploring Truths: A Systematic Approach to Learning English Through the Bible (Alpha Omega)

This is a complete study of parts of speech using Scripture. Use with *Diagramming* book below. This is a good tool for concentrating study of parts of speech rather than spreading it out over many years.

➧Exploring Truths through Diagramming: A Systematic Approach to Learning English Through Diagrams Based on the Book of Joshua (Alpha Omega)

This is a complete course for diagramming. Accompanies *Exploring Truths* above.

➧Grammar Songs - Learning with Music by Katherine Troxel (Audio Memory)

This is grammar instruction through music—appealing on junior high level and below. The songs are not too "young" for junior high as is true for so many other cassette instructional materials. The songs, professionally recorded on cassette tape, teach parts of speech, punctuation, sentence structure, capitalization, Greek and Latin suffixes and prefixes, and more. The basic set includes a seventy-two page student workbook and a teacher's guide that helps us coordinate the tape and workbook with a few extra activities. This really helps as a supplement, particularly for parts of speech, regardless of what other approach we use.

➧Practice Exercises in Basic English 7 or 8 (Continental Press)

This small workbook covers basic skills except diagramming. Use this with *Easy Grammar* or *Winston Grammar* and a writing supplement for a "minimalist" approach.(S)

➧Rules of the Game (Educators Publishing Service)

This is a series of three, softbound workbooks that teach grammar by the inductive method. That means that rather than telling students a "rule" and following it with exercises, students are led to discover a general principle or definition for themselves. In actuality, the amount of discovery is quite minimal, but it still is a more interesting way to introduce grammar concepts. Once the concept has been presented, students practice with a variety of exercises. Like *Easy Grammar,* this is a more concise means of learning grammar, and it can be used with children of widely varying ages—from about fifth grade through high school. Book 1 covers: nouns, pronouns, subjects, verbs, capitalization, punctuation, sentences, contractions, possessives, adjectives, adverbs, prepositions, interjections, conjunctions, compounds, and subject/verb agreement.

Book 2 briefly reviews the above, then continues with: direct and indirect objects, linking verbs, predicate nouns and adjectives, appositives, objects of prepositions, prepositional phrases, and punctuation. Book 3 works on dependent clauses, complex and compound-complex sentences, and verbals, while also supplying comprehensive application exercises for all previously learned grammatical elements. These inexpensive books are not reproducible, so purchase one for each student. Answer keys are also available at minimal cost.(S)

➠ Skills Bank Home Tutor [for IBM type machines] (Skills Bank Corporation)

See the description of the entire program where it first appears under math resources for junior high. The language module will help students with capitalization, grammar (including usage), punctuation, and spelling. While it is not comprehensive in all areas, it covers a lot of territory. Within each of the four areas listed, there are from eighteen to twenty-two topics covered at varying levels of difficulty. Some instruction is included with quizzes and on-line help. Student progress is tracked on each student's access disk, so we can see which topics have been covered and which of those have been mastered.(S)

➠ Winston Grammar by Paul Erwin (Educators Publishing Service)

This is a hands-on approach for learning parts of speech, some usage concepts, and sentence structure. Students use Clue Cards as well as worksheets which they mark with arrows, lines, and symbols to identify sentence components. Good for most students, it is especially recommended for those who have had difficulty with traditional methods. It is more fun than diagramming and accomplishes the same purpose. There are two kits, Basic and Advanced. The Basic level covers all parts of speech, noun functions, prepositional phrases, and modifiers. The Advanced level offers additional lessons on pronouns as well as verbals, clauses, and sentence types. However, *Winston Grammar* is not designed to offer complete coverage of all grammar topics that typically are taught in textbooks. The Teacher's Manual for each level has lesson plans and answer keys.

Composition

➠ Amsco School Publications (Amsco)

Amsco has a Language Arts catalog listing many resources appropriate for junior high through adult learners. Their books work well for home education because they are designed for independent learning, generally in a worktext format. They are inexpensively priced, and instead of costly teacher's editions, they sell very low priced answer keys. Available titles cover a wide range of topics. Examples: *Writing About Amusing Things* (good for paragraph development), *Writing Logically, Fifteen Steps to Better Writing*, and *Writing the Research Paper*.(S)

➠ Creative Writing (A Beka)

Use this creative writing workbook to round out A Beka's *Language* series. This is best used on younger levels, but if students have done no writing, it is a good place to begin.

➠ Easy Writing (ISHA Enterprises)

From the author of *Easy Grammar* comes a new approach to teaching writing. This is not a comprehensive writing program, but one that concentrates on sentence structure. Children learn how to write more interesting sentences by using conjunctions, subordinate clauses, particip

ial phrases, and other more complex structures. Each unit within the book is divided into an easier level and a more difficult level. Some children instinctively construct interesting sentences, but many do not. This book will help those children (and parents) who have difficulty writing sentences more interesting than "The boy chased the dog." Student work sheets are reproducible, so one book will serve for more than one child.

➠ Newspaper Workshop by Howard Decker (Globe Book Co.)

Students learn how a newspaper is written, then work through fun activities. Also purchase the teacher's manual.(S)

➠ Practicing the Writing Process (Educational Design)

This workbook on writing skills emphasizes technique. It contains a few sections that some might find objectionable, particularly a writing example about a dance performance that is used throughout the book. It is recommended for grades 4-high school, but it was designed for remedial teaching for older students. Students can work independently through this book to develop and improve writing skills.(SE)

➠ Report Writing (Continental Press)

Here is a concise book on how to do a research report, written in a very easy-to-read format. It is perfect for the reluctant researcher.(S)

➠ Skills Bank Home Tutor [for IBM type machines] (Skills Bank Corporation)

See the description of the entire program where it first appears under math resources for junior high. The writing module covers language mechanics (e.g., letter writing, error identification, quotations, comma usage), language usage (parts of speech in usage), sentence structure (syntax, patterns, construction, combinations), and paragraphs (organization and coherence). There are actually up to twelve separate topics addressed within each of the four described areas. Working through this module will help sharpen writing skills for students in preparation for high school level writing assignments.(S)

➠ Studying Poetry (Curriculum Associates)

Studying Poetry is a tool for introducing and developing poetry appreciation and writing skills. It begins with activities to develop awareness of what poetry is and helps tune students into sensory words and feelings which play a major part in poetry. The next section works on rhyming, followed by synonyms and antonyms. Students are then introduced to free verse, then the idea of painting pictures with words. (This middle section of the book is good for developing similar skills to use with any type of writing!) Students begin to search for just the right word to convey their meaning, while also learning how to use similes, metaphors, personification, hyperbole, and alliteration. Exercises that help students change general statements to specific sharpen their skills. Toward the end, various poetic forms are taught, including haiku, tercet, cinquain, limerick, quatrain, and narrative. The lessons do not get into meter, accent, and other more advanced poetic conventions.

The book is self-contained. Answers to pertinent exercises are in the back. Instruction and examples are provided, followed by activities or lines for writing exercises. Most junior high and all senior high students should be able to work through this book independently. There is a strong leaning toward feelings and emotions within the book (as is appropriate for poetry), but be aware that some students will find this type of study very uncomfortable and/or exceedingly difficult because of their personalities.(S)

➠ The Write Source, The Write Source 2000, Basic English Revisited, or Writers Inc (The Write Source)

Choose one of the first two books for junior high students or average to slow high school students. Choose either of the latter two books for advanced or more mature students. *The Write Source 2000* is the new, revised version of *The Write Source* (although the earlier version is suitable for students as young as fourth grade level); *Writers Inc* is a revised version of *Basic English Revisited*. Content in the newer editions emphasizes the writing process more than older editions. There are workbooks correlated to older editions.

These are student handbooks, to be used as reference tools by student writers. Writing is the primary emphasis, but also included are basics of grammar and speech as well as many extras to assist students in writing in every subject area. The books are easy to work with, coded for reference to exercises in the optional workbooks. These are terrific handbooks, with or without the workbooks. Handbooks can be used alone or with any language arts program, by all students at junior high or high school level. The cartoon style art work is especially appealing to teens.

A number of supplementary workbooks are available. *Basic Writing Workbook* reviews grammar with emphasis on the mechanics of writing (6th - 9th grades) and correlates to *The Write Source* and *Basic English Revisited* handbooks. Extra workbooks—*The Mechanics of Writing*, covering the mechanics of grammar, and *The Revising Process*, covering skills used in polishing written work—are available on two different levels for both *The Write Source* and *Basic English Revisited*.

Writers Inc and *Write Source 2000* reflect ideas from the new language arts frameworks with attention given to such things as the whole language approach, peer group work, and a more student-centered writing atmosphere. A teacher's guide to *Writers Inc,* called *Inc Sights,* is essential for figuring out how to use the *Writers Inc* handbook. It discusses various approaches to teaching writing, gives guidelines for evaluating student writing, tells when and how to refer students to the handbook, and provides more than 140 "mini-lessons" of writing ideas for high school students. *Writers Inc: Revising and Editing* (*Books* 1 and 2) "...provide students with instruction, strategies, and guidelines on revising, editing, and proofreading. The first book helps students with earlier stages of the writing process, while *Book 2* focuses on later stages. In most cases, choose *Book 1* for grades 9-10, and *Book 2* for grade 11-12. A teacher's guide similar to *INC Sights* is available for *Write Source 2000.* Workbooks for *Write Source 2000* are supposed to be purchased along with an expensive program binder for each level (grades 6, 7, and 8)—impractical for most home educators.

Write Source 2000 is loaded with ideas and activities to develop writing skills, while it also serves as a reference book for grammar, spelling, public speaking, study/test-taking/reading skills, and much more. Creative teachers can develop lessons from the handbook itself, while most others will prefer to work with the teacher's guide.

Do not depend upon the handbooks for elementary grammar instruction since they are designed for grammatical reference rather than as teaching tools. The *Mechanics of Writing* workbooks are helpful for grammar, but still assume that prior instruction has occurred.

Very inexpensive blank writing notebooks are also available. *A Daily Journal* is a blank book that has instruction and ideas for journal writing at the beginning. *Reflections* is another blank book that comes with helps for both ideas and idea development.(S)

➠ The Writer's Program, Books One through Four (Globe)

These are outstanding creative writing texts, that also deal with writing techniques. Each softbound book contains examples, pictures, instruction, and assignments. Most exercises are creative with no right or wrong answers. Students do not work in the books, so one book may be used with more than one student. The publisher offers these for ninth through twelfth grades, but they are appropriate for some seventh and eighth graders. There is some objectionable content that can easily be skipped.(SE)

➠ Writing A Short Story: A Creative Curriculum for 4th, 5th and 6th Grade Students by Lee Roddy and Lynn Brock (Roddy Publications)

Many of our home educated children list Lee Roddy's adventure stories at the top of their "favorite book" lists. Roddy knows how to grab a child's attention and keep the action moving toward a satisfying conclusion. In contrast, the stories our children write too often meander around in circles and dribble to an end when the author runs out of ideas. Now our children can write stories using the same techniques as Lee Roddy with the lessons provided in *Writing A Short Story*. Roddy wrote down the key steps in story writing, then turned it over to Lynn Brock, an experienced teacher, who organized the whole thing into manageable lesson plans.

The result is an easy-to-use teacher's manual, designed for teaching children working either individually or in groups. At the back of the book are reproducible pages for compiling a student "Story Book"—pages that help the student organize different aspects of the story writing process as they learn.

Objectives are clearly spelled out. Inexperienced teachers can follow lessons step-by-step, while more experienced teachers can choose elements from the lesson plans as they need. Brock has incorporated additional information about the lesson plans indicating which learning modalities (seeing, hearing, doing) are served within each lesson and which levels of Bloom's taxonomy of thinking skills are used. Preparation time is minimal. Any materials or background information needed are listed at the beginning of each lesson along with the approximate time the lesson should take. The entire book consists of fifteen lessons which you will probably want to use once or twice a week. This means that you could cover the material in a semester or less—unless your children won't stop writing.

Don't be put off by the 4th through 6th grade designation in the title. This book actually seems more appropriate for junior high because writing a short story requires the integration of many writing skills not yet mastered in earlier grades.

For the serious writers among our children, Lee Roddy has added a chapter at the end which shows how to prepare a manuscript for submission to a publisher. I expect that by using the techniques in this book, the efforts of some of our children will be good enough to publish!

➠ Writing for Life (Globe Book Co.)

This book is for the desperate parent who is concerned about his or her child's ability to write well enough to function. The book is written for the student writing at a very low level because of poor educational background, physical reasons, etc. The purpose is to develop functional skills. Students can work independently through the book because of its worktext format. However, most students who will need this type of book will also need supervision and interaction. Students begin by writing complete sentences, then paragraphs. Next they learn how to write telephone messages and notes as well as how to take notes about something they have read. Letters, addressing envelopes, writing invitations, directions, and thank-you notes are covered in the next section. Assuming that most students are in school, the next section covers class schedules, computerized test response forms, other school forms, and taking notes. (Substitute or add a job application here.) The last section deals with life: bank accounts, ordering by mail, and writing business letters.

Examples and exercises help students to break down tasks into manageable chunks before they tackle a task in its entirety. There is space for all work to be done in the book.(S)

➠ The Writing Program 7 and 8 (Modern Curriculum Press)

This series reflects the currently popular "whole language" approach. Reading and writing are strongly integrated to provide better motivation and understanding. Writing examples from literature, newspaper articles, plays, poetry, and other sources are used to illustrate writing principles. The examples are used also to stimulate ideas for writing. Excellent questions are provided within each exercise for students to evaluate and edit their own work. Sharing and "publishing" are the important conclusion to each lesson. Most lessons benefit from the interaction of two or more students, but they will still be effective used individually. This is a student text, not a workbook. Writing is done in a separate notebook. Parent/teacher involvement is essential and requires some lesson preparation time. Inexpensive Teacher's Guides are necessary at this level both for lesson presentation and the reproducible activity sheets found there. You might find some of the writing examples objectionable since they are secular in nature, but most home educators will have few problems with content.(SE)

➠ Writing Step by Step: Developing Paragraphs by Asking Questions by Mary Lou Ward (Builder Books)

Mary Lou Ward has developed some terrific ideas for helping children to see how simple the writing process can become with some "maps" to help them organize their ideas. She gives some basic questions for writers to ask themselves to get started with ideas, then shows how to string the ideas together with connective words to create a paragraph very simply. There are three sections in the book, one geared for lower grades, one for upper grades, and the last containing reproducible "maps" for students to use for writing projects. In the upper grades, students learn how to write a basic paragraph and organize their thoughts. Later they learn four other types of writing: explaining steps in a process, comparison and contrast, problem/cause, and cause/effect. Use this resource if your child is not yet able to write an orderly paragraph or has trouble organizing ideas.

➠ Writing Strands, Levels 6 and 7 (Revised editions) (National Writing Institute)

This is a great way to teach writing in the home school, especially for the parent with little writing experience. Lots of creative ideas, laid out step-by-step for (primarily) independent student work, set these books apart from others. Lessons are broken up into daily assignments to keep students from becoming overwhelmed. The strands (types of writing) within the books at these levels are argumentative, creative, explanatory, and report. (Developing skills in these areas will be important for high school level work.) The first editions of these books had content problems which are being corrected in the new editions.

The new Level 8 is not yet available, but author Dave Marks describes it for us. "Our new #8 is a fairly sophisticated creative writing book. It contains the creative writing assignments I have created for my son and used in my high school and college creative writing classes. It contains not just the assignments but the best of the papers and writings those assignments have produced. It is a program designed to teach a student to write short fiction."

Writing Strands is a good supplement to *Learning Language Arts through Literature* or *Understanding Writing*.

For extra help in developing good creative writing skills, check out the National Writing Institute's *Reading Strands*. It teaches parents how to use a Socratic method of instruction that can be used with children ages 4-18. Many of the sections that teach parents how to help children analyze what they are reading can be of great value as we are teaching writing. *Reading Strands* helps students develop reading interpretation skills, which in turn helps them think more about plot, characterization, motivation, etc. and how to translate those elements into interesting stories of their own.(S)

➠ Written and Illustrated by... by David Melton (Landmark Editions, Inc.)

Landmark Editions is the publisher of books which are written and illustrated by children. Every year they sponsor a contest to select such books for publication. *Written and Illustrated by...* is a teaching manual for helping children write, illustrate, assemble, and bind their own books. It has lesson plans, illustrations, and suggestions for working with all grade levels. Whether or not children choose to enter the contest, they can still learn to expand their creativity with the practical ideas provided here. To obtain a copy of the current Rules and Guidelines, send a self-addressed, business-sized envelope, stamped with $.52 postage to The National Written and Illustrated by... Awards Contest for Students at Landmark's address, listed in the appendix.(S)

➠ You Are the Editor (Fearon Teacher Aids)

This reproducible workbook has exercises for students to practice proofreading skills. This is good to use as they practice the writing process. Students should learn how to "proof" their own work and to read proofreading symbols (a form of shorthand) that are used to correct their work. The publisher will be discontinuing this book, so it will be available for a short time only.(S)

Listening Skills

➠ Learning To Listen (Educators Publishing Service)

For grades 7-9. This deals with the broader communication process rather than writing alone. This forty-eight page workbook takes students through eight basic listening skills: following directions, following a sequence, using context clues, using different skills for different subjects, finding topics and main ideas, listening for details, listening to make inferences, and taking notes while listening. The teacher's manual contains the "scripts" for the listening assignments, each of which will take no longer than three minutes to read. If preferred, there is a cassette tape of the selections that students may listen to so that they can work independently. Listening assignments are followed by workbook exercises.(S)

Grammar and Composition Resources for High School

Most high school students should have already acquired a mastery of basic grammar, so their energies should be directed toward improving composition skills. A poor knowledge of grammar can be corrected by reviewing material in any upper level English text or using any of the non-age-graded materials listed above such as *Easy Grammar, Rules of the Game*, and *Exploring Truths*.

Rather than having high school students do a complete grammar program, it might be just as effective to use only reference sources for grammar skills. The basics should have been mastered, so a reference book could be used for areas that present problems, either while writing or for correction afterwards. *Writers Inc* or other handbooks from the Write Source will serve well as handbooks. (See commentary below.) *BJUP's English Handbook* and many college level grammar handbooks are quite similar to each other, and most any will work well at high school level. Another resource, which you might have been using on a younger level is *Learning Grammar through Writing* (Educators Publishing Service), which presents the rules of grammar and composition listed with reference numbers. The teacher can use this to mark students' writing with reference numbers for the student to identify and correct errors. A similar but more comprehensive resource is *A Composition Handbook* (Longman Publishing). It can be used in the same manner, and it has more thorough grammar coverage suitable for older students.

Many students will need only a minimal amount of review to retain grammatical knowledge. *Daily Grams* (ISHA Enterprises) is recommended for such review.

➡ Basic English Revisited (The Write Source)

This is the original, older level of *The Write Source* listed above under seventh and eighth grade. Additional materials are available for the older level. For average ninth and tenth graders, use the *Basic English Revisited* handbook, with *A Study Skills and Writing Process Workbook*. For 11th and 12th graders use *A Practical Writing Skills Workbook*. With either you might wish to use the supplemental workbooks, *The Mechanics of Writing: Basic English Revisited*, for review of the mechanics of grammar, and/or *The Revising Process: Basic English Revisited* for polishing skills. Both supplemental books are very similar to books of the same title on the younger level for *The Write Source* and will only be necessary for students needing remedial work in either area. Emphasis in the program is on writing, but grammar is covered in the handbook. See the review of the updated version of this book, *Writers Inc*.(S)

➡ Basics of Systematic Grammar (Bob Jones University Press)

This 64-page booklet is for independent use by students who reach high school with little or no knowledge of English grammar. It covers parts of speech and basic functions in sentences. Programmed-learning is the instructional method.

➡ The Basics of Writing, Books 1, 2, and 3 (Globe Book Co.)

Each of these supplemental workbooks has an interesting format, is written on a fairly easy (remedial) level, and covers all forms of writing.(S)

➡ Creative Writing (A Beka)

This fairly easy book can be used for grades 7-10 as a supplement. It is recommended for those with little experience in creative writing.

➡ Easy Writing (ISHA Enterprises)

See description under seventh and eighth grades.

➡ English 9, 10, 11, and 12: Writing and Grammar (BJUP)

BJUP balances grammatical skills with their end goal of purposeful and effective communication by providing instruction, practice, review, and practical application throughout their English courses. Motivational themes trail through each course, with stories about the impact of writing as well as other "communication" experiences.

All levels review basic grammar. Levels 9 through 11 each introduce a few new grammatical concepts. There is a strong emphasis on writing skills throughout all levels. Grade nine emphasizes a wide variety of basic writing skills, concentrating on good description and organization. Grade ten works on outlining, writing, and revising. Students write a story in this course. Grade eleven teaches more types of writing, including persuasive writing and the research paper. Grade twelve helps students learn to use the power of the written word in formats such as literary criticism, essays, interviews, letters, tracts, resumes, and letters to the editor.

While there are student workbooks for each grade, the Teacher's Editions contain essential parts of the courses for each level. Students also need the English Handbook (BJUP) to use at all levels.

➡ English (McDougal, Littell, and Co.)[1989 editions]

There are separate texts for grades 9-12. This English series does an outstanding job of developing writing skills, moving beyond the mechanics of the writing process into mood, voice, tone, and other elements of style. Plenty of examples help to illustrate ideas clearly.

Grammar is taught separately in the last third of the book. Although grammar instruction is fairly straightforward, lessons for writing practice that link grammar with writing appear periodically throughout the grammar chapters. Diagramming is covered superficially in a small appendix.

Additional chapters address vocabulary development, speaking and listening, library skills, test taking, study skills, and business and college preparation.

This McDougal, Littell *English* series (there are other series that teach English from the same publisher, but they have different titles) is one of the best solutions for those who want a complete English course in one book. Students can work independently through the text, but developing writing skills always requires interaction and feedback from time to time. Parents who wish to have their teen work independently might want to set up a schedule that intermixes units on grammar and writing rather than concentrating heavily on writing first and grammar last.

The primary value of the Teacher's Edition will be as an answer key, although there are also some tips on teaching and evaluating writing.(S)

➡ English Handbook (BJUP)

This basic handbook for grades 9-12 is to be used with all levels of *BJUP's Writing and Grammar.*

➡ Getting Started in Journalism (National Textbook Company)

The focus here is on producing a school newspaper. Students learn how to put together a paper from the ground up, both writing and production. A discussion of ethics and legal restrictions is included.

➡ Grammar and Composition 3 and 4 (A Beka)

For grades nine and ten. These worktexts offer a thorough review of grammar with some work on writing skills. Students who have been studying grammar every year will find these repetitious, but those who have neglected grammar for a few years will find them sufficiently comprehensive. Purchase student book and teacher's edition (your answer key). *Teacher's Curriculum Guides for English 9* and *10* correlate language, literature, spelling, and vocabulary. You can supplement with A Beka's *Creative Writing* (if student has done no writing), *The Writer's Program* (Globe), or similar resources for composition work.

➡ Handbook of Grammar and Composition plus Workbooks A and B (A Beka)

Workbook A is for 11th grade and *Workbook B* is for 12th while the *Handbook* is used for both. The *Workbooks* have a strong writing emphasis with grammar review and application, although they are not as interesting as McDougal, Littell or BJUP. Purchase student books plus Teacher Editions (answer keys).

➡ Harbrace College Handbook (Harcourt Brace Jovanovich)

This is a classic handbook for grammar and writing skills, now in its eleventh edition. It is a handy, compact size, easy to use, yet comprehensive. In fact, I pull my eighth edition *Harbrace College Handbook* off my shelf for reference more than any of the other grammatical reference books I own. The new edition contains revised and updated examples and exercises. Newer topics addressed are word processing and how to avoid sexist language. There are also Instructor's Manuals and Instructor's Editions as well as workbooks to accompany the *Handbook.*(S)

➡ How to Write Clearly by Michel Lipman and Russell Joyner (International Society for General Semantics)

This short, fourteen-page book is an excellent tool for students (or others) who need to polish their writing skills. Examples and exercises work on editing for clear communication. Students work on developing a readable style with good sentence structure and effective word choices. Short exercises often feature poorly written samples for rewriting practice. Samples of effective rewrites are provided in the back of the book. Students can work through this book on their own if desired. Be aware that it is written at an adult level in terms of both content and vocabulary. This is a very inexpensive little book that makes an excellent supplement for any upper level writing course.(S)

➡ An Introduction to Christian Writing by Ethel Herr

Many home educated children envision careers as writers, but they do not know how to go beyond the basic writing instruction offered in their curriculum. Ethel Herr has written this book to help aspiring writers move from amateur to professional. Although the book is written for an adult audience, serious young people should find it easy to read and work with. Herr has woven together two strands involved in becoming a writer. She has done this by dividing the book into eleven, two-part lessons. "Part One of each lesson deals with the writer, his person, relationships, attitudes, market study, preparation, and work habits. Part Two gives specific instruction in writing skill areas." Herr includes numerous examples, checklists, and work sheets along with assignments for applying what she is teaching throughout the lessons. Herr has narrowed the focus of her book to Christian writing, that is, writing intended for the Christian market in book, magazine, devotional, or other formats. Because of that focus, she repeatedly stresses the need for a close relationship with God. Excellent content backed up by spiritual principles makes this a valuable book for aspiring Christian writers.

➡ Journalism Today! (National Textbook Company)

This text is written at a higher level than *Getting Started in Journalism.* The assumption is that students are working on their high school newspaper, where they will practice many of the skills they learn. Students learn about writing, interviews, newspaper production, ethics and responsibility, and careers. This is a hardbound student text. *The Journalism Today! Workbook* is a comprehensive workbook that covers the same basic topics, but in a different format which includes a "...large number of exercises, allowing flexibility in a variety of activity contexts." It can be used as a supplement to the hardbound text or another text, as well as on its own.(S)

➡ Language Arts (Alpha Omega LifePacs)

The LifePacs include grammar, spelling, composition, literature, and practical application. These may be repetitive on grammar or other skills that have been mastered previously, but you can choose the LifePacs that meet your child's needs by examining the scope and sequence from Alpha Omega which describes the content of each LifePac before you buy. Ninth grade level includes study of the play, *The Miracle Worker,* and the novel, *Twenty Thousand Leagues Under the Sea.* Tenth grade level studies *In His Steps;* eleventh grade level studies the play, *Our Town,* and the novel *The Old Man and the Sea;* and twelfth grade level studies *Hamlet.* It would be possible to use only the single LifePacs which cover each literary work without using the entire curriculum, but answer keys and teachers guides are designed to cover more than one LifePac, making it a bit more complicated to use in this way. It would be easier to use the entire curriculum, skipping previously mastered material. The high school language arts material from Alpha Omega is one of the publisher's strongest areas. Home schoolers generally have had quite favorable experience with it.

➡ Learning Language Arts through Literature (Family Learning Center)

Gold Book

The *Gold Book* for high school level is due in the Fall of 1992. See the description of the *Gray Book* for junior high for a fuller description. The format differs a little, since the *Gold Book* will be written in units rather than as individual lessons. Since it is not yet available, I will share Family Learning Center's description of it.

Dr. Greg Strayer, writer and former instructor of college English, is focusing upon American writing in the first book. [Author's note: more high school level books will follow.] The manual takes an in-depth look at American poetry, short stories and novels. Emphasis is on the elements of poetry and fiction as well as how to read and interpret the selections. A Section of the book is devoted to the essay. The composition skills are intended for college preparation and correspond to the reading selections.

Although the book is written for the 10th grade student, it could very easily be used by any high school student.

Four supplementary books will be required: *Great American Short Stories, The Mentor Book of Major American Poets, The Old Man and the Sea,* and *The Red Badge of Courage.* These books will be available through Family Learning Center.

➡**Look It Up** (Globe Book Co.)

Although I have not personally reviewed this workbook, it appears to be a worthwhile tool for improving reference skills using such reference works as a thesaurus, almanac, encyclopedia, atlas, reader's guide, and dictionary.(S)

➡**Warriner's English Composition and Grammar** (Harcourt Brace Jovanovich)

Third Course (Grade 9), *Fourth Course* (Grade 10), *Fifth Course* (Grade 11), and *Complete Course* (Grade 12). This is the popular English series by John Warriner, which has appeared in numerous editions. Cost is a major factor. Both student texts and Teacher's Editions are quite expensive. If students have a decent background in English grammar and composition from grammar school, then it makes the most sense to just purchase the twelfth grade *Complete Course* and use it over the high school years. Teacher's Editions contain answer keys to grammar exercises, and also help with the writing process and teaching instruction ideas. Parents strong in grammar could probably do without the Teacher's Editions, but they are recommended. Student texts are well written, with a good balance of grammar and composition instruction, although teaching methods are traditional rather than the integrated approach found in *Elements of Writing,* the new version described below. Practical application of skills is emphasized throughout the texts.

Following the merging of Harcourt Brace Jovanovich with Holt, Rinehart and Winston has come a revision of this series. The new series is entitled *Elements of Writing.* It is co-authored by Dr. James L. Kinneavy, who strengthens the composition aspects of the series. The books are updated in appearance with color and illustrations. The composition instruction is the heart of the book, with the grammatical instruction cross referenced through composition lessons and used as reference material. Literary models are included within each text as learning tools. This helps students learn both grammar and composition skills within the context of actual usage, which helps with motivation and retention of information. Writing assignments are defined more by process than topic, which gives students much more room to individualize their writing than do the assignments found in many other texts.

Grammar is presented separately in the second part of the book. It can serve as a handbook (particularly when used in conjunction with exercises in the first part of the book), but it also has exercises, diagnostic tests, review/posttests, and writing assignments. No diagramming

is in the *Complete Course* book, but I do not know if it appears in any of the other high school level books. (Diagramming is included in an appendix in the *Second Course.*)

Following the grammar section are chapters on topics such as speech, debate, library/media, dictionary, vocabulary, letters and forms, and studying and test taking. (Topics vary slightly from text to text.)

There is quite a bit of overlap in content from year to year in each text, although some new topics are presented at each level. Various types of writing activities would be the most prominent difference. Consider using a single text over a two-year period rather than buying separate ones for each year, since there is plenty of material in any one book. (The *Complete Course*/12th grade book is 1154 pages!)

The look has been updated with color and illustrations.

Both student and teacher books are even more expensive than the earlier series, but both are recommended. (Order from Holt, Rinehart and Winston.)(S)

➡**Warriner's High School Handbook** (Holt, Rinehart and Winston)

High school students can use this single book as a reference and study tool for grammar (including usage, mechanics, parts of speech, and sentence structure), composition, the use of reference resources, vocabulary, and study skills. However, it focuses primarily on grammar. High school students who have already had grammar instruction in earlier grades should be able to draw all the grammatical instruction they need from this book. An inexpensive Teacher's Manual serves as an answer key but also sounds like it is useful as an aid for parents who need help teaching and evaluating composition skills.(S)

➡**Writers Inc** (The Write Source)

This is the updated, revised version of *Basic English Revisited,* written for high school students. *Writers Inc* reflects ideas from the new language arts frameworks with attention given to such things as the whole language approach, peer group work, and a more student-centered writing atmosphere. This handbook elaborates on writing skills and the writing process much more than does the original. While it is still a handbook, it does some teaching with examples and explanations. A teacher's guide to *Writers Inc,* called *Inc Sights,* is essential for figuring out how to get full use from the *Writers Inc* handbook. It discusses various approaches to teaching writing, gives guidelines for evaluating student writing, tells when and how to refer students to the handbook, and provides more than 140 "mini-lessons" of writing ideas for high school students. Workbooks are not available for *Writers Inc.* (Also see the review of *The Write Source* under junior high for more information.)(S)

➡**The Writer's Program, Books 1, 2, 3, and 4** (Globe Book Co.)

These are excellent creative writing texts on a challenging level. Students are given many, many creative writing assignments with lots of variety. Some grammar work is included, but it is always presented in the context of improving writing. Texts are softbound. Students do not write in the books so they may be used with more than one student. There is some objectionable content, but it can easily be skipped. Highly recommended.(SE)

➡️ **Writing A Short Story: A Creative Curriculum for 4th, 5th and 6th Grade Students** by Lee Roddy and Lynn Brock

Valuable even at high school level, this book will help students who want to write short stories do it with the advice of an expert. See the complete description under junior high writing resources.

➡️ **Writing: Process to Product** (McDougal, Littell)

When I talk about teaching writing to teens, this book is number one on my recommendation list. It is an ungraded student "text" with a teacher's manual that is absolutely necessary. The author's goal was to provide a writing program with instruction in all facets of writing, including editing and revision, so that, as the teacher, he would have to spend less time instructing and could spend more time serving as final editor. He also wanted to provide a program that could be individualized to meet the needs of writers with varying degrees of skill. The book is designed to be used in a classroom, with peer group brainstorming and editing as an essential part of the process. If you can round up two or more teens to work together through this book, great. If not, consider getting involved in the writing process yourself and have your teen help evaluate your work. (If your skills are weak, you might then wish to have another person whom you can consult for final editing comments.) Even if you serve as teacher with one student, you can easily adapt lessons to fit your situation. Instructions are very clear with lots of examples. I particularly appreciate the numerous checklists of points to consider for evaluation—some for the student as he writes, some for the peer or teacher evaluator. Parents with poor writing skills often avoid teaching writing because they are not equipped to properly evaluate assignments. This book will help those of us in that situation.

The text is divided into three sections which can be used as desired. The first section teaches the writing process itself, then provides twenty-one different writing assignments such as narrative paragraphs, autobiographical essays, reviews, and business letters. The second works on content and organization, while the third section deals with style. The teacher's manual tells how to use the text and provides evaluation information and forms, activity ideas, and an answer key to the few discussion questions scattered through the text.

➡️ **The Writing Program 9** (Modern Curriculum Press)

See description under junior high composition recommendations.(SE)

Spelling and Vocabulary

Recommendations for Junior High

➡️ **Basic Goals in Spelling N** (7th grade) and **G** (8th grade) (Macmillan/McGraw-Hill—School Division)

This is a good secular spelling program that uses a phonetic approach.(S)

➡️ **Christian Liberty Speller Book 5** (Christian Liberty Press)

This speller is reprinted from a 1923 edition spelling book. It is recommended for eighth and ninth grade students, although older students might also benefit from it. Principles of phonics-based spelling are covered through both oral and written exercises. (But students do not write in this book.) Vocabulary development is also emphasized.

➡️ **Correct Spelling Made Easy** by Norman Lewis (Laurel/ A Division of Dell)

Mr. Lewis takes the 1,100 most commonly misspelled words (which are not necessarily the most commonly used words) and teaches us how to conquer them. This is a wonderful book for everyone, but especially for those who struggle with the same basic words over and over again. Words are grouped into lessons according to the problems they present—ise/ize words, ance/ence, hard and soft "c" and "g", etc. There is no memorization of rules, although rules are arrived at inductively as a tool for better memory. Exercises are done in the book to reinforce lessons. At the end of the book is a "Dictionary for Misspellers."(S)

➡️ **English from the Roots Up: Help for Reading, Writing, Spelling and S.A.T. Scores** by Joegil Lundquist

This book presents lessons for children to learn the roots of the English language that are found in the Greek and Latin languages. The goal is similar to that of *Vocabulary from Classical Roots* (from Educators Publishing Service). This book uses more interactive, teacher-directed teaching methods, while *Vocabulary from Classical Roots* is a workbook approach. However, older students might be able to use the book independently. In this approach, index cards, a file box, and a good dictionary are the primary tools for learning vocabulary. Actual teaching information provided is brief but loaded with activity suggestions. The teacher is on her own to implement the ideas. Examples of activity ideas: for the root "graph"—a number of related words are presented with accompanying ideas—"Telegraph—Let someone present a research report on Thomas Edison's early days as a telegrapher. Let someone do a report on Morse code and give a demonstration of it." or—"Lithograph—Discuss the process of lithography and talk about Currier and Ives. Their lithographs are still used every year as Christmas cards. Make potato or linoleum block prints." These activity ideas could be turned into great unit studies. This resource will be especially suited to the creative teacher who prefers general guidelines rather than detailed lesson plans.

➡️ **An Introduction to an Academic Vocabulary: Word Clusters from Latin, Greek, and German** by Horace G. Danner, Ph.D. and Roger Noel, Ph.D

"Memorizing vocabulary out of context is like trying to catch rain in a Kleenex...." according to the foreword of this book. The contexts provided by this book are the fascinating origins of words from Latin, Greek, and German (although references to other languages, particularly the Romance languages are present in each lesson). Unlike most vocabulary lessons, study is inductive; definitions are provided at the end for reference after students have studied word clusters to attempt to determine their common elements and meaning on their own.

Another difference between this approach and others is the author's inclusion of the stories behind the words, which are much more interesting than definitions alone. For example the description of "influenza" reads, "often shortened to flu; Italian; from influence; ancient astrologers believed that the infection was influenced by, or flowed in from, the stars."

The vocabulary words are definitely academic, reflecting medical, legal, and other specialized usage. For example the words from cluster number seven are: audit, inaudible, audiology, auditorium, auditory, audiovisual, audition, audient, audiogram, audience, audiencia, auditive, audile, subaudition, and audiometer. While many of the words studied are not in common use, the idea is that by becoming familiar with common word elements, we can easily figure out the meanings of unfamiliar words. One hundred word clusters are the basis of the same number of lessons. Extra information about word origins and usage is included along with pre- and post-tests.

The book is a consumable worktext, designed for independent study. Although originally written for high school juniors preparing for college entry tests, it has been successfully used by elementary teachers in gifted classes (presented by the teacher rather than used for independent study).

The word cluster approach should help students to boost their vocabulary with far less effort and more enjoyment than when using traditional methods of study.

➠ A Prescriptive Spelling Program, Books One, Two, or Three (Barnell Loft)

These books review spelling rules and apply them to spelling lists. They are recommended for students who have had difficulty in spelling. Reading levels of the three books are 3.5, 4.5, and 5.5 respectively.(S)

➠ The Riverside Spelling Program 7 and 8 (The Riverside Publishing Co.)

This program covers spelling rules very well and includes advanced word studies, dictionary usage, word usage, vocabulary, and word origins.(S)

➠ Rummy Roots Card Game

Rummy Roots is a card game that offers an alternative to book approaches for studying Greek and Latin roots. It is exceptionally well designed for learning purposes, because it includes instructions for four different games using a card deck of Greek and Latin roots plus English meanings. The first game helps us learn the meanings of the roots with a "Go Fish" type game. (Lists and glossaries for this and other games are included so we need not have a dictionary at hand.) Once we are somewhat familiar with root meanings, we move on to the next game of combining two roots to make an English word. The method of play is different, plus it includes the use of "bonus" and "stump" cards for fun. Players are supposed to say the meanings of their words, but we added that step after we played the game first just figuring out how to combine roots. (Take time to make sure players know the meanings of the roots before moving on to higher levels.) The third game allows players to make words combining up to three roots. Stump cards are now used to challenge players on word definitions. The fourth game adds yet another dimension of difficulty.

Some educational games are so busy teaching that they forget that games are supposed to be fun. *Rummy Roots* avoided that mistake by adding enough game elements, especially once we get past the introductory game.

Rummy Roots teaches "...42 Greek and Latin Roots, 193 Vocabulary words, and the knowledge to decipher half of over 2000 other words."

The publisher says the game is for players ages 8 to adult, but younger players will probably need to play mostly at the first two levels. Do not be in a hurry to push them on to levels where they might become frustrated. I think this game is ideal for junior high and high school students, although younger ones can be included.

➠ Spell-N-Meld (Behavior Development Products)

Junior high seems an ideal time to use Spell-N-Meld. This double-size card deck comes with a small, 38-page instruction book, with directions for fifteen different games. While younger children can play at least some of the games, the level of thinking required for many of them seems to be older. Some of the games compare to Boggle and similar more expensive games that have limited playing options. These games can be used to work on alphabetizing, phonics, vowel/consonant recognition, and parts of speech, as well as spelling. Some games can be played by a single player, while most require two or more. This is an excellent tool for improving spelling skills as well as other language art skills because of both design and flexibility. Hands-on learners as well as those who learn well in social situations such as game playing are particularly likely to benefit from this resource.

➠ Spelling Boosters: Easy to Use Enhancement Exercises for *The Writing Road to Reading* by Wanda Sanseri (Back Home Industries)

If you are also teaching younger children, this book will be a good investment. It is an idea book rather than an instruction manual or course. Many of the ideas are for younger children, but there are still quite a few for older students. I see this resource as particularly useful for teens who are tired of workbooks, yet who still need to spend a little time improving spelling skills. Although it was designed to reinforce phonics and spelling as taught in *The Writing Road to Reading*, almost everything here is useful for those who have not used that method. Suggested activities help children improve spelling, writing, and vocabulary skills, and there are even a number of ideas for working with Latin and Greek roots.

➠ Spelling, Vocabulary and Poetry 6 (A Beka)

Level 6 is considered sixth grade level by A Beka, but compares with seventh and eighth grade levels of others. The advanced level of difficulty is characteristic of all levels of A Beka spelling. The revised edition is colorful and includes more exercises and activities on usage, pronunciation, and word analysis than did the old edition. However, the basic method is still "teach, practice, and test" on the words themselves rather than working through exercises as in most such books.

➠ Spelling Workout G (7th grade) and H (8th grade) (Modern Curriculum Press)

These spelling workbooks include words frequently found in texts for science, social studies, and math at these grade levels. A Teacher's Edition is available for each grade level and includes an answer key.(S)

➠ Vocabulary from Classical Roots Books A, B, and C (Educators Publishing Service)

This vocabulary workbook series can be used from about fifth grade through twelfth. Each book is written at an increasingly difficult level.

Words with similar roots are grouped thematically for ease of study. A variety of exercises including work with synonyms, antonyms, analogies, and sentence completion helps students develop full understanding. Two unusual extras are included. Literary, historical and geographic references help develop cultural literacy. And suggestions for extended writing activities help students to apply new vocabulary.

Students with some exposure to Greek and/or Latin will immediately recognize the derivation of words from those languages. Other students without prior knowledge of those languages will develop some familiarity with Greek and Latin simply by using these workbooks.

A Teachers' Guide and Answer Key (in one book) for each level has teaching suggestions, exercise answers, and glossaries of some of the literary and historical references.

Book A is an easier starting point for this type of vocabulary study than *An Introduction to an Academic Vocabulary*.

➡ Vocabulary for Christian Schools (BJUP)

Levels C through F for grades 9 through 12. You will need both the worktext and Teacher's Edition for answers. According to the BJUP catalog new words are taught "...primarily through context. Students learn about word parts (prefixes, roots, and suffixes), word families, synonyms, antonyms, homonyms, and methods of word formation. The study of word parts helps students learn spelling as well as meaning. Some lessons also contain helpful spelling principles." *Book C* is the third (following *Books A* and *B* for younger levels) concentrating on Latin word parts. *Book D* teaches Greek word parts, *Book E* covers words originating from French along with some Greek and Latin words, and *Book F* broadens to cover words from many languages. There is also some crossover to grammar and writing skills. The format is more interesting than that of many vocabulary workbooks because of the background information and application in the lessons. Christian content is another plus.

➡ Vocabulary/Spelling/Poetry I and II(A Beka)

This new, colorful edition from A Beka has more exercises and practice for both spelling and vocabulary built into the student book than did the old edition. Spelling rules are reviewed throughout the lessons. Many vocabulary words are drawn from seventh grade level A Beka literature texts, and word lists are generally more difficult than those in other seventh and eighth grade spelling books. Excellent poetry from authors such as Longfellow, Scott, and Tennyson is included for appreciation. A Teacher's Edition, Test Booklet and an answer key to the Test Booklet are also available.

➡ Vocabulary Workshop by Doris Bain Thompson (Harcourt Brace Jovanovich)

This is a series to improve vocabulary, typical of those used in schools. It is not exciting, but it is effective.(S)

➡ Vocabu-Lit, Book 1, 2, or 3 (Perfection Learning)

All books are appropriate for sixth through eighth grades. Choose the book with literary excerpts that appeal to you the most. (Titles are listed in the *Perfection Language Arts Catalog*.) These books use a different approach to vocabulary. Start with a short literary excerpt with ten key words to be studied in bold print. Students then do dictionary work, synonym/antonym application, analogies, a crossword puzzle, and fill in the blanks of sentences guided by context clues. A glossary is provided at the end of each book. Student books are available either in soft cover (can be written in) or hard. Teacher's editions contain the answers.(S)

➡ Wordly Wise, Book Four (Educators Publishing Service)

This is an excellent vocabulary workbook with inexpensive answer key. Students use one list of words through four or five different types of exercises to become familiar with the word's usage in different contexts. Exercises include definitions, recognition of proper usage, word origins, prefixes and suffixes, synonym substitution, and crossword puzzles. The Answer Key is relatively inexpensive. The *Wordly Wise* series is popular with home educators because they are both effective and easy to buy from home school sources.(S)

Spelling and Vocabulary Recommendations for High School

➡ English from the Roots Up: Help for Reading, Writing, Spelling and S.A.T. Scores by Joegil Lundquist

See review under recommendations for junior high.

➡ An Introduction to an Academic Vocabulary: Word Clusters from Latin, Greek, and German by Horace G. Danner, Ph.D. and Roger Noel, Ph.D.

See review under recommendations for junior high.

➡ The Childs Spelling System: The Rules (Educators Publishing Service)

This can be used as a reference tool just as *Learning Grammar through Writing* can be used for grammar.(S)

➡ Scholastic Aptitude Vocabulary by Joseph R. Orgel (Educators Publishing Service)

This 128-page book is recommended for eleventh and twelfth grade students preparing for college entrance. It lists one thousand words that show up frequently on versions of the SAT and gives meanings, related forms, synonyms, antonyms. Four specimens of vocabulary examinations are included along with twenty vocabulary mastery drill tests. You will want to also purchase the answer key.(S)

➡ A Spelling Workbook by Mildred B. Plunkett (Educators Publishing Service)

This book is helpful for students struggling with spelling. Students who cannot spell well by high school sometimes have a related difficulty with reading. This book seeks to help by emphasizing spelling rules and generalizations, providing phonetic drills, and working on syllabication. Using such methods helps students improve spelling and phonics skills, both essential for good spelling.(S)

➡ Visual Vocabulary [four video cassettes with four eighty-page accompanying guidebooks] (NeuroEducational Associates, Inc.)

Students preparing for the SAT test can improve their scores significantly by concentrating on vocabulary. While other SAT preparation books also teach and review vocabulary, this series of videos uses a different methodology. Cartoon illustrations showing the meanings of words are accompanied by audio explanations. The theory is that by using both right and left brain activities, students better remember words and their meanings. This multi-sensory approach should help all types of learners, but it should be especially helpful for strong visual/spatial learners who have trouble making associations from words only. (Adults desiring to improve vocabulary will benefit as well.)

Each of the four tapes covers 250 words and is two hours in length. There are ten words per lesson and twenty-five lessons per tape. Each lesson should take between five and ten minutes to complete. There are pre- and post-tests in booklets accompanying each tape, with review exercises after every set of five lessons. Answers are at the back of the booklets.

Tapes can be purchased individually or as a set. Since they are quite expensive, consider buying them for a group of families and sharing them.(S)

➡Vocabulary for College (Harcourt Brace Jovanovich)

These are basic vocabulary books used by many schools. Books A through D are appropriate for grades 9-12. Tests and teacher's manuals are available.(S)

➡Vocabulary from Classical Roots, Books A, B, and C (Educators Publishing Service)

See review under recommendations for junior high.

➡Vocabulary, Spelling, and Poetry (A Beka)

Levels 8 - 12. The level of difficulty is very advanced. You will need to have your student practice using the spelling and vocabulary words in sentences and other forms of application on your own.

➡The Vocabulary Wordshop, Blue, Red, or Green Concourse (Perfection Learning)

For eighth through tenth grades. Choose the book with literary excerpts that appeal to you the most. (Titles are listed in the *Perfection Language Arts Catalog*.) Here we find a different approach to vocabulary. Start with an excerpt from classic literature with ten key words to be studied in bold print. Students then do dictionary work, a spelling exercise, synonym/antonym application, analogies, a crossword puzzle, and fill in the blanks of sentences guided by context clues. A glossary is provided at the end of each book. This series is essentially the same in methodology as the *Wordpak* series below and the *Vocabu-Lit* series described under junior high, but reading selections are longer than in *Vocabu-Lit*. Student books are available either in soft cover (can be written in) or hard. Teacher's editions contain the answers.(S)

➡Vocabulary Workshop by Doris Bain Thompson (Harcourt Brace Jovanovich)

Six volumes and teacher's manuals are available for junior high and high school levels. This is a good series of worktexts used by many schools.(S)

➡Wordpak vocabulary series [three books]: Spec-Trum, Rangefinder, and Lexicon (Perfection Learning)

All three books are appropriate for tenth through twelfth grades. This series is almost identical in format to the *Vocabu-Lit* and *Vocabulary Wordshop*. Reading selections are longer and more challenging than in the other two series. All three *Wordpak* books are written at the same level of difficulty, so the choice is arbitrary. Student books are available either in soft cover (can be written in) or hard. Teacher's editions contain the answers.(S)

➡Wordly Wise, Books 6 - 9 (Educators Publishing Service)

Excellent workbooks for vocabulary. See description of *Wordly Wise*, Book Four, under junior high recommendations.(S)

Literature

Recommended literature anthologies and readers for approximately seventh and eighth grade levels:

➡Christian Liberty Eclectic Reader, Books G, H, and I (Christian Liberty Press)

These reprinted readers are collections of stories, many by famous authors. They are very similar to the various McGuffey readers in format and content. The vocabulary is more challenging than that of most junior high reading anthologies. Excellent discussion questions and activity assignments for selected stories are included at the end of the

Guides for Reading the Great Books

➡ Read for Your Life by Becky Elder (Christian Worldview Library)

Read for Your Life is a resource guide that provides ideas for putting together a world view study, primarily with books. It lists recommended reading arranged in chronological order. Recommended books can be used as part of any reading program. The Christian Worldview Library lends a huge assortment of books, cassettes, and videos on Bible study, American history, world history, economics, business ethics, abortion, current events, home education, and many other topics.

➡ The Great Adventure: A Life-Time Reading Plan for the Great Works of the Western World by Robert D. Linder and Eileen D. Roesler (Mulberry Books)

This booklet is very useful for helping us select books or excerpts from among recognized classics. Titles are listed under topics and time periods, making it easy to select those that will supplement a chronologically-based study from the time of the Greeks to the present. Topical areas include literature, history, autobiography/biography, politics and society, and religion and philosophy. A thematic listing at the back offers the alternative of creating unit studies for topics such as "Fantasy and Utopianism," "Good and Evil," "Humor," and "Man and the State."

This book helped me to coordinate readings from A Beka's *Masterpieces from World Literature* with some from other sources into a literature course that both correlated with our history studies and served as a vehicle for studying world views.

book. (These have been added to the original text by CLP.) Very detailed instruction on elocution and articulation is included at the front of each book. While I suspect that most of us would skip this because "nobody else does it these days," I wonder if it would not be a worthwhile endeavor to better train our children in speaking skills using these lessons.

➡Excursions in Literature (BJUP)

This eighth-grade-level text covers a variety of themes portraying a Christian's journey through life, including choices he must face. The novel, *Wine of Morning*, is studied in the final unit. A video cassette of the story is also available.

The Teacher's Edition contains all commentary and is highly recommended. You might also want to use the TestBank (softbound book) or TestBank Data Disk (computerized version which requires the *Ask It* program).

➡Explorations in Literature (BJUP)

The seventh-grade-level text covers a wide variety of themes. It includes some Christian authors. One of the main purposes seems to be helping students to progress beyond simply reading for pleasure to the point where they enjoy reading for inspiration and wisdom. All teaching material and commentary is contained in the Teacher's Edition, which I recommend that you purchase. A TestBank (softbound book) or TestBank Data Disk (computerized format that requires the *Ask It* program) will save time on test preparation if you wish to test your student.

➥Language Arts (Alpha Omega LifePacs)

See description under "Grammar and Composition Materials for High School." Ninth-grade-level includes study of the play, *The Miracle Worker*, and the novel, *Twenty Thousand Leagues Under the Sea*. Tenth grade level studies *In His Steps*. Eleventh grade level studies the play, *Our Town*, and the novel *The Old Man and the Sea*; and twelfth grade level studies *Hamlet*.

➥Moore-McGuffey Readers 3 and 4 (The Moore Foundation)

These readers cover a wide range of reading skill levels. Most eighth graders will still be in the third reader. Stories are morally uplifting and emphasize positive character development.

➥Of People (A Beka)

Reading selections all reflect different aspects of character—most of them positive. They are followed by information about authors, discussion questions, and speed reading charts. Questions are much more thought-provoking than those found in younger level A Beka readers.

➥Of Places (A Beka)

Selections are from renowned authors with different settings as the themes. It is recommended for eighth grade level but appropriate for many seventh graders. See comments on *Of People* above.

➥Original Mott McGuffey Reader, Third Reader and Fourth Reader (Mott Media)

These readers have some archaic expressions and stories but excellent content. The third level is appropriate for many eighth graders.

➥A Time to Gather (Rod and Staff)

This seventh-grade-level reader includes stories, poetry (including selections of both from the Bible), and composition themes. Vocabulary lists and exercises follow each lesson. The inexpensive Teacher's Guide contains answers as well as teaching suggestions. An eighth-grade-level reader should soon be available.

Teaching Literature with "Real Books"

Good literature should be an essential part of the curriculum. Students at this level should primarily be reading full length books rather than anthologies, although anthologies are useful for introducing more variety into students' reading and providing discussion ideas. Discussion and oral reading should take place from time to time, especially when students are doing most of their work independently.

Suggested books for junior high level:

Rip Van Winkle and the Legend of Sleepy Hollow by Washington Irving
Twenty Thousand Leagues Under the Sea by Jules Verne
Life on the Mississippi by Mark Twain
Call of the Wild by Jack London
Kim by R. Kipling
The Adventures of Sherlock Holmes by A. C. Doyle
Danger to Windward by Armstrong Sperry
The King's Beard by Leonard Wibberley
America's Robert E. Lee by H. Comager

Ben and Me by Robert Lawson
Kidnapped by R. L. Stevenson

The following recommended books, listed in the first edition of *Model Curriculum Standards, Grades Nine through Twelve* (California Department of Education), are more appropriate for junior high than high school level and can be added to the above list:

The Red Badge of Courage by Stephen Crane
Johnny Tremain by Esther Forbes
Tom Sawyer by Mark Twain
The Pearl by John Steinbeck
Sounder by William H. Armstrong
Julie of the Wolves by Jean Craighead George
Adam of the Road by Elizabeth Janet Gray
A Wrinkle in Time by Madeleine L'Engle
Island of the Blue Dolphins by Scott O'Dell
The Bronze Bow by Elizabeth George Speare
Where the Red Fern Grows by Wilson Rawls
Ivanhoe by Sir Walter Scott

With the recent revision of *Model Curriculum Standards, Grades Nine through Twelve, first edition* (California Department of Education), the English Language Arts sections were removed and printed in two separate publications: *English Language Arts, Model Curriculum Standards Grades Nine through Twelve* and *Recommended Literature, Grades Nine through Twelve*.[6] Both are updated and expanded versions of the original material in the first edition. *Recommended Literature* is likely to be the most popular volume among home educators. It lists recommended reading, first broken down into two basic catergories—"core and extended materials" which are considered basic, and "recreational and motivational materials." Both categories are then broken down into biographies, drama, folklore/mythology/epics, nonfiction, novels, poetry, and short stories. Additional core categories are essays, speeches, and books in languages other than English.(SE)

The library is a good source for all of these books. For those who want to purchase books, Troll Books sells inexpensive, unabridged classics under the name Watermill Classics. Alpha Omega is another source for both classics and good literature. They both carry some titles listed above, as well as many others.

➥Amsco Literature Series (Amsco)

For those who want to study full-length selections, the Amsco Literature Series offers reasonably priced assistance. Unabridged editions of books are available that have large, readable type. In the Reader's Guide Editions of these books, the text of the book is first, followed by "...explanations, questions, and activities to bring out the details of plot, characterization, theme, style, and vocabulary." Included are questions of all types, which vary depending upon the book being studied. For example, background information and questions for *Hamlet* and *The Scarlet Letter* are very different because of the nature of each work. Representative titles: *Great Expectations, Hamlet, Jane Eyre, The Red Badge of Courage, The Odyssey, The Scarlet Letter,* and *Treasure Island*. (Shakespeare volumes also provide vocabulary assis-

---

6   *Recommended Literature* lists more than 1200 titles. Entries represent both classical and contemporary works and include numerous works for students whose primary language is Chinese, Hmong, Japanese, Khmer, Korean, Philipino, Samoan, Spanish, or Vietnamese.

tance on facing pages within the text, making them much easier to use.) Separate answer keys are available and recommended.

Supplements

To challenge students to read beyond the surface meaning, you might wish to use one of the following books as an aid to studying novels:

➡ Digging into Literature (Fearon Teacher Aids)

This is a guide for studying seventeen novels such as *Johnny Tremain*, *Bridge to Terabithea*, and *Phantom Tollbooth*. Student pages are reproducible.(SE)

➡ Inside Stories, Book 4 and Book 5 (Dandy Lion)

Each of these books covers ten novels, with questions that take students from basic comprehension levels through higher levels of thinking. Each book is studied through a number of lessons with questions for discussion following every few chapters. Conclusion and summary discussion questions stretch students' thinking, and activities take them beyond the boundaries of the novel itself. For example, after studying *Across Five Aprils*, a novel of the Civil War, students are directed to research two political figures mentioned in the book and present it as either a first-person speech or autobiographical paper. Novels such as *Johnny Tremain*, *Bridge to Terebithia*, *The Witch of Blackbird Pond*, *Sing Down the Moon*, and *Wrinkle in Time* are studied in Book 4, suggested for grades 6-7. In Book 5 for grades 7-8, novels such as *The Incredible Journey*, *The Pearl*, *Across Five Aprils*, *The Grey King*, *Jonathon Livingston Seagull*, and *A Swiftly Tilting Planet* are included. Use discretion about novels that you choose for study. All are not worthwhile reading for Christian students.(SE)

You might want to work on reading comprehension with one of the following:

➡ Reading for Comprehension H and I (Continental Press)

Half-page, interesting stories are followed by multiple choice questions.(S)

➡ Reasoning and Reading, Level 1 and Level 2 (Educators Publishing Service)

160-page workbooks help students understand and evaluate what they read. Recommended for grades 8 and 9.(S)

➡ Skills Bank Home Tutor [for IBM type machines] (Skills Bank Corporation)

See the description of the entire program where it first appears under math resources for junior high. The reading module in this program will still be useful at junior high level. It has three sections: reading comprehension, vocabulary building, and word knowledge. The most difficult sections within each area address topics such as hyperbole, personification, Latin and Greek roots, and suffixes that form nouns and adjectives. This is a good way to review reading skills before moving on to more difficult literature.(S)

High School Level Literature

English Language Arts, Model Curriculum Standards Grades Nine through Twelve (California Department of Education) is recommended for specific ideas in the study of literature at all high school levels. A separate companion volume, *Recommended Literature, Grades Nine through Twelve* (California Department of Education), lists recommendations for different literary forms.(S)

Among core literature recommendations taken from the first edition are the following:

Little Women by Louisa May Alcott

Pride and Prejudice by Jane Austen

"The Devil and Daniel Webster" and other works by Stephen Vincent Benet

A Man for All Seasons by Robert Bolt

Martian Chronicles and other works by Ray Bradbury

Jane Eyre by Charlotte Bronte

Wuthering Heights by Emily Bronte

The Good Earth by Pearl Buck

Alice's Adventures in Wonderland by Lewis Carroll

Don Quixote by Miguel de Cervantes

Canterbury Tales by Geoffrey Chaucer

Robinson Crusoe by Daniel Defoe

David Copperfield, Great Expectations, A Tale of Two Cities, and other works by Charles Dickens

The Hound of the Baskervilles and other works by Sir Arthur Conan Doyle

"The Hollow Men" and other works by T.S. Eliot

The Great Gatsby by F. Scott Fitzgerald

Anne Frank: The Diary of A Young Girl by Anne Frank

"The Road Not Taken" and other works by Robert Frost

The Miracle Worker by William Gibson

Lord of the Flies by William Golding

The Scarlet Letter by Nathaniel Hawthorne

The Odyssey and *The Iliad* by Homer

Brave New World by Aldous Huxley

"The Legend of Sleepy Hollow" and other works by Washington Irving

To Kill a Mockingbird by Harper Lee

Perelandra, Out of the Silent Planet, and other works by C.S. Lewis

Billy Budd, Moby Dick, and other works by Herman Melville

1984 and *Animal Farm* by George Orwell

The Death of Socrates and other works by Plato

"The Pit and the Pendulum" and other works by Edgar Allen Poe

Men of Iron by Howard Pyle

The Yearling, Cross Creek, and other works by Marjorie K. Rawlings

Light in the Forest by Conrad Richter

Hamlet, Henry V, Macbeth, Midsummer Night's Dream, Othello, Merchant of Venice, and other works by William Shakespeare

Pygmalion by George Bernard Shaw

"Ozymandias" and other works by Percy Bysshe Shelley

Oedipus the King, Antigone, and other works by Sophocles

The Grapes of Wrath, The Pearl, The Red Pony, Of Mice and Men, and other works by John Steinbeck

Treasure Island, Kidnapped, and other works by Robert Louis Stevenson

Uncle Tom's Cabin by Harriet Beecher Stowe

Gulliver's Travels and other works by Jonathan Swift

"The Charge of the Light Brigade" and other works by Alfred Lord Tennyson

The Trilogy of the Ring by J. R. Tolkein

Anna Karenina, War and Peace, and other works by Leo Tolstoy

The Adventures of Huckleberry Finn and other works by Mark Twain

Twenty Thousand Leagues Under the Sea, Around the World in Eighty Days, and other works by Jules Verne

The Aeneid of Virgil by Virgil
All the King's Men by Robert Penn Warren
The Bridge of San Luis Rey by Thornton Wilder
    I would add to the above (or use instead):
In His Steps by Charles M. Sheldon
Pilgrims' Progress by John Bunyan
The Divine Comedy by Dante
Paradise Lost by John Milton
The Spy and other works by James Fenimore Cooper
The Marquis' Secret and other works by George MacDonald
    (updated versions)

Also look for top-quality fiction from Christian authors such as Frank Peretti, Bodie Thoene, and Stephen Lawhead. Christian publishers are making a determined effort to publish more such fiction, so look for many new titles from them over the next few years.

Ideally, students should be reading full-length books in both British and American literature along with other classical literature such as some of the titles listed above. Critical thinking skills can be developed in discussing and reporting on what they read. It is often helpful to have Christian literature textbooks to help as we study secular literature. Themes that might sound objectionable in themselves, can be used to illustrate the results of evil or immorality.

Literature Textbook Recommendations

General Literature

➡ Christian Liberty Eclectic Readers J and K (Christian Liberty Press)

Similar to the McGuffey Readers, these books are reprints of early readers. At this older level, the content is similar to many other anthologies in that they draw primarily from recognized authors, often using excerpts from classic works. Public speaking skills receive attention in the first part of each book, since students should be exercising those skills as they read aloud some of the selections. These books will be quite challenging for most of today's students, although they are listed for ninth and tenth grade level. Excellent discussion questions and writing activities for selected stories are included by CLP at the end of the books.

➡ Elements of Literature (BJUP)

Suggested for tenth grade. This text teaches students literary analysis at a more challenging level than the ninth grade level *Fundamentals of Literature* from BJUP. It delves into topics such as themes, allusions, symbolism, irony, as well as teaching more about the forms of literature—fiction, poetry, biography, drama, etc. The course includes use of the separate book, *Great Expectations* by Charles Dickens. There are separate Teacher's Editions for the basic student text and for *Great Expectations*, both of which include reproductions of the student text pages as well as teaching information and helps.

➡ Fundamentals of Literature (BJUP)

Suggested for grade nine. This new textbook is the foundation for the study of literature. It studies conflict, character, theme, structure, point of view, and moral tone through both traditional and contemporary selections. The drama *Cyrano De Bergerac* is included for study in the text, with a videocassette also available. Interpretation and evaluation from a Christian point of view are a major emphasis. Reading selections are not necessarily Christian, since interpreta-tion and evaluation can be truly taught only by studying examples written from more than one perspective. The Teacher's Edition contains reproductions of the student text pages as well as helps for discussion and analysis. A Test-Bank to accompany this text is available in both softbound book and computer disk formats.

➡ Norton Anthologies (W.W. Norton and Co.)

There are a number of anthologies published by Norton including *Norton Anthology of English Literature, Norton Anthology of American Literature (two volumes), Norton Anthology of Literature by Women, Norton Anthology of Poetry*, and others. These books emphasize classical selections unlike most anthologies written for high school students. Commentary is included, although it is written at college/adult level. Various editions of these books have been printed over many years, so it is fairly easy to find them in used book stores at fantastic prices.(S)

➡ Themes in Literature (A Beka)

Suggested for ninth grade. Character qualities such as courage, joy, justice, and humility are the themes of selections from authors including Tolstoy, Hawthorne, and Chaucer. Included in the student text are information on authors and literary devices, vocabulary lists, and discussion questions.

➡ Working with Poetry (Educators Publishing Service)

This book is designed for eleventh and twelfth grade students who lack experience reading poetry. According to the catalog description, students analyze a variety of poems, focusing on words, images, rhythm, and rhetorical devices.(S)

American Literature

➡ American Literature (BJUP)

Suggested for grade eleven, this text covers American literature from colonial time up through this century. Representative authors are William Bradford, Jonathan Edwards, Benjamin Franklin, Nathaniel Hawthorne, Herman Melville, Samuel Clemens, Thornton Wilder, and Bruce Catton. Selections are organized by historical literary periods, while addressing some of the philosophical movements that influenced literature. Background information, analytical help, discussion suggestions, and a reproduction of the student text are in the two-volume, spiral-bound Teacher's Edition.

➡ Beginnings of American Literature (A Beka)

Suggested for first semester of eleventh grade. This book has students study types of American literature. The end of the book includes a study of *The Scarlet Letter*.

➡ The Literature of the American People (A Beka)

Suggested for second semester of 11th grade. Use this book with *Beginnings* listed above. Nineteenth and twentieth century American authors are studied by "periods" in literature, with selections from the different genres of each period.

British Literature

➡ British Literature (BJUP)

Suggested for twelfth grade. This book covers eight literary periods from Old English to Modern. Selections are often chosen to illustrate philosophical and cultural issues from a Christian perspective. Religious developments receive far more attention here than they do in other British Literature texts. Representative authors include John Wycliffe, Geoffrey Chaucer, Thomas More, Shakespeare, Ben

Jonson, William Wordsworth, and Robert Browning. The play *Macbeth* is also included for study. The Teacher's Edition is highly recommended.

➠Introduction to English Literature (A Beka)

Suggested for first semester of twelfth grade. It covers the development of English literature from the Anglo-Saxons through the Puritans. Both *Macbeth* and *Pilgrim's Progress* are included for study. Background information is included in the student text.

➠The Literature of England (A Beka)

Suggested for second semester of twelfth grade. Use with *Introduction* listed above. Selections from the Restoration through the twentieth century are chosen to reflect the spiritual state of England through those periods. Selections are from Dickens, Defoe, Boswell, Tennyson and others.

➠Shakespeare Parallel Texts (Perfection Learning)

Perfection has published Shakespeare's plays of *Hamlet, Julius Caesar, King Lear, Macbeth, The Merchant of Venice, A Midsummer Night's Dream, Othello, Romeo and Juliet,* and *The Taming of the Shrew* in parallel editions. On one page is the original version of the play and on the opposite page is a line-by-line paraphrase. Each book contains a supplement with study questions, vocabulary work, and further activities. If you are reluctant to study Shakespeare with your children because you do not understand it, this is your key to success. One inexpensive answer key covers all nine books.(S)

World Literature

➠Backgrounds to World Literature (A Beka)

This book is suggested for first semester of tenth grade. It includes an introduction to literary devices and uses art masterpieces for illustrations. Purchase only the student text.

➠Masterpieces from World Literature (A Beka)

Suggested for second semester of tenth grade. Use this book with *Backgrounds* listed above. *Masterpieces* presents selections in historical order with commentary on the time period and its effect on literature. A test booklet and answer key also available. (See mention of use of this text as part of world view studies in Chapter Five.)

Speech

What good does it do if our teens recognize the importance of communication, yet their only experience is in written communication? Most of our communication is oral, not written!

The lack of a group class should not deter us from helping our teens develop speech skills. We can involve the entire family in speech activities, with each family member offering something on his or her level. An older teenager might present an original speech about a current event. A junior high student might present his own entertaining version of a radio commercial. A younger child could present a dramatic reading of a poem, while a still younger child could "show and tell." Ideally, Mom and Dad should also get involved. Plan opportunities for oral presentations and speeches as often as possible.

Our teens need to practice making oral presentations to more than just their family members. I strongly recommend getting together with other home educators to provide settings for frequent oral presentations, possibly as a group class.

Many of us need guidelines and ideas for training our children in the skills for oral presentations.

Bob Jones University Press publishes the only Christian speech text with which I am familiar. Most secular speech texts will also be suitable. The principles of effective speech have not changed, so we can save by purchasing older, used textbooks from second-hand book or thrift stores.

➠National Textbook Company

The English and Communication Arts catalog from National Textbook Company has a number of resources for speech, drama, and debate. Some titles are *Contemporary Speech, Getting Started in Public Speaking, Getting Started in Debate, Basic Debate, Strategic Debate, Coaching and Directing Forensics, The Book of Scenes for Acting Practice, Stagecraft, Theatre and Drama,* and *The Dynamics of Acting.* Get their catalog for descriptions of these and other specialized resources.

➠Speech for Christian Schools (BJUP)

Recommended for tenth through twelfth grade. It covers the basic topics that we encounter in secular speech texts, but with a Christian perspective. There is also strong emphasis on the areas of debate, dramatic interpretation, broadcasting, and drama with some scripts included in the text. Speech skills are presented with many practice assignments to help students develop communication skills as a means of both glorifying God and benefiting others.

➠Speech for Effective Communication (Harcourt Brace Jovanovich)

This high-school-level, hardcover textbook covers all major speech communication topics.

➠Speech: Principles and Practice (Scott, Foresman and Company)

This high-school-level, hardcover textbook covers both interpersonal and public communication.

➠The Write Source, Write Source 2000, Basic English Revisited, and Writers Inc (The Write Source)

All four handbooks offer brief lessons on public speaking with criteria and checklists for evaluation. See complete descriptions earlier in this chapter.

Chapter Thirteen

History/Social Studies/Geography

Foundations

Teaching history will be much easier if it is interesting to our children. Actually, history has been one of the more popular subjects with home schooling families, at least partly because of the inspiration of such men as Richard "Little Bear" Wheeler (Mantle Ministries) and Marshall Foster (Mayflower Institute). They have a talent for creating an excitement and enthusiasm for history that we missed when we were in school. Surprisingly, they accomplish this by teaching more historical facts rather than substituting entertainment for factual information. The true facts about history are eye-opening and thought provoking, even to children. We also have some excellent (truth and fact-filled) history books and teaching aids available to us. For many of us parents, it is like discovering a brand new subject that we never knew existed. It certainly bears little resemblance to what we were presented in school.

Many of us who have been able to teach our children at home for the elementary grades have had opportunities to try some of these ideas and materials, and we discovered that our children learned a great deal and enjoyed history.[1]

There are certainly some home educators who never quite got into this sort of history in earlier years and missed out on the fun. There are many more just beginning home schooling, possibly facing the task of undoing the last six to eight years of history as taught in the school system. The task for both is much more difficult. They must provide both the "foundation" and the "building" in a much shorter time span.

Our children need a historical foundation beginning with the Bible. Laid out in the Bible is the motivation for all that has happened since the beginning of creation. Man acts according to his heart as evidenced by stories throughout the Bible. The historical truth of the Bible provides crucial information about the development of cultures and societies. For instance, the story of the Tower of Babel explains why and how men were scattered throughout the world, and how each group began speaking an individual language. All of history ties in to the Bible either factually or motivationally.

A second layer for that historical foundation should consist of a chronological overview of history. Students must have some idea of the sequence of events to be able to form a coherent picture. For instance, an understanding of the Enlightenment and the changes it produced in the philosophies of entire nations is dependent upon an acquaintance with the general time frame of those events.

A third foundational layer consists of basic geographical knowledge. We cannot refer to third world countries without some idea of where those countries might be located. We cannot conceive of the difficulties of exploration without knowledge of geographical barriers.

A fourth layer should consist of cultural awareness. We need not spend undue amounts of time studying about obscure African tribes to ward off charges of racism, yet our children do need to understand some of the basic differences in social structures, philosophy, and beliefs of cultures other than our own.

The public school system has placed a lop-sided emphasis on the fourth layer, with little emphasis on the second and third layers, and total rejection of the first. We must reverse their approach to provide a satisfactory foundation.

Upon such a foundation, we can then erect a building. That building will be constructed of details—the color of history that makes it come alive.

Avoiding Name-Date Syndrome

If you were given a list of names and dates to commit to memory with no additional information about the people or events represented by those names and dates, you would find it difficult to retain such information for very long (unless you are a whiz at mnemonic devices or other such memory tools.) It does not connect to anything else you know, and there is nothing of interest in the bald information itself to cause you to reserve a corner of your memory for it.

When we teach history, we too easily fall into the "name-date syndrome," assuming that if our children know all the recognizable names and dates, they know history. Yet, those names and dates rarely find a lasting home in children's memory banks beyond the upcoming test.

If we have been teaching our children at home through the elementary years, we have probably gone beyond names and dates and provided our children with the stories of history that make it come alive. Our children are probably "acquainted" with many of the important players and dramas from past ages through biographies, historical novels, well-written textbooks, Richard "Little Bear" Wheeler's presentations, movies, etc. Rather than relying solely upon textbooks, we have drawn upon other interesting resources that have drawn our children into the stories of history in a more personal way. It is similar to the feeling that we have toward a main character after watching a movie. We feel as if we have come to know the character more intimately because we became momentarily involved in his or her life.

---

1   J. Steven Wilkins has a new two-cassette tape set called *Teaching and Learning American History* (Covenant Publications) which is designed to help parents teach American History as described above. He outlines specific goals for different age levels, and suggests helpful resources to use.

At junior and senior high levels, we should not be always repeating factual information, but rather we should be building upon information that is already there, linking threads of history together. Our children should already have basic knowledge to which they can "hook" new knowledge. Unfortunately, for some junior high students this will be a time of laying foundations rather than adding on to their building; and it is important that we take time to cover foundational concepts if that has not yet been done.

When our children have had poor history instruction through the elementary grades, we have a tendency to want to rush them through material to bring them up to date. Yet, in these cases, it is more profitable to concentrate on basic ideas than a wealth of information. There is no point sowing more information if there is no soil in which the seeds can take root.

Why Learn History?

Even if our teens have a foundation for historical knowledge, they will not correlate information to it if they do not believe that the information is of value to them. Most teenagers will not naively accept our statement that something is important to learn without some evidence to back support it. But, do we really believe that history studies are important for any reason other than that this is one of the subjects we have to teach? If we do not see the value, our children will sense our lack of conviction.

Yet, there are excellent reasons for studying history, especially for Christians. The Bible repeatedly talks about the importance of remembering and learning from what has gone before. Our own country was founded upon Christian principles, although our founding fathers took care to make sure we would have neither a government controlled by any one church nor churches controlled by the government. They had seen the abuses when either institution controlled the other throughout centuries past. They decided upon a republican form of government, having studied all pre-existing governing systems because of their desire to avoid the mistakes of others. They decided upon these principles based upon their knowledge of history. Our present day legislators generally do not know history as did our founding fathers, and we are suffering the consequences of their ignorance. A thorough knowledge of how our government operates is more than ever necessary for Christians in an increasingly hostile society.

As Christians, we are also instructed to share the Gospel of Jesus Christ to the ends of the earth. Yet, to approach another person in total ignorance of his cultural background is presumptuous and possibly foolish. We might be so offensive in our approach that the door is slammed shut before we can even begin to share. We need to know about other people's beliefs or we will have difficulty contrasting them with the truth. We gain that knowledge through studies of other cultures and philosophies.

Economics

Economics is tightly linked with history and government, so it makes sense to integrate the study of all these subjects. Understanding the driving force of economics upon events is crucial to real understanding of history. Beyond that, our children should have a basic grasp of economics (particularly free market economics since it is often not taught in colleges) before they leave home. They are likely to face indoctrination with false economic ideologies from most other sources, particularly colleges. An economics course of one or two semesters (or a course integrated with other studies) should provide them with enough information to identify major differences in economic philosophies. Even though economics is not a universal requirement for graduation, and is seldom a college entry prerequisite, I urge you to make it part of your course of study.

Newspapers

The newspaper should be an important resource in our curriculum. Teenagers should be studying and analyzing past events, contrasting these with current events from the news. (Television news is not an adequate substitute.) Editorial pages help point up controversial issues if we have trouble identifying them ourselves. While teens are learning historical, geographical, and cultural information through current issues and events, they are also developing and sharpening their thinking skills. See "Current Events" for details and suggestions.

High School Requirements

States require up to three years of history/social sciences for high school graduation. This should include:
1. United States History and Geography
2. World History, Culture, and Geography
3. American Government, Civics, and Economics[2]

College entry requirements for history/social studies vary considerably. For instance, the California State University system requires only one year of U.S. History. Biola University, a Christian university in California, requires two years of social studies with no specific courses listed. Many college catalogs list a vague social studies requirement, assuming that whatever the states' school systems have set as graduation requirements will be adequate to meet the college's desire that students be prepared for further study in the history/social studies area.

In states where we have freedom to set our own course of study, we then have plenty of choice in history/social studies. I personally feel that we should be covering all of the above areas at high school level for two reasons: the topics should be covered when students are mature enough to understand the philosophical ideas that motivate history, government, and economics (they are not mature enough in

---

2   In California, one semester of economics became a required course with the 1988-89 school year. It can be covered as a one semester course (the other semester can be spent on U.S. government and civics), or economics can be incorporated into both world and U.S. history studies. Economics textbooks, videos, games, and other learning materials are available to home educators on a "library checkout" basis from the Center for Economic Education with centers located at nineteen California State University campuses. Contact your closest State University's Economics Department to see if they have this program.

elementary grades); and this may be the last or only chance for our children to study these topics from a Christian, patriotic, conservative, free-market perspective (or whatever your personal viewpoint happens to be).

World History Resources

(listed in approximate order of increasing difficulty)

➡ World Studies (BJUP)

Suggested for 7th grade. This outstanding book covers world history at an introductory level. It is interestingly written, well illustrated, and has worthwhile questions. The emphasis on foreign cultures is stronger than it is in the tenth-grade-level *World History*. The student text can be used alone. Excellent comprehension and discussion questions are included, although answers are in the Teacher's Edition. As with some BJUP books, the student text is also contained in the Teacher's Edition so we can buy only the Teacher's Edition, unless we prefer the durability of the hardback text. A TestBank (softbound book) containing a variety of types of test questions for us to use is also available.

➡ Social Studies LifePacs (Alpha Omega) 700 level - 7th grade

Introduces social studies concepts: history, geography, anthropology, sociology, economics, and political science for both the United States and the world. Although this is a more boring approach, it does the job fairly well. It is recommended for parents with little time for direct instruction and children who work well independently.

➡ The History of the World in Christian Perspective: Since the Beginning (A Beka)

Suggested for seventh grade, this text covers ancient history. Watch the reading level since this text is also used on high school level. (A revised edition is due in January of 1993.) This is a good chronological history text, reflecting A Beka's Christian, patriotic, conservative perspective. The Teacher's Guide/Curriculum is useful only for answers. A *Student Test and Map Booklet* and accompanying Teacher's Key are also available. Questions in both the text and test booklet are too detailed, so use them with discretion.

➡ The Modern Age: The History of the World in Christian Perspective (A Beka)

Suggested for eighth grade. This is the chronological continuation of *Since the Beginning*, covering modern history. Watch the reading level since this text is also used on high school level. The format is the same as *Since the Beginning*, listed above.

➡ Streams of Civilization Volumes 1 and 2 (Christian Liberty Press)

Christian Liberty has updated and reprinted a notable history text that went out of print about ten years ago. Volume 1 is presently available, with Volume 2 to follow, probably in the next year. These are Christian texts that recognize the importance of religious and philosophical views throughout history. Coverage of history is broad, yet not as in depth in either content or the handling "ideas" as other high school texts such as those from BJUP. It can be used at either junior or senior high level, since the reading level is not difficult. Black-and-white or two-color illustrations are numerous. At the end of each chapter is a list of suggested projects which range from discussion questions through building projects. For instance, among the options for chapter eleven are writing a detailed report on one of the key figures of the chapter, comparing Mohammed and the

founding of Islam with Joseph Smith and the founding of Mormonism, and make a cut-away model of a donjon. A list of key vocabulary/concept words is also found at the end of each chapter. A separate test packet with answer key is also available for a small additional fee.

➡ World History (BJUP)

This is one of BJUP's best books. Suggested for tenth grade, this book studies world history from a Christian perspective. It includes politics, economics, geography, the arts, and science, concentrating more on the abstract facets of history than on wars and conquests as we generally see in younger level history books. Use this text with BJUP's supplemental maps. The Teacher's Edition contains helpful information but is not essential. A TestBank is also available either in book format or computer data disk.

➡ World History and Cultures in Christian Perspective (A Beka)

This world history text covers both ideas and factual material. The Teacher's Edition contains the actual student text with teacher information in the front of the book. A test booklet and answer key are also available, but, as with other A Beka materials, there is often too much emphasis on detail. The novel, *Animal Farm* is used along with the textbook. The student text includes research suggestions and map projects, while the Teacher's Edition includes suggestions for supplementary materials, a list of objectives, chapter overviews, answers to chapter questions, and more map projects. The perspective is strongly Christian, capitalistic, patriotic, and anti-communist.

➡ Modern Times: From the Twenties to the Nineties Paul Johnson (Harper Collins Publishers)

Serious history students must have this book! Johnson uses Einstein's Theory of Relativity and its impact on society in mid 1919 as a dividing line ushering in "modern times." While this is not a Christian book, a key theme is the abandonment of moral absolutes and the results. Johnson traces this theme through the Russian Revolution, rise of Hitler and the Third Reich, expansion of Communism, changes in Europe, and the moral decline and simultaneous dependency upon government-based solutions in the United States. While that theme is evident, the book can still be viewed on a simpler level as a valuable history resource.

The historical information is loaded with details that enlarge our understanding, yet at the same time will overwhelm many readers. Because Johnson builds his presentation, it is really not practical to use the book as a reference, picking and choosing scattered sections to read. However, there are some sections that you might feel that you can skip while maintaining overall understanding. I suspect that this book will most often be read by adults who will excerpt information to share with their teens, but if your teen is seriously interested in history, I highly recommend that you make this book a part of his library.

American History Resources

➡ The American Republic (BJUP)

Written for eighth grade students, this book is an introduction to United States history. If your child has already studied United States history at an elementary or junior high level, skip to the BJUP eleventh grade level *United States History*. Good discussion questions and well-written text make either BJUP U.S. history book a good choice, although questions in the older level text do require a higher maturity level than do those in the eighth grade text. An AskIt Test Bank Data Disk as well as a TestBank in book form are also available.

Social Studies LifePacs (Alpha Omega) 800 level - 8th grade

United States history is covered in greater depth than at previous levels. See comments directly above.

American Government and Economics (A Beka)

Suggested for ninth grade. American history is prerequisite although this provides quite a bit of review. It presents a conservative, free enterprise, Christian, patriotic perspective, contrasting our government with other governmental systems. The text leans too strongly towards the "America can do no wrong" outlook, but any differences of opinion we might hold should merely provide extra discussion material. Watch for slanted questions such as " Why should all men register for the draft?" (How do pacifists deal with this?) Thought and discussion questions are included in the student text. The student text is sufficient by itself although a Teacher's Guide and Student Test/Review Booklet are also available. While we may not agree with everything, this is an excellent text. Two supplements help to keep things interesting. *We Choose America* is a delightful supplement of short essays and political cartoons. *Animal Farm* by George Orwell helps to round things out even more with its allegorical story of a socialistic government set up by animal characters. (*Animal Farm* is supposed to be used with *World History and Cultures*, but works well with this text.) Both books are available from A Beka.

American Government for Christian Schools (BJUP)

This text, like A Beka's, teaches about our government by interrelating history, including the influences of Christianity. It also incorporates an introduction to economics, comparing different economic systems, while promoting the free enterprise system. The student edition contains both content and application/discussion questions. Student text pages are reprinted in the Teacher's Edition (spiral-bound with a hardback cover rather than the old three-ring binder) which also has objectives, annotations to the text, answers to questions in the student text, and suggested activities in the margins. Instructions for a mock Congress and a mock trial are included, and both activities would be great to do if you can gather a group. The student book can be used on its own if we do not need the answer key in the Teacher's Edition and prefer to have our students work independently; or, students could read the text from the Teacher's Edition rather than purchasing the student text, although they would then have access to answers to questions. This book has been written for twelfth grade students, but may be used with younger students who have developed their thinking skills and have a good background in American history. A TestBank (softbound book) is available. BJUP now has a separate economics text.

Heritage of Freedom (A Beka)

Suggested for eleventh grade. This is a study of United States history from the conservative, patriotic viewpoint. It strongly promotes the benefits of capitalism. Purchase the student text only.

A History of Christianity in the United States and Canada by Mark A. Noll (Wm. B. Eerdmans Publishing Co.)

Since Christianity has played such a key role in the history of both the U.S. and Canada, author Mark Noll has written a history text that focuses in on that topic. Since both countries are closely intertwined historically, he expanded coverage beyond just the United States. Mexico receives brief mentions occasionally, but otherwise has not been included. Noll states in the introduction that for purposes of definition in this book, "...the church consists of all who name the name of Jesus Christ." Because of this, Mormons, Jehovah's Witnesses, Catholics, Seventh Day Adventists, Pentecostals, Presbyterians, and Baptists are all lumped together as Christians with no distinctions made as to what it truly means to be a Christian. While this manner of treatment will offend some, the overall content of the book is valuable for understanding the changes that have taken place in the more private realm of religion as well as in the public arena due to the influence of Christianity.

What appeals to me about this book, is that Noll tries to balance different aspects of people and situations, rather than trying to arrive at some conveniently simplified description. He tells about figures such as Christopher Columbus, showing the strength of courage and spiritual convictions, while also demonstrating that he was sometimes driven by less lofty motivation.

Use this book as a reference tool or as an adjunct to history studies. (Available in either hardback or soft bound editions.)

United States History, 2nd edition (BJUP)

Suggested for eleventh grade. This is another outstanding text from BJUP. It offers an excellent, balanced treatment of history up through the Bush administration, including the role of religion. Rather than simply presenting information, this text looks deeper into philosophies and ideas out of which arise the issues and events of history. The perspective is less extremely conservative/patriotic than A Beka's texts, yet it is still unquestionably conservative in outlook. The Teacher's Edition is not essential if we read the text and keep up with our student. However, it is helpful for answers, activity ideas (many only practical for the classroom), and occasional "additional background." One of the strongest features differentiating this text from A Beka's is the excellent, thought-provoking discussion questions which are included in the student text. The student text is one, large, hardbound book. The Teacher's Edition comes in two, spiral-bound books, with student pages reproduced in only two colors. An AskIt Test Bank Data Disk as well as a TestBank in book form are also available.

I was apprehensive when I saw that BJUP had come out with a second edition of this book, since the first was so good. My fear that the second edition would be weaker than the first seems to be groundless. However, if you will fill in the gaps for recent history, the first edition of this book is still highly recommended. (Try to purchase the accompanying Map Packet if possible.)

A Basic History of the United States by Clarence B. Carson (American Textbook Committee)

This series of five books is written at college/adult level, so it is appropriate for very mature students and might be most useful as a reference tool. Carson presents a conservative's view of United States history from 1607 to 1985. The role of religion in history is discussed yet this is not an obviously Christian series. Carson writes in a more entertaining literary style than is generally found in history texts. He also includes much background information to enhance understanding of events. A Teacher's Guide contains summaries, points to emphasize, discussion questions, lists of people and terms to identify, and activity suggestions that can be used at the teacher's discretion.

➡ **The Primary Source Document Series** (The Perfection Learning)

The series includes seven separate, softbound volumes, each with ten to fifteen source documents. A study guide comes with each book. In addition to each document, we get a brief summary of its origins and thought provoking questions. Topics: Volume 1—Pre-revolutionary America; Volume 2—The Founding Period; Volume 3—Expanding America; Volume 4—Modern America (liberal ideas are heavily represented); Volume 5—American Court Cases; Volume 6—Early American Speeches; and, Volume 7—Modern American Speeches (weighted towards humanistic ideas and Democratic influence). The documents from earlier periods and court cases make interesting reading and serve as excellent supplements to history studies.(S)

If you are interested in the conservative, patriotic viewpoint, you might also use *We Choose America*, by Thomas Williams (A Beka), *Masters of Deceit*, by J. Edgar Hoover (A Beka), and *You Can Trust the Communists*, by Dr. Fred Schwarz. All are excellent books that give a reasoned analysis of the evils of communism without being "hysterical."

Easier Level Texts

For students who have lower reading levels we recommend three books that can be used as a series to cover United States history and government: *America's Early Years, Twentieth Century America*, and *Democracy in Action* (Steck-Vaughn). These are thinner books, in worktext formats, which cover the basics. They ignore religion's role in our country's formation and instead include women and blacks as do most secular textbooks. The general tone is anti-communistic. The discussion questions are very good for thinking and application of principles covered. Vocabulary study helps students better understand what they read. These are recommended for remedial high school level.

Geography

The best way to teach geography is to travel, referring to maps as we go. Since travel is too expensive for most of us, the easiest way to teach geography is to always refer to maps, globes, or historical atlases as we study history or read other books with actual geographical settings. Other materials can serve as supplements. Workbooks, atlases, and other materials are available from Nystrom Publishers, Hammond Inc., or American Map Corporation. Current periodicals such as *National Geographic Magazine* (SE) are wonderful, in spite of their evolutionary outlook. National Geographic maps that come with some issues are superb, often providing much more information than just the geographical locations. Many of these maps actually teach history, science, geology, sociology, and other topics. These should be filed and used as needed rather than left in the magazines. Some thrift stores bind and sell old *National Geographic* maps. This is a very inexpensive way to get some of these maps. The National Geographic Society also publishes many other, little-known instructional materials. Among these is *Teaching Geography: A Model for Action Handbook*—a resource manual to help us incorporate geography instruction into our curriculum. It includes lesson plans and lists of resources. Write to The National Geographic Society

for more information about this and other geography teaching materials.

Computer fans learn geography and reference skills by role playing as detectives tracking down notorious criminals in the *Carmen Sandiego* games (Broderbund) reviewed above. The first three games are fun but a little young for high schoolers. *Where in Time* is written on an older level and also teaches some history. This is the one to get for older students.

Most students will prefer games far above textbooks for geography studies, so I also include reviews of two excellent geography games.

➡ **Geography** (BJUP)

Although titled "Geography," this appears to be more of a social studies course since it includes much more than geographic information. This makes the course more interesting than if it dealt only with geography. A missionary and spiritual context raises it above the level of typical secular social studies texts. This is a large (616 page) book, written for ninth grade level, with an accompanying activity book that should also be used. The Teacher's Edition is helpful, and a TestBank book with a variety of questions that we can use to create tests is also available.

➡ **Global Pursuit** (National Geographic)

This well-designed game for teaching geography has the excellent National Geographic quality we find in their magazines. Questions are very challenging—too much for students below fifth grade at the easiest level of questions—so buy it for upper elementary through high school levels. There are different levels of questions and a few variations in the way the game can be played. Unlike some educational games, this is one that some (not all!) children will choose to play because it is fun.(S)

➡ **Mapping the World by Heart** by David Smith (Tom Snyder Productions)

Would you like your children to be able to draw a map of the entire world, including latitude and longitude markings without copying or referring to another map? David Smith's methods are designed to enable children to do just that. This geography curriculum is recommended for grades 5-12, although if fits most appropriately in upper elementary and junior high levels. It uses an assortment of activities to develop map skills, but the most important are the actual map-drawing activities. Besides properly locating and identifying places, children learn geographical knowledge that includes map reading skills, i.e., directions, symbols, topographical maps (great activities for learning how to make these!), the various types of map projections, the earth's rotation/seasons, dimensions, and more.

This ungraded program comes in a nicely designed three-ring binder. It can be used as a one-year program or it can be used as a supplement over a number of years, perhaps studying continents in conjunction with history topics. Lessons are well-designed and easy-to-follow. Great illustrations and layout make it especially easy to use.

Lessons need to be presented by the parent/teacher, but after the presentation students do much of the work on their own using reproducible work sheets from the binder. With the binder we get one set of 9 double-sided 11" x 15" maps to be used by students for initial work. We also get three projection maps (three different types) drawn on grids, plus three blank, 11" x 17" grids (reproducible) for students to use for their final map which will be done from memory. Additional maps are available in sets.

There are lots of extras included in the program that we can use or not as we please—games, activity ideas, mnemonics, addresses for resources, and instructions for putting on a "World's Fair."

This method of learning geography has proven to be much more effective and less painless than traditional methods since it involves a variety of activities that interest and challenge students.

I suggest using it either while doing United States and World history studies in upper elementary and junior high levels or else as a concentrated course just before starting U.S. and World history study at high school level. I say this because at younger levels students lack knowledge of people, places, and events to which they can relate geographical knowledge, so they are less likely to be interested. Older students need the concrete geographical knowledge to help them understand and link events as they are presented in upper level studies.

➡Where in the World (Aristoplay)

This game contains four different game variations. Players of different skill levels can play together by selecting easier or more difficult questions. Play can be concentrated on one geographical region being studied if desired. Along with geography, players learn some economic and cultural information. At the top level, current events are incorporated into game play. I recommend it because of the quality construction, educational value, and great variety of usage. For ages eight to adult.(S)

Studying the U.S. Constitution and Law

➡Constitutional Law for Christian Students by Michael P. Farris, Esq. (Home School Legal Defense Association)

Serious students at the junior and senior levels of high school will develop a much better understanding of the present state of Constitutional law from reading this book. It contains actual text of Supreme Court decisions that have helped to shape law into its present form, along with the original texts of the foundational documents of our government. Commentary by Mr. Farris prior to each document guides students in their reading to key points in the decision. Study questions which can be used either for written work or discussion help to enlarge understanding.

The first unit discusses the "Historical Background of the Constitution." Farris uses an interesting analogy, comparing the Declaration of Independence and the Constitution to a present day corporation's articles of incorporation and by-laws respectively. Other related documents such as The Articles of Confederation and The Bill of Rights are included in the discussion.

Unit II addresses "The Constitution as Higher Law," covering the roles of state and federal constitutions and the establishment of the principle of judicial review. Unit III deals with executive and legislative branches and limits to their constitutional authority. Unit IV tackles the thorny problem of the judicial branch acting as lawmaker, and also the proper limitations on the scope of judicial activity. Unit V uses the last third of the book to cover religion-related constitutional issues, which should be of special interest to Christian students.

While the commentary is very readable, some of the justices' writing takes perseverance to unravel, so make sure your teen is able to work at this level. This book is also recommended for all adults. The accompanying, inexpensive teacher's handbook is recommended.

➡The Making of America: The Substance and Meaning of the Constitution by W. Cleon Skousen (National Center for Constitutional Studies)

Recommended for advanced students in grades 10-12. This book includes some U.S. history and biographies, with emphasis on the constitution. It is written from a Christian perspective, although it is not overtly Christian in content. Check out other books from the National Center for Constitutional Studies, such as biographies of George Washington, Benjamin Franklin and Thomas Jefferson and *Soldiers, Statesmen, and Heroes*, which is about the first seven presidents. Avoid their tapes and workbooks. The tapes are boring to listen to, and the workbooks work on simple recall of facts already covered in the book.

➡The Story of the Constitution (Christian Liberty Press)

This paperback edition is a reprint of a 1937 book, but with a few additions and updates. The first and most interesting section is the background information, followed by brief biographies of the signers, then the text of the Constitution and amendments. Next is an alphabetical analysis of the Constitution (similar to a concordance), then a few interesting writings such as Washington's "Farewell Address." Last is a section of random questions and answers to pass on interesting tidbits of information such as the number of lawyers who were members of the Constitutional Convention. This book was designed to be used with *The Land of Fair Play* (a CLP book) for a complete civics class. *The Land of Fair Play*, an in-depth civics textbook, is in the process of being updated and expanded. Wait for the new edition which should be available in Spring of 1993.

➡Whatever Happened to Justice? [from the "Uncle Eric" series] by Richard J. Maybury (Bluestocking Press)

The author of *Whatever Happened to Penny Candy?* has done even better with *Whatever Happened to Justice?* Written for a slightly older audience (age twelve and up), it discusses how our justice system has changed from a reliance upon common law to a reliance on political law. He shows how the abandonment of common law has left us with a fickle system that reacts to pressure as much as to any more important factor of law.

Maybury has a gift for translating what sounds like tedious information into very personalized examples. He follows the *Penny Candy* format where Uncle Eric is writing letters to nephew or niece Chris (could be male or female). Each letter is reasonably brief, so students will not be overwhelmed with too much information at once.

Some "chapter" titles are "Two Kinds of Law," "The Lawless West," "Instability, Nuremberg, and Abortion," "Competing for Privilege," "The Constitution: Highest Law of the Land?," and "Are Lawyers and Judges Corrupt?" Final letters address "unsolved problems" such as risk, capital punishment, the environment, and poverty.

Use this book as a supplement to American history or government studies. It will not take much time to read through, although it might generate lengthy discussions. No matter what else you use, this book is a must!(S)

America's Christian History

There is tremendous interest in America's Christian history, partly as a result of the determination by some Christians to set aright the falsehoods that have been taught for so many years. There are now many excellent books, cassettes, and videos that correct the historical record.[3]

➠America, The First 350 Years [audio tapes with study guide] by J. Steven Wilkins (Covenant Publications)

This is a more in-depth study than either *The Light and the Glory* or *The American Covenant*, yet it is very easy to understand because of the excellent presentation. The set comes with 16, ninety-minute cassette tapes (with two lectures per tape), a three-ring binder notebook, and a study guide that can also be inserted into the binder. Mr. Wilkins' goal is to teach the truth about American history—to correct the misinformation that has been taught as fact in the schools and the media. He covers selected historic events and ideas from colonization through the Civil War, with an underlying theme of how far our country has strayed from its original ideals and the need to resurrect those ideals. He does have some strong theological leanings (e.g., postmillenialism) that you may or may not agree with, but these play a minor part in the presentation. Mr. Wilkins is speaking to an adult audience, yet the tapes could be used with junior high or high school students. Ideally, this should be used as a family study with older children. (Younger children will probably have too short an attention span to listen through the tapes.) The notebook clearly outlines each presentation with the key ideas noted. Documentation of quotations and bibliographies are included. The notebook itself can be used as a refresher course for review. The Study Guide has a page of discussion questions (which could also be writing assignments) for each tape. This set would also work well with an adult study group. Components can be purchased separately or as a set. The price is very reasonable for so many tapes.

➠America's Godly Heritage [video] (Wallbuilders)

David Barton sets forth the beliefs of many of the famous founding fathers concerning the proper role of Christian principles in education, government, and the public affairs of our nation. Excerpts from court cases show that for 160 years Christian principles were upheld. Graphics show the degeneration in America since rejecting the founders' beliefs.

➠The American Covenant, The Untold Story by Marshall Foster and Mary Elaine Swanson (The Mayflower Institute)

This book is about America's Christian history and also relates to the Principle Approach. It has workbook exercises and can be used alone or with two other Principle Approach volumes, *Teaching and Learning America's Christian History* and *The Christian History of the Constitution of the United States of America* (published by Foundation for American Christian Education, but also available through American Christian History Institute and others). *The American Covenant* presents the key events which shaped America's history, emphasizing the Christian character of our founding fathers as well as the biblical principles which were an intrinsic part of our country's history. This book is probably the easiest to work with of all those available that address America's Christian history.

The American Covenant Audio Seminar—an eight hour seminar on eight cassette tapes—dramatically enhances the information in the book.

The American Covenant Movie is a video tour of ten of America's great monuments, which provide a backdrop to Marshall Foster's presentation on the forgotten roots of our country.

➠God and Government—Volume 1: A Biblical and Historical Study; Volume 2: Issues in Biblical Perspective; and Volume 3: Restoration of the Republic by Gary DeMar (American Vision, formerly published by Wolgemuth and Hyatt)

This series of three books was written to help Christians develop a biblical world view and an understanding of the Christian foundations of our country. Begin with *Volume 1* and use the books in sequence. (It is not necessary to use all volumes.) Written for junior high level or above, *God and Government* works well as a supplement to history, government, and Bible study. DeMar quotes widely from both Scripture and historical documents to provide evidence for his assertions. Essay type questions for discussion or writing are at the end of each chapter, with answers provided in the book. (There is no separate teacher edition or answer key.)

➠The Light and the Glory by Peter Marshall and David Manuel (Baker Book House, formerly published by Fleming H. Revell)

If you have teens who have already taken secular history courses in school, this is a great book to introduce them to a different viewpoint for studying early American history. It tells the stories of famous men in our country's early history, including in those stories the often ignored influence of God in their lives. This is the history that most of us never learned! A Study Guide workbook is also available. Follow this book with the sequel *From Sea to Shining Sea*, which covers the period from the Constitutional Convention up to pre-Civil War times. No study guide is available for the second book.

➠The Mayflower Institute offers seminars featuring Marshall Foster on topics relating to America's Christian history. Many of these are available on audio and/or video cassette. Write for their brochure of available titles and descriptions.

➠Story of America's Liberty [video] (American Portrait Films)

This is an educational documentary on America's Christian heritage. The key idea which it communicates is that America was founded on Christian principles and with a recognition of God's providence in the challenges faced by our founding fathers. There was recognition that they were dependent upon God's continued blessing to survive, an important truth seemingly lost in modern America. Video footage of historical sights, documents, paintings, statues, etc., provide evidence along with quotations from original

---

3   Sources that specialize in America's Christian history materials are *American Christian History Institute, Foundation for American Christian Education, The Family Educator, The Horne Booke*, and the *Mayflower Institute*.

writings. While junior high students will learn much from this video, I think that senior high students will benefit most, especially if they take time to discuss the people, events, and ideas presented.

The Principle Approach

The Principle Approach requires much study and planning on the part of the teacher/parent, but the results are worth the effort. Most people using the Principle Approach have children keep a notebook for recording information that has been researched and studied. The application of concepts is also recorded in the notebook.

Seven principles are identified, studied, and used as a foundation for further learning. The principles are:
– God's principle of individuality
– The Christian principle of self-government
– America's heritage of Christian character
– Conscience is the most sacred of all property
– The Christian form of our government
– How the seed of local self-government is planted
– The Christian principle of American political union

History is an important aspect of the Principle Approach—primarily America's Christian history—but the Principle Approach can be applied to all subject areas as explained in Mr. Rose's book listed below.

If the Principle Approach appeals to us, junior high and high school would seem to me the ideal time to pursue this with our children since they are now able to deal with abstract ideas better than at elementary levels (although many families are implementing this method very successfully at younger levels.)

Below are listed books based upon the Principle Approach. Contact Foundation for American Christian Education (F.A.C.E.) or the American Christian History Institute for more information.

➡️**America's Christian History** by Jean Ryland-Smithies (Intrepid Books)

This is a series of eight books written for grades one through eight, but also usable on older levels. The language and vocabulary are purposely on a higher level than today's textbooks written for those grades. Mrs. Ryland has made the Principle Approach very accessible with these books. They are thought provoking without being overwhelming.This is not a typical U.S. history course since it concentrates on particular points to illustrate principles.

➡️**The Christian History of the American Revolution** by Verna M. Hall (Foundation for American Christian Education)

This volume provides the Biblical background of the American Revolution by comparing the liberty of the Gospel with American political liberty.

➡️**The Christian History of the Constitution of the United States of America, Volume I and Volume II**, subtitled **Christian Self-Government with Union** (Foundation for American Christian Education)

These books by Verna Hall provide the primary source references that help to form the philosophical foundation for the Principle Approach. They also lay out the basic principles. They are rather confusing to use on their own but work best as source books in conjunction with other books listed below. These are beautiful, hardbound volumes as are

the other books from Foundation for American Christian Education.

➡️**A Guide to American Christian Education for the Home and School, The Principle Approach, second edition** (available late 1992) by James B. Rose (American Christian History Institute)

This is THE book about how to teach the various subjects by the Principle Approach. It is a beautifully bound, very large book—550 pages, requiring a significant study effort. However, it attempts to answer all the questions that arise over implementation of the Principle Approach. It defines the Principle Approach and the Seven Principles. It discusses application of the Principle Approach in both the school at home and the Christian school. Some of the most valuable information in this book is that which tells how to "4=R" a subject and how to use the Principle Approach to teach literature, geography, history, economics, science, mathematics, and typing.

➡️**The Rudiments of America's Christian History and Government: Student Handbook** by Rosalie J. Slater and Verna M. Hall (Foundation for American Christian Education)

The purpose of this book is to introduce students to the reasoning and writing of biblical principles applied in *The Christian History* volumes and *Teaching and Learning America's Christian History*.

➡️**Study Guide to the Christian History of the Constitution of the United States of America, Volume II** by Mary-Elaine Swanson (American Christian History Institute)

The purpose of the *Study Guide* is to focus on materials in Volume II of *Christian History of the Constitution* which tell how and where our Founders discovered and developed the seeds of American unity and union. The principles underlying the choices of our founding fathers are stressed, demonstrating their reliance upon a Christian world view. The *Guide* may be used by adults or mature high school students. The use of a notebook as outlined in *The Principle Approach* (by Slater) is strongly recommended.

➡️**Teaching and Learning America's Christian History: The Principle Approach**, by Rosalie Slater (Foundation for American Christian Education)

This volume outlines the seven basic principles with lesson plans and background information. Each topic is frequently cross referenced to the above *Christian History Volumes* by Verna Hall. This book will get you started, but will not carry you through into all subject areas as does the book by James Rose.

Extra Resources for the Principle Approach

➡️**Physical Geography** by Arnold Guyot (American Christian History Institute)

This is a reprint of the 1885 edition of this book. It serves as a companion to the section on teaching geography in James Rose's *A Guide to American Christian Education*. It is also quoted and referred to in *Teaching and Learning America's Christian History*, although it is not required for that book. I am not knowledgeable enough to critique the geographic content of the book, and I assume that it is accurate, although there are certainly recent discoveries that shed more light on some topics (such as earthquakes and plate tectonics). When the author ventures away from geographical facts the content of the book becomes debatable. I am bothered by Guyot's approach to the "Human Family"—the white caucasian is held up as the ideal with every other race as inferior. He also makes other simplistic generalizations about continents and historical movements that are more philosophical than factual. However, his explanation of racial differences (physical, mental, and moral) presents an interesting perspective which is valid to some degree. This is a heavy duty geography textbook. It is not very readable alone but serves better as a source book.

➡ **June Keith Book Catalogue** (Foundation for American Christian Education)

This catalog lists books to be used for a Christian History Literature Program as recommended by James Rose and other leading figures advocating the Principle Approach. The selection of books promises to be very helpful to all home schoolers. Books are chosen for their contributions to our understanding of the principles taught through the Principle Approach. Some of these are very difficult to find from other sources. They also carry syllabi to enhance study of some of the books.

➡ **The American Dictionary of the English Language, a facsimile 1828 edition** by Noah Webster (Foundation for American Christian Education)

A dictionary seems an unusual item to list under history, but this one is different. Webster provides Biblical references within many definitions to clarify the meaning and usage of words. Definitions of many words have changed since 1828, and this dictionary helps us to properly interpret source documents from America's beginnings by defining words as their original writers intended. The use of this dictionary is also a vital part of the Principle Approach since one of the first steps in studying a subject is to properly define it.

In Addition to Textbooks

History Games

➡ **By Jove** (Aristoplay)

Before playing the game, we "meet" the mythological characters by reading the included storybook, *By Jove Stories*. Then we allow our children to experience for themselves the capriciousness of the so-called gods that were worshipped by ancient civilizations as they play this board game. Children learn about classical mythology characters such as Hercules, Ulysses, and Achilles while also learning about the religious beliefs that spawned them. For ages ten to adult.(S)

➡ **Hail to the Chief: The Presidential Election Game** (Aristoplay)

This game reviews American history and helps students understand how our electoral system works. This is a high quality game with a full color game board, and numerous play options. Questions assume a basic knowledge of United States history.

➡ **Made for Trade: A Game of Early American Life** (Aristoplay)

Learn about the history, culture, trades, and economy of colonial America with this outstanding game for ages eight to adult, with four different levels of play.(S)

➡ **Where in the U.S.A. is Carmen Sandiego?, Where in the World is Carmen Sandiego?, and Where in Europe is Carmen Sandiego?** (Broderbund)

These highly recommended computer software programs (IBM and Apple) require research through the enclosed guidebooks, maps, encyclopedias, and more as the player tracks down the villains. The incentive to learn geographical information along with some history is enhanced when the computer (rather than the teacher) tells a child to go look something up. Games can be saved, and players advance in rank as they capture gang members until they capture Carmen Sandiego herself. Recommended for upper elementary through adult.

➡ **Where in Time is Carmen Sandiego?** (Broderbund)

This is the newest computer game in the *Carmen Sandiego* series. It is available now in IBM format but should be in Apple format before too long. Graphics are improved over other *Carmen Sandiego* games, and funny, little graphic "extras" have been added throughout the game. It is slightly more difficult than others in the series, according to my on-site game testers. *The New American Desk Encyclopedia*, a two-inch-thick reference book, comes with the game. The format is the same as the others—detectives tracking down Carmen Sandiego and her gang members. The detective in this case jumps on his chronoskimmer from country to country, and back and forth through time, following clues to track down his prey. Some of the historical data that comes up on the screen can be ignored by players without affecting the game, and children quickly learn which things they need to pay attention to. So they do not learn everything to which they are exposed. Yet, the value as a learning tool is still terrific. Do you know to what country and in what time period you would go to find William the Silent? If the player doesn't know, he can find out from the *Desk Encyclopedia*, but, if he's too slow he will use up all of the time allotted to him for solving the case. Recommended for upper elementary through adult.

Current Events

The study of current events is essential for informed citizens. Skip the television news reports that are more entertainment than information. Instead read newspapers, news magazines, or weekly publications from God's World Publications[4]. God's World publishes elementary level newspapers and two older level resources that interest us here: *God's World Today* for junior high or the adult level *World* magazine. Teacher's Helper sheets that come with individual orders of *God's World Today* give in-depth study ideas for current news topics. Both present Christian perspectives on current events with some commentary.

Missionary and evangelistic outreaches also provide wonderful incentives for cultural studies. Supporting a mis-

---

4   *God's World Today* is published every week through the school year. *World* magazine is published weekly most of the year, with the exception of biweekly publication in May, June, July, August, and December, for a total of 40 issues per year.

sionary organization and reading their newsletters or magazines gives us a much better picture of particular cultures than we could ever get from textbooks.

For current events from a broader and more comprehensive perspective, check out the *National Public-policy Resource Theme-packets*. These are an unusual resource that can do a great job of turning our older students on to learning. C. Bernard Schriver, an educational and public affairs consultant, has researched many current event topics, summarized background information for us, compiled articles, and suggested activities for student involvement. Schriver says, "Analysis includes contemporary application of the principles of traditional American concepts of individual rights, private property, free markets, and limited Constitutional government." While Schriver's conservative philosophy is usually evident in the analytic material, the articles and other material he includes present a range of viewpoints to encourage thinking.

Some topics of earlier *Theme-packets* are "America's First Post-Cold War Challenge" (the Persian Gulf crisis), "Taxpayers' 'Bill of Rights'," "Goals of America's Homosexual Lobby," "Supreme Court and Separation of Powers," and "Clarence Thomas' Supreme Court Bid." There are four *Theme-packets* on free-market economics and eight in a Constitutional series entitled "Beyond the Bicentennial/America's Third Century."

Some topics on the agenda for the 1992-93 school year are "Election Year 1992," "Christopher Columbus' Quincentennial," "Flat-Rate Income Tax," "Multiculturalism," Environmentalism in the 1990's," and "Ex-Soviet Union in the Post-Cold War Era."

Packet prices range from $5-$15, depending upon the size of each, with most close to $10. We can "subscribe" and receive nine packets for the school year, mailed monthly as they are compiled. However, the cost ($100) might be prohibitive for many families. They can instead purchase only the packets that seem most pertinent to their studies. (Select a free packet with orders of $50 or more.) Another alternative is sharing the cost of the series through a support group or with other families.

The value of these packets lies in the fact that Schriver does the research that most of us do not have time and money to do. He pulls together information and presents it within a context that stimulates students to examine issues on a deeper level than occurs when they simply read through textbooks. Consider using some of these as supplements to history, government, and economics courses or as part of world view studies.

Mr. Schriver is offering home educators their choice of one packet from his catalog at half-price as an incentive to check them out. The free catalog describes the packets clearly, so we can easily identify those most useful for our studies if we choose to purchase them individually.

Test Taking Skills for Social Studies

➠ Mastering Social Studies Skills (Amsco)

This unusual book is not a social studies course, but a resource which teaches some basics of social studies while primarily teaching test-taking skills. The social studies content consists primarily of geography—map reading, latitude and longitude, climate zones, time zones, and the various types of maps. Test-taking skills are not limited to the social studies area, just as most social studies tests do

not usually test social studies knowledge as much as they do reading and thinking skills.

These test-taking skills include reading; writing; use of reference tools; reading tables, charts, and graphs; and interpreting photographs, drawings, and cartoons (editorial or political).

Of particular interest to me is the writing section where the book helps students understand the difference between a single sentence answer and a paragraph answer to a question. It shows them how to expand on a brief answer, an important skill to develop for essay questions.

Junior or senior high students who have had little exposure to standardized tests or those who have weak backgrounds in social studies will benefit from this book. It is in worktext format, with many practice exercises on the above topics. I reviewed the softbound edition, but it is also available as a hardback book. Inexpensive answer keys are available.(SE-watch cartoon section particularly for subtle biases.)

Economics

Introductory Economics

➠ Whatever Happened to Penny Candy? [from the "Uncle Eric" series] by Richard J. Maybury (Bluestocking Press)

For the economically illiterate, begin with the book *Whatever Happened to Penny Candy?*, a simple, entertaining introduction to economics. *Penny Candy* introduces the economic facts of life where they touch us most—continuing increases in the cost of things. The book is written as a series of letters from fictional Uncle Eric to Chris, who could be either his niece or nephew. Uncle Eric explains simply the economic facts of life, adding interesting historical tidbits along the way. Doses of economic theory in each letter are just enough to prod thinking without overload. The author has also included an excellent annotated bibliography with suggestions for where to go next to learn more about economics. The newly revised version includes a pamphlet of Teacher Support Materials—essay and discussion questions, activity suggestions, a quiz, and answer key.

Canadians can order a twenty-page supplement to *Penny Candy* that explains the differences between American and Canadian monetary and economic history, which will help Canadian students better understand and apply the principles taught. Order the supplement from Window Tree Learning Project or Bluestocking Press.(S)

➠ Young Thinker's Bookshelf: Books, Software, Movies, Toys, Games, Music, and Audio Cassettes to Encourage Independent and Critical Thinking by Jane Williams (Bluestocking Press)

This is a guide to books, cassettes, computer software, and movies relating to literature, history, law, business, economics, communication, learning/education, and critical thinking. The author believes in free market economics and recommends materials which support that viewpoint.(S)

➠ Biblical Economics in Comics (Vic Lockman)

Biblical Economics in Comics teaches economic principles in story form with great comic illustrations. As children learn principles of economics they also find out how government intervention makes a mess of things. Lockman includes at the end a Biblical view of government and economics. This book is for all ages, although teens and adults will better understand Lockman's views while younger children may simply perceive the book as entertainment. This is an inexpensive supplement everyone can use.

➡ **Get a Grip on Your Money: A Young Adult Study in Christian Financial Management by Larry Burkett (Focus on the Family)**

High school students will find Burkett's approach to personal economics much easier to understand than most textbook presentations. Topics covered from a Biblical perspective are choosing a career, looking for work, resumès, job interviews, budgets, record keeping, checking accounts, loans and credit cards, coping with budget busters, insurance, buying a car, buying a first home, and giving to God. The student text has reproducible forms/work sheets in the back. A student can work independently, and the thirteen lessons should take about one hour each to complete. As far as I can tell, the Teacher's Guide is not essential for students studying independently, but it is very useful for class instruction with suggestions for presentations, discussions, and activities. There are quizzes in the student book, but the answer key is found in the back of the student book. Cartoon illustrations that make the book user-friendly, practical illustrations, and solid teaching make this the best resource I have seen for covering these topics with teens.

➡ **Money, Banking, and Usury (Vic Lockman)**

Vic Lockman teaches how banks use fractional reserves to enrich themselves, and how the government creates money. He also covers the subject of debt, including scriptural injunctions against debt. He uses his trademark cartoon presentation format. This book should be understandable for most junior high students and is appropriate for anyone older.

➡ **Introduction to Business (Educational Development Corporation)**

From Usborne's line of outstanding books, comes *Introduction to Business*, a guide to setting up and running a business. This is on elementary/junior high level. As in all of the Usborne books, wonderful illustrations make a dull subject interesting.(S)

➡ **Surviving the Money Jungle: A Junior High Study in Handling Money by Larry Burkett (Focus on the Family)**

Larry Burkett does just as good a job on the junior high level as he has done for years for adults. He presents financial principles and practical guidelines from a biblical perspective, making them easy to understand. In this book he discusses attitudes toward work and work habits; the secret of contentment; honesty in money handling; debt; the difference between needs, wants, and wishes; hoarding versus saving; tithing; and how to decide with whom we should share our wealth (charity). There are thirteen lessons in all. Cartoon illustrations help capture attention. Students can work through the student workbook independently, although the course was designed for class presentation. The optional Teacher's Guide has tips for class presentation, activities, and discussion. There is no answer key, since the workbook is more for personal development and application than for review of material studied. Older students can work at a more mature level in Burkett's *Get A Grip on Your Money*.

More Challenging Resources for Economics

➡ **American Government (BJUP)**

This text, reviewed above, also covers economics. Note that BJUP also has a separate economics text reviewed below.

➡ **A Banker's Confession by Gary Sanseri (Back Home Industries)**

This is an easy-reading book about debt, thrift, and wise use of resources from a Christian perspective. Sanseri offers practical suggestions for Christians trying to live by biblical principles in a world which has rejected them. His use of history and stories helps to illustrate and explain his reasoning. Sanseri, a banker by profession, also advocates prepayment of home mortgages, demonstrating mathematically the huge financial savings that can result. This is an excellent book for older students who will soon be involved in the treacherous financial marketplace. I recommend it also to college students and adults. A companion study guide with questions to reinforce and expand ideas in the book is also available.

➡ **Basic Economics by Clarence Carson (American Textbook Committee)**

Some students may want to go beyond the basic introduction to economics that is presented in government and economics texts from A Beka and BJUP. Carson's book draws very much upon history and government for an understanding of economics and, again, reflects a conservative, Christian philosophy, but with a strong emphasis on free enterprise and private property rights. It is recommended only for very capable students or else as a resource text for selected readings.

➡ **Larry Burkett books**

The Coming Economic Earthquake (Moody Press), *Surviving the 90's Economy* (Moody Press), *Investing for the Future* (Victor Books), and other books by Larry Burkett offer a Christian outlook upon our shaky economic situation. The contents of many of Burkett's books overlap each other, so it is not necessary to read all of his books. Teens can choose topics that are of most interest.

The Coming Economic Earthquake predicts a rather dismal economic future based upon factors such as the deficit, financial shortcomings on state and local levels, the savings and loan collapse, personal debt, social security's likely shortfall, stock market cycles, and foreign loans. He suggests strategies for Christians such as becoming debt free and changing investments. The book includes a very practical list of helpful resources.

Surviving the 90's Economy reviews many of the causes of economic decline mentioned above plus others. Then Burkett offers broader coverage of solutions and strategies for government, business, and family to manage in tough times.

Investing for the Future focuses in on investment strategy. While it reviews some common Burkett themes such as becoming debt free, it goes much further in personal financial planning. Of particular interest to teens should be his suggestions for the first "financial season of life" where he addresses situations faced by young couples. (Parents should be interested in the specific advice Burkett offers.)

Teens interested in financial careers will find any of these books very helpful as a Christian balance to the typical education in economics and financial planning.

➠Economics for Christian Schools (Bob Jones University Press)

BJUP's new economics text is designed for use at twelfth grade level. It deals with economics in business, government, the marketplace, and the home. The ideas taught reflect free-market philosophy and Christian values, although students do learn about conflicting ideas. Students are introduced to many key people in economics on both philosophical and practical levels through brief biographical sketches. Brief sketches on different countries help us understand global implications of any country's economic policies and choices. Chapter reviews include terms (definitions), content questions, and excellent application questions. The Teacher's Edition is useful to home schoolers as an answer key, but it also contains margin notes, objectives, activity suggestions including an interesting stock market project, supplementary ideas, a resource directory, and a bibliography. A TestBank (softbound book) and AskIt are also available.

➠Economics: Principles and Policy, Second Edition by Tom Rose (American Enterprise Publications)

This is a basic economics course from a Christian perspective, written at a challenging level. A teacher's manual is available which provides teaching helps and answers to the textbook questions. Recommended for grades 11 or 12.

➠Economics: The American Economy by Tom Rose (American Enterprise Publications)

This is a companion text to the above book. A teacher's manual is available that provides teaching helps and answers to the textbook questions.

➠Economics: Work and Prosperity (A Beka)

This new text by Dr. Russell Kirk, one of the leading conservative writers in the United States, seems less like a textbook than other A Beka books, probably because it is so well written. Rather than teaching dry economic theory, Dr. Kirk uses our daily encounters with economics (at the grocery store, the shopping mall, etc.) to illustrate principles. As we would expect from this author, he explains and de-

fends the free enterprise system. Competition, supply and demand, and government influence upon economics are also covered. Discussion questions are interspersed where appropriate rather than at the end of each chapter. The questions are dramatically different from those found in most A Beka texts—they are interesting and relevant. The book is listed in the catalog as a one-semester course for twelfth grade level, but the reading level is appropriate for most high schoolers. The limiting factor is that students must have the familiarity with modern history that is necessary for full comprehension of this text.

➠Free Enterprise Economics (American Enterprise Publications)

This eighteen-page pamphlet provides a concise explanation of free enterprise economics.

➠Government and Economics (A Beka)

See description above. The viewpoint is Christian and supports the free market.

➠The Myth of the Robber Barons by Burton W. Folsom, Jr. (Young America's Foundation)

This is a GREAT book. The author divides entrepreneurs into the two categories of market and political entrepreneurs. Political entrepreneurs depend on the government for financial backing, political favors, real estate bargains, etc., while market entrepreneurs rely on the free market to accomplish their ends. The author shoots down the traditional lumping together of nineteenth and twentieth century capitalists under the description "robber barons" by pointing out the differences in approach between a good businessman and a businessman who uses the government to "steal" from others. Presented in biographical story fashion, the book makes interesting reading, although the closing chapter (where the author attempts to sum things up) is superfluous. Key figures featured in the book are Cornelius Vanderbilt, James J. Hill, The Scrantons, Charles Schwab, John D. Rockefeller, and Andrew Mellon. My thanks to Anne Beams, a terrific historian and economist from San Diego for putting us on to this book.

Chapter Fourteen

Science

Junior High Science: Preparing for High School

Students should have a good foundation in basic science concepts when they enter ninth grade. *Model Curriculum Standards, Grades Nine through Twelve* , first edition (California Department of Education), lists these prerequisites that teens should have before taking high school level science:

1. Knowledge of environmental phenomena that children experience as they grow. This includes biological principles such as the growth of plants and animals and interrelationships among living things, and physical events such as lightning and thunder, sounds, and energy sources.

2. Skills of scientific investigation learned in previous laboratory science classes. This includes using the scientific method, understanding cause and effect relationships, and following safety precautions.

3. Attitudes about the role science plays in understanding and manipulating our environment. (Author's Note: The state's ideas about what our attitudes toward science should be, as listed in the rest of the prerequisites, reflect a humanistic value system, so I do not include them.)

4. Basic skills of reading and mathematics. The prerequisite skill in reading enables students to read science texts, laboratory manuals, and periodicals as well as to decode new vocabulary and terminology. Mathematical abilities, especially computation, problem solving, algebraic concepts, and measuring/graphic skills are integral to successful performance on the topics contained in these model curriculum standards. (Author's Note: Students will have varying needs for math skills depending upon which science courses they choose to take.)

These prerequisites are not as difficult as they sound. If we have our young people read books about science-related topics, perform experiments, go on field trips, and take time to explore science they will have done most of it. Scientific method is essentially logical thinking and recording of information. It need not be any more difficult than doing an experiment with seed growth under different conditions, recording results, and suggesting reasons for the recorded results.

If one or more of the above areas are weak, choose materials or activities that will help fill the learning gap so that students will be prepared for high school science.

Junior High, Recommended Texts

➡ Earth Science [revised, second edition text and Teacher's Edition] (BJUP)

This is a well-written book with interesting and worthwhile activities. However, the scope and sequence seems to be different from many other earth science texts with more emphasis on astronomy and less on topics such as oceanography than is typical. Purchase both the student text and the Activity Edition for experiments. Since most of the experiments can be done at home, but not necessarily indoors, it is practical for home schoolers to use. Teacher's Editions for both the text and the Activity Edition are available. It is written for eighth grade level, but could be used for junior or senior high. If the activities do not fit your needs, consider substituting *Affirmative Guides Volume II-Our Wonderful Earth* (Science Projects, Inc.).

I understand that the major change in the second edition is a reordering of chapters into a more logical progression. The old *Activity Edition* can still be used with the second edition text by simply choosing activities in the order topics are studied.

➡ Investigating God's Orderly World 1 (Rod and Staff)

This is part one of a basic science course covering life, physical, and earth science topics. Unit topics include the definition of science, astronomy, gravity, heat energy, weather, planet earth, life on earth, fire, parasitic diseases, food and digestion, and agriculture. Study and review exercises are included in the student book. Some experiments are described in the text. The Teacher's Guide suggests teaching methods, lists equipment needed, and serves as an answer key. Test booklets are also available. It may be spread out over two years to remain within material available through Rod and Staff, but it has about one year's worth of material. Like other Rod and Staff science books, it glorifies God as Creator, relating science to Scripture throughout.

➡ Investigating God's Orderly World 2 (Rod and Staff)

This is part two of a basic science course. Topics covered include light, sound, the body, behavior, work and machines, energy and engines, principles of chemistry, elements, electricity and magnetism, reproduction and heredity, and care of the body. Study and review exercises are included in the student book. Some experiments are described in the text. The Teacher's Guide suggests teaching methods, lists equipment needed, and serves as an answer key. Test booklets are also available. This text might be used for either eighth grade or high school level depending upon how fast the student goes through the first book. However, this is a general science course and will not satisfy the college requirement for either life or physical science.

➡ Life Science (BJUP)

This is one of BJUP's best books. Get the student text and the Activity Edition for experiments, most of which you can do at home. Even though this book was written for seventh grade, it is quite comprehensive. Some home educators are using it to satisfy the life science requirement for high school. Teacher's Editions for the text and the Activity Edition are available. There is also a TestBank with questions for us to use to create our own tests. To help with lab work, you might want to use the dissecting kit and instructions available from both Nasco and BJUP.

➡ **Life Science Work-Text** (Amsco)

This life science book is an easier option than the BJUP *Life Science*. First of all, it is a worktext, with instruction, lab activities, and questions all in one book. Each unit begins with lab activity. These include such things as microscope work, dissecting, fairly simple chemistry experiments, plant activities, physical tests, and growing cultures. Most of these should pose little difficulty for home use, although they require the acquisition of a microscope, specimens, and a minimal amount of lab equipment. Questions and charts for data recording are included with the lab activities.

Instruction is not as comprehensive as in the BJUP text, although it will be sufficient for junior high and, in some cases, for senior high.

Topics range from cells through a wide range of plants and animals, the human body (studied by body systems as well as under other headings), reproduction, heredity, genetics, energy for living things, food production, ecology, and conservation.

The book is illustrated, primarily with black-and-white line drawings. It is softbound and printed on inexpensive paper, both of which keep the cost very reasonable. We will need the answer key which is also very inexpensive.

The emphasis on lab activity (and the fact that it is right there at the beginning of each unit) makes this a good choice for Wiggly Willys who need hands-on involvement.

Evolutionary content offers some problems throughout the book, and particularly in a discussion about dinosaurs. The dinosaur feature is one of a number of "Science, Technology and Society" features scattered throughout the book. These are the most likely to expose world view clashes such as the evolution/creation debate, and they can either be omitted or used for discussion without detracting from the course.

Since this is a new publication, it is not listed in the current catalog. The order number is N 567 W.(SE)

➡ **Science: Order and Reality** (A Beka)

Although written for seventh grade, this text may be a bit difficult for some junior high students. The content is good, but questions tend to be too detailed. Place less emphasis on memorization of detail. Follow with A Beka's *Matter and Motion*. (A revised edition of this textbook will be available in the Spring of 1993.)

➡ **Science: Matter and Motion** (A Beka)

Since this is the sequel to *Order and Reality*, use both books to provide a thorough introduction to various areas of science. Watch for excessive detail and memorization.

➡ **Science LifePacs** [700 - 7th grade level or 800 - 8th grade level] (Alpha Omega)

Alpha Omega presents each year's program in ten LifePacs per subject. You also need Answer Keys and the Teacher Handbook which are usually sold separately. The Teacher Handbook contains basic instructions for using the curriculum, tests, discussion topics and questions, and activities—all of which are important for a complete course. Alpha Omega sells a basic science laboratory kit that can be used for elementary and high school. The kit is quite expensive, yet, while you might be able to create alternative methods for doing many of the activities with household equipment, the kit will save you time and energy. If you are uncertain about purchasing the lab kit, first purchase the LifePacs to see what will be needed throughout the year, then make your decision about lab equipment. Topics covered in 700 for seventh grade are: tools and methods of science, science careers, measurement and graphing, astronomy, the sun, the moon, the atmosphere, weather and climate, and the human body. Topics in 800 for eighth grade are: science and society, the structure of matter, health and nutrition, energy, machines, balance in nature, and science and technology.

Extras or Supplements

➡ **AC/DC: The Exciting Electric Circuit Game** (Ampersand Press)

Introduce the principles of electric circuitry with this game, and I guarantee they will understand it better than if they try to get it from a textbook. The circuitry concepts are fairly basic—series or parallel circuits, power sources, switches, wiring, fuses, and energy users. An extra sheet

---

Science Fair Projects

➡ **The Complete Science Fair Handbook** by Anthony D. Fredericks and Isaac Asimov (Good Year Book)

Everything we need to put on a science fair is included here. Instructions are given for teachers, parents, and students. There are tips on how to make your science fair a success, timetables for planning, suggestions for projects by grade levels, chapters on conducting research and the scientific method, ideas for presenting and displaying projects, criteria and forms for judging, and more. Even if there is no science fair, students can work on science projects on their own using guidelines and ideas from this book.

➡ **A Science Project** (A Beka)

This is a resource book offering step-by-step explanation of scientific investigation, research papers, presentations, and science fair exhibits. Recommended for grades 7 - 12 for projects.

➡ **The Ultimate Science Project Notebook** (Castle Heights Press)

Subtitled "Ideas for Truly Great Science Projects," the goal of this little, thirty-four page book is to help students come up with truly interesting projects that stimulate real learning. A secondary goal is to offer unusual ideas that have not been done hundreds of times before. There are forty-five project ideas described here. Some of the ideas have to do with electronics. (Some of these require building your own radio frequency detector or light meter. Directions for these are found in Castle Heights' *First Steps in Electronics Kit*.) A few of the ideas: using the light meter to test the reflectivity of light off of plant leaves which would be related to productivity of the plant in areas with limited light exposure; determining the bursting strength of chip packages, ketchup packets, or hot sauce bags; designing an energy 'clean' house; and a comparison of hacksaw blade construction and durability.

Basic science project information and a planning chart are included, although this information presented here is less extensive than that found in other books. You will want this book for the ideas and perhaps another one for more help on organization and presentation.

which sums up the basic information (titled "What You Always Wanted to Know about Electricity But Were Afraid to Ask") is included. Diagrams of workable and unworkable circuits also help us figure some of this out. "Shock" and "Short" cards are included to keep the play interesting, although neither is really explained.

Three, twelve- to thirteen-year-old boys figured out how to play the game in about ten minutes on their own and gave it a thumbs up for fun. That means the rules are easily decipherable, and the game playing aspect is strong enough that they will play it more than once—something we cannot say about many educational games.

➡️Affirmative Guides [Lab kits] (Science Projects, Inc.)

Five different sets of kits, called "volumes," each consist of four different boxes containing lessons, experiments, and lab equipment. These are shipped quarterly in August, October, January, and April. Each volume contains instructions and materials for twelve lessons that will provide plenty of lab work for the school year. These kits can provide some high school level lab work for chemistry, biology, or physics, although they are not designed for any one age group or to fulfill the requirements of a particular course. Use them with the entire family, then have high school students do further research and experimentation on appropriate subjects. Topics of the five volumes are *The Chemical Realm, Our Wonderful Earth, Life About Us, Physical Forces,* and *How Do We Fit.* (Twenty-two volumes are planned, and some of the future kits will be more challenging for high school students.)

Everything needed comes within each kit—instructions, equipment, materials, and lesson plans.

These kits are unusual in design, but they are also unusual in that they are biblically-based, teaching that science is part of God's creation. The Bible principles are correlated with each lesson plan. The cost is over $100 per volume, a reasonable expense if they provide all that they claim.

If material within a kit is not challenging enough for your teen, consider having him or her teach younger children using the materials.

➡️AIMS Education Foundation Program

This series of activity-oriented books combines science with math activities in fun projects for experiencing science in action. For example, one activity has to do with the amount of popped corn obtained from various brands of popcorn. As they proceed, students learn about ratio, volume, value-for-cost, etc. Reproducible work sheets are included for recording data from the activities. Books are offered covering various grade levels, but our interest here is with the oldest level of books covering grades 5-9. There are books on topics such as food, flight, and the human body. These are particularly good for students who struggle with both math and science, since the fun activities provide positive experiences in those subject areas as well as real life application of math and science skills.(S)

➡️The Exploratorium Science Snackbook

The San Francisco Exploratorium is one of the world's best hands-on science museums for children. In this book, teachers have adapted Exploratorium exhibits and demonstrations for children to recreate at home. Topics range over the areas of chemistry, physics, and life science, but visual effects seem to be an important part of many activities. Each project has clear directions with illustrations of both the original Exploratorium exhibit and the homemade version.

Scientific explanations follow each activity. I appreciate the fact that the explanations are easy to understand, using analogies to familiar phenomena and occasional illustrations. For those of an investigative bent, there are often follow-up activities under the heading "Etc."

These projects range from simple to very complicated—learning about air with a hair dryer and a ping pong ball on the easy end as compared to a gravity experiment using clear plastic, rigid-walled tube, rubber stoppers, copper tubing, vacuum tubing, vacuum pump, and clamps. Most materials for projects can be obtained at places such as hardware and toy stores, although you might have to obtain some items from sources listed in the book's resource guide, found in the back. Remember that these projects were designed by teachers for classroom use, so many are more complicated than what a single family might tackle at home. (Consider doing some of the more complicated or expensive projects with home school groups.) Some projects require some serious power tool usage for cutting wood to precise measurements or routing work, offering an excellent challenge for older students. Science concepts will be most easily understood by students at junior high level or older, although younger children can certainly begin to understand some scientific principles. With 107 experiments to choose from, there are plenty of challenging projects for older students. Some of these projects might even provide "jumping off" ideas for science fair projects.

Check out the Exploratorium's catalog for other unusual science resources.(SE)

➡️Pollution Solution Game (Aristoplay)

Junior high students can learn about pollution, consequences, and solutions by playing this game. Watch out for popular assumptions such as the one that population control will automatically help the situation. Use this game as an adjunct to science study and as an opener for discussing hot current events topics.(SE)

➡️TOPS Learning System (TOPS)

Individual books (called Worksheet Modules) titled *Magnetism, Balancing, Electricity, Pendulums, Metric Measuring, More Metrics, Animal Survival, Green Thumbs: Radishes,* and *Green Thumbs: Corn and Beans* incorporate math and thinking skills for learning about scientific principles through activities. Activity instructions are simple to understand and easy to do successfully. The *Electricity* book provided the first successful electricity experiments I was able to do with my children after a number of previous attempts with other methods. Equipment needed is minimal and inexpensive. Activity work sheets are reproducible so one book can be used for many children. Lessons can be used with children in grades 3-10. These activities will generally be too easy for the child with a good science background, but they will help children with little science background to overcome their fears that science is difficult.

TOPS also publishes 23 *Task Card Modules,* written for students in grades 7-12. A number of topics are available in the *Task Card* format. Choose those that relate most closely to the area(s) of science to be studied each year. Sample topics are *Graphing, Probability, Oxidation, Heat, Pressure, Electricity, Motion,* and *Machines.* Each packet or module contains a teacher's manual, two sets of student task cards, plus a class management guide. We can ignore the classroom instructions and, instead, guide our children in independent study using the task cards. Two-thirds of these have been fully revised and are now available in reproducible book format.

TOPS also will send their combination catalog/magazine to homeschoolers at no charge. You can read more about the products there, but every issue of the catalog also includes a couple of complete science lessons from the books or task cards so you can try before buying.

➠ The Weather Wizard's Cloud Book by Louis D. Rubin, Sr. and Jim Duncan (Algonquin Books of Chapel Hill)

For budding meteorologists this is an outstanding resource. It is written for all ages, rather than as a textbook for children. However, because the teaching is done with illustrations and the reader's own observations, it is practical for teens to use. A subtitle/description on the book's cover reads, "A unique way to predict the weather accurately and easily by reading the clouds," and this is the main thrust of the book. However, we do not merely memorize cloud shapes and colors, but go much deeper into cloud formation, thunder and lightning, hurricanes and other storms, and the effects of volcanic activity on weather. A brief chapter at the end tells how to build your own weather station.

I suggest using the companion book, The Weather Wizard's 5-Year Weather Diary. While it conveys some "how tos" and definitions on observing weather, it is primarily a weather journal for recording observations, as well as data on wind, barometer reading, humidity, precipitation, temperature, and clouds. The page for each date has space for recording five years, so that comparisons and trends are readily seen. Setting up a weather station and the initial reading/study will take a significant amount of time (perhaps a few months), but ongoing observations will require much less, although on a daily basis. Consider using these resources as part of an earth science or general science course.(S)

About Microscopes

Laboratory work in the life sciences should include work with a microscope if at all possible. Cheap microscopes (most of those in the under $100 range) are just about useless. In most cases you will be better off with small magnifiers that magnify images ten to thirty times. Hand-held, pocket-size instruments will usually give you clearer views than you can get with cheap microscopes. (Nature's Workshop sells a small 30x illuminating microscope—a pocket instrument that sells for less than ten dollars. This is a good alternative for those who do not want to invest in a "real" microscope.)

Microscopes, even in the fifty to hundred dollar range, usually are difficult or impossible to focus at high magnification. While they can be focused more easily at low magnification, preparing good slides is still a challenge. An exception is the Blister Microscope (General Science Service Co.). The Blister Microscope sells for about forty dollars. It comes with a 50x magnification lens (25x and 100x lens are available at extra cost) that can be used to view both slides and thicker, opaque objects that cannot be viewed with a regular microscope. The microscope uses a much more efficient appliance-size light bulb rather than the frustrating mirror set-ups common to lower priced microscopes. It plugs in rather than operating on batteries. Special blister slides make slide preparation much easier than traditional slides although regular slides may also be used. This micro-

scope is much easier for children to focus and operate successfully. It is made of heavy duty metal, and the cost is much less than for regular microscopes. I have used both a Blister Microscope and a seventy dollar microscope (a popular brand that is carried by many suppliers) in our home school science classes. Opinions are unanimously in favor of the Blister Microscope.

Another viewing tool to consider is the Discovery Scope™ (Discovery Educational Systems). This instrument provides magnification that changes depending upon focal distance, but is at least 10 times actual size. It features a unique design that can be used indoors but is especially useful for outdoor/field work. It comes with clear plastic chambers which can be filled with three dimensional samples (pond water, creatures, etc.), then quickly snapped into place atop the viewer. Students can actually study small living creatures this way without having to kill them to make observation possible. It uses natural light rather than artificial, and allows a variety of adjustments for viewing and focusing. It also has a special clamp that can be used to hold items such as flowers (that we do not want to crush) for viewing. Optional attachments are available for video recording or photographing observations. Ease of use and versatility make it a practical alternative to the hand-held illuminating microscope mentioned above. I particularly recommend it to those who will be doing botany field work, but it will be very useful for other environmental studies.

The Blister Microscope, together with a hand-held viewer such as the illuminating microscope or the Discovery Scope™ (because they can be used in the field since they are not dependent upon electricity), should provide for all indoor and outdoor magnification activities.

If you prefer to purchase a quality, standard microscope, they are available from Nasco, Schoolmasters Science, Edmund Scientific, Carolina Biological Supply, and many other sources. (Nasco tells me that they are able and willing to special order other microscopes than those described in their catalog.) However, the people at Nature's Workshop sound like they have searched for microscopes with home schoolers' needs in mind. They describe their microscopes clearly so you can more easily choose one to meet your needs. (They, too, can order other microscopes than those described in their catalog.)

For those unfamiliar with slide preparation, many of the sources listed under "For Labs," later in this chapter, sell prepared slides.

One very inexpensive option that will provide viewing opportunities, but not the complete experience of operating a true microscope, is the Microslide Viewer (available from Nasco and Schoolmasters Science). Prepared strips of slides, called Microslides, are available to use with the Microslide Viewer, or an extra lens can be added to the top for viewing three-dimensional objects. Microslides are already enlarged views of objects, with the Viewer providing only a minimal increase in magnification.

High School Level

If the student does not already have a good foundation in science, you might begin with basic science texts (seventh or eighth grade level) such as those listed above.

Meeting Requirements

The minimum high school graduation requirement for most states is two years of science including physical science and life science. Which courses actually fulfill requirements is rather vague, depending primarily on college admission requirements. For non-college bound students, a general science course and a life science course are ususally satisfactory. Keep in mind that students who graduate by taking the GED or Proficiency Examination need only be concerned about college entrance requirements and their personal educational needs.

For college preparation, courses should usually be biology and chemistry or physics. However, it should be acceptable to substitute classes such as botany or zoology for biology. Similarly, we should be able to use other equally challenging courses that would come under physical or life science headings as long as they include enough laboratory experience.

The laboratory aspect of many high school science courses seems to pose the most problems. Laboratory classes are not required by some states for high school graduation but are often required by colleges for admission.

As far as I can tell, high school chemistry classes will qualify students for advanced placement in college chemistry courses, but high school biology classes will not unless students take advanced placement exams. This might influence our decision about which courses to use for high school. (Check with potential colleges for their policy.)

If our teen plans to finish high school at home and go directly from there to a well known four-year college or university, he had better plan to do as much science as possible at home rather than settle for the bare minimum. If science is difficult for whatever reason, check out video courses such as those from A Beka[5](add your own lab work) , correspondence courses such as chemistry courses from Seton or the North Dakota Division of Independent Study, part-time school, or other options discussed in Chapter Eight.

Those who plan to spend some time at junior college or enroll in a small college, usually have more leeway in science preparation. Some home schoolers purposely skip science lab classes at home and take them at junior colleges.

Recommended texts

General Science

➠ Basic Science Text plus Activity Edition (BJUP)

This is an excellent text for physical science, but it should be preceded by BJUP's eighth grade *Earth Science* for astronomy, meteorology, geology, and oceanography to ensure broader science coverage. Teacher's Editions for the text and Activity Edition are available. A TestBank (softbound book) is also available.

➠ Earth Science (Science Workshop Series), Books 1, 2, and 3 (Globe Book Company)

This is a remedial science course for students who are not college bound. The three worktexts contain instruction, work pages, and experiments/activities. Topics in Book 1 (*Geology*) are an introduction to scientific methods, studying the Earth, rocks and minerals, erosion and weathering, building up the Earth, and fossils. Book 2 (*Oceans and Atmosphere*) covers the hydrosphere, atmosphere, weather, ocean currents, pollution, hurricanes, and tornadoes. Book 3 (*The Universe*) discusses space exploration, the solar system, the Earth's motion, stars, satellites, and exploration.

The activities do not require school lab setups, so they are practical for home educators.

The Teacher's Editions for each book contain teaching strategies, answers, and review tests.(SE)

➠ Achieving Competence in Science (Amsco)

Achieving Competence in Science does not fit into any of the categories I am using. I envision this unusual book fitting two possible purposes. This first might be to provide an overview of science subjects for the student who has put little time into studying traditional high school science topics, yet needs that information for test taking, meeting requirements, or personal benefit. The second purpose might be to assist the parent who will be teaching junior and senior high science, yet lacks background knowledge.

There are three chapters on earth science, three on life science, two on physical sciences, one on energy sources and issues, and a final chapter on interactions of science, technology, and society.

Throughout the book are helps for learning "process skills," such as interpreting data in a table, designing a controlled experiment, and designing an observation procedure.

Vocabulary terms are emphasized in the text (also with a glossary at the end), an important part of the knowledge required for test taking. The reading level is fine for average high school students.

Each chapter presents the information with illustrations, followed by multiple choice questions. The presentation seems just right for the purposes of this book—not so much detail as to be overwhelming, yet enough to develop understanding. Process skills instruction also includes multiple choice questions. At the end of the book is a comprehensive, seventy-question practice test, similar in format to standardized tests.

This book is very inexpensive, yet it is almost 200 pages long.

Evolution is given a brief nod of approval, but is not a significant theme throughout the book.(SE)

---

5   A Beka's video courses might be a good method for covering high school science classes. Actual lab work might still present difficulties, but the videos are a convenient option for quality science instruction which is sometimes beyond our capabilities. All of A Beka's science textbook courses are available on video. We can choose courses individually at the high school level, so it is not necessary to do all or none with the A Beka videos.

➡ **Physical Science (Science Workshop Series), Books 1, 2, and 3** (Globe Book Company)

As with the *Chemistry* series from the Science Workshop described later, these comprise a simpler course than typical high school textbooks, although you can still grant credit for an introductory high school physical science lab course. This particular series combines chemistry and physics topics, fulfilling the physical science requirement of most high schools, but not meeting the requirements of most four-year colleges. The format is worktext with instruction, work pages, and experiments all within each book.

Topics in Book 1 (*Matter and Energy*) are introduction to scientific methods, states of matter, atoms and elements, motion, and simple machines. Book 2 (*Chemical Changes*) covers heat, compounds, mixtures, solutions, acids and bases, and chemical reactions. Book 3 (*Electricity and Magnetism*) includes sound, light, electricity, magnetism, energy, nuclear power, and conservation.

Easy experiments are included. The Teacher's Editions for each book contain answers, teaching strategies, and a test.(SE)

➡ **Physical Science [Computer Video Interactive course]** (ACE School of Tomorrow)

See description of the computer video interactive courses under A.C.E.'s *Algebra I* course. This course functions in the same manner, covering physical science.

➡ **Science LifePacs [900 - 9th grade level: General Science]** (Alpha Omega)

This ninth grade level material includes ten LifePacs, Answer Keys, and Teacher Handbook. Students work independently through LifePacs for most of the course, while important discussion and activity is directed by the parent using the Teacher Handbook. Alpha Omega sells a basic science laboratory kit that can be used for elementary and high school. The kit is quite expensive, and you might be able to create alternative methods for doing many of the activities with household equipment. Buy the LifePacs first to see what will be needed. You might find that purchasing the laboratory kit saves you much time and energy in rounding up materials and equipment. Topics within the "General Science" LifePacs are: atomic energy, volume, mass, density, physical and historical geology, body health, astronomy, oceanography, science and the future, and scientific applications.

➡ **Science of the Physical Creation** (A Beka)

This text further illustrates the laws of general science and their application covering meteorology, oceanography, geology, chemistry, and physics. Recommended for ninth grade.

Extras

➡ **Discover Nature at the Seashore** by Elizabeth P. Lawlor (Stackpole Books)

This is the book I wished I had when we made our numerous field trips down to the Bolsa Chica saltwater marsh in past years. It is divided into three sections: The Rocky Shore, The Salt Marsh and the Mud Flats, and The Beach. This book is much more than a field guide. It does not attempt to be comprehensive, leaving that for the field guides. However, it provides in-depth information on each topic along with activities. Some of these activities can get quite involved, so choose which to do according to your needs. Data charts within the book can be used with the activities, but it would be better to keep a separate notebook.

As I mentioned, the book strives for depth rather than breadth as evidenced by the six chapters within The Rocky Shore section. Chapters cover the six topics of barnacles, sea stars, slipper limpets, blue mussels, seaweeds, and periwinkles. Within those limited topics, related and associated species are discussed.

Activities can be used with younger children also, so this is a good book for whole-family studies. The book works well as part of a self-designed life science course, although it will be a valuable supplement to textbook studies.(SE-evolutionary assumptions at the very beginning)

➡ **Krill** (Ampersand Press)

If students are studying marine life, this is a helpful way to understand interactions and their food chains. It will actually be more useful with younger students, since teens will quickly tire of the narrow focus of the game. Purchase it primarily for use with elementary students, but do pull it out for older students for a relief from book learning.

➡ **Suburban Nature Guide: How to Discover and Identify the Wildlife in Your Backyard** by David Mohrhardt and Richard E. Schinkel (Stackpole Books)

Many of us who live in the suburbs lack easy access to the wilds of nature. If you live in the eastern United States (east of the Mississippi River), you will find this guide a wonderful way to begin nature studies without leaving home. It includes sections on mammals, birds, reptiles and amphibians, insects, spiders, trees and shrubs, vines, flowers, grasses, ferns, mosses, fungi, and the interesting category of "creatures in moist places." If you cannot find examples from one category, you certainly will find them from others. In case you need to attract wildlife, an appendix tells how to construct bird houses and feeders.

The reason I particularly like this book is that most of us cannot afford to have guides on hand for every one of the above categories. There are a number of species that are common to many areas, and by showing and describing those that we are most likely to encounter, this book has summarized information from a number of guides into one. Fleas, silverfish, cockroaches, toads, sparrows (many kinds), squirrels, snails, yellow jackets, mulberry trees, yarrow, bermuda grass, and lichen are a sampling of the more common living things we can learn about in this book. In addition to descriptive information, there is a good deal about habitats and habits.

Even though we live on the west coast, the majority of the living things described in this book can also be found here. In fact, this book helped me identify the stinkhorn (it smells as bad as it sounds) my son recently discovered growing under our apricot tree.(S)

Biology

➡ **Biology [Computer Video Interactive course]** (ACE School of Tomorrow)

See description of the computer video interactive courses under A.C.E.'s *Algebra I* course. This course functions in the same manner, covering biology. Students are required to do written reports documenting their understanding of experiments they view. The catalog says that all material covered in the standard PACES is covered with the addition of ten percent added academic information.

➠ Biology (BJUP)

This very difficult text is recommended only for parents with excellent knowledge of biology and teaching bright, mature students. The essential Teacher's Edition comes in two spiral-bound books and contains reproductions of the student pages. Answers to questions appear in the borders around the pictures of the student pages, so most people will want students to use a separate text. The laboratory manual is appropriate only for school classrooms. Consider substituting the seventh grade level *Life Science* text with either the accompanying lab manual or lab experiments that you put together yourself.

➠ The Biology Coloring Book by Robert D. Griffin (HarperCollins)

This 233-page coloring book was designed for students in college biology courses, but it will be a valuable tool for high school level students also. It covers basic processes and structures of plant and animal life in detail.(S)

➠ Biology: God's Living Creation (A Beka)

This is an excellent text that differs from most others. It is unusual in that it proceeds from the "whole" to the "part," the opposite of other texts. For instance, botany study introduces types of trees and plants, moves on to parts of stems and flowers, then into cellular structure, whereas other texts begin with cellular structure and work up towards complete organisms. All material is contained in the student textbook so the Teacher's Edition is unnecessary. *A Field and Laboratory Manual* provides instructions for twenty-seven labs and three projects, but many are difficult to do at home. For lab work, consider using a dissecting kit with instruction manual from Nasco or BJUP, or use Castle Heights Press' *Experiments in Biology for Small Schools.*

➠ Different by Design - Frog by Richard Green (Creation's Ambassador Press)

Those who choose to dissect frogs as part of their biology studies should consider using this book. It is primarily a step-by-step guide for frog dissection. However, it offers commentary with a creationist slant which helps students both understand the design of the frog and appreciate God's character as the designer. Mr. Green offers helpful hints throughout the process, especially valuable to those of us who have never dissected a frog. He also poses questions about design and function to keep students thinking about what they are observing. At the end of the book are suggestions for putting together our own dissecting kit for practically nothing by using substitutes for actual dissecting instruments. I recommend that you also purchase the separate lab notebook for students. Both are very reasonably priced.

Three more books are scheduled for the *Different by Design* series: *Microscopic Study* (due Fall of 1992), *Earthworm* (due Winter 1992-93), and *Perch* (due Spring 1993).

➠ Experiences in Biology for Small Schools by Kathleen Julicher (Castle Heights Press, Inc.)

While biology lab experiments are much easier to do at home than chemistry experiments, lab manuals that accompany textbooks still assume that we have access to a wide array of lab supplies. Kathleen Julicher recognized that this is a problem shared by both home educators and small schools, so she developed lab experiments that are practical for schools with limited supplies.

In this book, she offers thirty investigations from five biological areas: zoology, human anatomy and physiology, cellular biology, botany, and ecology. The investigations include a number of dissections (with illustrations and instructions), work with a microscope, lab experiments, and field study. Materials needed for each investigation are conveniently listed at the front of the book. Students follow scientific method to describe the investigation, record information, analyze results, and state conclusions, all in a notebook they maintain. They also make drawings as a means of recording information.

In the back of this book, is a description of the fundamental requirements of a biology class (very useful to home educators who are designing their own classes), information on record keeping (notebooks and reports), instructions for lab drawings (with a reproducible form to use), instructions on microscope usage (with a work sheet for identifying parts of the microscope), plus a detailed explanation of scientific method.

While we are encouraged to make copies of the drawing pages and some of the data pages, the book is designed for each student to have his own book and complete many work and activity sheets within the book. Thus, it is a consumable book and is not designed for reproduction for classroom use.

Castle Heights Press has made arrangements with The Science Projects Store to offer the materials needed for dissection. Contact the store directly for information.

➠ Science LifePacs 1000 - 10th grade level: Biology (Alpha Omega LifePacs)

LifePacs were designed to be used independently by students for most of the course work, but they do require some teacher interaction as directed by the Teacher Handbook. Purchase the ten LifePacs for level 1000, Answer Keys, and Teacher Handbook. Lab experiment materials are available at significant extra cost. Consider purchasing the LifePacs and determining which experiments you feel are crucial. Then think of inexpensive ways to do them. Check the *Nasco Science Catalog* for materials you might wish to order. You might decide that Alpha Omega's laboratory kit is a worthwhile investment to save you time and energy.

➠ Schick Anatomy Atlas (American Map Corporation)

For those studying the human body, this is an excellent reference resource. Thirty, full-color anatomy charts are each overlaid with transparent identifying overlays as we see in college physiology books. Teens (and younger children) will find these fascinating to look at aside from their studies. It sells for about $25, but is an excellent investment and well worth the cost. (Order number 1448-2)

➠ StudyWare for Biology [Computer program for IBM or Macintosh machines] (Cliffs Notes)

This program can be used to supplement a biology course. It is designed for review rather than instruction. Questions are posed on the screen, with multiple choice answers. Both correct and incorrect answers are explained. An on-line glossary, hints, and illustrations are easily accessible.(S)

➠ Reviewing Biology (Amsco)

Students who want to take New York State Regents Exams or other achievement tests can use this book to review all the key concepts of biology. It reviews at two levels of difficulty, marking with asterisks those topics that are beyond a typical high school biology course, such as biological structure formulas (learned from chemistry). A brief chapter on evolution will prepare students with information to fit the biases they will encounter on tests, especially important for students who have studied only from Christian texts.

Since this book is intended for review, it covers each topic very succinctly, followed by multiple choice questions. A glossary is included. Almost half of the book is sample tests (New York State Regents Exams). The inexpensive answer key is also necessary.(SE)

Chemistry

While A Beka, BJUP, Alpha Omega, and Basic Education all offer chemistry courses, it can be difficult to set up a laboratory at home if you are trying to follow their lab work outlines. Alpha Omega is easier than the others since they offer laboratory materials in kits that can be used in the home. Accredited courses such as those available from the North Dakota Division of Independent Study, University of Nebraska-Lincoln, and American School are an option that many will be interested in. However, Seton's chemistry course described below might be the best alternative of all since the course is designed for home educators and the cost is very reasonable. You might also wish to check with private schools, junior colleges, public high schools, etc., for opportunities to enroll your child in chemistry with a good lab program and save yourself the hassle of doing it at home.

➠Building Blocks of the Universe by Isaac Asimov (Abelard-Schuman, out of print)

This out-of-print book is a wonderful introduction to the study of chemistry if you can find a copy. (Check used book stores.) Asimov introduces twenty-three of the most common elements, teaching basic chemical principles without the mathematical explanations for valences and bonding. It is more of a "get acquainted" approach, telling about characteristics and uses of each element. For every element, there is an unusual or interesting association, such as neon gas and neon lights. Building Blocks is a good book for preventing "chemistry-phobia" right from the beginning. Read this before beginning a chemistry course.(SE)

➠Chemistry [correspondence course] (North Dakota Division of Independent Study)

It takes two, one-semester courses to comprise a complete high school chemistry course. The same textbook, Basic Chemistry by Seese and Daub, is used for both parts. Laboratory experiments are included, and students need to order the lab kits for each semester. As of this writing, the Lab Kit for Chemistry I costs $83.50; the Lab Kit for Chemistry II is $76. Out-of-state students pay a little less than $50 for enrollment in each course, plus the cost of the text ($48), study guides for each semester ($15 each), plus the lab kits.

➠Chemistry [correspondence course] Seton Home Study Program

Seton offers a chemistry correspondence course. The course includes the A Beka Chemistry text, lesson plans, tests, and lab experiments. However, the lesson plans were written to correlate with the textbook that Seton formerly used (which is no longer available). It can be a little confusing trying to use that manual with the A Beka text. However, the lab experiments, designed by a home schoooling father, are much more appropriate for home study than those found in the A Beka lab manual or most others. Household items are used for lab work, with the exception of just a few chemicals that you will need to order. The lesson plans will be rewritten to correlate with the A Beka text by late 1992 or early 1993. The course is very reasonable in cost and offers a fairly easy method for providing a comprehensive lab class.

Seton also offers the Castle Heights Experiments in Chemistry for Small Schools as a supplementary option for lab work. (It can provide all lab work if we choose to use it for that purpose.)

➠Chemistry—Science Workshop Series—Books 1, 2, and 3 (Globe Book Company)

This is a chemistry course including laboratory work that is practical for home schoolers who do not need a rigorous chemistry course. (It is written as a remedial course.) The books have shorter reading passages in a worktext format requiring brief responses. Lots of diagrams and photographs are included along with many activities. The first book is introductory—many students will have already covered the content in elementary school or junior high. Topics in Book 1 (Atoms and Elements): introduction to scientific methods; states of matter; atoms and elements; and compounds. You might want to skip Book 1 and begin with Book 2. Book 2 (Mixtures and Solutions) covers mixtures, solutions, acids and bases, pollution, toxic waste, and acid rain. Book 3 (Reactions): matter, chemical reactions, metals, oxidation, and reduction. Older editions of this series covered slightly more difficult content, so use them if you can find them.

This course does not compare with typical high school chemistry courses in scope or depth although you could grant high school credit for it as an introductory course. College preparatory students will usually need a more challenging course depending which college they plan to attend and what studies they will be pursuing. The experiments in these books can be done easily at home and will satisfy the need for a lab class.

The Teacher's Editions for each book contain answers, teaching strategies, and tests.(SE)

➠Experiences in Chemistry for Small Schools by Kathleen Julicher (Castle Heights Press, Inc.)

"This uncomplicated chemistry laboratory manual was written for the small school with modest resources," according to the author. The experiments described in this book have been tested in both regular and home schools. Experiments cover a breadth of topics comparable to the basic content of high school chemistry courses. Although experiments are not written to correlate with any particular textbook, the topics are common enough that we should be able to correlate them with any text we choose. Experiments are arranged under the general topic headings of density, kinetic energy and molecular motion, chemical reactions, and types of reactions.

Introductory information about basic goals for high school chemistry knowledge, safety rules, and chart making are found in the front of the book, while in the back are lists of supplies and sources plus a description of scientific method.

Experiments are well organized. Materials needed are listed in a box at the top of the page. Background information and the purpose is explained. Step-by-step procedure is followed by questions about the experiment itself and about related topics. Some questions direct students to do outside research that will expand their understanding. Observation charts for recording data are also included in most experiments. The author has frequently inserted information about "real life" situations where the chemistry knowledge can be observed or applied, which makes learning far more interesting to many students. An answer key is included.

Parents who have had chemistry before should not find this book too difficult, but parents without any background knowledge might have some trouble. (Familiarity with lab procedures is helpful especially when we have to make substitutions or figure out alternative methods to use.) Overall, I think that most parents will find this book a very practical tool for helping them create chemistry lab courses.

➠Reviewing Chemistry (Amsco)

Students who want to take New York State Regents Exams or other achievement tests can use this book to review all the key concepts of chemistry. It reviews at two levels of difficulty, marking with asterisks those topics that are beyond a typical high school chemistry course. Even the lower level of review assumes solid knowledge of algebraic equations used in chemistry.

Since this book is intended for review, it covers each topic very succinctly, followed by multiple choice questions. A glossary is included. About one-third of the book is sample tests (New York State Regents Exams). The inexpensive answer key is also necessary.(S)

➠Science LifePacs [1100 - 11th grade level: Chemistry] (Alpha Omega)

This is a challenging course. Algebra I is prerequisite. This course integrates laboratory work throughout the lessons. Alpha Omega will sell you a chemistry lab kit to use with the LifePacs. (However, you need both the core kit and chemistry kit which becomes very expensive.) You might buy the LifePacs and Teacher Handbook first, then make a list of necessary chemicals and equipment in order of priority. Those with more limited resources might try to provide chemistry experiments by purchasing a chemistry kit from the toy store and doing whatever experiments can be done with it and other household resources.

➠StudyWare for Chemistry [Computer program for IBM or MacIntosh machines] (Cliffs Notes)

This program can be used to supplement any chemistry course. It covers topics such as scientific notation, atomic structure, the periodic table, acids and bases, orbital structures, electrochemistry, nuclear chemistry, quantum theory, biological chemistry, and organic chemistry. It is designed for review rather than instruction. Questions are posed on the screen, with multiple choice answers. Both correct and incorrect answers are explained. An on-line glossary, hints, graphs, and figures are easily accessible.(S)

Chemistry for Future Homemakers

➠Kitchen Science: A Guide to Knowing the Hows and Whys for Fun and Success in the Kitchen by Howard Hillman (Houghton Mifflin)

Future homemakers might benefit more from the practical approach to chemistry in this book than from a traditional chemistry course. Here is information that everyone can use every day. No knowledge of chemical bond structures and valences is necessary to understand that chemical reactions take place in foods. The concern is more with practical results and how to control them than with complete technical explanations. Find out why refrigerated eggs are easier to separate than room temperature eggs; why you

should not cook avocados; what happens when you deep fry foods at too high or too low temperatures; what are the functions of the various ingredients of yeast breads; why foods to be frozen should not be wrapped in aluminum foil; and much more. The book is arranged topically in a question and answer format—not as a textbook. The index helps in locating necessary information quickly. While this book does not meet chemistry course requirements, it makes a good substitute (as a supplement) for non-college bound students who are taking general science courses.

Physics

➠Conceptual Physics by Paul Hewitt (HarperCollins/Scott, Foresman and Company)

This award winning physics text keeps popping up as the most recommended textbook. The Colfax's write in *Homeschooling for Excellence*, that this book "...was less comprehensive than we would have liked but more accessible than anything else we could locate." (p.89) It is written as a college text, but can be used at high school level. It does not require a background in higher math for understanding. Hewitt writes about physics in clear, non-mathematical language understandable to those lacking science background. (Parents might even read the book and adapt the information to fit all ages.) Each chapter has a section called "Home Activities," which describes fairly simple lab/experiment type activities which can easily be done at home without fancy equipment. Using these activities can make this a complete lab course. Topics covered are: mechanics, properties of matter, heat, sound, electricity and magnetism, atomic and nuclear physics, and relativity and astrophysics. It is an expensive book, but it is hardcover and 650 pages long. You will want the relatively inexpensive Teacher's Manual as an answer key. (Order through the high school division, not the college division, even though the book is advertised as a college textbook.)

➠Electromagnetic Spectrum Chart (The Exploratorium)

This is an "extra" for those students who are into wavelengths, frequencies, x-rays and other physics concepts related to waves. It is a large reference chart displaying "the full range of the electromagnetic spectrum." Information on all types of electromagnetic radiation is included.

➠Physics (BJUP)

This is a twelfth-grade-level text with an accompanying *Physics Lab Manual*. A Teacher's Manual for the text and Teacher's Edition for the *Lab Manual* are both recommended. Like most physics texts, this one draws on logic and math learned in high school math courses, so algebra and geometry are minimal prerequisites. The *Lab Manual* uses inexpensive equipment and also gives instructions in the Teacher's Edition for making homemade variations of standard equipment. This text should work if the teacher/parent is fairly good at science and can work closely with the student.

➠Physics (ACE School of Tomorrow/Basic Education)

Prerequisites: Algebra 1 and geometry. This is a self-contained Basic Education physics course that requires no supplementary books. No laboratory work is included. The newer A.C.E. physics course will eventually have videos to accompany the PACES. Videos will demonstrate laboratory experiments.

➠Physics: The Foundational Science (A Beka)

Prerequisites are Algebra I and II. This new text from A Beka should work for home educated students. It moves from the familiar—matter, energy, solids, liquids, gases, and mechanics—to the less familiar concepts—thermodynamics, wave phenomena, light, electricity and magnetism, quantum theory, special relativity, and electronics. For better understanding, practical examples are given and ideas are related to everyday experiences. The harmony between the Bible and science is repeatedly demonstrated. The text can be adapted for students of varying ability by choosing from various options within the text. A video tape of lab demonstrations will help with lab work. A Teacher's Guide, Solution Key, Test Packet, and Quiz Booklet are available as well as a Lab Manual and accompanying Teacher's Guide, which I have not reviewed.

➠Reviewing Physics (Amsco)

Students who want to take New York State Regents Exams or other achievement tests can use this book to review all the key concepts of physics. It covers mechanics, energy, electricity and magnetism, waves, and "modern physics," with optional units on motion in a plane, internal energy, electromagnetic applications, geometric optics, nuclear energy, and solid state physics. The math required to understand concepts as presented in this book is at least through precalculus.

Since this book is intended for review, it covers each topic very succinctly, followed by multiple choice questions. A summary of equations, reference charts, and a glossary are included. About one-third of the book is sample tests (New York State Regents Exams). The inexpensive answer key is also necessary.(S)

➠Science LifePacs [1200 - 12th grade level: Physics] (Alpha Omega)

Prerequisite: Algebra I. Designed for independent work, the course consists of ten LifePacs, Teacher Handbook, and Answer Key. LifePac topics include: kinematics, dynamics, work and energy, introduction to waves, light, static electricity, current electricity, magnetism, and atomic and nuclear physics. This course does not have to be used as a lab course, but it is strongly recommended. Alpha Omega sells physics laboratory equipment in a kit that can accompany the LifePacs. The kit is very expensive, and you might find that you can construct enough experiments of your own with household equipment at a fraction of the cost of the kit.

Botany

Botany is not a required subject, but it is life science. Students who do not need to have biology, might consider botany as a substitute. Anyone wishing to study botany should probably first get a hold of the *Science and Nature Catalog* from Acorn Naturalists. They have the most complete and diverse catalog of resources for nature study that I have seen. Activity kits, books, and supplies useful for all ages are included. The emphasis is on field work using reference books rather than on textbook learning. Those who are concerned about providing courses more like those in schools can look for botany textbooks from used or college book stores. (These books tend to be uniformly gray and boring in appearance.) While texts can be useful for background information and detailed explanations, field guides and field study usually provide the most effective and interesting learning.

In searching for effective botany resources, I was frustrated by the almost universal inclusion of evolutionary theory throughout the books. Evolution is used to explain and identify plant groups by showing how they supposedly all are descendants from simpler life forms. I have not found any botany textbook that is not based upon evolution. (Let me know if you find one.) Even the children's books are loaded with it, so we have to watch content most of the time.

➠The Amateur Naturalist's Handbook by Vinson Brown (Simon and Schuster)

A terrific book for all levels of nature study, this book divides activities by level of experience, then by topic. Thus, we have a section for beginners which covers animals (observing, collecting, and skinning/taxidermy), plants (observing, collecting, pressing, and mounting), rocks and minerals (identifying and collecting), climate (basic "laws" and study of clouds, temperature, wind, and water), and ecology (interrelationships). The next level is for the minimally experienced student naturalist, then the advanced naturalist, and finally the explorer naturalist. At each level, children study the same topics, but at deeper levels. For instance, animal studies at the student naturalist level include making your own zoo (for small critters) and studying classification and anatomy of animals. The advanced naturalist studies larger animals as well as pond and stream life and sea creatures. The explorer naturalist section is brief, offering suggestions for in-depth study for the various areas.

If you have the time, this book can be the foundation of a complete hands-on science course for all family members. If you have a budding scientist who likes to work independently, just turn him loose with this book.(SE)

➠The Book of Forest and Thicket: Trees, Shrubs, and Wildflowers of Eastern North America by John Eastman (Stackpole Books)

"It is one thing to recognize a plant or animal. It is another to know where to look for it, to become familiar with its way of life, to achieve a sense of its links to other organisms and its existence as a community dweller." This introductory statement highlights the difference between this guide and so many other field guides. Identifying plants is better done with a field guide, but for those who want to know more, this is a wonderful book.

A description of each plant is given along with alternate names, and a listing of close relatives. Next is a section on each plant called "Lifestyles." This is where it gets interesting. We learn about the plant's habits, likes, dislikes, and peculiarities. "Associates" describes plants, animals, and other insects that are typically in the surrounding environment. "Lore" delves into man's use of the plant and its history, as well as folkloric uses and associations.

This book will add a dimension to botanic studies which appeals to learners who want to know more than just the basic information and want to truly understand nature. (Note that it is specific to Eastern North America rather than a comprehensive book.)(S)

➠Botany Coloring Book by Paul Young (Barnes and Noble Books/division of Harper and Row Publishers, Inc.)

This book is similar to *Botany Illustrated* in format. The content emphasizes structure and function rather than plant families. There are sections on plant genetics, reproduction, growth, leaf structure, pollination, monocots/dicots, fruit types, and much more. Extensive sections cover fungi and algae. This book is useful as a supplement rather than as a primary learning tool. Coloring and reading about the illustrations will help students better understand the various topics covered. This book is directed toward college level students and might be overwhelming to those working on a much lower level.(S)

➡ **Botany Illustrated** by Janice Glimn-Lacy and Peter B. Kaufman (Van Nostrand Reinhold Company)

This is a botany study guide in coloring book format for serious botany students. Plants are illustrated and described in great detail. They are grouped by families so that it is easier to learn common characteristics. All plant families, including fungi, molds, and algae, are covered. In addition there are extensive sections on cells, cell division, various types of plant tissue and cellular structure, and photosynthesis. Use this book by selecting appropriate pages to accompany plant studies rather than by trying to complete the entire book.(SE)

➡ **Peterson's Field Guides** (Houghton Mifflin Trade Ordering Dept.)

These guides are for those willing to first familiarize themselves with botanic vocabulary. To use the guides, we follow a key which classifies plants according to structural characteristics such as the number of petals and their arrangement, the number of stamens, placement of the ovary, etc. While illustrations of these features are provided in the books, some knowledge is necessary to use them properly. On the other hand, these books can be much more efficient to use than others such as the Audobon that require us to look through many pages to try to find a matching picture. Peterson's Field Guides titles for botany are *Pacific States Wildflowers, Southwest and Texas Wildflowers, Eastern and Central Edible Wildplants, Mushrooms, Ferns, Eastern Trees, Western Trees, Trees and Shrubs, Eastern Forests, Rocky Mountain Wildflowers, Wildflowers of Norheastern/Northcentral North America,* and *Medicinal Plants.*(S)

For Lab Work

You can order individual laboratory kits, dissecting materials, and other lab supplies to do experiments from the following sources:

➡ **Blue Spruce Biological Supply**

I understand that Blue Spruce offers a basic dissection kit that includes seven specimens (worm, frog, starfish, grasshopper, perch, clam, and crayfish), instructions, and tools for a very reasonable price.

➡ **Bob Jones University Press**

The BJUP catalog lists scientific supplies, with quantities appropriate for home educators. The list includes a dissecting kit similar to that available from Nasco.

➡ **Carolina Biological Supply Company**

Their huge catalog offers anything you could want concerning science, including small lab kits for you to set up your own individual subject lab experiments.

➡ **Creation's Ambassadors**

Creation's Ambassadors' *Need Meeter Catalog* is designed to provide basic materials for home schoolers. We can get some things from them that we cannot get from larger suppliers. They offer laboratory apparatus, chemicals, lab kits, microscopes and slides, living material, preserved material, dissection kits, teacher resources, books, and videocassettes.

➡ **Edmund Scientific Company**

Edmund's has a variety of science equipment, including microscopes and laboratory supplies.

➡ **Fischertechnik** (available through Timberdoodle)

This is a big line of mechanical and electrical construction kits that can even work with computers (robotics). They are more complicated and more expensive than *LEGO*, but very intriguing and very well built. In our experience, *Fischertechnik* constructions hold together better than *LEGO* constructions.

➡ **Frey Scientific**

This is an economical source for equipment and supplies.

➡ **American Science and Surplus**

American Science and Surplus (formerly Jerryco) has a lot of surplus science-type items at fantastically low prices. However, stock changes constantly, and you never know what they have from month to month. Catalogs are published about seven times a year (showing a cover price of $1.00) and provide detailed descriptions of their weird and variable products. They usually have motors, mechanical and electrical devices along with many other items that defy classification (e.g., diagonal mirrors for telescopes, dental tools, foldup stereo optic viewers, and bicycle seats.) Some of these items should suggest science projects to the invention-minded.

➡ **LEGO** (LEGO Dacta)

LEGO makes educational Technic sets that come with teacher's guides and individual lessons on mechanical principles such as levers, pulleys, gear ratios, and rack and pinion steering. They also sell computerized sets for Apple and IBM (and compatible machines). These are reasonably priced and make terrific teaching tools for some physics principles. There are some *LEGO* kits in stores labelled as Technic sets, but stores rarely carry the educational sets with teaching materials. Write to *LEGO* for information on educational sets or order from one of the suppliers shown in the Appendix.

➡ **Nasco**

Request their free science catalog. They have a large selection of just about everything you could possibly need, and their prices are very reasonable. For biology, they offer a complete dissecting kit with tools, "creatures," and instructions.

➡ **The Science Projects Store** (Science Projects, Inc.)

Science Projects will provide almost any science material and equipment at very competitive prices without a minimum purchase requirement. (They will even ship a single test tube if we are willing to pay the freight!) They have a free price list, but call to confirm availability, lead time, and pricing, especially on unusual items.

Health

Note: Also see "Sex Education" in Chapter Seventeen, "Beyond the Three R's."

➡ **Encyclopedia of Good Health: Nutrition** (Facts on File)

This book is one of a series of six. Other titles are *Exercise, Stress and Mental Health, Human Sexuality, Substance Abuse,* and *Maintaining Good Health.* The series was written for junior high students but not as classroom textbooks. The *Nutrition* volume was the only one that I reviewed, so I cannot vouch for the content of any of the others. *Nutrition* is divided into two parts. The first part explains what nutrition is and how it affects each person. The second section discusses ways to improve and maintain good health through proper nutrition. There is nothing radical here; the author promotes widely accepted nutritional viewpoints, including such things as recommended daily allowances. It includes helpful information such as the calorie count of popular fast foods and the numbers of calories burned by participating in different types of activities. E.g., a double cheeseburger will take 238 minutes of half-court basketball playing to work off. A book like this should help our teens make wiser food choices.

➠A Healthier You (A Beka)

This health text is designed to complement science studies. It should take from 9 to 18 weeks to complete. Unlike secular texts, this one focuses on both inner and outer health. Topics include: emotional changes, self-control, attitudes, courtesy, posture, grooming and appearance, drugs (with a strong stand against drugs, alcohol, and cigarettes), and spiritual fitness. Recommended for seventh or eighth graders.

➠Let's Be Healthy (A Beka)

Topics in this health text for grades 8-10 include nutrition, diets, food abuse problems, AIDS, and first aid. This is a 9-18 week course, designed to supplement science.

➠Foodworks and Sportworks (Addison Wesley)

These are two separate books, originally from the Ontario Science Center. Each is a combination of information and experiments. *Foodworks* has over 100 activities plus all kinds of information—some interesting, some disgusting—about food. Perfect for junior high kids! *Sportworks* will help teens to identify their basic body shape, learn how to react intelligently when someone mentions "lats, pecs, and delts," understand the dynamics of movement in different sports, and much more. More than fifty activities are scattered through the book. Both books have lots of funny illustrations and are written humorously. These are books that teens will enjoy reading and using. They will learn and remember more practical information from these books than they will from textbooks.(S)

Creation Science

Our beliefs about the origin of life play a major part in our world view if we think through the implications of our beliefs. It is vital that we work with our teens to help them explore the ramifications of a belief in evolution as well as a belief in biblical creation.

The *Understanding the Times* curriculum excels in this area. However, everyone is not going to be using that course. Some of the resources listed below will be more easily available to some of us, and will do a good job of exploring world view implications of evolutionary doctrine. *Evolution Conspiracy* (Jeremiah Films) and *The Genesis Solution* (Films for Christ) are two examples that immediately come to mind. See the descriptions below.

➠The Case for Creation [video] (Films for Christ)

This forty-five minute video, hosted by Dr. D. James Kennedy, challenges the primacy that has been given to the theory of evolution, especially in the classroom. The video demonstrates the lack of evidence to support evolution. Kennedy uses the same logic that was used by the defense in the Scopes trial, that is, that we should be able to discuss all of the evidence and weigh conflicting theories to choose which we believe to be right or wrong. Interviews with scientific authorities, both Christian and non-Christian, are used to add weight to this argument and also to buttress the creationist view. I suggest using this video as an introduction to the creation/evolution controversy with teens.

➠The Evolution Conspiracy by Caryl Matrisciana and Roger Oakland (Harvest House Publishers)

This book is not primarily a comparison of creation science versus evolution, but goes beyond the debate into the history of evolution and the implications of the evolutionary mindset. While it does discuss scientific evidence (or lack of evidence) for both theories, it goes beyond that discussion to talk about evolution as a position of religious faith. One very interesting section deals with evolution's connection with the New Age. Recommendations for further reading along with addresses for creationist organizations in both the United States and overseas are provided.

The authors have researched and footnoted their information providing much factual evidence for their opinions. However, this book is published in what is called a popular trade edition, which means that it is fairly easy to read and interestingly written. Most teens should find it easy reading.

➠Evolution Conspiracy [video] (Jeremiah Films)

Caryl Matrisciana, author of the book of the same title, is also one of the creators of the Jeremiah Films, so we see quite a bit of overlap in content in the book and video. The video explores the development of evolutionary thought, discusses evolutionists' claims for mutational and transitional forms in light of the fossil record, and demonstrates the theological ideas implicit in evolutionary theory (showing also the links to New Age beliefs). The film is more tightly organized than the book, making it easier to follow the line of reasoning throughout. I highly recommend this video. (This video is available only for "home-use/private exhibition." It is not licensed for public showings.)

➠The Genesis Solution (Films for Christ)

This video makes an excellent lead-in to the study of creation versus evolution. Speaker Ken Ham's theme here is how foundational a belief in either creation or evolution is to the rest of a person's world view. He shows the importance of the book of Genesis for understanding all of Scripture as well as God's relationship with and plan for man.

Ken Ham, a native Australian, is a talented speaker who skillfully lightens the presentation with humor. Animation is very effectively intermixed with Ham's presentation, making the presentation even more entertaining and also visually memorable.

If you have to pick just one film on creation and evolution, the choice might be between this film and *The Evolution Conspiracy*.

Viewing restrictions apply to this video. It is sold at two prices; the lower price allows viewing only within homes, not in larger gatherings such as churches or schools. The more expensive price licenses viewing in the larger settings. Those who purchase originally for home viewing may pay the difference for licensing for larger group viewing at a later date.

Both book and video versions are also available from Master Books.

➠The Illustrated Origins Answer Book by Paul S. Taylor (available through Films for Christ, published by Eden Films)

Films for Christ rents or sells a film/video series entitled *Origins: How the World Came to Be*. The videos are excellent, but since there are six videos in the series, home educators might prefer to purchase only one or two from the series.

The Illustrated Origins Answer Book follows the sequence of the videos, presenting the same information, so if you use only selected films, you can fill in with the book. The six topics are Origins of the Universe, The Earth, a Young Planet?, The Origin of Life, The Origin of Species, The Origin of Mankind, and The Fossil Record. Both book and films present a more scientifically-based, in-depth look at the issues than we find in many other resources. Science plays the starring role, proving the validity of the evidence for creation and undermining evolution.

The book has space to provide even more research information than do the films. The first half of the book is a presentation of the topics, while the second half is references—definitions, bibliographical information, scientific explanations, and quotations.

Those who want to really understand the scientific discussion of origins will appreciate either or both resources.

➠A Scientist Looks at Creation (American Portrait Films)

Dr. Robert Gange presents scientific evidence for creation in this two-part video. In relies largely on astronomical evidence, but does delve into other areas of science and mathematics to prove his point. He believes that the earth was created as recorded in the Bible, yet, unlike many creation scientists, he believes that creation took place billions of years ago. This video spends most of the time building the scientific evidence and much less time on the religious implications. At the end of part two, Dr. Gange simplifies the implications of the evidence into two basic philosophic choices—materialism or theism. He suggests that scientists are continually making new discoveries about the origin of the universe that are forcing them to arrive at the same place Christian theologians have been for centuries. The video incorporates Gange's presentation with illustrations and film clips so that it maintains the visual interest of the audience. Science topics are quite advanced, so use this video with older students.

➠Unlocking the Mysteries of Creation

Because of its comprehensiveness, one of the very best creation science books is *Unlocking the Mysteries of Creation* by Dennis Petersen. This is an outstanding book for all ages. It includes thorough discussion of creation, bringing in history and science. It incorporates scripture, science, and interesting information in a nicely illustrated format. We can pick and choose information to read as we adapt to the ages of our children.

➠Water...Water... Everywhere! (Evidence for the Worldwide Biblical Flood) (Vic Lockman)

Lockman presents scientific evidence for a young earth, reflecting his belief that creation took place in six, twenty-four hour days, as well as for the worldwide flood as described in the Bible. As in his other books, abundant cartoon illustrations are used to present information in an easy-to-understand format. This book is an excellent tool for introducing the scientific evidence although it does not provide the depth of information that we find in books such as *Origins: Creation of Evolution* or *Unlocking the Mysteries of Creation*.

Bible-Science Association

The Mid-Kansas Branch Chapter of the Bible-Science Association operates a lending library for videos, audio tapes, and books on creation and evolution. They ask out-of-area borrowers to cover return postage and, if they can, make a donation to help cover their postage costs as well as other costs of operating the library.

Videos and books are available for children through adults, while all audio tapes are for adults. Numerous videos are recommended for teens. Videos feature many different speakers including such notables as Dr. Henry Morris, Ken Ham, and Dr. Richard Bliss. Some videos are featured as courses so that we can set up a regular program. Some videos reviewed in this book are available: *Evolution Conspiracy, The Genesis Solution*, and *Gods of the New Age*. They include audio and video tapes on a broader range of topics (hundreds of items listed!), so send for their free catalog.

Master Books

It is also worthwhile to supplement science studies with some of the creation science books from Master Books. (Write for their catalog for complete listings.) One of their most highly recommended books is *Origins: Creation or Evolution* which compares the two models of how our world began. Written for teens and classroom use, this is an easy and effective resource to use. A companion video and video teacher's guide are also available.

Voyage to the Stars is the first of a series from Master Books, written for junior high students. It teaches astronomy through a story format. Content is high level, but the presentation, using characters and dialog, makes what generally is reserved for college study understandable to younger students.

Master Books has many other books written at adult level, but there are at least two others appropriate for teens that you might consider: *Fossils: Key to the Present* and *Origin of Life*.

Master Books publishes most of the resources that come out of the Institute for Creation Research. However, you might want to contact ICR directly for information on their museum and other resources. (Their address is in the appendix.)

Chapter Fifteen

Foreign Language

Foreign language should be of importance to us as Christians, since knowledge of other languages permits us to communicate with more people. With the huge influx of immigrants from other countries into the United States, almost all of us have opportunities to share with people who speak other languages. We cannot foretell what languages we may need to learn in our lifetime, but the study of one foreign language makes it easier for us to learn others. This is especially true for related languages such as the Romance languages—Latin, Spanish, French, and Italian.

Study of foreign language provides many students with their first real need to use the grammar vocabulary they have been accumulating over the years. Grammatical knowledge from the study of English helps us to understand similar constructions in other languages. Thus, foreign language study indirectly becomes a reinforcement tool for English grammar.

Most states require one year of foreign language for high school graduation, although no such requirement is reflected in GED tests. (The State of California requires one year of study in either foreign language or visual/performing arts—a choice that reflects the low priority that both subjects have in California schools.) A minimum of two years of study in one foreign language is preferred by most universities, and this is the requirement with which we should be concerned.

We might find it quite difficult to teach our child a foreign language if we have not already studied that language ourselves. Libraries offer tapes on many languages so we can experiment with a few to see what seems most interesting. Then we will have to find a text or materials to work with. If we feel that we are just not able to teach a foreign language, we need to consider other options: summer school, community college, tutoring, or trading skills with another home schooler.

The reviews presented here reflect my familiarity with Latin and Spanish. For more information about Hebrew and Greek, check Mary Pride's *Big Book of Home Learning: Volume Four* (Crossway) which covers foreign languages.

Sources for foreign language materials

Miscellaneous

➡️Harcourt Brace Jovanovich

HBJ publishes three levels for each of French, Spanish, and German. These can be used for either junior or senior high.

We used an earlier edition of the HBJ Spanish (*Nuestros Amigos*) which I found easier to use than most standard textbooks that I have reviewed. Because vocabulary translations were often included in the lessons, the books could be used more easily than most without the teacher having prior knowledge of the language. This is true of the older HBJ French and German programs as well.

The new series for each language should maintain these same characteristics.

➡️There are many supplements that can be used with these courses. Among them are exercise workbooks, activity workbooks, test booklets, audio or video cassettes, and computer software for IBM type machines. Check their catalog for complete information, as well as availability of older editions.(S)

➡️Hebrew Tools (Parakletos)

This computer program functions like *Greek Tools*, described below.

➡️Houghton Mifflin Publishers

They publish foreign language texts similar to Harcourt Brace Jovanovich above, but not quite as easy to use.

➡️The Learnables—French, German, Spanish, Russian, Chinese, Japanese, Hebrew, Czech, or English (International Linguistics Corporation)

This unusual approach uses picture books (no text with the pictures) and cassettes to build up vocabulary and teach sentence structure from repeated usage. The same books are used with each language. You get four books with twenty-one audio cassettes. Tapes begin with words and short phrases whose meaning is obvious from the pictures. Translation is not given. If you are in doubt, repetition of a word in another picture will likely clear things up for you. Sentences become more complex as do the pictures. This approach is certainly more enjoyable than typical programs of either the textbook variety or the records that have you simply repeat the foreign language phrases after the speaker. You have to think about what is happening in the pictures to understand the meaning.

The drawback is that students do not develop the ability to read or write the language they study since they are not exposed to the written form. *Basic Structures* supplements *The Learnables* to provide some reading and writing practice. *Basic Structures* (available in French, Spanish, German, and Russian, with Hebrew coming in 1993) consists of one book and four cassettes that give students listening, reading, and writing practice. Begin using *Basic Structures* after completion of Book 1 of *The Learnables*.

An intermediate *Learnables* program in German has four more books with five cassettes to accompany each, so students can pursue German studies to a higher level of proficiency which includes reading German. The *Spanish Language Series*, *French Language Series*, and *German Language Series* (published by International Linguistics) also provide intermediate study programs which include reading practice.

Grammar is not taught directly in any of these programs, but students acquire grammatical knowledge from actually using the language. At elementary and junior high levels this does not present a problem, but it does for high school where formal grammar is often required.(S)

➡National Textbook Company

Their catalog lists hundreds of language resources for a number of languages—more than I have seen in any other catalog. They have both conversational and grammatical instruction materials for all ages. In addition, there are many supplemental items that will be helpful with other courses we might use. The primary languages they provide for are Spanish, French, German, and Italian, but they also have materials for Latin, Russian, Japanese, Chinese, Korean, Greek, Hebrew, and Portuguese.

➡North Dakota Division of Independent Study—foreign language courses

Accredited high-school-level courses are available in French, German, Latin, Norwegian, Russian, and Spanish. Two years of every language except Russian are offered. Most courses come with audio and/or video cassettes. Computer-assisted Spanish I and II courses are available for those with Macintosh computers. Prices vary greatly depending upon the materials required, so consult their catalog for complete information.(S)

➡Vis-Ed Vocabulary Cards

Vocabulary Cards for French, German, Spanish (choose the bilingual Spanish-English edition rather than the classical Spanish edition), Greek (both classical and biblical), Hebrew (biblical), Italian, Latin, and Russian. Each very inexpensive set includes about 1,000 flash cards (1 1/2"x 3 1/2" each) and a study guide containing simple instructions and a mini-dictionary, all packaged in a sturdy box. Extra helps such as the principal parts of irregular verbs are shown on the cards. Many words (in the Spanish set reviewed) have related forms which appear as nouns, verbs, and adjectives, so all are shown. For instance, the noun "el calor" (heat) has an adjectival form—"caluroso/a." The foreign language is printed in black on one side, and the English equivalent is printed on the reverse in green. Use these cards to review and expand your vocabulary for any of the above languages. As with the *Think Spanish (French,* etc.) sets, the cards could also be used with a game board.

French

➡French 1 (Bob Jones University Press)

This French course teaches both grammar and conversation so that students actually practice using the language. Grammatical explanations are provided within the text, so students can work independently for much of their study. However, conversational practice and oral drill should be done for effective learning. Since this text is designed for Christian students, "...dialogues and readings center on events in the life of an American missionary and his family in France." Folk songs, Christian choruses, and Bible memory verses—all in French—help to reinforce learning. Course components are the hardbound student text; spiral bound Teacher's Edition which includes notes and answers; nine audio cassettes; softbound, consumable Student Activity Manual; and Teacher's Edition of the Student Activity Manual, which includes a tapescript of the cassettes.

➡French 1 (Nouveaux Chemins) and 2 (Langue et Louange) (A Beka)

A Beka now has instruction in the French language. Available components in addition to the two student books are a teacher's guide, pronunciation/Scripture cassette, *Oral Mastery Exercises,* student test booklet with separate answer key, and vocabulary cassettes. Courses are available on video through A Beka's Video School.

➡French 1 (Bob Jones University Press)

BJUP's new French course uses French folk songs, Christian choruses, Bible memory verses, and interesting readings about French lifestyle and culture to make study more interesting and useful. Components are the student text, a student activity manual, and teacher's editions for both books. A set of nine audio cassettes is also necessary for learning proper pronunciation and developing fluency.

➡Think French, Levels I and II (Vis-Ed)

The concept is the same as *Think Spanish,* reviewed below under "Spanish."

German

➡Praktisches Deutsch - Grundstufe I, Grundstufe II, and Mittelstufe I (BJUP)

Bob Jones University Press has the only German language program written from the Christian perspective that I know of. This is a three-year program that uses the total immersion approach. Student worktexts are entirely in German. Vocabulary is learned through association, description, and illustrations. Students also complete written exercises for reinforcement. The subject matter sounds interesting: German history, art, literature, travel, amusement, politics, and religion. The textbook authors assume a teacher's knowledge of German, so it will be difficult to use if the parent/teacher lacks that knowledge. Audio cassette sets are available for the first two textbooks which will help with pronunciation. Instruction, practice, and exercises are all contained in the worktext. No Teacher's Edition is available. Purchase a German-English dictionary from another source for reference.

Also check out German materials from *The Learnables,* Harcourt Brace Jovanovich, and Houghton Mifflin listed under "Miscellaneous."

➡Think German, Levels I and II (Vis-Ed)

The concept is the same as *Think Spanish,* reviewed below under "Spanish."

Greek

➡Basic Greek in 30 Minutes a Day by Jim Found (Bethany House)

Because this book relies heavily on cognates (words that sound very similar to familiar English words), learning is simplified. A parent with no background in Greek should be able to teach from this book (or learn Greek for him or herself).

➡Greek (Alpha Omega LifePacs)

This is a one-year course, with supplemental materials including *Greek Manual, Textus Receptus, and Lexicon.*

➡A Greek Alphabetarion [book, audio tape, and computer program] (Trivium Pursuit)

These materials serve as an introduction to the study of Greek. The book teaches letter identification, formation, sound, and articulation as well as relationships to the letters of our alphabet. Learners are encouraged to practice writing as they learn. Charts are used to help organize the information and make it easier to learn. A set of Greek letter cards (to be copied from the book) can be used for learning activities and games. Historical and linguistic background information as well as a lesson on numerical values of the Greek letters are also included.

The computer program will run on IBM type machines. It is written in Basic and will run with EGA or CGA cards. (A CGA adaptor for a monochrome monitor will work.) The program offers essentially the same information that is in the book, but has expanded historical information as well as quizzes and work sheets.

The audio tape gives us auditory input of the same information.

All three media (book, tape, computer) help provide multisensory learning for greater effectiveness.

➡ **Greek Programmed Primer** by John Werner (Trivium Pursuit)

This is a three-volume, programmed-method course in both classical and biblical Greek. Written for adults it can be used for very bright junior high students, and most high school students. *The Greek Alphabetarion* is a useful supplement that should be used before starting this course to provide good foundational knowledge of the Greek alphabet and pronunciation.

➡ **Greek Tools** (Parakletos)

This computer program for IBM machines comes with the book *Learn New Testament Greek*, a Greek primer. The software uses a flash card method, and includes a grammar guide and reference. It includes a basic word processor so that we can practice writing what we are learning. The primer is correlated with the software to offer a total college equivalent course.

Latin

➡ **Artes Latinae** by Waldo Sweet (Bolchazy-Carducci Publishers)

While Bolchazy-Carducci publishes many classical language materials, the most interesting to home educators is *Artes Latinae*. This is a programmed Latin course for independent learning. It includes texts, readers, reference notebooks, teacher's manuals, test booklets, cassettes, and optional audio-visual materials for levels 1 and 2. Students first become familiar with pronunciation and the sound of the language in sentences. Later they look at sentence elements and develop vocabulary. Knowledge builds in small increments that are constantly repeated for reinforcement—the essential description of the programmed method. It does teach Latin grammar, but in an unusual way. I have some concern about the methodology beyond the programmed method itself. For instance, in Book One, before nominative and accusative cases are named, students are told to identify subjects and objects by endings of "s" or "m"—a fact which will not hold true with plurals and other declensions. Later, the proper terms and other endings are introduced, but I personally find this confusing. Proper grammar is taught as the program progresses, on a "need to know" basis. The program moves slowly (at least through the first half of Book One) with much repetition, although students can zoom ahead through this at whatever rate is comfortable for them. Coordinating the teacher's manual and other materials with the textbook is also quite confusing, but we really do need all the extras except the audio-visual materials, which are recommended but not essential.

Many knowledgeable people do not share my misgivings about *Artes Latinae*. Because of this, I suggest that you compare this review with others before deciding whether or not to try *Artes Latinae*.(S)

➡ **Basic Language Principles with Latin Background** (Educators Publishing Service)

This small book combines English grammar review with a beginning course in Latin. Students improve their understanding of English grammar and learn the basics of Latin grammar and some Latin vocabulary. This is especially appropriate for use with junior high students.(S)

➡ **Cambridge Latin Course** [third edition] (Cambridge University Press)

This Latin program is a three- or four-year course. The third edition consists of Units 1, 2, 3, and 4. To begin at junior high level, use Units 1 and 2 each for an entire year. To begin at high school level, plan to cover both Units 1 and 2 in one year. Units 3 and 4 each will take a year. This program assumes teacher familiarity with Latin. It provides cultural background information and teaching hints in the teacher manual. Grammatical information and a Latin-English dictionary are included in the third edition student text. Translation work is from Latin to English but not the reverse. A student workbook is available for each unit. Answer keys to both students textbooks and workbooks are available separately from North American Cambridge Classics Projects (NACCP) Resource Center. Although this program is challenging, it is also interesting because of the historical tidbits and use of a story format for much of the student work. Pronunciation is covered on an optional cassette (for Units I and II) rather than in the text. Filmstrips are also available, but not essential. Grammar is incorporated from the beginning. Cambridge also offers a Latin grammar and Latin readers.(S)

➡ **Ecce Romani** (Longman Publishing)

This is the best intermediate (not childish, yet not overwhelming) Latin course that I have found. It is not as challenging as typical high school courses, yet it is quite comprehensive—equivalent to a two-year Latin course. It should work with bright fifth or sixth graders, junior high, and high school students. Rather than stories of Caesar's wars, the story of an upper class Roman family is carried through the series. Cultural tidbits also make the text interesting. You need to get all of the components: student's text, Teacher's Handbook, Language Activity Book and accompanying Teacher's Edition. The text assumes the teacher's familiarity with Latin, but not to the extent of most other programs. The Teacher's Handbook is easy to read and very helpful. It does not give direct answers to exercises in the book, but does address unusual constructions and new concepts. The teacher should work with the student, learning together, so that they can do book exercises together. The Teacher's Edition for the Language Activity Book does contain answers to Activity Book exercises, so you might prefer to concentrate on those exercises because of the availability of answers. The student text contains a Latin-English glossary, but not the reverse. If students need English-Latin help, there are reproducible sheets in the back of the Teacher's Handbook. One irritation is the listing of new vocabulary in order of introduction in the story rather than alphabetical order, making it time consuming to find words that were not remembered the first time they occurred.

Student texts are available in three different formats: paperback books for each of five different levels, "original" version with two hardback books that combine books 1, 2, and 3 in Volume I and books 4 and 5 in Volume II, and the "new" version which combines books 1 and 2 into Volume I and books 3 and 4 into Volume II. All other components are purchased for each of the five levels separately. Tests and a cassette tape to help with pronunciation are also available.

➡ **The Jenney Latin Program—First Year Latin, Second Year Latin, Third Year Latin, Fourth Year Latin [1987 edition]** (Prentice-Hall, School Division)

Many newer Latin programs have moved away from the classical approach by using fictional stories about children and everyday situations rather than the classical writings, and by de-emphasizing grammar, instead using a more conversational approach. The Jenney series has been updated (there is a 1990 edition, with the previous update only having been published in 1987) so that it is more interestingly written than our old, classical high school Latin texts from the 1940's and '50's. However, it still uses classical writings and a strong grammatical approach. Colored pictures, cultural background, famous Latin quotations are intermixed with solid grammatical study. The student text is hardcover, and a workbook is also available for the first two years. The Teacher's Resource Guide has answers for both text and workbook, teaching suggestions, additional exercise practice, composition work, and tests. This is a high school course and assumes that students already have a good foundation in English grammar and understand grammatical vocabulary. We have tried a number of Latin programs, but I wish that we had started with the Jenney series.

The Teacher's Resource Guide for the newer 1990 edition costs over $100, while the Teacher's Resource Guide for the 1987 edition is only around $20. The price increase is because of the inclusion of cassette tapes and "tapescripts" which are not essential. Since there is no option to purchase only what we need for an answer key for the 1990 edition, choose the earlier edition to save money.

➡ **The Phenomenon of Language** (Longman Publishing)

This book is not a Latin course in itself, but rather an introduction to study of languages with Latin used as the example. Concepts learned here apply to English and many other foreign languages. Prior knowledge of a foreign language by the teacher is unnecessary. The book is in work-text format with good cartoon illustrations and interesting information tucked in here and there to keep students' attention. This would be great to use in junior high or early high school to overcome foreign language phobia. For non-college bound students, it may be enough in itself. In addition to the student worktext, there is a Teacher's Answer Key and Tests with accompanying Tests Answer Key. No lesson preparation time is necessary. Students can work independently although parent/teacher interaction is highly recommended.(S)

➡ **Preparatory Latin, Book 1and Book 2** (Longman Publishing)

This series was designed for upper elementary and junior high students, yet it looks more appropriate for junior high or as a beginning course for senior high. Reading material is interesting, although the book itself looks rather boring with only three or four pictures of ancient ruins for illustrations. Unlike most other Latin programs, this one gets right into verb conjugations and tenses. It is actually quite heavy on grammar considering the intended audience. New topics are introduced in small increments with clear explanations. Translation of Latin into English takes precedence, although some exercises for the reverse are

given. Oral exercises are encouraged. High school students might be able to work independently through these books, but most junior high students will need some parent/teacher involvement. Although the authors designed the course as an introductory course for students who would then go on to Latin I in high school, I suspect that students who complete both books would be ready for Latin II. The softbound books serve as textbooks, with written exercises to be done on separate paper. The only components are the texts and answer keys. In spite of the fact that the teacher's knowledge of Latin is assumed, those without Latin background should be able to use this series.

➡ **Latin** (Seton Home Study School)

Seton offers a Latin correspondence course using the Henle *Latin* series from Loyola University Press.

Sign Language

➡ **Say It by Signing** (Audio-Forum)

Here is a course on video cassette for learning sign language which can be used by learners of all ages.

➡ **Sign Language for Everyone [video and book]** by Cathy Rice

This four-hour video course teaches over 600 signs of American Sign Language. This is the only introductory signing course that I know of that also teaches signs for witnessing. The signs are taught in groups with logical associations so that they are easily remembered. A 170-page, hardback book comes with the video, making it easier to review and practice what we have watched on the video. The course is appropriate for all ages.

➡ **Modern Signs Press**

Modern Signs Press offers a wide variety of sign language materials.

Spanish

➡ **Curso Primero: Workbook for a First Course in Spanish** (Amsco)

Parents who have a reasonable grasp of Spanish might want to use this inexpensive tool for teaching Spanish. Instruction is cursory, reflecting the book's design to be used as a supplement to another form of instruction. There is strong emphasis on grammar throughout, taking students through present tense verbs, nouns, articles, adjectives, "to be," numbers, time, preterite tense, and pronouns. Optional chapters cover commands, present participles with estar, position of object pronouns, and future tense. Grouped vocabulary words, relating to such topics as school, home, and food, can be used to extend vocabulary before actually getting to the exercises in those chapters at the end of the book.

Reading and listening practice exercises are included at the end, requiring assistance from someone familiar with proper pronunciation and at least the basics of Spanish.

Students using this book can develop a solid grasp of Spanish grammar as well as good reading and writing ability. However, I do not recommend this book to parents with no Spanish background because they will find it difficult to determine important points of each lesson and fill in meanings for words whose definitions have not yet been taught.

Verb charts and vocabulary lists (English-Spanish and Spanish-English) are at the back of the book. An inexpensive answer key is available.

Second and third courses in the same format are also available from Amsco.(S)

➡ Spanish I (Alpha Omega LifePacs)

This is a one-year course with 30 audio cassette tapes (3 for each of the 10 LifePacs) that are essential to the course.

➡ Spanish I, Por Todo El Mundo and Spanish II, Mas Que Vencedores (A Beka)

This is a fairly traditional approach to learning Spanish, yet there is a strong emphasis on Christian witnessing. You will need to buy a student text, Teacher's Guide, *Vocabulary Manual*, and Teacher's Edition to the *Vocabulary Manual* for each course. Two coordinated cassette tapes are also needed for *Spanish I*. A Student Test Booklet is optional. Courses are also on video cassette through the A Beka Video School.

➡ Logos Language Institute Spanish [plus introductory study of 21 other languages]

Logos assumes that their students are studying independently. They provide everything we need to learn to speak a basic conversational level Spanish. There are six books with a cassette tape accompanying each book. An *Introductory Study Packet* is the first book. This book provides us with a pronunciation key, everyday phrases to use for basic communication and witnessing, and key Scriptures. The intent is to get us "up and running" with some immediately usable Spanish. The other five books are the actual course. They are called *In Depth Study Packets*, Levels One through Five. (A sixth level book might also be available within the next year.) The first four levels correspond approximately to a first-year-high school Spanish course. Adding level five approximates completion of a first-year-college level Spanish course. I would use the *Introductory Study Packet* if starting with younger students who are weak in grammar, but skip straight to Level One if beginning with older students.

The people at Logos view foreign languages through "missionary eyes." Much Christian vocabulary is included in keeping with the purposes of the Institute. The Institute advances no particular denomination. The Spanish study does include some Catholic words since a majority of Spanish speaking peoples are Catholic. Tapes alternate male and female speakers saying the words and phrases to be repeated, first at slow speed then a little faster. Books include grammar instruction, sample sentences, fill-in-the-blank exercises, speaking exercises, and a little bit of cultural background information. The emphasis is on practical usage of Spanish rather than translation. Students need a basic knowledge of grammatical vocabulary—nouns, adjectives, gender, etc. (The level one book includes a brief review of English grammar.) This is a terrific way to reinforce grammar learned in English studies, as students see how they can apply grammar knowledge. Upper elementary grades or junior high would be a good time to start this program, although it is appropriate for all ages in content. Students should also buy a Spanish/English dictionary.

➡ Speedy Spanish

This is a good conversational Spanish course written by a Christian family. It can be used with all ages, although it is best suited for younger learners who need to be taught with a conversational approach. Components are the *Elementary Spanish Book* and a set of four, ninety-minute, cassette tapes. One book is needed for each student since many activities and exercises are done in the book. One set of tapes will do for all. I was particularly impressed by the creativity and variety of the program. Each of the thirty-six lessons is set up to take one week of study. New vocabulary words and practice sentences are studied while listening to a cassette tape. Match-up exercises in the book have children identify Spanish and English words and phrases that mean the same thing. Children can check their own answers by listening to the tape. Bible verses and short worship and praise songs are taught in Spanish. (The songs are in the book and on the tape.) At the end of each lesson, children practice vocabulary with a lotto type game called Quiz-nish. Vocabulary cards are included at the back of the book, to be colored, cut out, and used for study and for Quiz-nish. The variety of activities is bound to prove interesting to children and encourage learning. The only thing lacking in this program is grammatical instruction (although declension charts are provided), but it is intended as an introductory course rather than a complete grammatical course. Even so, many grammatical concepts are picked up through usage. The program's authors believe that children should have fun with the language and learn to speak it correctly, then learn the whys and wherefores later when they get into more formal language study.

Speedy Spanish, Book 2 comes with five, ninety-minute cassettes. It teaches more complicated sentence structure while continuing to build vocabulary. Declension charts are provided in the back of the book, and a pronunciation chart is in the front. Development of a biblical/Christian Spanish vocabulary is stressed throughout, in lessons and songs as before. It is recommended that students obtain and read a Spanish Bible.

The inclusion of games, songs, and flash cards make the material appropriate for use with young children, although you might eliminate one or more of these elements with an older learner.

➡ Think Spanish, Levels I and II (Vis-Ed)

Here is an inexpensive supplement for any Spanish course. Level I contains 400 flash cards and a cassette tape. 200 of the cards, called Concept Cards, have cartoon-type pictures with a question in Spanish on one side. The answer, also in Spanish, is on the reverse. A featured vocabulary word heads the reverse of the card (e.g., a noun with its article). Irregular words show the regular form beneath so you can find them in a dictionary if necessary. The cartoon situations provide clues to the sentences, but they are not entirely self-explanatory. You need to have a beginning Spanish vocabulary to start using these cards or you will be frustratedly looking up 90% of the words. The cassette tape is over an hour long and features native Spanish speakers reciting the sentences from the concept cards to help with pronunciation. The other 200 cards deal with grammatical constructions, with questions on one side, and answers on the reverse. They are designed for practice in usage with an emphasis on verb forms. This is not a stand-alone Spanish course, but can be used along with any other course. I would suggest that you not begin using it until you have studied Spanish for at least three months and have a foundation. (Suggestion: The concept cards could later be used along with a game board—answer correctly and move ahead.) Level I covers the content of one year of high school Spanish or one semester of a college course. Level II covers a second-year high school course or second semester college course.(S)

Also see Harcourt Brace Jovanovich, Houghton Mifflin, and *The Learnables* which offer Spanish materials under "Miscellaneous" above.

Chapter Sixteen

Visual and Performing Arts

Visual or performing arts courses are optional in most situations. However, this does not mean that we should ignore education in the fine arts. We Christians have neglected the arts in recent years, and seem to be just beginning to rediscover our God-given talents for artistic expression. Francis Schaeffer's *How Should We Then Live?* (Crossway) will help us understand the tremendous impact the arts have on life and how they serve as a reflection of our society.

Objectives for studying the arts might include: how social, political, economic and technological events have influenced the development of artistic styles; how art can be used as a means of non-verbal communication; how to use art to express concepts; how dance, drama, music, and visual arts are expressed in different cultures and in history; interrelationships between art and other subject areas; art as a reflection of the ideals and values of cultures; learning self-expression through the arts; learning to make aesthetic judgments of various art forms; study of particular art forms to achieve skill; preparation for a career in one of the visual or performing arts.

A resource for an integrated study of the arts is Konos Curriculum's unit on *Creativity* . This was formerly a part of Volume 3, but since it needed to be portioned out over more time than a typical Konos unit, it is offered separately. The unit addresses the arts, music, and literature of western civilization according to historical time periods. It should tie in nicely with history studies.

Art

You should plan to use an assortment of the recommended materials along with others you find to meet the above objectives. If those objectives sound too philosophical, perhaps it is easier to think of art study in terms of: technique (methods), history, and appreciation. The library is a source for books on art history and artists' biographies, although college libraries are even better.

➠Adventures in Art (Cornerstone Curriculum Project)

Here is the tool to balance any art instruction with the Christian perspective. Those familiar with Francis Schaeffer's book *How Should We Then Live?* will spot Schaeffer's theme that philosophy and ideas are reflected in art. Charlotte Mason's ideas (popularized in the book *For the Children's Sake*) also are foundational. Cornerstone has carefully gathered together top quality prints of famous art works that illustrate how art reflects ideas. Four levels are planned for the series. Accompanying the fourteen art prints at each level is a teacher's manual that provides us with the dialog to use with our children as we study each one. Material has been written on a level to use with children as young as first grade. It should be studied and presented a little differently to older children. These sets could be used over a long period of time, returning to applicable art works as topics arise in history.

➠Art Extension Press

This company offers prints of the world's masterpieces for study in either small (3" x 4") or large (7" x 9") sizes, grouped by levels (primary, intermediate, and upper). The levels seem to be somewhat arbitrary—there is not a great difference in the text or subject matter from primary to upper. I suggest starting with the primary print set with children of all ages. *Learning More About Pictures,* by Royal Bailey Farnum, is the "teacher's manual" for art studies based upon the prints. It provides an outline of art history and commentary on the 100 prints offered. Purchase the book and one or more of the sets of prints. These are great for those of us who have little art background. Special subject groupings of art prints are also offered.(S)

➠Audio-Visual Drawing Program—Drawing Textbook, and other book and video titles by Bruce McIntyre

Bruce McIntyre, a former Disney illustrator, has been teaching drawing (including a nationally broadcast telecourse) for many, many years. He presents techniques of drawing in a simple manner that anyone can comprehend. His goal is artistic literacy—the skill of being able to sketch out an idea quickly because you know the principles of drawing. The books are as easy to understand and apply as his telecourses. Telecourses designed for elementary grades (but not childish) are for sale, and your local educational station might be showing McIntyre's older level *Freehand Sketching* program. All of McIntyre's resources are excellent for both aspiring artists and those who simply want to acquire basic skills.(S)

➠Davis Publications

Davis sells many excellent art books, including some of the most popular art history textbooks. Write for their catalog to get full descriptions. A number of Davis Publications books are reviewed below—some actual curricula, while others are likely to be of general interest.

➠Art in Your World by Brommer and Horn (Davis)

This introductory art course is written for seventh through twelfth graders. It covers the role and importance of art in the environment; differences between fine art, industrial art, commercial art, and crafts; art careers; elements and principles of design; art history; the influence of art in contemporary culture; and art skills including drawing, painting, printmaking, sculpture, graphic design, and crafts.(S)

➠The Big Book of Cartooning, Books I and II (Vic Lockman)

Students interested in drawing cartoons can learn from a Christian cartoonist. Step-by-step lessons with examples make it easy for just about anyone to be successful. Topics taught in *Book I* include faces, figures, hands and feet, animals, scenery, perspective, layout, lettering, inking, and special effects. *Book II* is on animals, and it expands to cover many types of living creatures including dogs, horses, elephants, insects, birds, and sea creatures.

Lockman has a new book due out in September of 1992, titled *The Big Book of Cartooning—Machines*. Teens who like to draw cars, motorcycles, airplanes, spaceships, and robots will have lots of fun with this one.

➥Discover Art (Davis Publications)

Two books continue Laura Chapman's outstanding *Discover Art* program up through junior high. *Discover Art* teaches art history, appreciation, and techniques as related topics. For example, within a chapter on drawing, we examine representative samples from major international collections, learn about Leonardo da Vinci (art history) and see samples of his work, discuss ideas for drawing, learn drawing techniques, learn about drawing media, explore design concepts, look at samples of student work, and discuss related careers. Activity is a major part of each chapter, and supplementary or alternative activity ideas are provided. Written assignments (which can also be done orally) are suggested at the end of each chapter under the headings "Aesthetics and Criticism" and "Art History." There are many color and black-and-white illustrations within each chapter so students can experience the variety of outcomes that might result from using one technique or variations on that technique.

These two books are different than earlier levels, primarily in format. In younger level Teacher's Editions, the student text pages are reproduced within teacher's pages and it was possible to purchase only the Teacher's Edition. The junior high books are much larger, hardbound books, and Teacher's Editions are separate spiral-bound volumes. The Teacher's Editions are important to help us get the most out of each course. The seventh grade Teacher's Edition which I reviewed includes lesson plans, presentation methods, lots of background information, reproducible student pages (some hands-on activities, some written activities/study sheets), a lengthy bibliography, lists of print and audiovisual resources, a glossary, and a transparency for teaching color theory.

Chapter titles in the seventh grade book, entitled *A World of Images*, are Basic Art Concepts, Careers in Art, Design: The Language of Art, Seeing and Discussing Art, Art History before 1900, Art History: The Twentieth Century, Art: A Global View, Drawing, Painting, Printmaking, Graphic Design, Sculpture, and Crafts.

Chapter titles in the eighth grade book, entitled *Art: Images and Ideas*, are The Creative Process and Careers in Art, Design: The Language of Art, Aesthetic Perception and Art Criticism, Art: A World View, Early Art in North America, North American Art: Twentieth Century, Drawing, Painting, Printmaking, Graphic Design, Sculpture, and Crafts.

Even though some chapter titles are the same in both books, the content is different at each level. However, there is so much within each book that we might need two years to adequately cover just one.

The art history content can be useful for studying world views (see Chapter Five's discussion of teaching world views), although we will have to add commentary to the information presented.(SE)

➥Discovering Art History by Brommer (Davis Publications)

Brommer concentrates on relationships among art, culture, and society throughout history. An excellent resource for tying together various subject areas.(S)

➥Drawing on the Right Side of the Brain by Betty Edwards (Jeremy P. Tarcher, Inc.)

Betty Edwards helps adults and older children to develop an artistic eye by teaching us to look at things as they truly are—in terms of line, angle, positive/negative space, etc.—rather than through our preconceived ideas of what particular things look like. (Think of how the majority of children represent any tree with a lollipop shape.) This book is big on theory and philosophy, some of which you will have to weigh for yourself, deciding whether or not it is useful. Right brain/left brain theory receives much attention, including some exercises to help those dominated by the left brain hemisphere develop artistic abilities, which are localized in the right brain. The book is written on an adult level, but activity ideas can be presented to any age group. Lessons quickly advance in difficulty getting into perspective, mathematical proportions in the human body, and methods of cross-hatching to achieve shading. An extra chapter on handwriting has been added to the latest edition. Edwards emphasizes the value of consistent, legible handwriting, both as a message about the writer to the reader and as an art form in itself. She gives some excellent ideas and exercises to help us recognize and improve upon our sloppy handwriting habits. Because of the quick pace of *Drawing on the Right Side of the Brain*, teens and adults with at least some minimal drawing experience will benefit most from it.(SE)

➥Drawing with Children by Mona Brookes (Jeremy P. Tarcher, Inc.)

Mona Brookes has helped many people discover that art is not only for those who feel they were born with talent, but that anyone can "do art" with just a few lessons. The first few chapters of the book deal with attitudes and preparation. She gives specific instructions about materials. Expensive art supplies are not necessary—just begin with a pen, then move on to felt pens and colored pencils. If we want to experiment with pastels and watercolors, simple instructions are supplied. Parents can use the book as a guide to work with children as young as three or four, or anyone able to read the book can use it as a self-teaching tool. Teens should be able to use it independently, but most would receive much more motivation from working with someone else. Lessons begin with the five elements of shape. Next we draw from two-dimensional pictures, then from still life (three-dimensional). Instructions for drawing people are excellent without being overwhelming; she shows the general shapes that can represent body parts, their relationships, and some positions without getting into mathematical proportions. Mona Brookes gives a few specific assignments of things to draw, but for the most part it is up to us to draw what we wish utilizing the techniques that she has taught. *Drawing with Children* would be a good starting place for most younger children and for teens with little drawing experience.(S)

➥Drawing for Older Children and Teens by Mona Brookes (Jeremy P. Tarcher, Inc.)

Mona Brookes carries further her successful method of teaching drawing. There is a lot of material here. It might even be a little overwhelming for some. Beginners might prefer to start with the simpler ideas in *Drawing with Children* until they feel more confident. For those who are ready for something more, all the important principles of drawing are introduced.

A parent could use this book to set up a full year's art course for their high schooler. Teaching tips are included. One important feature of the book is its emphasis on accep-

tance and enjoyment as well as an absence of criticism. The feeling Mona Brookes conveys is, "Yes, you too can draw!"
                                              - reviewed by Valerie Thorpe

History of Art for Young People by H.W. Janson and Anthony F. Janson (Abrams)

Francis Schaeffer's book *How Should We Then Live?* prompted me to use H.W. Janson's *History of Art* (Prentice-Hall Order Dept.) as a primary resource for our world view studies. (See Chapter Five.) The adult level book is lengthy, heavily illustrated, and expensive. It has been around for many, many years (updated periodically), so older editions might be available through used book stores at lower prices. A more practical alternative for most of us will be the somewhat condensed version of the book entitled *History of Art for Young People* (Abrams). The style of writing (and actual words) are essentially the same, although some portions of the text are rewritten, and others have been omitted. There are fewer illustrations, yet there are still 519, with 219 of those in full color!

Janson's books are valuable resources because he follows an historical outline. Information about art, architecture, and sculpture as well as religion, philosophy, science, and other subjects is skillfully intertwined. All of this, together with biographical information about key historical figures, provides a helpful background and expansion of ideas presented by Schaeffer in his book. In fact, the abundant illustrations in both books include most paintings, sculptures, and building referred to by Schaeffer in *How Should We Then Live?* Chronological Charts (time lines) are included in *History of Art for Young People*, showing links between political history, religion and literature, science and technology, architecture, sculpture, and painting. A glossary and index both help to make it easy to understand and locate information in the book.

Janson's books are not Christian, so they must be used with care. I recommend them to those who are knowledgeable about both the Bible and Bible history, and who are able to interpret historical events in Biblical context. For instance, if we are studying Greek sculpture (lots of naked bodies) we do have to consider the philosophical view of the Greeks. We need to discuss why they glorified the human body, and we also need to discuss their pantheon of gods who seemed to differ from humans only in their immortality and power.

In terms of teaching world views, both of Janson's books provide visual proof of Schaeffer's assertion about art reflecting man's spiritual status through the ages. We can see the progressive changes reflecting man's view of man and his purpose in life.

I recommend using *History of Art for Young People* as a read-together activity with discussion rather than for independent reading by teens. I also suggest incorporating readings with world history studies so that the history studies (hopefully from a Christian text) are fleshed out with the content of Janson's book, while the content of *History of Art* is balanced with the Christian perspective. Another option is to choose selected sections to read rather than trying to cover the entire book.(SE)

Investigating Art by Moy Keightley (Facts on File)

This book comes highly recommended by Kim Solga, author of *KidsArt*. Designed for older students, it teaches line, color, pattern, texture and form. Lots of illustrations and projects are included, along with complete instruction

on equipment and technique. Kim says, "With this book, young people will be able to develop confidence in their own creative abilities and find the approach to art that suits them best." I like the practicality of the projects for students working at home. They can learn art techniques by following the suggestions here without a huge financial outlay for materials. The book uses many illustrations that have a "modern art" look to them, so this book might not be for you if you have a strong aversion to modern art.(S)

KidsArt

KidsArt provides art instruction, appreciation, and activities for all ages and abilities in a newsletter format. A one-year subscription brings us four, sixteen-page issues for only $10 (at this writing). Each issue features a main topic—for instance, a recent issue on "Faces" studies famous portraits (art history and appreciation), then gives instruction for drawing portraits; then it shows how to enlarge pictures using diagonal or square grids; activities include making "blockhead" portraits and clay sculptures. *KidsArt* also includes tips on art products, materials, and resources. Activity instructions are complete and easy-to-follow for even the least experienced non-artist. *KidsArt* also has a free 48-page catalog full of sample activities and art resources as well as unique arts and crafts items.(S)

Mark Kistler's Draw Squad (Simon and Schuster)

Kistler, a student of Bruce McIntyre (see *Audio-Visual Drawing Program*), decided that he wanted to help spread the good news that everyone could learn how to draw by learning just a few basic techniques. He teaches the same basic ideas that McIntyre does, but his book has a "jazzier" format with some cartoon characters popping up occasionally to make things more interesting. Lessons are well laid out and easy to follow—a fourth or fifth grader can use it on his own, and the format is such that it appeals equally to adults.(S)

The National Gallery of Art

The National Gallery of Art has an Extension Service Program which has designed audio-visual art programs. The programs are set up as topical studies. Some are historical, such as "700 Years of Art" and "The European Vision of America." Some are technical such as "The Artist's Hand: Five Techniques of Painting." Others are narrow in scope, such as "Picasso and the Circus" and "The Treasures of Tutankhamun." Programs are available in different media—slide with audio cassette, film, and videocassette—but all programs are not available in all media forms. The only cost for using these materials is that of return postage. Requests must be made many months in advance, so planning ahead is essential. Send for the free *Extension Programs Catalog* which describes programs, available formats, and borrowing procedures.(SE)

University Prints

This company lists 7,500 fine art prints in their catalog. These very inexpensive prints, all 5 1/2" by 8", cost only $.07 (black and white) and $.15 (color) each. These would be suitable for study of art history more than technique since the detail is not usually fine enough to make out brush strokes. Prints are not just of paintings but also of sculptures, and some prints are of photographs of famous buildings. Prints can be purchased individually or in topical sets which are very affordable. For instance when you study about ancient Egypt, you might purchase the set of 66 prints entitled "A Visit to Ancient Egypt" for only $4. The

Topic Study Sets brochure lists six pages of grade-level prints on hundreds of topics.(SE)

Telecourses

Some public television stations offer drawing courses that can be taken for college credit if desired. Some of these are excellent. Look for courses that give students "tools" for developing their own skills rather than courses that ask students to simply mimic the teacher. Check with your community college for information.

Music

The library should be an excellent source of records and books on various musical styles, music history, and composers. Students should be encouraged to try playing at least one type of instrument and learn the rudiments of note reading.

Recommended resources

➡ Basic Library of the World's Greatest Music (M/L International Marketing, Inc.)

This is a broader, classical music appreciation resource than *Music and Moments with the Masters* since it includes works from thirty-one different composers representing "nearly all the orchestral forms in the world of Classical Music." However, there are fewer selections on average per composer than in *MMWM*—selections are chosen to be representative of various musical forms rather than "biographical." Forty-six complete works are presented on twenty-four cassettes. They come packaged in two cassette albums. An important part of the *Library* is the *Listener's Guide*. In the *Listener's Guide* are biographies (well-written); background information on the musical pieces; timetable charts of musical periods which also shows musical history in relation to other historical events; a dictionary of musical phrases; listening activities; extended activity suggestions in art, writing, dramatization, etc.; questions and answers; and puzzles. The biographies and musical background are the most useful parts of the *Listener's Guide*. Children are unlikely to pick up the *Listener's Guide* and read on their own, so it will require parental assistance to make full use of this resource.

➡ Children Sing the Word, Volume 1 (Volume 2 is in preparation)

This is a Christian, biblical approach to teaching music written especially for home schooling families. The songs are from Scripture and the instruction is built upon biblical precepts. *Volume 1* consists of three books and a cassette tape. Optional Flash Cards and Teacher's Manual (containing teacher helps and answer keys) are available. The three books are distinctive in purpose, rather than a progression in teaching skills. Book 1 teaches singing and can be used with very young children through adults. The cassette tape contains recorded versions of the twelve songs. Book 1 also has drawings and brief histories of ancient musical instruments. Book 1, used with the teacher helps found in the Teacher's Manual, is designed for preschool level. Book 2 contains basic music theory—note reading, key signatures, timing, following step-by-step precepts. Biblical precepts, building good habits for music study, are taught first. A "practice keyboard," printed on heavy paper and eleven notes (white piano keys) long, is provided for children to practice beginning exercises. Book 3 completes the program

with lessons for guitar and piano. Included in the lessons are staff writing practice, review, and daily practice schedules. The entire set is very reasonably priced and appears to be a practical method. As with many small companies, quality is improving with each new printing and revision. *Volumes Two* and *Three* are in the planning stages and will soon follow.

➡ Davidsons Music

Those who want to learn to play the piano but cannot afford lessons, should consider Davidsons' guaranteed, self-teaching courses by Madonna Woods. Courses for playing by ear, by note reading, or both are offered. Much of the music is oriented toward church and gospel. Courses for organ, guitar, electronic keyboard, and a number of other instruments are offered, but the bulk of the business concentrates on piano instruction and playing for different age and ability levels. Typical piano courses include a book, audio cassette, chord chart, keyboard decals (for learning notes), and sound set-ups for playing the organ.

Davidsons' newest release is the *Piano Course for Christians*. Six levels (labeled Preparatory and Levels 1-5) cover beginning through advanced material, teaching music theory and technique particularly aimed at those who want to play in church type settings. However, students will be able to play any type of piano music after completing the course. Instruction is set up so that it can be used by an experienced teacher, inexperienced parent, or even by older students working on their own. The typical home schooled teen can truly teach himself or herself with this course. A book and one or two audio cassettes come with each level. The first two levels (Preparatory and Level 1) cover music fundamentals. Because this requires more explanation/teaching, each of the first two levels have two cassettes. Children begin playing familiar songs (hymns or tunes of a Christian nature) almost from the very beginning. Madonna Woods teaches the use of chords and other musical elements that are essential to true musicianship. The difference is apparent in Level 2. (Students who have already learned the fundamentals through some other means can probably start in Level 2, skipping Preparatory and Level 1.) Courses are very reasonably priced. If you have foregone piano lessons because of the cost, here is your answer.

➡ The Gift of Music—Great Composers and Their Influence (Crossway)

This book examines great composers and their music from a Christian perspective. Detailed biographies of composers are written on an adult level.

➡ God Made Music series (Praise Hymn)

This Christian music curriculum is available for kindergarten through adult levels. The seventh grade book presents all needed material in one student book which can be used at upper elementary levels through junior high. Correlated music books are available at each level. Interesting format and content make this series outstanding, although it may be overwhelming for non-musicians.

➡ Homespun Tapes, Ltd.

Homespun offers hundreds of instructional video and audio tapes for a wide variety of musical instruments. They offer lessons for country, bluegrass, folk and many other styles. *Easy Gospel Guitar, Flatpick Country Guitar, 5-String Banjo, Learn To Play Autoharp,* and *Making and Playing Homemade Instruments* are just a few of the titles that might interest you. Homespun has lessons for guitar (acoustic and electric), fiddle, banjo, mandolin, autoharp, dulcimer, drums, keyboards, bass, synthesizer, harmonica, penny whistle, dobro, jaw harp, and musicianship. Vocal instruction (including yodelling) is also available. Tapes are for skill levels from beginning through advanced intermediate. Homespun also sells some books, strings, and small instruments.(S)

➡ **Keyboard Capers: Music Theory for Children** (Elijah Company)

The title almost does this book a disservice by designating it only for children. Somehow, with four years of piano and five years of violin plus assorted music classes in school, my music theory knowledge is pitiful. This book really covers the basics and the things that I have missed! It is recommended for children because the author presents the material in short lessons with visual aids and games that are designed for early-elementary-age children. There are a couple of little poems that are used, but the games are not cluttered with too many cutesy gimmicks. Most learning takes place with the visual aids and activities. If you are short on time, purchase the prepared visual aids sold by the publisher. For older students or adults, pick and choose the games that are useful and get right to the heart of the lesson. Lesson plan headings are the musical alphabet, orientation to the piano, musical notation, rhythm, intervals, note identification, music vocabulary, ear training, and major scales. The piano or keyboard is the primary teaching tool used with the book. A xylophone could be substituted, but an inexpensive electronic keyboard would be preferable. The basic knowledge of music learned is applicable to any other musical instrument and to singing.

➡ **Meet the Classics** (Toys To Grow On)

Choose either the Introductory set of six cassettes featuring Bach, Mozart, Beethoven, Chopin, Tchaikovsky, and Brahms or the Complete Library featuring the above six plus Handel, Strauss, Schubert, Foster and Sousa, Verdi, Haydn, Wagner, Mendelssohn, Schumann and Grieg, Vivaldi and Corelli, Berlioz, and Dvorak (eighteen cassettes in all). These cassettes are the same Allegro cassettes as the biographical tapes found in Music and Moments with the Masters. Brief passages of each composer's music is interspersed throughout each life story. There are no complete musical performances. However, those who already own a library of classical music will appreciate this source for biographical tapes.

➡ **Music and Moments with the Masters** (Cornerstone Curriculum Project)

Cornerstone sells four different sets of excellent quality recordings. Each set has eight cassette tapes covering four composers—two tapes per composer. There is a biographical tape that intersperses the composer's music with his story, and there is a tape of some of the composer's most popular pieces. Biographical tapes are so well done that they will appeal to all ages. The book, *A Gift of Music*, is included for background information. The first set features Bach, Handel, Haydn, and Mozart. Set two features Beethoven, Schubert, Berlioz, and Mendelssohn. Schumann, Chopin, Verdi, and Grieg are in Set three. Wagner, Brahms, Tchaikovsky, and Dvorak are in Set four. This is a wonderful way to introduce your family to classical music if we don't know where to start. It has extra appeal since our children can listen and learn entirely on their own.(S)

➡ **Music Education in the Christian Home: The Complete Guide** by Dr. Mary Ann Froehlich (Word Inc., formerly Wolgemuth and Hyatt)

Dr. Froehlich has written this book based on her belief that music education is not an option but a scriptural command for Christians. She uses the first two chapters to buttress her statement by discussing music in Scripture and its practical application.

Once we are convinced that we need to teach music, we then need to know how to go about it. Froehlich discusses the most popular methods of music education (for those of us who have no idea whether Suzuki is the best method or if there are any other possibilities).

The rest of the book is practical information that can be used whether or not we have chosen one of the methods that were discussed. The author assumes that at some point we will be choosing some type of lessons for our child. However, a well-rounded music education will go beyond the scope of what is learned in lessons from a single teacher. It is the parent's responsibility to work on a comprehensive plan for music education. A Music Education Checklist in the book will help us identify goals for music education. The author provides suggestions for meeting those goals. For example, listening is a major part of music education, so the author includes lists of musical examples from medieval times through modern. Since a book this size could not possibly provide us with all of the details that we need to actually teach music, a large proportion of the book consists of listings of music resources including books on education, history, reference, techniques, and theory. Those of us who like the integrated approach might use the timelines in the back of the book to tie musical history to other history-based studies.

The non-musician might find all of this intimidating, but he/she should just choose a starting place such as listening to some of the works by major composers. (Check if your library has tapes, records, or CD's for loan.)

It helps to work with a music teacher who includes parents in children's lessons as do Suzuki teachers. In this way we learn along with our children and get guidance on what we can do on our own.

➡ **Practical Theory Complete : A Self-Instruction Music Theory Course** by Sandy Feldstein (Alfred Publishing Co.)

This ninety-six page workbook is a consolidation of three smaller workbooks (although we can choose either format). It covers basic music theory useful for all instruments and singing. It begins with the staff, clefs, and note naming. At the end it is teaching harmonizing a melody, composing, and chord progressions in minor keys. It seems to cover everything important in between—scales, dynamics, intervals, inversions, and much more. Students write in the book. Most lessons are simply practicing with information provided and no answer keys are provided for these. However, occasional review lessons have answer keys at the end of the book. It should work fine for children at least nine or ten years old through adults. Computer programs (IBM, Apple, Commodore, and Atari) are also available that correlate with the workbook and give aural feedback.

➡ **Tretter Violins**

If you need to purchase or rent a violin, check prices from Tretter Violins before you do anything. They sell beginners' violins (all Suzuki sizes) at very low prices. Even better, they have a buy back policy that makes it cheaper to

buy, then sell back the instrument than to rent one from another supplier. They also have a wide variety of quality violins for experienced players. I list this resource for
instruments because owner, Frank Tretter, is a Christian
businessman who has experience working with home
schooling families (including our own).

Drama

Drama can be difficult without a larger group, but support groups and community theaters offer possibilities. On
the other hand, dramatic reading can be practiced with an
audience of only one if that is all that is available. All of our
teens should at least attempt to do some dramatic reading,
even if their dramatic efforts never blossom any further.

Many of the poems and stories in literature books lend
themselves to dramatic reading. Most literature books also
contain at least one play script that can be used for practice.
(With only a few family members, each person can take on
more than one role, changing voices and mannerisms to fit
the characters.)

Bob Jones University Press is now offering packets containing scripts for five different plays that are consistent
with biblical values and appropriate for high school level
(see descriptions in the BJUP catalog). BJUP also offers
Speech for Christian Schools which is reviewed under Language Arts.

Chapter Seventeen

Beyond the Three "R's"

Thinking Skills

Developing thinking skills will primarily depend upon interaction between parent and child on various subjects—going beyond the obvious, encouraging deeper questions. For instance, we read an article on a controversial subject from the newspaper, then everyone comments about it. If everyone is well informed about the subject, the discussion can provide some lively debate. Becoming well informed does not occur overnight, but happens gradually as we and our children read newspapers, books, and magazines—accumulating a background of information. There are often reaction-provoking articles in the editorial section of the newspaper. This is a good place to start.

Thinking does not have to center around current events. If our children can take information that they have picked up somewhere and then apply it in a new way in a different situation, they are operating at the higher levels of thinking. If they can read an advertisement and identify the half-truths and propaganda, they are thinking critically.

Curriculum to teach thinking skills is not really necessary if we are debating ideas and challenging opinions (but not arguing) as a normal part of our family interaction. But some of us are not comfortable with debates and discussions, and prefer not to stir up family emotions over current events. For the calmer folk, some of the thinking skills materials are more practical. Even the outspoken among us might prefer to use some of the materials just because they are fun.

➡**Critical Thinking Press & Software (formerly Midwest Publications)**

Critical Thinking Press & Software specializes in supplemental book and software activities to sharpen thinking skills for better academic performance at all grade levels. Subject areas covered are mathematics, language arts, science, and social studies.

Two of their more basic books appropriate for teens are *Building Thinking Skills, Book 3—Figural*, and *Building Thinking Skills, Book 3—Verbal*. They are suggested for grades 7-12.

For high school students, I particularly like *Critical Thinking Skills, Books One* and *Two*. This is a fun course in logic that will challenge parents too. Some of the exercises are silly, but effective. You can skip around to a certain extent, choosing lessons that are most interesting, easier, or more challenging. These books need to be used interactively, since they are not designed for independent work. You will also need the teacher's manuals for each book.

➡**The Elements of Clear Thinking (Educators Publishing Service)**

The Elements of Clear Thinking is actually a series of three workbooks designed for high school level. The individual titles are: *Sound Reasoning*—how to distinguish between good and bad arguments, characteristics of deductive and inductive reasoning, pitfalls and fallacies, and identifying arguments; *Accurate Communication*—the use and misuse of language (slanted language, connotations, ambiguity, jargon, etc.); and *Critical Reading*—prereading, choosing reading rate to fit subject matter, organizational patterns. Here students also write a precis, a paraphrase, and evaluations. Choose one or all three titles. Teacher's keys are available for all three. One thing that I noticed, particularly in the first book, sets these apart from some of the other "logic" courses—the author introduces each formal logic principle or thinking skill, but always moves to practical application in typical situations such as conversations, advertising, or politics.(S)

➡**Just Think® 6 or 7 or Stretch Think® 3 (Thomas Geale Publications, Inc.)**

While these particular books in the publisher's series are designed to be used through junior high, because they were designed for gifted classes they can easily be used in high school also. These books develop thinking skills through a variety of creative methods. While all books include activities from almost every subject area, some place more emphasis on one area. *Just Think® 6* has a strong American History component, so consider using it the year that you study American History. *Just Think® 7* includes many activities that challenge students to consider current problems and issues. *Stretch Think® 3* seems to have more science-related topics than the others. One book can be used with any size group. Any pages that students need to use are reproducible. These are not workbooks, but teacher's manuals. The teacher must read through each activity before presenting it, but there are no extra teaching aids to prepare.(S)

➡**Wff N' Proof**

Wff N' Proof makes logic games that can easily overwhelm the faint hearted. Their *Equations* game is probably easier to tackle than most of the others. The original *Wff N' Proof* game is very difficult, but if you have a student who needs a challenge, here it is.

➡**Critical Thinking Activities (Dale Seymour Publications)**

The activities in this reproducible book hail from the field of mathematics and are divided into the three areas of patterns, imagery (not the new age type), and logic. Written for grades 7-12, the activities vary in difficulty to reflect that grade span. We can pick and choose appropriate activities by topic and difficulty level.

The patterns section goes far beyond "fill in the missing number" to include work with such topics as equations, charts, Venn diagrams, exponents, geometric formulas, and designs. Imagery has to do with developing visual skill in "seeing" accurately as well as predicting such things as how a shape will look from a different angle or when combined with another shape. A lot of the activities here resemble those I have seen on intelligence tests. Geometry skills get some extra practice here. The logic section includes Venn diagrams, logic statements, deductive exercises, and even one word logic game. While almost all activities are related to math, the skills are transferrable to other subject areas as well as to life situations.

There are 163 pages of activities, and the answer key is found at the end of the book.

➡️ **How to Lie with Statistics** by Darrell Huff (W.W. Norton and Company)

There is one last book that I would like to mention here, even though it might more properly belong under mathematics. *How to Lie with Statistics* is a small, paperback book that was originally written in 1954. It has been reprinted at least thirty-six times according to my copy of the book. The author introduces us to all of the shady ways that statistics can be interpreted to say whatever one desires. In a very humorous way, he talks about how advertisers carefully choose just the right numbers, and manipulate those numbers to enhance their products. Advertisers are not the only culprits targeted by Mr. Huff. Pollsters and politicians are equally exposed. While teens can read this on their own, it is the type of book that is fun when shared out loud. Watch out for a few references to the Kinsey sexual research. These can easily be skipped. Also, be aware that data has not been updated since the originally printing. Even so, the author's point still comes across clearly—we have to be alert and thinking logically when we evaluate information, such as that in advertisements and commercials, that has been designed to influence our behavior.

Electives

Typing

Typing is very important for each student to learn, whether it be learned on a typewriter or a computer keyboard. Typing courses can be taken in summer school or studied at home with a text from a used book store or college book store. One typing course of particular interest to Christian students is *Keyboarding with Scripture* (Association of Christian Schools International). Exercises consist of either KJV or NIV versions of Scripture, from small segments through long passages. Set up in traditional format, exercises progress in difficulty, with numbered lines to help determine the number of lines typed within specified times. If you have a computer, *Type!, Typing Tutor*, and other good programs, including free or inexpensive public domain programs are available.

Computer Literacy

We seem to have grown beyond the idea that all students should understand basic computer programming. For the general public, computer technology is moving in the direction of requiring less and less understanding of the computer's internal functioning, but more familiarity with applications such as using data bases, word processors, and other software. There will be those who are interested in computer programming, who will certainly need to study mathematical languages, Basic, Pascal, Fortran, and electronics. Those interested in using the computer as a tool should be devoting time to learning about the applications, not the technology that makes the applications possible. For instance, a person interested in desktop publishing needs to study word processors, publishing software, graphic art software, printing, and other aspects of the field.

Nevertheless, programming can be a worthwhile course for anyone as a tool for teaching logic. Writing flow charts is a logical challenge which depends upon good thinking skills. An understanding of programming may also turn out to be of value to a computer user trying to figure out why a program does not behave as it should.

At the same time, there seem to be many home educated teens with a true avocation for computer programming. The computer industry is their career goal. These students need to be learning what they can about computers now rather than waiting to begin in college.

For computer education, check your local computer bookstore for materials or consider the following resources:

➡️ **Introduction to Computers** (BJUP)

This text is available in either hard or soft bindings and is recommended for seventh through ninth grades. It is truly an introduction, covering how computers can be used, applications (word processing, spreadsheets, and data bases), and the process of programming (how programming works, but not actual programming). The Teacher's Edition contains a usable copy of the student text, so you need purchase only the Teacher's Edition.

➡️ **Computer Science** (BJUP)

Recommended for grades ten through twelve, this book teaches computer programming along with Christian philosophy. Students learn BASIC computer language. The course can be used with IBM compatible, Apple II series, Commodore, and some Radio Shack models. The Teacher's Edition contains a usable student text, explanations, notations for each different type of computer, and a floppy disk containing programs in the student text. Purchase the Teacher's Edition appropriate for your type computer.

➡️ **Using the Personal Computer** (A Beka)

This text teaches applications rather than programming. Students learn how to work with word processing, data bases, spreadsheets, and graphing. Fundamentals of typing are covered at the beginning for those lacking keyboard skills.

No computer program comes with the text. Instead students must work with programs to which they have access for their own computer. Lessons give general instructions such as "Center the title and use 12 point bold" since it would be impossible to provide instructions for particular key strokes to accomplish this within all of the different programs. For a student with no prior knowledge of any of the applications, this means that he will have to rely heavily upon the program manuals for chosen application programs. He will have to learn the basics of each program before he can work on the lessons.

Exercises include business, school, and home applications, using Christian hymns and Bible verses for some exercises.

➡️ **Programming A: Basics of Basic** (ACE School of Tomorrow)

This computer programming course for the BASIC language is presented in one, self-instructional book of twelve units. It comes with a computer disk that integrates with each unit. Students study from the workbook, practice applications on the computer, then do workbook exercises to reinforce learning. Available only for IBM compatible machines.

Computer Software

There are hundreds of sources for educational software. Because of the lack of time and space, I have not tried to review all of the good software available.

In spite of my limitations, there are a few software sources that I want to let you know about.

Fas-Track Computer Products carries home and school software for Apple, Macintosh, and IBM machines. Prices are significantly discounted, and descriptions in their catalog are useful.

Learning Services offers discounted educational software for a number of computers. They are selective in their offerings but still have a large selection of quality products. They also carry multi-media products (e.g., CD Rom and laser disc players plus software). Send for their free catalog.

Telemart is another good source for software of all kinds at discount prices. They do not specialize in educational software, yet you might find what you are looking for here, especially word processors and application software, often at the best prices. Telemart sells to everyone. Credit card orders can be taken over the phone.

Public domain software and shareware are programs that vary greatly in quality, but they are available free or at minimal cost. You can obtain these programs free by downloading them from bulletin boards or copying from a friend's disks. If neither of these avenues is open to you,

---

➡ **Pride's Guide to Educational Software** (Crossway Books)

This is the one "must have" book for anyone who wants to have anything to do with a computer. Bill and Mary Pride have written this 608-page book to help us with both hardware and software decisions for educational computing. They cover just about everything. I can't figure out why major word processors such as Word Perfect and Word are not included since many older students should be working on more sophisticated word processing programs such as these rather than the simpler versions that are reviewed. Aside from that, the Prides must cover everything else that is worth looking at.

They dedicate a bit of space up front (and in an appendix) to discussion of various hardware choices, including new technology, especially CD-ROM. Pros and cons of IBM type machines, Apple, Macintosh, Atari, Amiga, and Commodore are aired, along with personal recommendations from the Prides' vast experience.

Software reviews are divided into categories: interdisciplinary; preschool; language arts; math; science; social studies; culture; and high school, college, and beyond. There are multiple chapters within each of these sections.

Reviews include price information as well as rating by concept, usability, educational value, and an indication of what level of sophistication the program has.

Totally green beginners will find lots of help that will forestall some expensive mistakes, and experienced computer buffs will find the reviews (especially when comparing similar programs) much more helpful than those typically found in computer magazines or advertising write-ups.

---

there are catalogs offering public domain software at very low prices.

Shareware differs from public domain in that these programs are sometimes samplers of more comprehensive programs that the author would like you to purchase. The idea is—try it first; if you like it, you pay for it (sometimes this is called registering) and receive update information when available. Shareware is run on somewhat of an honor system. If we use and do not pay, the authors do not have the resources to develop more software for our benefit. The cost of shareware is generally much less than for equivalent programs sold in stores.

[NOTE: In most public domain and shareware catalogs, there are included programs which Christians will find objectionable—programs with wizardry and spell casting, sexually explicit material, astrology, gambling, and other trash. There are a few selective catalogs such as the ones from The Shareware Source and AccuSoft.]

AccuSoft has a selective catalog of 150 public domain and shareware programs for IBM type machines. Selections are based upon overall program quality and also on content. AccuSoft says, "As a Christian owned and run business, AccuSoft refuses to distribute any pornographic, obscene, occult, or otherwise offensive material." Catalog listings are very helpful with both descriptions and configuration requirements, and their favorite programs are marked.

Experimenting with public domain software can be frustrating and time consuming, so I was pleased to receive a catalog from **Micro Star**, a company selling public domain software (present prices are $2.99 to $12.95 a disk) that rates these programs. The Micro Star catalog describes IBM compatible, public domain software and shareware, and rates programs with one to five stars. Micro Star also provides information about necessary machine configuration such as memory, color/monochrome cards, joysticks, etc.

Another firm that deals with both public domain and shareware is **Public Brand Software**. Like Micro Star, they rate software to help us sift through the options, but they provide much more detailed descriptions of programs. Shareware programs are purchased for $5 a disk from Public Brand Software, and if we choose to use and register them, costs range from $5 to $89 or more. We can find word processors similar to the full featured and very expensive *Word Perfect* and *Microsoft Word*; data base programs similar to *DBase* and *Lotus*; educational, Bible, and game programs, plus much more.

The Shareware Source has a free descriptive catalog of public domain and shareware educational programs for early childhood through high school. Their offerings are limited, but do not include objectionable titles. Disks are only $2 each.

Computer Bulletin Boards

Computer Bulletin Boards are much more than places to stick things. There are all kinds of treasures available through bulletin boards once you figure out how to use them. (It is not really supposed to be all that complicated.) The great news is that there are bulletin boards for home schoolers. CompuServe (call 1-800-848-8199 for information about joining) has an Education Forum for all sorts of information relating to education. One special section of that forum (Section 16, I understand) is dedicated to home education. Two other bulletin boards are strictly for home educators.

Bloomunit BBS for Homeschool Families offers an outstanding library of educational shareware available for download, as well as an extensive collection of other family-oriented programs. Each program posted for download on Bloomunit has been thoroughly tested; you will find no "junk" files on the Board. In addition to shareware, the BBS offers over 40 national and international message conferences through VirtualNet, including such topics as "Family Living," "Alternative Education," and "Kids Only, 12 and Under." Computer and BBS beginners, including children, are welcome and encouraged to call. There is no charge for access to or use of the BBS. Bloomunit has been in service since March of 1991, available 24 hours a day, 7 days a week, in West Palm Beach, FL, at (407) 687-8712. High-speed communications are supported by a PM14400FXSA v.32bis modem; set your terminal program for 8n1.

Another bulletin board service for home school families is just now beginning. The homeschooling Arnold family in College Station, Texas goes on line with the **National Homeschool Computer Bulletin Board (NHBB)** on September 1, 1992. It will have 24-hour-a-day phone lines with many different services available such as home school legal news, teaching tips, free classified ads, shareware for downloading, pen pals, letters to the editor, health and nutrition, poems and stories by home educators, curriculum information, and more. The BBS number is (409) 690-HOME.

Choosing Computers

While Apple machines and software dominate the elementary schools, the situation changes at high school and college level. IBM and Macintosh become the standards. IBM family machines seem to be the standard on college campuses, so this may be a factor to consider if you are making a computer purchase. (Now that Macintoshes are becoming much cheaper and can run DOS disks, the situation might change dramatically.) Other machines such as Commodore and Atari can be used, but you might run into unforeseen communication problems when you want to swap disks of information with friends. Sooner or later most computer users want to share computerized information with others, and it can be expensive (and a lot of bother) to transfer that information from one machine to another if you do not have compatible machines. Some computer users never encounter this problem, so be aware of likely uses for your computer before making your purchase. Computer technology is changing so rapidly that the situation could be quite different within a few years. The agreement between IBM and Apple to work together is only one example of present situations which will likely result in fundamental changes in personal computers which will inevitably influence our choices. Buy the latest technology you can afford if you need to communicate with other computers through yours. Those who are only looking for a low-priced word processing tool for their children can look for the best buy that appeals to them. However, remember that higher education today often expects that students have access to either IBM or Apple type computers. If teens are close to college entry time, take extra care in choosing.

On a practical level, Apple and Macintosh computers are easier to use but more expensive than IBM type computers. Upgrading and options are both usually much less expensive and more easily obtainable for IBM type machines. Apple and Macintosh machines are basically the same wherever we purchase them. However, IBM type computers can vary dramatically according to the components used to assemble each. This makes it more challenging for the novice buyer.

For a lengthy discussion of the above topics as well as insight into the future of computing, check out *Pride's Guide to Educational Software* (Crossway Books).

Home Economics

I have a personal aversion to home economics courses. I was very interested in cooking, sewing, and related subjects in high school, so I enrolled in home economics courses. I persevered for two years hoping to learn something. I even tried a summer school class. But it was hopeless. My mother had already taught me far more than any of the classes without hardly even trying.

At home we already have the tools and the motivation for learning the arts of homemaking. Planning menus, purchasing food, preparing it, then getting the family's reaction is eminently more practical than the limited experience we get in a class or from a book. We can acquire more information from a friend, the library or bookstore if needed.

There are times when it is worth looking for outside help. If mom does not know how to sew, perhaps a mentor could be found within the family, neighborhood or church. Adult education and college classes are available for more complicated sewing techniques such as pattern making and tailoring. Cake decorating or other specialty classes can also be fun and worthwhile.

Work with the assets on hand for basic homemaking skills, then seek out sources for help with special needs or interests.

Chris Ellyson of Georgia passed on a great suggestion for developing the less obvious homemaking skills—the things that make a home an inviting, comfortable place to be. She suggests reading Edith Schaeffer's book, *The Hidden Art of Homemaking* (Tyndale House Publishers), one chapter a month, and allowing our children to practice and embellish Mrs. Schaeffer's ideas in our own homes.

I would like to mention *Kitchen Science* (Houghton Mifflin) again here even though it is reviewed under the Chemistry heading in the Science chapter. Many moms, including me, do not know the information in this book, yet there are tips here that will help us prepare more nutritious meals for our families. It is the kind of book that we dip into for a topic at a time rather than read straight through, so pick it up to have for handy reference.

Child Development

Future parents, but most especially future mothers, should have an understanding of child development—what children normally do at what ages. There is great comfort in knowing that just because all of the other little children you see are potty trained by one year, your child is not developmentally delayed because he is not trained until two.

The most widely recognized standard references that are easily read and understood are those from the Gesell Institute by F.L. Ilg, A. Gesell, and L. B. Ames entitled: *Child Behavior, The One Year Old* (separate books are available for each year up to nine years old) (Dell Publishing), *The Child from Five to Ten* (Harper and Row), and *Your Ten to Fourteen Year Old* (Dell Publishing).

Child development texts are available from college bookstores. However, most such texts as well as the Ilg, Gesell, and Ames books have a socialistic, humanistic bias.

Driver's Education

Driver's education is conceded as a must because insurance rates, prohibitive as they are for young drivers, are usually astronomical without evidence of driver's education. (The certificate from driver's ed will, in some states, enable teens to get their licenses at a younger age and lower insurance rates.) Unfortunately, Dad is not generally considered a competent instructor, so it is necessary to enroll under a recognized instructor. You can find such instructors at public schools (usually free) and private driving schools (expensive). Some driving schools offer group discounts so consider gathering a group of teens who would like to take driver's education together. When I called about a half dozen driving schools to check costs when three teens took the class together, all but one offered a discount. (Perhaps driving lessons would be an appropriate birthday or Christmas gift for a fifteen- or sixteen-year-old.)

Check the yellow pages for driving schools. They sometimes offer specials during spring break and summer vacation so you might save money by knowing about bargain times and planning ahead. If you request information, they often put you on a mailing list and send notices of special discounts.

Summer school is the time to take driver's education at your public high school if available. Some home schoolers have run into problems such as refusal because of lack of space, or the requirement of taking health education at the same time. (Health education classes often include sex education or other material offered from a humanistic viewpoint.)

Sources for Electives

Outside of the fundamental academics, there are many ways of enriching our curriculum that should be considered not only as options, but rather as essential to a well-rounded curriculum. Classes in arts and crafts, physical education, music, mechanical arts, and much more are available through many sources. Check your parks and recreation department, museums, community colleges (including television courses), private lessons, tutors, and other home schoolers with special talents.

Personal Development

In addition, there are a number of things that we should be doing that fall outside the area of standard curriculum, or at best are on the fringes.

An easily overlooked area is preparation for adulthood and increased responsibilities. While all of this is fairly obvious to some, others of us will wish to have some resources to draw upon.

Bob Jones University Press offers an eleventh and twelfth grade level text entitled *Family Living*, which covers preparation for family life along with personal development. Included topics are time management, grooming, friendship, dating, budgeting, and consumer education.

A similar book comes from A Beka—*Managing Your Life Under God*. Written for tenth through twelfth graders, this book covers relationships, sex and drugs, preparation for marriage, responsibilities, job success, safety, abortion, and evolution. Course content should take between nine and eighteen weeks to complete.

Another BJUP book is *Beauty and the Best*, dealing with personal conduct for young women.

Wayne and Emily Hunter are the authors of *Man in Demand* and *Christian Charm* (Harvest House), Christian courses in personal development for young men and women. Physical development, relationships between the sexes, manners, personal hygiene, smoking, drinking, drugs, and other topics are discussed from a conservative, fundamental viewpoint. Because of the sensitive nature of the content, it is appropriate that *Man in Demand* be taught by the father and *Christian Charm* by the mother, although teens can read either book independently.

As teens look to their futures, the challenges facing them can seem discouraging and overwhelming. *How To Plan Your Life* by Jim Davidson (Pelican Publishing Company) offers very practical advice for "being successful." He addresses the question of what it means to be successful, writing as a Christian (although non-Christians will also find the book valuable).

The book is full of wisdom. Even Davidson's short piece on acting versus reacting is worth the price of the book. But there are many more reasons to read this book such as his discussion about cause and effect, and his ideas about service as a key to success. Topics he addresses are self-image, importance of goals, a personal inventory, the use of our minds, choices, healthful living, success, setting and achieving goals, careers or jobs, natural laws, true, long-lasting success, self-examination, spiritual life, the role of traditional families, free enterprise, planning for future security, time management, personal habits, communication skills, and life-long learning.

How To Plan Your Life is a splendid book for older teens and adults.

Sex Education, Dating, and Preparation for Marriage

Everyone does not need a book to learn what they should know about relationships between the sexes, dating, sexually transmitted diseases, and so on. Ideally, these should be topics for ongoing discussion and learning, with the appropriate information passed on as the child matures. However, the ideal situation seldom exists, and many of us will want to rely on books to help us make sure that all of the important issues have been covered. Current issues, such as the AIDS epidemic, will require teaching that was not needed in the past. Following are reviews of resources which address these areas.

➡**AIDS: What You Haven't Been Told [video]** (Jeremiah Films)

This hour-long video offers a comprehensive and frightening overview of the AIDS crisis. Interviews with medical and political authorities as well as AIDS victims provide both statistical and personal information that is often glossed over by the popular media. The political issues linking the homosexual movement, AIDS research, and civil rights are explored, while exposing the dangers imposed upon our society by governmental fear of the power of homosexual organizations. The idea of safe sex is exposed as a fraud, while abstinence is promoted as the best defense. The film is Christian although most information is presented in a factual manner without being dependent upon belief in the Bible. Christians are urged to demonstrate a Christ-like attitude in helping to care for AIDS victims without accepting or approving of the sin involved in most cases. This film is used as part of the *Understanding the Times* course. Jeremiah Films also has a shorter version, *No Second Chance*, which is reviewed below.

➠ Learning About Sex series (Concordia)

This is a series of books on sex education. Titles for older children include *Sex and the New You* by Richard Bimler, recommended for children eleven to fourteen; and, *Love, Sex, and God* by Bill Ameiss and Jane Graver, for ages fourteen to young adult. Concordia is a Lutheran publishing house and reflects that denomination's attitudes. In these books, strong stands against abortion and homosexuality are taken, while birth control (within marriage) and teen dating are treated as acceptable. Alcohol, drugs, AIDS, venereal diseases, and other related topics are covered in *Love, Sex, and God*, making this quite a comprehensive book. Generally, most Christians will have no trouble with the basic information presented. The format of each book is interesting and age appropriate. For parents who would rather retain more control than just handing their child a book, Concordia published *How to Talk Confidently with Your Child about Sex*, by Lenore Buth. The beginning of the book is more of a marriage manual than sex education, but the rest of the book covers essentially the same information that is in the books written for children. Here the writer is speaking directly to parents rather than children, so we would use this book to study a topic and then share with our child rather than reading it to him or her.

➠ Love, Dating and Sex: What Teens Want to Know by George B. Eager

If our teenager is ambivalent about his or her relationship with God, biblical arguments for chastity hold little weight. This is unfortunately the situation we have with many of our sons and daughters. Most teenagers are not convinced solely by scriptural guidelines. Thus we have the "Just say no" campaign, designed to spread the message that chastity is a good choice purely from the self-centered viewpoint. What arguments will help these teens to buy the "Just say no" propaganda? There are a number of books available, but one of the best is *Love, Dating and Sex: What Teens Want to Know*. This book carries a clear message that sex before marriage brings nothing but grief. It teaches a pragmatic morality—there are good self-serving reasons for chastity as well as avoidance of drugs and alcohol. I would rather have my teens choose to do what is right because it is God's desire and pleasing to Him, but if that does not work, an appeal to their self interest is probably the next best argument. Mr. Eager does an excellent job of discussing the emotional aspects of dating and sexual relationships, and he speaks to teens on their wavelength. Although the author discusses sexually transmitted diseases, with brief descriptions of some of the most prevalent ones, this is not a clinical book on sexual functioning or a how-to manual. Mr. Eager deals with the underlying reasons why so many teens get into sexual relationships—feelings of inadequacy, desire to be accepted, pride, peer pressure, etc.—and sends a clear message of encouragement to stand strong and resist temptation. (The book is also available on audio cassette tapes.)

➠ Men and Marriage by George Gilder (Pelican Publishing Company)

Gilder challenges the commonly accepted theory that the differences between men and women are minimal, and that their roles should be interchangeable. In just the first chapter, he will shake up your thinking about gender roles and society's attitudes, and he does it uncommonly well. The book demonstrates an uncanny insight by Gilder that goes well beyond any other books of which I am aware. I find myself nodding and affirming what he says, then sitting back in surprise when he connects that information to a sequence of topics.

He discusses marriage and family, the breakdown of monogamy, homosexuality, women in combat and in the work place, plus many other related topics, following a thoughtful progression of ideas.

Gilder writes to an adult audience, frankly discussing adult topics, so this is a book for mature teens only. In fact, I think of it as appropriate for most teens as they graduate from high school, and for younger teens only if they are into exclusive dating relationships. (Parents should read it first to determine if it is appropriate for their teen.) It should help both young men and women better understand their expectations and needs.

➠ No Second Chance [video] (Jeremiah Films)

This thirty-minute video describes what AIDS is, how it is transmitted, and promotes abstinence as the only reasonable protection against the disease. It features interviews with AIDS victims to demonstrate the horrors of the disease. A nurse speaking to a classroom of teenagers serves as the film's vehicle for reinforcing key points and presenting the biblical view of sexual behavior. The film also promotes a compassionate Christian attitude toward AIDS victims. *AIDS: What You Haven't Been Told*, a lengthier video from the same company, uses many of the same interviews and scenes to present a more comprehensive overview of the AIDS issue.

➠ Preparing for Adolescence (Regal Books)

Many of us are already familiar with this classic book by Dr. James Dobson. Dr. Dobson, speaking to teens in a friendly, non-threatening tone, covers physical, emotional, and spiritual angles of physical (primarily sexual) development, boy-girl relationships, the sex act, grooming, and more. This book should be required reading for both parents and teens and probably even pre-teens. *A Growth Guide Workbook* for *Preparing for Adolescence* is available from the publisher. *Growthpak*, which includes the book *Preparing for Adolescence*, an eight, audio-tape version of the book, and the workbook, offers an alternative that may appeal to many teens.

➠ Sex, Love, and Romance: Sex Education from the Bible (A Beka)

This book, written for junior and senior high students, "...details God's plan concerning dating and marriage and the consequences of disobeying His moral commands in these areas." Unlike most secular sex education books, this one does not deal with physical details but with attitudes and standards. While it is "preachy" in tone, it is still a refreshing change from the humanistic view of sex education which, because of its moral depravity, spends most of its time on teaching about birth control, safe-sex, and AIDS.

➡️**The Shaping of a Christian Family** by Elisabeth Elliot (Thomas Nelson Publishers)

The jacket of this book says, "More than a manual on raising children or a treatise on the biblical basis of family life, *The Shaping of a Christian Family* sheds light on the many facets of family living: homely joys and shared troubles, triumphs and tragedies, difficult choices and rich rewards.

Sound advice is woven around Mrs. Elliot's stories of her childhood and parenting. Her godly wisdom shines through every chapter. This book is the ideal "textbook" for a parenting class, even though it is too special a book to be thought of as a schoolbook.

Also, parents who were not raised in godly homes can draw on Mrs. Elliot's experience as a model for themselves to improve their own parenting skills.

Abolishing the Dating Custom

As teens become more aware of and interested in those of the opposite sex, we confront the issue of dating. Some home schooling families (and others) have decided that dating is an unbiblical concept, and then have restricted boy-girl activities to group events. Single couple, boy-girl (or should we say man-woman?) relationships then are saved for the time when both are ready to consider marriage commitments. This approach helps teens to avoid morally dangerous situations, prevents broken hearts over break-ups, helps teens to maintain balanced relationships with a wider variety of people, and stabilizes groups because they aren't constantly being disrupted by changing loyalties within the group.

Jonathan Lindvall has been presenting his ideas along this line for many years. State groups, such as CHEA of California, have audio tapes of his workshops. Mr. Lindvall's ministry, Bold Parenting Seminars, also sells his tapes. Of particularly interest on the romance and dating issue are *Preparing for Romance* (for the entire family) and *A Talk to Godly Teens About Sex and Romance* (for teens and older audiences). Order the most recent *Preparing for Romance* version (taped at the CHEA of California 1992 Convention), consisting of two tapes, which covers more material than earlier versions. Contact Bold Parenting Seminars for a list of available tapes.

John Holzmann, another home schooling father, has also dealt with the dating issue in his book, *Dating with Integrity* (Word Inc., formerly Wolgemuth and Hyatt). Instead of recommending a prohibition against dating, he redefines it.

The basic guideline he suggests is that everyone should treat everyone else (male or female) just as they would a biological brother or sister. For instance, he raises the question to a young man, "Would you hold hands with your biological brother or sister?" If not, don't do it with anyone. The same idea applies to conversations and all other activities. This guideline permits some single-couple, boy-girl activity, yet keeps it on a strictly-friends level.

An important part of making this concept work is in communicating the idea behind it to those with whom a person associates. Otherwise, because a young man or woman is operating in such an unusual way, people (particularly those of the opposite sex) will probably not be able to understand the arms-distance approach and rejection of going-steady type commitments. I find Holzmann's ideas very practical. The only problem I can foresee is that introverts might have trouble communicating their relationship guidelines to others. But, if we can establish such guidelines within home school support groups, young people will find it much easier to hold to such standards within the supportive group. That experience might then enable them to continue on in the same way when they move beyond home school circles. (*Dating with Integrity* is highly recommended reading for all teens and parents.)

Still another resource on dating is an audio-tape series, *Preparing Your Children for Courtship and Marriage, From Toddlers to Teens* by Reb Bradley. In seven, ninety-minute tapes Pastor Bradley instructs parents of children of all ages about romantic relationships, teaching children the sanctity of sex, sexual values, understanding true and false love, and choosing a mate. His goal is to instill in parents a "...biblical vision for preserving their children's sexual purity."

Like the previously mentioned resources, *Preparing Your Children* challenges many of the accepted notions about relationships, dating, and marriage, recommending biblical guidelines in their place. Bradley's approach is broader than Lindvall's or Holzmann's, covering more background and related issues while spending less time specifically on the dating/courtship issue. Tapes are actually directed at a multi-age church audience, so they are appropriate for teens to listen to on their own. However, I recommend listening as a family activity, followed by discussion. The accompanying twenty-page *Syllabus and Study Guide* can be used by older family members as seems appropriate.

Bradley's speaking style is professional and entertaining, a real plus when we want our teens to listen. Even so, since each tape is ninety minutes long, you might want to listen to half of each at a sitting so that you do not lose the interest of those who have a hard time just listening for such a lengthy period.

Gregg Harris offers some insight on courtship and marriage with one of his tapes from the Advanced Home Schooling Workshop titled *Arranged Courtship for a Lasting Marriage* (Christian Life Workshops). In this tape, he "...encourages parents to avoid the dating scene entirely by accommodating the courtship of their young people within the context of normal family routines."

Part Three

Testing and Resources

Chapter Eighteen

Testing

There are two aspects of testing to consider—the everyday tests that reflect student mastery of material being studied at that time, and standardized tests which reflect the overall level of competence.

Mastery Testing

The first type of test is used widely in schools since teachers have few other means of ensuring that students are learning anything. They do not have time to read everything that students write, listen to oral reports, or participate in discussions with every student. At home, with constant interaction, we can use these other methods of evaluation. However, when children are working independently, as they usually are in high school, testing becomes more necessary. If we are home educating more than one child, we cannot possibly read everything that we assign, which makes it difficult for us to use interactive methods of evaluation. Teens will figure out quickly that they know more about the subject than we do. Some teens will gladly share their new-found knowledge, but others will take advantage of the situation to skim through lessons.

We must determine which subjects most need discussion and interaction, then read those assignments so that we can help our teens. Leave the cut-and-dry subjects that are more objective for our teens to study on their own, and use the tests that are available from the publishers to monitor progress if necessary.

Some students will have developed a love of learning and recognized its value. We will not need to check up on them with frequent tests. Others need to know that someone is monitoring them regularly.

Standardized Testing

Some of us give our children standardized tests without clear ideas of what we expect to learn from such testing. Many of us feel that this is a necessary part of education because "the schools do it." In some states it is required by law for home educated children to be tested periodically. Some of us want to demonstrate to skeptical relatives that we are indeed educating our children by sharing with them our children's standardized test results. A few of us, whether we admit it or not, want proof that our children are more intelligent than others. Then, there are those of us want to find out if we are doing an adequate job as teachers.

Schools test children regularly for a number of reasons, most having little to do with the individual child, but more to do with statistics, politics, and money. We need not be concerned with testing for these purposes.

When the state demands standardized testing, there is little we can do but go along with the requirement. Skeptical relatives can be a definite problem, and sometimes good test results will relieve the pressure on us. But, more often, skeptical relatives are impressed with the results that they see in our children after a year or two of home education. All of us want to be proud of our children, but that is not adequate reason to submit them to standardized testing. The concern over our adequacy is legitimate. Usually we can tell how well our children are doing just because we are working so closely with them every day. But it can be difficult to step back and objectively examine what we are accomplishing. A standardized test will not give you a total picture. It does not measure curiosity, creativity, social wisdom, attitudes, and the other intangibles that can be of utmost importance. A standardized test will tell us to some extent how well our child has mastered and retained basic subject matter, and how well he applies reading and thinking skills.

The most important reason for testing, and one which few of us identify, is to test for gaps in knowledge. If a child misses every problem having to do with fractions, but answers correctly every other math problem, there is a definite learning gap.

Test Results

It is important that we receive a complete breakdown of standardized test results, showing what particular skill or skills within a subject area show weakness. A general score showing poor language usage is often of little value. More valuable would be a breakdown showing that most punctuation questions were answered incorrectly, while other skills were satisfactory. Standardized test results are returned to us in various forms—some providing only a minimal amount of information and others giving a thorough breakdown of subject areas. We must know what kind of result interpretation we will get from the testing before we send in our money. If we need a thorough breakdown of results, we must make sure that that is what we will receive.

Testing Services

Bob Jones University Press offers a testing service using the *Iowa Test of Basic Skills* (a standardized test) for junior high, the *Test of Achievement and Proficiency* for high school, and the *Cognitive Abilities Test* for grades 3 - 12. Tests scored from April through September are machine-scored, giving you very detailed and useful results. Because fewer children are tested at other times of the year, tests scored in the fall and winter are hand-scored with little breakdown for detailed results. In addition, they offer *Metropolitan Math, Reading,* or *Language* diagnostic tests, and *Personality Profile* testing. Tests from BJU, except for the *Personality Profile,* must be administered by either a credentialed teacher or someone with a four-year college degree. Contact Testing Services Department for more information.

Christian Liberty Academy Independent Achievement Testing Service offers *California Achievement Tests (CAT)* to both enrolled and non-enrolled families. Testing may be administered by parents. Student test form (answer sheet only) and grade equivalent results for individual subjects are returned to you. The cost is very reasonable and there are no restrictions on who can administer the test, making this a favorable alternative for many families.

For a small additional fee, Christian Liberty Academy will also use the test results to provide you with curriculum recommendations for the coming school year, if you so desire. Recommendations are not limited to materials used in CLA courses. While recommendations will be chosen to suit the obvious grade level placement, there is no avenue for evaluating learning styles, family situation, individual interests, or other factors that are important in curriculum selection. This service would probably be most appealing to those just beginning, who need to start somewhere and feel unable to evaluate all of these other factors until they have had some experience. This service does help to solve the major problem of grade level placement, and it will be likely to pick up learning gaps from earlier years and recommend materials to fill in.

Home Education Center, in conjunction with Family Christian Academy, offers the *Stanford Achievement Test* in the Spring of each year. They also offer diagnostic tests and a curriculum recommendation service.

McGuffey Testing Service is available to home schoolers in grades K-12 whether or not they are enrolled in McGuffey Academy. The *Stanford Achievement Test* is offered and may be administered by parents without special qualifications unless a certified teacher is required by your state. McGuffey Academy will hand-check each test and will send you a copy of the results along with an evaluation and letter that will help you to interpret the scores accurately. The results show a detailed breakdown of skills within subject areas.

Covenant Home Curriculum offers an adapted version of the 1964 SAT test. (Older SAT tests were more challenging than present editions.) **Covenant Home Achievement Tests** evaluate English and math skills of students in grades K-12. Tests are hand-scored and provide results under general headings such as grammar, reading comprehension and spelling. Test scorers include some observation comments that might pinpoint specific problems. The English section of the test is tied to the Warriner English series, although it should adequately evaluate skills of students using other English programs. Tests are available to all home educators, and no credentials or degrees are required for those administering the tests.

Summit Christian Academy offers the *Iowa Basic Skills* test in the Spring for younger students in grades 3-8. They also offer the *Test of Achievement and Proficiency* for grades 9-12. Both tests are computer-graded with results sent to the parents. The cost is $30 for enrolled students and $40 for others.

Sycamore Tree offers the *Comprehensive Test of Basic Skills* for K-12. There are no restrictions on who can administer the test. Tests are scored professionally on May 15 and August 15, providing a very detailed and helpful breakdown. The rest of the year, tests are hand-scored with a much less comprehensive breakdown of results. Testing is free to families enrolled in Sycamore Tree.

Write to these organizations for information. Many of the independent study programs arrange standardized testing for those who desire it. In states requiring testing, contact your local support group for the best means of meeting those requirements.

Outside of these testing services (and others not listed), standardized tests such as the Iowa test are available only to qualified teachers, schools, and school services.

Diagnostic Testing

If we wish to identify gaps in learning, a shorter diagnostic test might do the job just as well as a standardized test, but with a lot less hassle. Most diagnostic tests can be administered by parents without strict guidelines. Diagnostic tests are available from Bob Jones University Press, Home Education Center, Summit Christian Academy, Alpha Omega, and A.C.E. (Accelerated Christian Education) for anyone who wishes to order.

Regarding the Alpha Omega and A.C.E. tests, use only the Math and English tests, since the others will not be useful for general purposes. These are parent-administered and graded. The tests are not perfect. Since they were designed to place students in the publishers' curricula, they do ask some questions that pertain only to each particular curriculum. You should look for and cross out these questions before your child takes the test. The tests also reflect each publisher's scope and sequence, which might differ from yours or that of the publisher whose material you wish to use. Use the results to (1) identify weak areas; (2) compare with your scope and sequence (what you plan to teach and when) to identify areas that should already have been mastered or are next to be taught; and (3) plan the child's course of study to either review or teach areas as needed.

Alpha Omega diagnostic tests (in Bible, English, math, science, and social studies) are offered by Summit Christian Academy along with the more widely accepted *Wide Range Achievement Test.* This combination of tests is offered for diagnostic purposes for $30. Tests are teacher-graded, and results are sent to parents.

A more specific diagnostic tool for reading is *The Blumenfeld Oral Reading Assessment Test* (Paradigm). This audio tape is designed to analyze a person's ability to decode and pronounce words, progressing from very simple three-letter words to difficult multi-syllabic words. Easy administration instructions are on the tape as well as in the printed material which comes with the tests. Words are also pronounced on the tape for the parent/teacher. There are 380 words on the test, arranged in increasing order of difficulty. There is also a post-test to use later on to check for improvement. Five copies of each test are included with the kit, and extras are available at reasonable cost from the publisher. While the test can be used with any age from beginning reader through adult, it will be especially useful for the parent who begins home schooling in the mid-elementary grades or later and suspects that her child might have difficulty with decoding or phonics. The test will help to identify whether reading problems are caused by lack of phonetic knowledge or lack of experience with words (vocabulary). It is not designed to identify learning disabilities or comprehension problems, although dyslexia problems might show up during test administration.

There are other diagnostic tests, but these are the most easily accessible to home educators.

Preparing Children for Testing

There are many materials to help children do well on standardized tests. Familiarity with test-taking strategies will help them do their best. Two tools for help in test preparation are the *Scoring High* series (American School Publishers) and *On Target for Tests, Book C*, for grades 7-9 (Continental Press). Of particular interest to teens who plan to take college admissions tests is the *College Admissions Practice Test* offered by Bob Jones University Press. (Also see SAT and ACT test preparation helps in Chapter Seven.)

Learning Difficulties/Disabilities

However we choose to label them, there are definitely home educated children who are having difficulty learning by traditional methods. For inexperienced parents, this can create an overwhelmingly frustrating situation. There is a strong temptation to put these children into the public school system so that they will get special education. Too often the special education programs provide nothing more than band-aids to pass children ahead in subjects by simply giving them very, very simple work to do as a substitute for normal classroom activities. Rarely do schools take time to address the underlying causes of learning problems. This is because they do not have the necessary time to spend with each individual child to help overcome problems. It is a lot faster to use band-aids.

There are a number of avenues which might lead to cures for learning disabilities. Although most disabilities are still present to some degree no matter what we do, there are things we can do to try to alleviate major problem areas. Two of the most successful strategies for curing learning disabilities are vision therapy and perceptual motor training.

A child's eyes must do more than just see words and numbers. They must send the proper information to the brain. Then the brain must send the proper response to be spoken or written or acted upon. There is much room for errors in transmission. If the eyes do not see well or do not send the proper message to the brain, the result often appears to be a learning disability. Visual therapy involves exercises to help improve eye function, which in turn can help the learning process.

If the message is properly perceived by the eyes, it may yet be lost in transmission by garbled transmission lines. If the proper connections are not made by nerve cells, this too interferes with learning. Perceptual motor exercises are designed to help improve the connections within the nervous system so that messages promptly reach their proper destinations.

If some of this sounds like hocus pocus to you, you are not alone. However, I have seen the results of a number of children working through both methods. While neither method can guarantee improvement for all children, a large proportion of those who faithfully follow a program of exercises (visual or perceptual motor or both) do achieve some measure of improvement.

Unfortunately, we often have trouble determining whether our child's learning difficulty is caused by a learning disability rather than other factors such as immaturity, laziness, or rebelliousness. This is the question facing many of us when we feel that our child is functioning below level in one area or another. We don't want to shell out hundreds of dollars for a professional evaluation unless we are fairly certain there is a problem. And, even if we are looking for professional evaluation, many of us have no idea where to find an evaluator or what type of evaluator we need.

It is helpful to have some guidelines of symptoms to look for that indicate learning disability problems before rushing off to the professional. The books described below—*How to Identify Your Child's Learning Problems and What to do About Them, The Learning Connection*, and *20/20 is Not Enough* —provide such guidelines. Some of the problems we encounter are minor enough that we can deal with them ourselves with just a little guidance, such as is provided in most of the materials described here. Rosner's *Helping Children Overcome Learning Difficulties* (published by Walker, sold by BJUP), which I have listed last, offers more specific help for working in each subject area to overcome a range of difficulties.

If you suspect that your child has a significant problem, you really should see a specialist. He or she is trained to identify things that we might easily miss. Also, because of their experience, specialists can often suggest the best methods to use to overcome problems. Some testing services which offer services to home educators are described under "Developmental Testing and Testing for Special Problems." You might ask other home educators for referrals to such services in your area.[1]

➡ How To Identify Your Child's Learning Problems And What To Do About Them by Duane A. Gagnon (Pioneer Productions)

"Do you suspect your child of having a learning problem but would like to know for sure? Do you have a child that has already been identified as having a learning difficulty, but you would like to have activities you can do with him/her at home that will help?.... Or would you just like some practical activities to do at home with your children to help develop their learning skills?" These are the questions the author poses to his readers.

He has written an easy-to-read tool for laymen (parents) who suspect their children can use help with a learning problem. Part one helps us evaluate strengths and weaknesses in both auditory (hearing) and visual (seeing) skills in nine areas: attention, analysis, synthesis, sequenc-

---

1   I am not an expert on learning disabilities, so I offer these reommendations to you, trusting that you will check them out yourself, asking questions about the programs, asking for references, and using discernment about what is best for your child.

ing, short term memory, long term memory, comprehension, abstract reasoning, and expression.

Part two consists of methods and activities to help in areas that show weakness. These activities are NOT perceptual motor activities such as those found in Lane or Shapiro's books, but are instead school-like activities typically used by special education teachers. For example, to improve visual comprehension, show the child a picture of a person and have him indicate the various parts of the body and what they do. These activities can be useful, but if you identify a serious problem, consider both a professional evaluation and the use of perceptual motor therapy, vision therapy or some other means of curing the problem.

➠ The Learning Connection book and Stepping Stones Kit (Vision Development Center/Steven R. Shapiro)

Vision Development Center has combined both visual and perceptual motor therapies into a single program that can be undertaken at home with professional supervision. Mom and Dad can be the therapists at much lower cost than if they take their child to a specialist for regular visits.

To read more about the program before investing in the whole kit, Steven Shapiro has written *The Learning Connection*. Here he tells the background of his work, using many stories of children he has worked with as examples. He writes in a friendly, easy-to-read style, unlike that of most other books on the treatment of learning disabilities. He includes tips on symptoms to look for that generally indicate learning disabilities. There are charts of normal developmental patterns for children of kindergarten age through eighth grade. The last section of the book provides directions for many perceptual motor activities along with a chart showing which exercises will help in which developmental area. These exercises/activities can be used by anyone without purchasing anything else. However, many children will also need visual therapy.

Materials for the complete program, which integrates both visual and perceptual motor therapies, are found in *Stepping Stones Learning Therapy Kit*. The kit includes: the book, *The Learning Connection*; vision development training video (contains easy-to-follow instructions); step-by-step instruction manual; student activity manual (which includes the same descriptions of perceptual motor exercises as *The Learning Connection* plus a large number of visual activity pages not found elsewhere); 3-D pictures, focusing-lens flippers, special glasses (used only with exercises), vision development progress charts for visual therapy; and a built-in follow-up program for retention of skills. (I am told that much of the cost of the kit is due to the inclusion of the focusing-lens flippers which have expensive lenses.)

The cost of testing by a learning disabilities specialist can easily be equal to or greater than the cost of this kit. The methods which are used appear to be similar to those used by reputable therapists. Steven Shapiro has many successful case histories on file to substantiate his claims. This should be a good alternative for those who need to do something and cannot get to a specialist for help. The kit does not provide a simple cure-all. A substantial time investment (20-30 minutes per day) will be required to faithfully keep up the exercise program. Shapiro reports that most children show improvement in four to six weeks.

Mr. Shapiro is also available for seminars if you want to gather a group of people interested in learning about learn-

ing disabilities (also available on video). He can offer personal testing along with these seminars.

➠ Developing Your Child for Success by Kenneth A. Lane, O.D. (Learning Potentials Publishers, Inc.)

Dr. Lane has written this book based upon years of work in vision therapy. In the first chapter, he explains the many factors involved in the reading process (in fairly technical language). Next he explains how we can help children develop perceptual motor skills for reading success. The remainder of the book is divided into eight sections of activities, each focusing on a developmental area. Activities are arranged according to level of difficulty so that parents can begin at easy levels, then work up to more complex levels. The sections are titled as follows:

Section I - Motor Therapy Procedures: Activities to Develop Balance and Gross Motor Skills

Section II - Visual Motor Therapy Procedures: Activities to Improve Eye-Hand Coordination and Writing Skills

Section III - Ocular Motor Therapy Procedures: Activities to Improve a Child's Eye Movements and Eliminate Rereading and Losing His Place When He Reads

Section IV - Laterality Therapy Procedures: Activities to Develop a Child's Body Imagery and Understanding of His Left and Right

Section V - Directionality Therapy Procedures: Activities to Help Children Develop Directionality Skills and Eliminate Reversals

Section VI - Sequential Processing Therapy Procedures: Activities to Improve a Child's Ability to Remember Things in Sequence

Section VII - Simultaneous Processing Therapy Procedures: Activities to Improve Visual-spatial, Letter Position and Visualization Skills

Section VIII - Vision Therapy Procedures: Activities to Improve Focusing, Eye Teaming and Overall Visual Skills

A list of materials and equipment needed for the exercises is included. (The most expensive item probably is a small trampoline.)

The author does not recommend that this book be used as a substitute for professional evaluation. However, he outlines a very comprehensive program covering a multitude of activities that are generally recommended for overcoming various learning disabilities. Parents could work through the activities with their children without professional assistance.

Compared to Steven Shapiro's *Learning Connection*, this book is much more comprehensive in explanation and illustration of activities, although it lacks some of the checklists to help identify problem areas. (See information below about diagnostic assistance available through Dr. Lane's office.) It does not require the use of the lenses and other visual tools that are in Shapiro's *Stepping Stones Kit*.

In this book, there are few tools to help identify problem areas and no differentiation of therapy programs according to individual needs. Instead, all children should do all of the exercises. A book such as *How to Identify Your Child's Learning Problems and What to do About Them* might be useful in helping to pinpoint problem areas if you are unable to afford professional evaluation. However, Dr. Lane has developed a reasonably-priced diagnostic program. Parents can administer a developmental test to their child which Dr. Lane then grades, or he can screen children through diagnostic software.

Dr. Lane has also developed five workbooks that can be used as part of a total perceptual program to work on specific areas. Workbook titles are *Recognition of Reversals, Spelling Tracking, Visual Tracing, Visual Scanning,* and *Visual Memory.*

Dr. Lane offers even more assistance. He says, "To further help parents, I am also offering a daily lesson plan. Depending on the diagnosis from the computer screen or the developmental test battery, I can write out a daily lesson plan that will give them five activities to do a day for six months. These activities are taken from my workbooks and *Developing Your Child for Success.*"

➠Smart but Feeling Dumb by Dr. Harold Levinson (Warner Books)

This intriguing book suggests that many learning disabilities are based upon inner ear problems. Dr. Levinson advocates use of temporary medical treatment to achieve a permanent cure. I know of one well-known learning disability practitioner who incorporates such medical treatment into his program with sometimes successful results.

➠20/20 is Not Enough by Dr. Arthur S. Seiderman and Dr. Steven E. Marcus (Alfred A. Knopf)

Experts often find that vision problems are at the root of learning difficulties or disabilities. Doctors Seiderman and Marcus believe that vision therapy can be of tremendous help to many struggling learners and also to those who are near-sighted. Through case histories, they discuss various vision problems, provide the medical explanation, and describe possible treatments. This is not intended to be a do-it-yourself manual, but rather a guide that will help us identify possible problems. (It provides checklists of possible symptoms of vision problems.)

In addition to vision problems that hinder education, the book deals with sports and vision, the work place and video display terminals, aging and vision, and the possibility of curing myopia (near-sightedness).

An appendix summarizes various vision research studies and lists bibliographical information both for the studies cited and for further related reading.

➠Helping Children Overcome Learning Difficulties by Jerome Rosner (BJUP)

Rosner offers help to both parents and teachers, assuming that they are functioning within traditional school settings. In spite of that limitation, his book is packed with helpful information. Strategies for both teachers and parents to use when dealing with learning disabled children go beyond teaching into relationships and life functioning.

He begins with discussions of the various forms of testing, explaining how they work. While he directs us to professionals for physical tests (vision and hearing), he gives instructions for doing perceptual testing ourselves. Part II has instructions for working on visual or auditory perceptual skills as well as general motor skills. Part III offers specific help for school subject areas—reading, arithmetic, spelling, and handwriting. At the end, Rosner offers preventive suggestions for preschool children.

All of the foregoing make this book more comprehensive than the others described here. However, Rosner does not emphasize large-muscle, perceptual motor exercises as do the others, relying instead on more specific, small-motor exercises in combination with teaching techniques.

Allergies

One further problem that some parents have discovered at the root of their child's learning difficulties is allergies. If you have been puzzled by your child's ability to learn well and easily one day, and a seemingly contradictory inability to function the next, maybe allergies are the culprit. In her book, *The Impossible Child* (A Guide for Caring Teachers and Parents/ In School At Home), Dr. Doris J. Rapp describes and gives examples of behavioral and appearance clues to help spot allergy-related problems. Next she deals with possible environmental or food sources. Suggestions follow to help teachers deal with problems, including behavioral problems such as unresponsiveness in learning situations, that have been caused secondarily by allergy problems . A later section provides suggestions for parents to help alleviate problems under their control. Rapp points out that many children who have been labelled as learning disabled are in reality suffering from allergies. There are a number of methods for dealing with allergies which are discussed. A lengthy section of references will direct parents to sources for more information or assistance.

Although written for teachers and parents in typical school settings, almost everything in this book will be equally applicable for home educators.

The Practical Allergy Research Foundation carries other books by Rapp such as *Allergies and Your Family* and also provides helpful information such as a Multiple Food Elimination Diet that can be used to identify or eliminate possible food allergens.

Developmental Testing and Testing for Special Problems

Developmental tests will help to identify maturity levels and learning styles that can help guide us in determining methods for teaching each child. Tests for learning disabilities will help us identify specific problems. For developmental testing or testing for learning disabilities or handicaps, we refer you to the services below. These services will also be helpful in advising methods to overcome problems.

EDAN. This is an educational consultation service based on use of the Structure of Intellect-Learning Abilities (SOI-LA) tests. Testing is available for kindergartners through high school. Two options are offered: Option 1 includes the tests, which are administered by parents in the home, and computerized evaluation. Option 2 adds extended interpretation by professional developmental specialists on audio cassette. Tests identify strengths and weaknesses, including learning disabilities, developmental vision problems, areas of particular strength, and learning styles. The evaluation provides recommendations for teaching methods along with training materials for remediation or enhancement. The cost is very reasonable and accessible to all families since it is all handled through the mail. Request a free brochure for full description.

Charlene Forsythe. Charlene is a registered nurse with a masters degree in education with an emphasis on learning handicaps and perceptual-motor development. She has studied under Elizabeth Davies, one of the foremost authorities in the area of perceptual-motor development, who in turn was trained by Dr. Newell Kephart. (Those who are familiar with some of the key people and ideas in perceptual-motor development will recognize Kephart and be familiar with his methods.) Charlene will evaluate your child and prescribe a program to help overcome both physical and learning disabilities. This approach is often very effective for children with dyslexia, dysgraphia, kinesthetic deficits, and other problems. The cost is very reasonable.

Linda Howe. Linda's background is in teaching. She has done advanced study and received special training in perceptual-motor development from Elizabeth Davies, and her training and methods are similar to those of Charlene Forsythe. Linda Howe has had great success working with many home-educated children, even those who have tried other methods that did not work. The cost is very reasonable. The prescribed program is done by parents with their child at home, with occasional re-evaluations.

Dr. Stephen Meyer, A Child's Life. Dr. Meyer offers a full range of diagnostic services for educational or learning disabilities and emotional problems of children. Counseling and psychotherapy are available. Dr. Meyer is familiar with resources for sensory-motor therapy. Physical therapy and sensory-integration therapy for brain-injured children, and speech and language therapy are also available. (Dr. Meyer is a committed Christian who is actively involved with Christian schools.)

Dr. Ray Nadeau, Nadeau Reading Clinics. Dr. Nadeau offers developmental testing for all ages. His clinics usually try to administer testing to young children in large groups (at schools or other centralized locations). Older children will need to go for individual testing. Nadeau provides parents with detailed results and recommendations for exercises and methods to use with their children. (Secular organization)

Dr. Stanley Walters, Center for Children and Parents. The center offers a full range of testing and interpretation. They provide follow-up services for those who need them. Many parents begin with the full Educational Check-up for their child, then have monitoring check-ups annually. Dr. Walters has a tremendous amount of experience and insight into methods and materials appropriate for different children as well as effective parenting. He is especially good at identifying potential problem areas and suggesting preventive measures. Dr. Walters has a number of publications that are very helpful for parenting/teaching. Some of the most highly recommended are: *Implementing Positive Shaping in the Home, Temperamental Children—Diagnosis and Treatment, Learning Theory for Parents and Teachers*. For information on publications write to Center for Children and Parents, 2509 Meadowgrove Rd., Orange, CA 92667 or call (714) 543-1212. Note that the address for publications is different from that for testing services. (Secular organization.)

Chapter Nineteen

Sources for Materials

Once you have made your decisions, you are ready to order textbooks and other resources. How on earth do you go about it? Won't publishers refuse to sell textbooks to individuals?

It can seem very intimidating to set out to order curriculum on your own. However, there are many different ways to get these resources. The least expensive way is generally to order directly from the publisher.

If you enroll in a correspondence course, independent study program, or school service simply as a means to obtain textbooks without hassle, you will be paying much more than you need to for books. If the services offered (other than supply of textbooks) are helpful to you, then enrollment is worthwhile. On the other hand, if you are only using this method because you do not know how else to get the books, you will be wasting money.

There are several businesses set up particularly to serve the home school community with materials. Others offer materials appropriate for home education although that is not their primary purpose. All of these offer a free catalog or brochure of their materials unless otherwise indicated.

Codes are used to alert you that resources or companies are not Christian or present some potential problems. Even Christian companies carry materials from secular suppliers, most of which will present no problems at all. (S) indicates a company that is secular in outlook rather than Christian. (SE) indicates that they are secular and also that they carry some items that are in conflict with Christian beliefs or morals.

Acorn Naturalists

Their catalog, subtitled *Resources for Exploring the Natural World*, is a naturalist's delight. Tools such as a plant press, combination compass/thermometer/wind chill calculator, and an aquatic net help the do-it-yourselfer. Kits designed for westerners provide instructions, equipment, and activity cards. They offer hundreds of books, some on general topics, such as *The Amateur Naturalist's Handbook*, and some on specific topics under headings such as western habitats, weather, fossils and rocks, plants, invertebrates, amphibians and reptiles, birds, and mammals. In addition, they offer games and videos. Home schoolers in California will find many items specific to the state, but there are still many options for those who live elsewhere.(SE)

Activity Resources Company, Inc.

This company offers only math materials, but they have searched out the best materials. They offer Cuisenaire® and Base 10, plus many other books and materials appropriate for preschool through junior high levels.(S)

Alpha Omega

Alpha Omega, publisher of the LifePac curriculum, has over the past few years developed one of the largest catalogs of learning materials for home educators entitled *Hori-*

zons. While most items will supplement the LifePacs, some will replace them. Games, literature, hands-on helps, and supplementary books form the bulk of the catalog items. Resources for grades K-12 are included. Visa, MasterCard, and Discovery cards are accepted. Their customer service personnel will try to help with curriculum selection decisions.

Blue Mountain Book Peddler

This business obviously grew out of a very personal love and appreciation for good books. The choices are very eclectic and wide ranging in topic and perspective. They carry some titles reviewed in this manual, such as the Brown Paper series, Saxon math, *Easy Grammar, Scienceworks, Foodworks,* and *Ecce Romani*, plus good literature.

Send for free catalog.(S)

Blue Spruce Biological Supply, Inc.

Blue Spruce is a good source for science lab materials. From their catalog, it appears that schools are a large part of their market, but they do sell to individuals. They carry materials that might be needed in the elementary grades as well as those for older levels. While they carry a few books, the bulk of their inventory consists of specimens (live and preserved), dissecting equipment, slides, and lab equipment.(S)

Bluestocking Press *(Educational Spectrums Catalog)*

Bluestocking Press carries a different line of materials than any of the other suppliers. They feature resources for an integrated approach to history (American history emphasis) and economics (free market), as well as books on entrepreneurship and alternative methods of higher education. They sell their own very unique publications: *Special Report: Selling to the Other Educational Markets, How to Stock a Quality Home Library Inexpensively, Whatever Happened to Penny Candy?, Whatever Happened to Justice?,* and *Uncle Eric's Guidelines for Selecting Books That Are Consistent with Basic American Principles.* In addition they sell helps for critical thinking and writing skills, reading guides, rubber stamps, and basic home schooling books.Send $1 to cover first class shipping of their catalog for immediate delivery. Money back guarantee. MasterCard and Visa accepted.(S)

Builder Books

Send $1 for catalog with full descriptions.

Builder Books carries a full line of materials for home education including many items recommended in this manual. They are very knowledgeable and carefully research the products they sell. They are a good source for traditional materials as well as educationally-sound alternatives to traditional curriculum. For many years they have been providing dependable service to home educators.

Children's Books

This is a source for children's reading books which have already been screened for ungodly content. The catalog lists all types of books—biographies, classics, educational, beginning reading, preschool, and fiction—along with a few games and flash card sets. They carry books from Troll, Dover, Usborne, and others, including Christian literature from publishers such as Mott, Bethany House, and Moody. Both reading levels and interest levels are listed under book descriptions. Discounts of 10-20% on all orders.

Visa and MasterCard accepted. Send for free catalog.

Christian Book Distributors (CBD)

CBD is a discount source for Christian books. Memberships are available, but are not required for ordering. Nonmembers can remain on the mailing list and receive free the bi-monthly regular catalogs. Members also receive sale catalogs and newsletters (alternating months with the regular catalogs) with special bargains. They carry over 5000 titles with discounts usually ranging between 20% and 75%. CBD is similar to Great Christian Books, but they do not list a section of materials specifically for home education. CBD also publishes special academic and family catalogs, available upon request. Memberships are $5 for U.S. and Canada, $8 for all other countries.

Christian Life Workshops

Christian Life Workshops is Gregg Harris' business. CLW offers a free magazine/catalog called *Our Family Favorites*. In it they offer information as well as resources that the Harrises have found useful in their ten years of home schooling. Many items such as *The Christian Home School* by Mr. Harris and *The Christian Family Complete Household Organizer* are published by CLW. Others are books on home education, teaching resources, parent helps, as well as a few hard-to-find items.

CLW has developed a publishing arm called Noble Publishing Associates. This is a cooperative publishing business which should very well suit the needs of those who develop ideas for home schoolers and Christian families, but need help getting them published and marketed. Contact CLW for details.

Christian Teaching Materials Co.

Their 104-page catalog is $2 for the first issue. After customers purchase from CTM, they then receive catalogs free. (Catalogs are updated frequently, reflecting current stock.) This is a source for new textbooks and learning materials. Stock includes Fischertechnic, Usborne, Christian Liberty Press, Rod and Staff, Saxon, Mortensen, ACSI, Mott Media, Master Books, Key Curriculum Press, Alpha Omega, Little Folk Visuals, Weekly Reader, and others.

Creation's Child

Send SASE for free brochure.

They offer world and U.S. history time lines, books on America's Christian heritage, and more.

Creative Kids Learning Co.

This Christian family business carries materials for all subject areas plus special education, with an emphasis on creative/alternative learning more than on textbooks. They list many items reviewed in this manual such as books by Ruth Beechick, Troll Books, *TOPS*, Crossway books, Usborne, and materials from Educational Insights. They can also order items from many publishers which are not listed in their catalog. Send for free catalog.

ed-tex Arlene Mickley

This company represents leading publishers of educational textbooks and media materials for careers and special education. Representatives can help you locate appropriate materials for specific needs in both educational areas. Among publishers represented are Fearon/Janus/Quercus, Phoenix Learning Resources, Education Associates, Hammond, Educational Technologies, Inc., Chronicle Guidance Publishers, EconoClad, EDL, and The Right Combination.(S)

The Elijah Company

The newest Elijah Company catalog reflects a greatly expanded line of resources, particularly the extensive reading lists and history and science sections. This business, operated by a home schooling family, has selected quality materials that reflect their philosophy of home education. These include more real books and less textbook-type resources. A large part of the catalog is devoted to history resources, listed by topic/time period. However, they also sell resources for all subject areas.

Send $1 for catalog.

The Family Educator

This business is strong in history and literature materials with a Principle Approach orientation. They also stress the three R's with selected materials.

Great Christian Books

A $5 yearly membership fee enables you to purchase Christian books at good discounts. (If you mention *Christian Home Educators' Curriculum Manual*, they will waive the membership fee!) Membership is automatically extended for another year at no charge with each purchase. GCB has more than 7000 items from about 400 different publishers. While GCB is not exclusively a home education source, they have greatly expanded their home education line. They also carry commentaries, study guides, and other books, in addition to titles from A Beka, Chariot, Family Learning Center, Alpha Omega, and Crossway. Many of these books are difficult to find at local Christian book stores. No returns are permitted unless the wrong item was shipped or merchandise arrives in damaged or defective condition.

Growing Without Schooling (Holt Associates)

They offer a newsletter, books, games, instruments, tapes, and more for home educators. Their catalog is entitled *John Holt's Book and Music Store*. While items reflect a wide (primarily non-Christian) philosophical range, they tend to be very creative and unusual. They carry some recommended titles that I have found nowhere else. They will accept telephone orders using MasterCard or Visa.(S)

Hewitt Research Foundation

Hewitt has made many significant changes over the past few years. They are reflected in their new catalog *Blueprints for Building Great Children*. Offerings are primarily for elementary grades, but they include selected materials for junior and senior high.

Home Education Center

This company has a 54-page catalog listing a wide variety of materials, although mostly for elementary grades. They also serve as a clearing house for some used materials (we can send in our used materials for them to resell if they are on Home Education Center's "Accepted Used Materials" list.) They will either buy our used materials, or we can use the value as credit toward a purchase. They have four walk-in stores with regular business hours, located in Knoxville, Nashville, Memphis, and New Orleans. Call for locations and hours. In addition, they offer testing services.

The Home School Books and Supplies

They sell a full line of home education materials (over 7200 items in stock), including A Beka, Alpha Omega, Modern Curriculum Press, Saxon, and many other items listed in this book. (No used books or materials.) They have access to thousands more items, so call to see if they can supply what you need. If you are in the Washington area, they have a store (with regular business hours) where you can browse through their huge selection. Send for free catalog.

Overseas delivery at only 10% (book rate) shipping. Mail, call, or FAX orders. Visa or MasterCard accepted.

Home School Supply House

They have made some top-quality choices in materials for the basic subject areas, even though their line is smaller than those of some of the largest distributors. Included are many items from Modern Curriculum Press, Harcourt Brace Jovanovich, and Dover.

The Horne Booke

They carry Mott Media's Classic Curriculum, Principle Approach materials, the Sower series, children's classics, an excellent selection of books on America's Christian history, Little Bear Wheeler's tapes, *Webster's 1828 Dictionary*, and Stansbury's *Elementary Catechism on the Constitution*.

Josh Jr. Christian Book Club

Flyers advertise book club offerings aimed at three different age groups: pre-kindergarten through second grade, third through fifth grade, and sixth grade and up. The goal is to offer quality materials with Christian values. Books, videos, audio cassettes, stickers, pencils, and t-shirts are listed. Book offerings include classics, biographies, games/puzzles, educational, spiritual growth, and Christian fiction. Free gifts, discount pricing, and "Bonus Bucks" help bring the costs below retail prices. Send for free flyers.

Library and Educational Services

Although they do not carry textbooks, they do offer many other children's books at discounted prices (at least 30% off of list price). A recent catalog lists books from Troll (biographies, classic literature, nature, history), literature (primarily Christian), videos, and many other items.

Four separate catalogs list their offerings. Catalog titles are *Religious Products, Secular Products, Everything for Kids Only*, and *The Best of Everything*. Catalogs are $3 for the first and $1 for each additional OR all four for $5. Mini-catalogs are sent to those on special mailing lists, and include items from all four categories. A mini-catalog will be sent free upon request. They frequently add new items to the catalogs, and they have occasional special sales of both adult and child books.

Lifetime Books and Gifts (Bob and Tina Farewell)

Lifetime's descriptive catalog offers a wide variety of materials for home educators including good literature and history material, plus a complete line of resource books for *Konos* curriculum. The newest catalog is much larger than earlier editions, reflecting a big expansion in their product lines. Mrs. Farewell also offers a special book search service for out-of-print books such as old editions of *The Book of Life, Child's History of the World*, and *Child's Geography of the World*. Send $3 for *The Always Incomplete Catalog*.

Modern Talking Picture Service

Modern Talking Picture Service's job is to help those who make educational videos get those videos to their intended audiences. They have a huge variety of videos for elementary and secondary levels that can be borrowed for FREE. Films are usually available in either 16mm or VHS format. The videocassettes (VHS format) even come with prepaid return labels, so we do not even pay return shipping. However, the borrower does pay return shipping on 16 mm films. Most films are produced by government agencies, corporations, and under grants. They usually are promoting an organization, product, or idea, although it is more obvious in some films than others. The quality varies from poor to excellent. Films can and should be requested for viewing dates well in advance. Following are just a very few sample titles with descriptions to give you an idea of what is available:

Committed to the Land from Union Pacific Corporation traces the history of Union Pacific from its dramatic beginnings in the 1860's through its modern roles in rail and truck transportation, environmental services, computer technology, and land development.

Electronics...Your Bridge to Tomorrow from Electronic Industries Association. This film was made to motivate high school students with technical aptitude to pursue careers in the electronics industries. It visits schools, businesses, and electronic service centers to show students what careers are available and how to prepare.

Request a free catalog for either elementary or secondary grades. The secondary catalog is much larger than the elementary, and it categorizes films under subject headings. Films are available under the following headings: science, home economics/consumer education, health/safety, social studies, agriculture, driver's education, career guidance, business/marketing, education, the arts, sports, the environment, energy/ecology, and a special selection of films about Germany.(S)

The Moore Foundation (Dr. Raymond and Dorothy Moore)

They offer all of Dr. Raymond and Dorothy Moore's books, the *Moore-McGuffey Readers, Winston Grammar, Math-*

It, a newsletter—*The Moore Report International,* and variety of materials in accord with their educational philosophy including *The Weaver, Konos, Usborne books,* and more. They plan to increase the number of resources offered, so send for a brochure for a complete list.

Rainbow Re-Source Center

Send $2.50 for the current issue of their newsletter (which includes an inventory list and helpful suggestions and recommendations from other homeschoolers) or $12 a year for 6 issues. This is a clearinghouse for used books and teaching materials, with selected new materials also available. The inventory includes a broad range of both basic and supplemental materials, most at bargain prices. They will also help you sell your no-longer-needed materials.

Shekinah Curriculum Cellar

Shekinah sells a full line of home education materials, books, and games, including many items recommended in this manual such as A Beka, Basic Education, Alpha Omega (English and all high school subjects), Saxon, and Usborne. They guarantee the lowest prices. Shekinah also has a store, albeit with limited shopping hours. If you are in the area, call for a recorded message about store hours.

Send $1 for catalog. No phone orders.

Sycamore Tree

They offer Alpha Omega and Rod and Staff curriculum, plus a huge selection of books, games, and toys. Sycamore was the first home school supplier on the scene and has a long-standing reputation for dependability.

Send $3 for their catalog, which includes a $3 certificate redeemable on your order. The catalog will be sent to you free if you mention *Christian Home Educators' Curriculum Manual.*

T & D Christian Sales

Discount source for Christian books and Bibles.

Teacher's Laboratory, Inc.

Materials range from those for studying environmental sciences, design and technology, magnetism, measuring, and magnification, through a variety of math resources. They also sell a selection of resource books. Included in their catalog are some items reviewed in this book that are not widely available such as *Conceptual Physics, LEGO Simple Machine* and *Robotic* sets, balances, and *Gee Whiz!* Teacher's Laboratory includes "Notes to Teachers" free with most major kits and equipment. These will help you get the most from your investment.

Send for their free catalog of hands-on math and science materials for all ages.

Windows to Learning

Windows to Learning (formerly Beverly's Books and More) carries a broad line of materials somewhat similar to that of Builder Books or Shekinah Curriculum Cellar. They have materials for all subject areas including books from A Beka books, Modern Curriculum Press, Educational Publishers Service, and many more. They also have a walk-in store in addition to their mail order service. The store has limited hours, so call first.

Free catalog to the continental United States.

Window Tree Learning Project

Canadians will be glad to know that there is a source in Canada for home education materials. Their catalog includes textbooks, workbooks, resource books, reference materials, and manipulatives from many publishers. Special titles include *Starting from a Walk, Whatever Happened to Penny Candy?* (with a Canadian supplement), *A Child's Story of Canada,* and other materials on Canadian history and geography.

We hope to see this business grow to help Canadian home educators more easily get what they need. Window Tree also puts out a newsletter called *Learning Leaf* with practical teaching tips, student activities, and book reviews. In British Columbia testing, consultation, and workshops for parents are offered.

Special sources

a) Schools often discard outdated or unneeded books. Keep your eyes open. Library book sales and thrift stores are often surprising sources for good materials. Encyclopedia sets, reference books, classic literature, and just about anything else can be found sooner or later at one of these sources.

b) The national magazine, *The Teaching Home,* carries advertisements and information on resources that will keep you up to date on what is available. Their perspective is fundamentalist Christian.

Home Education Magazine also reviews materials and carries advertisements. They differ from *The Teaching Home* in being open to all philosophies.

c) *How to Stock a Quality Home Library Inexpensively,*
    by Jane A. Williams (Bluestocking Press)
This inexpensive little book should be one of the first purchases that you make. Most of us do not have unlimited budgets, so we need to get the most that we can for our money. Jane Williams knows all the bargain sources, but she does not just list them and leave us to fend for ourselves. She gives us all the information we need to really make the most of it. She also shares some money making/money saving hints to help us subsidize our home library. The Appendix gets even better. It has source lists of names and addresses (plus details), the most valuable being one listing sources for discounted and remaindered books and publisher's closeouts—some mail order, some walk-in.

d) **O.T. Studios** has assisted Christian Home Educators Association of California by taping workshops at major conventions for many years. Other state organizations will also have tapes of conventions or seminars available. Tapes address just about every aspect of home education, although the quality varies from tape to tape because of the convention setting. Write to O.T. for a list of the "best" tapes from CHEA events, or write to your state organization for information on their tapes.

Sources for special needs

While in this book I spend a minimal amount of time addressing special learning needs resulting from disabilities, physical handicaps, or (on the other extreme) giftedness, I realize that some children will need materials that are more challenging, move at a slower pace, or are designed to help overcome a particular handicap. Following are some useful sources. All offer free brochures or catalogs.

Braille Institute

The Braille Institute operates only in southern California, but they have a toll free number that anyone may call to obtain referrals for assistance in their area. There are many organizations other than the Braille Institute helping those who are blind. Many of them offer classes in life skills, free library loans, and other services. A series of five public service videos dealing with problems encountered by blind people at different ages is available for borrowing at no charge through many video stores.

For referrals call (800) Bra-ille. Our local Braille Institute will answer written inquiries. Write to the Anaheim address for the Braille Institute, listed in the Appendix.

Contemporary Books, Inc.

Contemporary offers books for adult learners who lack educational background or for ESL students. They emphasize math and language arts, although they do address a few other areas with a couple of items. The materials are designed to help students build basic skills (both life and educational) and/or help them pass the GED examination.(S)

DLM Teaching Resources

DLM offers materials for the learning disabled for all subjects. Their catalog includes educational software and assessment instruments.(S)

Edmark Corporation

They sell software and print resources for special education.(S)

ed-tex

(listed above under general sources at the beginning of this section)

This company represents several of the publishers of special education items that are listed here.(S)

Educators Publishing Service

EPS offers materials for both average and below average learners. This is one of the best sources for materials for children with "minor" disabilities such as dyslexia and dysgraphia. Books range from general materials useful with all children to those addressing very specific needs, and they are very reasonably priced.(S)

Fearon/Janus/Quercus Education

They have academic curriculum for junior and senior high, written at elementary reading levels, covering all the basic subject areas, life and consumer skills, and health. They also sell material for adults who have learning difficulties.(S)

The Gifted Child Today Catalog (GCT, Inc.)

Their large catalog of materials for gifted learners is free. They also publish two magazines. *Gifted Child Today* is written for parents while *Creative Kids* is written for children.

Samples of the magazines are available for $5 and $3 respectively.(SE)

Gallaudet Bookstore Catalog

They offer materials for the hearing-impaired for all subjects.(S)

Modern Signs Press, Inc.

This is a good source for sign language materials.(S)

Phoenix Learning Resources

They offer *Programmed Reading* plus other materials for students with learning disabilities.

A Positive Approach Magazine

This unique Christian magazine is written for the "physically challenged" person. Published quarterly, it ranges wide in covering many topics related to various handicaps at all age levels. The magazine features articles by Joni E. Tada, Joni and Friends, and other ministries. The issue I reviewed had articles on topics such as osteoporosis, rehabilitation, deaf workers, photography for the blind, "International Hearing Dog," balance disorders, career strategies, and incontinence, along with inspirational stories and helpful advertisements.

Resources for the Gifted

They offer supplementary materials for math, language arts, science, computer, thinking skills, and social studies for above average learners.(SE)

Ordering

When ordering from publishers, it is a good idea to use school stationery for a more professional look. Some publishers will sell to us only if orders are written on school letterhead. To create school stationery/letterhead have a typesetter create a heading on a plain 8 1/2" by 11" piece of paper as you have seen on other business stationery. It need not be fancy, but it should look professional. It should include school name, address, and phone number. Typesetting and printing can be very expensive. A better option is to use a computer/laser printer service that will create and print stationery for us in the small amount that we will need. Joshua Harris' Kid's Stuff business offers such a service—*Just Enough Stationery* (Kid's Stuff). He will provide custom, computer-created school-letterhead stationery at a cost far lower than that charged by typesetters and printers. *Educational Support Foundation* offers a package that, in addition to school stationery, includes envelopes (unprinted), report cards, transcript forms, business cards, small and large labels, and master copies of all forms personalized for your school.

A very few publishers have policies stating that they will not sell to individuals. Some say they will sell student texts but not teacher's editions to individuals. Their concern is usually to prevent regular school students from getting teacher's editions for purposes of cheating. If we order on school letterhead, or send a copy of a school affidavit, we will usually have no problem with any of the publishers that we have listed. If someone in the ordering department of a publisher tells you that you must have a letter of authorization from your school district or some other authorization that is difficult or impossible to obtain, do not give up. Recognize that they want to establish your legitimacy, then suggest other possibilities such as an order on letterhead, copy of an affidavit, or anything else that might reassure them. Usually, just sending the order on school letterhead without making prior inquiries raises no questions at all.

Some publishers charge extra fees for small orders. This means that it might be more economical for us to order their materials from one of the distributors that carry them(shown by the code letters at the end of appendix entries).

It is a good idea to order books for the fall well in advance—at least by early summer—to avoid back orders and long waits. Many publishers will offer an examination/return period, although they will ask for payment ahead of time. You can then return books that do not satisfy you. This can be a lot of trouble and the postage can be expensive, so do try to examine textbooks at conventions, other home schoolers' homes, Christian schools, or wherever else you have the opportunity so that you can avoid problems.

A few last thoughts before you order:

Costs vary greatly among publishers, yet the cost will still be far less than the cost of Christian school. Cost does not always guarantee the best quality. Paying more than is necessary to accomplish our goals is a waste of our resources. On the other hand, choosing the cheapest option might cost more if we have to buy something else to replace it because it did not suit our purposes.

Do not judge books solely by their appearance. Flashy graphics and color can sometimes be a cover-up for poor content, particularly with the secular publishers. If the appeal of color and pictures is important for the child, that is one thing, but the content needs to be worthwhile. Paperbacks will generally be less expensive but also less durable than hardbacks. If it is very likely that books will be used by more than one child, purchase hardbacks whenever possible.

And finally, do not buy curriculum for children far ahead of schedule. It is impossible to tell what will be best for them a year or two from now.

Appendix A

Sources and Addresses

Source addresses for all materials I have referred to in this manual are included here. When I list only the publisher's name under an item, you will find a separate listing for the publisher which includes its address. You can usually contact the publisher directly, but sometimes publishers would rather not sell to individuals. In these cases, they have distributors to sell us their products. In most cases we will pay the same price whether ordering from a distributor or a publisher.

If you need to order teacher's editions, answer keys, or solution keys from the large secular publishers, be sure to read the ordering instructions in the previous chapter.

I have referred you to a number of sources that carry lines of products for home educators in the section entitled "Sources." It can be very time consuming and expensive to write to every publisher and distributor who might have something of interest. I have tried to make things easier by providing a key to help you identify a source that might carry a number of the items in which you are interested. Then you can place one larger order, saving on shipping costs and hassles. In the key, I list again some of the sources described more fully under the "Sources for Materials" section. These particular sources were chosen because of the number of reviewed products that they carry, their established reputations, and their ability to fill orders from all over the country. Obviously it is difficult to keep track of who is selling which items, and that information changes from time to time. Because I do not indicate that an item is carried by a certain distributor, it does not preclude the possibility that they do indeed carry it. The best approach is to obtain catalogs from a number of these sources for reference.

I have chosen not to include prices which I know is an inconvenience to many. The primary reason for this decision is the fact that prices change so frequently that it is almost impossible to keep up with changes. Since this book will be in print for about two years, many prices will undoubtedly be incorrect in a short period of time. Also, people tend to order from books such as this long after the original printing date. This means that publishers and distributors have to spend a lot of time sending orders back for the correct payment. It seems more efficient to send for catalogs from a number of distributors and publishers (another reason for the key used here) and compare current prices.

Distributors	Code
BUILDER BOOKS	A
GREAT CHRISTIAN BOOKS	B
THE HOME SCHOOL BOOKS AND SUPPLIES	C
LIFETIME BOOKS AND GIFTS	D
SHEKINAH CURRICULUM CELLAR	E
SYCAMORE TREE	F

Reading the Codes

Code letters of each of these sources appear in parentheses (). If that source carries only selected items from this publisher, the parentheses with code/s follows immediately after that item. Otherwise, the parentheses with code/s indicates that all items from that publisher are carried by the indicated sources. Sometimes a distributor has access to a resource although they do not always keep it in stock. Such items are marked in the key with an "x" following the code letter. For example, (B,Cx,D) indicates that B and D carry the item in stock, while C can easily order it for you.

All of the publishers and sources listed will send a free catalog or brochure unless otherwise specified. Check for complete details on distributors under "Sources for Materials."

Many publishers and sources have toll free telephone numbers. This means that they pay for the cost of our call. These numbers all have (800) as their area code prefix. If an (800) number is for orders only, please call the other number listed with other types of questions.

A Beka Book Publications
Box 18000
Pensacola, FL 32523-9160
(800) 874-2352
(800) 874-3590 FAX; place orders using MasterCard, Visa, or Discover
See "Major Publishers" for a more detailed description. (B,C,E)

A Beka Book Correspondence/Video School
Box 18000
Pensacola, FL 32523-9160
(800) 874-3592
(800) 874-3593 FAX

Abrams (Harry N. Abrams, Inc.)
100 Fifth Avenue
New York, NY 10011
(212) 206-7715

History of Art (D) and *History of Art for Young People*

ACE School of Tomorrow (A.C.E./Basic Education)
P.O. Box 1438
Lewisville, TX 75067-1438
(800) 888-9338
See "Major Publishers" for a detailed description.

AccuSoft
P.O. Box 360888
14761 Pearl Rd., Suite 309
Strongsville, OH 44136
(800) 487-2148 telephone orders only ($20 minimum) with Mastercard, VISA, Discover, check or money order. Call M-F, 1-5 p.m.

(216) 225-2340 Canada
no minimum on FAX or mail orders

Acorn Naturalists
17300 East 17th St.
Suite J-236
Tustin, CA 92680
(714) 838-4888
(714) 838-5309 FAX
 (F-some items)

ACT testing
See American College Testing program.

ACTPEP
P.O. Box 168
Iowa City, IA 52243
College credit by testing

Addison-Wesley
Jacob Way
Reading, MA 01867
(800) 447-2226
(617) 942-1117 FAX
High school math, *Foodworks,* and
Sportworks. They also take orders for Long-
man Publishing titles: *Composition Hand-
book, Ecce Romani, Preparatory Latin,* and
The Phenomenon of Language. (C)

Advocates for Self Government
3955 Pleasantdale Rd., Suite 106A
Atlanta, GA 30340
(800) 932-1776
*Does Wrong Become Right If the Majority
Approves?*

AIMS Education Foundation
P.O. Box 8120
Fresno, CA 93747-8120
(209) 255-4094

Alfred A. Knopf Books
Order from Random House, Inc.

Alfred Publishing Company, Inc.
P.O. Box 10003
Van Nuys, CA 91410-0003
*Practical Theory Complete: A Self-Instruc-
tion Music Theory Course.* Available
through local music stores. Do not order directly from the publisher.

Algebra
See Professor Weissman's Software.

Algonquin Books of Chapel Hill
P.O. Box 2225
Chapel Hill, NC 27515-2225
(919) 967-0108
(919) 933-0272 FAX
*The Weather Wizard's Cloud Book, The
Weather Wizard's 5-Year Weather Diary*

Alpha Omega
P. O. Box 3153
Tempe, AZ 85280
(800) 821-4443
(602) 438-2702 FAX
See "Major Publishers" for a more detailed
description. (B,C,E,F)

Alpha Omega Institute
P.O Box 3153
Tempe, AZ 85280
(602) 731-9411

American Christian History Institute
James Rose
P.O. Box 648
Palo Cedro, CA 96073
(916) 547-3535
*A Guide to American Christian Education
for the Home and School, The Principle Ap-
proach.* Some ACHI materials are also
available from Foundation for American
Christian Education and Horne Booke. (Cx)

American College Testing Program
P.O. Box 168
Iowa City, IA 52243
ACT testing

The American Covenant: The Untold Story
See The Mayflower Institute.
Also available from Foundation for Ameri-
can Christian Education and American
Christian History Institute.

American Enterprise Publications
R.D. 6, Box 6690
Mercer, PA 16137
(412) 748-3726
Economics: Principles and Policy, Second
Edition; *Economics: The American Econ-
omy; Free Enterprise Economics* (pam-
phlet) (Cx)

American Information Newsletter
2408 Main St.
Boise, ID 83702
6 months, $25; 1 year, $48

American Map Corporation
46-35 54th Road
Maspeth, NY 11378
(718) 784-0055
(718) 784-1216 FAX
Schick Anatomy Atlas, maps, and atlases.
(A,C,E)

American Portrait Films
P.O. Box 19266
Cleveland, OH 44119
(800) 736-4567
(216) 531-8355 FAX
*No Alibis, The Silent Scream, The Massacre
of Innocence, The Right to Kill, A Scientist
Looks at Creation, Aids: What You Haven't
Been Told, No Second Chance,* plus many
other videos on hot topics.

American School
850 E. 58th St.
Chicago, IL 60637
(312) 947-3300
Secular, high school correspondence course

American School Publishers
P.O. Box 5380
Chicago, IL 60680
(800) 843-8855
(800) 621-0476
(312) 984-7935 FAX
Scoring High series (F)

American Science and Surplus
601 Linden Pl.
Evanston, IL 60202
Source for surplus goods, lots of science related items.

American Textbook Committee
Route 1, Box 13
Wadley, AL 36276
Basic Economics and *A Basic History of the
United States* (also available from Blue-
stocking Press). (C,D)

American Vision
P.O. Box 724088
Atlanta, GA 30339
(800) 628-9460 credit card orders only
(404) 988-0555 other orders and inquiries
God and Government (B)

**America's Christian History: Christian Self-
Government**
See Intrepid Books.

Ampersand Press
P.O. Box 1205
Point Reyes Station, CA 94956
(800) 624-4263 orders only
(415) 663-9163
(415) 663-9203 FAX
O! Euclid, Krill, AC/DC (A,C)

Amsco School Publications, Inc.
315 Hudson St.
New York, NY 10013
(212) 675-7005 orders
(212) 675-7000 information
Source for inexpensive textbooks, all subjects, primarily high school/college level.
Send for free catalogs. The Educational List
& Net Prices catalog is simply a title and
price listing. Specific Mathematics, Language Arts, and Social Studies catalogs provide descriptive information. Titles
reviewed: *Achieving Competence in Science, Curso Primero (Spanish), Algebra I,
Algebra: An Introductory Course, Life Science Work-Text, Reviewing Biology, Reviewing Chemistry, Reviewing Physics, The
Reader as Detective, High Marks,* and the
Amsco Literature Series. (Cx)

Arco Books
Distributed by Globe Book Company. See
Globe Book Company.
*Preparation for the SAT, Preparation for
the GED, Preparation for the American
College Testing Program* (Cx)

Aristoplay
P.O. Box 7028
Ann Arbor, MI 48107
(313) 995-4353
Games: *By Jove, Hail to the Chief, Where
in the World, Made for Trade, Pollution Solution.* Send for free catalog. (A,B,C,D,E,F)

Art Extension Press
P.O. Box 389
Westport, CT 06881
(203) 227-6637
Art prints and teacher's manual for art ap-
preciation

**Association of Christian Schools Interna-
tional (ACSI)**
Box 4097
Whittier, CA 90607-4097
Keyboarding with Scripture (B,C,E)

Audio-Forum
96 Broad St.
Guilford, CT 06437
(800) 243-1234
Say it by Signing (VHS) video cassette (C)

Audio Memory Publishing
2060 Raymond Ave.
Long Beach, CA 90806
(800) 365-SING
Grammar Songs audio cassettes (A) and *Love, Dating and Sex* book (C,D,E,F)

Audio-Visual Drawing Program
Bruce McIntyre
1014 N. Wright St.
Santa Ana, CA 92701
(714) 542-0344
Send for free descriptive, illustrated catalog. (C,D,E-*Drawing Textbook* only,F)

Back Home Industries
Gary and Wanda Sanseri
P.O. Box 22495
Portland, OR 97222
A Banker's Confession, Spelling Boosters (B,D)

Baker Book House
P.O. Box 6287
Grand Rapids, MI 49516-6287
(800) 877-2665
(616) 676-9185
(616) 676-9573 FAX
Worlds Apart, Battle for the Family, The Light and the Glory (A), *From Sea to Shining Sea* (A) (B,C,D)

Barnell Loft Publications/SRA
P.O. Box 5380
Chicago, IL 60680
(800) 843-8855
Specific Skills, Prescriptive Spelling (E).(C)

Barnes and Noble
1 Pond Road
Rockleigh, NJ 07647
(800) 242-6657 for orders only
(201) 767-6660
Discount bookseller. Bargain source for *The Synonym Finder.*

Barnes and Noble Books/division of Harper and Row, Publishers
10 East 53rd Street
New York, NY 10022
Botany Coloring Book (C,D,F)

Barron's
250 Wireless Blvd.
Hauppauge, NY 11788
(800) 645-3476 for orders only
(516) 434-3311
Algebra the Easy Way (A), *Calculus the Easy Way, Survival Mathematics* (E), *How to Prepare for the GED* (A), college preparation and Spanish books. (C,Dx)

Basic Bible Studies
See Tyndale House Publishers.
Available at Christian book stores. (B,E)

Battle for the Family
See Baker Book House
Available at Christian bookstores. (B,Cx)

Peter Bedrick Books
Alphabetically listed under Peter

Behavior Development Products
Rt. 2, Box 291-N
San Marcos, TX 78666
(512) 353-2833
Spell-N-Meld and *Operations*

Berg Christian Enterprises
P.O. Box 66066
Portland, OR 97290
(503) 777-4101
Certificates for graduation and other occasions

Bethany House Publishers
6820 Auto Club Rd.
Minneapolis, MN 55438
(612) 944-2121
Basic Greek, Kingdom of the Cults (B,C,Dx)

Bible Memory Association
P.O. Box 12000
Ringgold. LA 71068-2000
(318) 894-9154

Bible Science Association
Mid-Kansas Branch Chapter
1429 N. Holyoke
Wichita, KS 67208
(316) 683-3610

BloomUnit BBS
Linda R. Bloom
4986 Palm Beach Canal Rd.
West Palm Beach, FL 33415-3101
(407) 687-8712 (bulletin board number)

Blue Mountain Book Peddler
15301 Grey Fox Road
Upper Marlboro, MD 20772
(301) 627-2131

Blue Spruce Biological Supply
221 South Street
Castle Rock, CO 80104
(800) 825-8522
(303) 688-3396 (in Denver area)

Bluestocking Press
P.O. Box 1014G4
Placerville, CA 95667-1014
(916) 621-1123
How to Stock a Quality Home Library Inexpensively (E), *Whatever Happened to Penny Candy?* (E,F), *Whatever Happened to Justice, Uncle Eric's Guidelines for Selecting Books That Are Consistent with Basic American Principles, Young Thinker's Bookshelf* (A,B,C)

Bly Academy
P.O. Box 5878
Kingwood, TX 77325
(800) 648-4574
(800) 826-4262
Videos

Bob Jones University Press
Greenville, SC 29614
(800) 845-5731
See "Major Publishers" for a detailed description.

Bolchazy-Carducci Publishers
1000 Brown St., Unit 101
Wauconda, IL 60084
(312) 526-4344
Artes Latinae (C)

Bold Parenting Seminars
Jonathan Lindvall
P.O. Box 820
Springville, CA 93265
(209) 539-0500
Preparing for Romance and *A Talk to Godly Teens About Sex and Romance* (D)

Boston University
Office of Admissions
121 Bay State Road
Boston, MA 02215
(617) 353-2300

Braille Institute
Orange County Center
527 North Dale Ave.
Anaheim, CA 92801
(800) Bra-ille for referral information
(714) 821-5000

Broderbund
P.O. Box 6125
Novato, CA 94948-6125
(800) 521-6263
Geometry, Where in the World is Carmen Sandiego?, Where in the USA is Carmen Sandiego?, Where in Europe ...?, Where in Time...? computer games. Available from most computer software outlets or from the publisher.

Builder Books
P.O. Box 5291
Lynnwood, WA 98046-5291
(206) 778-4526
Send $1 for catalog with complete descriptions.

CBN Educational Products
CSB 336
Virginia Beach, VA 23465-9989
(800) 288-4769 for orders
(804) 523-7700 for information
Winning (Sing, Spell, Read, and Write's version for adult or remedial reading)

Calculus the Easy Way
See Barron's.
Sometimes available in secular and teacher supply stores. (C)

California State Department of Education Publications Sales
P.O. Box 271
Sacramento, CA 95802-0271
(916) 445-1260
Model Curriculum Standards for Grades Nine through Twelve, first edition; English Language Arts, Model Curriculum Standards Grades Nine through Twelve; Recommended Literature, Grades Nine through Twelve.

Calvert School
Dept. 2CCM, 105 Tuscany Road
Baltimore, MD 21210-9988
(410) 243-6030
(410) 366-0674 FAX

Cambridge University Press
40 West 20th St.
New York, NY 10011-4211
(212) 924-3900
Latin series. Order answer keys and other
supplementary materials from North American Cambridge Classics Projects Resource
Center.

Career Pathways
P.O. Box 1476
Gainesville, GA 30503
(404) 534-1000

Carolina Biological Supply Company
2700 York Rd.
Burlington, NC 27215
(800) 334-5551
or Box 187
Gladstone, OR 97027
(800) 547-1733
Source for science kits and supplies.
The almost two-inch-thick catalog is free
when requested by a teacher on school stationery. Otherwise the catalog price is
$17.95 (postpaid).

Castle Heights Press, Inc.
Kathleen Julicher
106 Caldwell Dr.
Baytown, TX 77520
(713) 424-4066
Experiences in Chemistry for Small Schools
(F), Experiences in Biology for Small
Schools (F), Geometric Constructions, The
Ultimate Science Project Notebook, and
First Steps in Electronics .(B)

**Center for Applications of Psychological
Type**
2815 N.W. 13th St., Suite 401
Gainesville, FL 32609
(800) 777-2278
People Types and Tiger Stripes and *Please*
Understand Me (also available from Blue-
stocking Press)

Center for Children and Parents
See Dr. Stanley Walters.

The Challenge of Raising Cain
Debe Haller
P.O. Box 4458
Huntington Beach, CA 92605
(714) 373-HOPE
The Home Educator's Lesson Plan Note-
book; also seminars and books on motiva-
tion under the title: *The Challenge of*
Raising Cain: Creative Ways to Get Chil-
dren to Cooperate. (E)

Children Sing the Word
Box 183
Chesterville, OH 43317
(419) 768-3152 (B)

Christian Book Distributors (CBD)
P.O. Box 6000
Peabody, MA 01961-6000
(508) 532-5300

**Christian History of the Constitution of the
United States of America, Volumes I and II**
See Foundation for American Christian Ed-
ucation.
Also available from American Christian
History Insitute.

**Christian Liberty Academy/Christian Lib-
erty Press**
502 W. Euclid Ave.
Arlington Heights, IL 60004
(708) 259-8736
(A,B,C,D,E)

Christian Life Workshops
Gregg Harris
P.O. Box 2250
Gresham, OR 97030
(503) 667-3942
The Christian Home School, The Christian
Family Complete Household Organizer
(B,D)

Christian Light
P. O. Box 1126
Harrisonburg, VA 22801-1126 (B)

Christian Schools International
3350 East Paris Avenue S.E.
Grand Rapids, MI 49512
(800) 635-8288
The Church in History (B), *The Story of*
God and His People series

Christian Teaching Materials
14275 Elm Ave.
P.O. Box 639
Glenpool, OK 74033-0639
(918) 322-3420

Christian Worldview Library
(UPS address) 700 E. 37th N.
Wichita, KS 67219
or (mail address) P.O. Box 546
Wichita, KS 67201
(316) 838-0851

Classic Curriculum
See Mott Media. (B,E)

CLEP
P.O. Box 6600
Princeton, NJ 08541-6600
(609) 951-1026
College credit by testing. Send for two free
booklets: *Moving Ahead with CLEP* and
CLEP Colleges (published by The College
Board).

Cliffs Notes, Inc.
P.O. Box 80728
Lincoln, NE 68501
(800) 228-4078 orders and inquiries
(402) 423-9254 FAX
Test preparation and literature guides,
StudyWare computer programs (C)

**College Admissions: A Guide for
Homeschoolers**
Poppyseed Press
P.O. Box 85
Sedalia, CO 80135
(F)

The College Board
45 Columbus Ave.
New York, NY 10023-6992
(212) 713-8165 customer service
Also distributed by the Macmillan Publishing Company.
The College Board publishes many books
including *The College Handbook 1993,*
Moving Ahead with CLEP, CLEP Colleges,
test preparation books for SAT, ACT,
PSAT/NMSQT, CLEP, plus some college
preparation software. Most books may be
ordered through local bookstores.

College Board ATP
P.O. Box 6200
Princeton, NJ 08541-6200
(609) 771-7600 east coast, recorded information available 24 hours
(510) 653-1564 west coast
SAT and Achievement Test information.

Collegiate Cap and Gown Company
1000 N. Market St.
Campaign, IL 61820
(217) 351-9500
Write or call for the name of the distributor
in your area.

Comparing World Views
Roy Hanson
910 Sunrise Ave., Ste. A1
Roseville, CA 95661
(916) 786-9322
Send $3 plus $1.50 postage and handling.

CompuServe
(800) 848-8199

Conceptual Physics, 5th or 6th edition
Published by Scott, Foresman and Com-
pany. See HarperCollins/Scott Foresman
and Co.
Or order from Teacher's Laboratory or
Growing Without Schooling

Concordia Publishing House
3558 South Jefferson Ave.
St. Louis, MO 63118
Learning About Sex series.
Available through Christian bookstores.
(B,C,Dx,F)

Contemporary Books, Inc.
180 North Michigan Ave.
Chicago, IL 60601
(800) 621-1918
(312) 782-3987 FAX
Real Numbers, Number Sense, Number
Power, plus GED preparation helps

Continental Press
Elizabethtown, PA 17022
On Target for Tests, New Language Patterns and Usage, Practice Exercises in Basic English. (A,C,E)

David C. Cook Publishers
Alphabetically listed under David

Cornerstone Curriculum Project
2006 Flat Creek
Richardson, TX 75080
(214) 235-5149
Music and Moments with the Masters, Adventures in Art, Science:The Search, Principles from Patterns: Algebra I

Correct Spelling Made Easy
Laurel/A Division of Dell Publishing Co.
See Dell Readers Service. (C)

Covenant Home Curriculum
Stonewood Village
17700 W. Capitol Dr.
Brookfield, WI 53054
(414) 781-2171
Correspondence courses and testing service

Covenant Publications
224 Auburn Ave.
Monroe, LA 71201
America, The First 350 Years (B) and *Teaching and Learning American History.* Send a SASE for free brochure. They also carry cassettes (music) and books relating to America's history.

Cracking the System
Villard Books, NY
Available from Growing Without Schooling.

Creation's Ambassadors Press
P.O. Box 122
Fair Haven, NY 13064
(800) 745-5978
Different by Design series and *Need Meeter Catalog.* Also, source for the *Discovery Scope™.*

Creation's Child
P.O. Box 3004 #44
Corvallis, Or 97339
(C,D,E,F)

Creative Publications
788 Palomar Ave.
Sunnyvale, CA 94086
(408) 720-1400
Cuisenaire® Rods, Base 10 blocks, and other learning materials

Creative Teaching Associates
P.O. Box 7766
Fresno, CA 93747
(800) 767-4282
(209) 291-6626
(209) 291-2953 FAX
Educational games, AIMS Education Foundation materials. Some items available from Alpha Omega, Builder Books, Great Christian Books, Lifetime Books, Shekinah Cur-

riculum Cellar, Sycamore Tree, and teacher supply stores.

Critical Thinking Press & Software (formerly Midwest Publications)
P.O. Box 448
Pacific Grove, CA 93950
(800) 458-4849
Critical Thinking Skills, Building Thinking Skills, and many other titles on thinking skills. (A,E)

Crossway Books
Division of Good News Publishers
1300 Crescent Street
Wheaton, IL 60187
(708) 682-4300
(708) 682-4785 FAX
Mary Pride's *Big Book of Home Learning series: Getting Started, Preschool and Elementary, Teen and Adult, Afterschooling* (F); and *Schoolproof* (F); *The How and Why of Home Schooling; Books Children Love; The Gift of Music; The Great Evangelical Disaster; How Should We Then Live?* (available from Horne Booke); *Pride's Guide to Educational Software* (F); *Prospects for Growth; Prosperity and Poverty; Recovering the Lost Tools of Learning; Loving God With All Your Mind; Turning Point; Freedom, Justice, and Hope.* Available through Christian bookstores and home school suppliers. (A,B,C,D,E all carry some titles)

Cuisenaire® Rods
Cuisenaire® Company of America
P.O. Box 5026
10 Bank St.
White Plains, NY 10602-5026
(800) 237-3142 for orders
(914) 997-2600 for information
(800) 550-RODS FAX
Available from Activity Resources, Creative Publications, Shekinah Curriculum Celllar, Sycamore Tree, and Timberdoodle.

Curriculum Associates
Studying Poetry. Order through Hewitt Educational Resources/Hewitt Research Foundation.

D.C. Heath and Company
Listed under Heath

DLM Teaching Resources
P.O. Box 4000
One DLM Park
Allen, TX 75002
(800) 527-4747 from all states except Texas
(800) 442-4711 in Texas

Dale Seymour Publications
P.O. Box 10888
Palo Alto, CA 94303
(800) 872-1100
(800) 222-0766 in California
Mathematics for Trade and Industrial Occupations, How to Lie with Statistics, The Everyday Science Sourcebook plus many excellent resources for math and science. (Fx)

Dandy Lion Publications
3563 Sueldo #L
San Luis Obispo, CA 93401
Inside Stories, which is included in the "Homeschool Bookshelf" from Home School Supply House

David C. Cook Publishers/Chariot Family Publishing
20 Lincoln Ave.
Elgin, IL 60120
(800) 437-4337
(B,C,E carry many Cook titles)
How to Be Your Own Selfish Pig

Davidsons Music
6727 Metcalf
Shawnee Mission, KS 66204
(800) 488-1003 for orders
(913) 262-4982 for questions
Madonna Woods piano/organ courses

Davis Publications, Inc.
50 Portland St.
Worcester, MA 01608
(800) 533-2847
(508) 753-3834 FAX
Discover Art series (A,E), *Art in Your World, Discovering Art History,* and specialized art texts for high school level.

Dell Publishing
666 5th Avenue
New York, NY 10103
(800) 223-5780
Child development books by Ilg and Ames (C)

Dell Readers Service
Laurel/A Division of Dell Publishing Co.
2451 S. Wolf Rd.
Des Plaines, IL 60018
Correct Spelling Made Easy. Also check secular book stores.

Developing Your Child for Success
See Learning Potentials Publishers, Inc.

Discover Intensive Phonics
Communication through Language Development
325 E. Delaware Rd.
Burbank, CA 91504
(818) 845-9602
Send SASE for more information.

Discovery Educational Systems
P.O. Box 210633
Bedford, TX 76095
(800) 926-9462
Discovery Scope™

Eastgate Publishers
4137 Primavera Rd.
Santa Barbara, CA 93110
Pyschoheresy, Prophets of Psychoheresy (B)

Easy Grammar
See ISHA Enterprises. (A,B,C,D,E,F)

EDAN
P.O. Box 5823
Lynnwood, WA 98046

EdiTS
P.O. Box 7234
San Diego, CA 92167
(619) 222-1666
Career testing

Edmark Corporation
P.O. Box 3218
Redmond, WA 98073-3218
(800) 426-0856
Software and print resources for special education.

Edmund Scientific
101 E. Gloucester Pike
Barrington, NJ 08007-1380
(609) 573-6259 for product information
(609) 573-6250 or 547-3488 for ordering

ed-tex
Arlene Mickley
15235 Brand Blvd., Suite A107
Mission Hills, CA 91345
(818) 363-3379
Represents publishers of career and special education materials

Education Associates
P.O. Box Y
Frankfort, KY 40602
(800) 626-2950
Job seeking skills—books and audio-visual materials, plus *Project Discovery*

Educational Design Inc.
47 West 13th St.
New York, NY 10011
Practicing the Writing Process; Improving Your Spelling Skills (E); *Basic Algebra* (E). (A)

Educational Development Corporation
P.O. Box 470663
Tulsa, OK 74147-0663
(800) 475-4522
(918) 622-4522
(918) 663-4509 FAX
U.S. distributors for the Usborne books, including *Introduction to Business*. Some Usborne titles are carried by teacher supply stores. (A,B,C,D,E,F)

Educational Support Foundation
1523 Moritz
Houston, TX 77055
(713) 870-9194
custom stationery, diplomas, record forms

Educators Publishing Service
75 Moulton St.
Cambridge, MA 02138-1104
(800) 225-5750
(617) 547-6706 in MA
Learning Grammar through Writing (E), *The Childs Spelling System: The Rules* (E), *Basic Language Principles with Latin Background, Wordly Wise* (E), *Reasoning and*

Reading, Vocabulary from Classical Roots, Winston Grammar (E). (A,B,C,D)

William B. Eerdmans Publishing Company
Alphabetically listed under William

Elementary Algebra
W.H. Freeman (See Freeman)
Available from Growing Without Schooling

The Elijah Company
P.O. Box 12483
Knoxville, TN 37912-0483
(615) 691-1310
Keyboard Capers (C,F), *How to Tutor* (A,F), *Alpha Phonics* (A,F), plus distributor for many more.

English from the Roots Up: Help for Reading, Writing, Spelling and S.A.T. Scores
Joegil Lundquist
Literacy Unlimited
P.O. Box 278
Medina, WA 98039-0278
(C,D)

Essential Learning Products
P.O. Box 2607
Columbus, OH 43216-2607
Supplemental workbooks for math, grammar, study and thinking skills. (A)

Every Thought Captive
P & R Publishing Co.
P.O. Box 817
Phillipsburg, NJ 08865
(B)

Exploratorium Mail Order Department
3601 Lyon Street
San Francisco, CA 94123
(800) 359-9899
Electromagnetic Spectrum Chart and *Exploratorium Science Snackbook* (C)

FACTS (Financial Aid and College Tuition Scholarship Service)
4150 Ambrose N.E.
Grand Rapids, MI 49505
(616) 364-4438

Facts on File, Inc.
460 Park Avenue South
New York, NY 10016
(800) 322-8755
(212) 683-2244 in NY, AK, or HI call collect
But, What If I Don't Want to Go to College? ISBN # 0-8160-2534-7; *The Complete Guide to Nontraditional Education*; *Encyclopedia of Good Health: Nutrition* ISBN # 0-8160-1670-4; *Free Money for College* ISBN # 0-8160-2342-5; *Investigating Art* (available from KidsArt) ISBN # 0-87196-973-4 (Cx,Dx)

Family Academy
146 S.W. 153rd, Box 290
Seattle, WA 98166
(206) 246-9227

The Family Educator
P.O Box 309
730 Forest Avenue
Templeton, CA 93465-0309
(805) 434-0249

The Family Learning Center
Rt. 2, Box 264
Hawthorne, FL 32640
(904) 475-5869
Learning Language Arts through Literature (A,B,C,D,E)

Family Walk
Walk Thru the Bible Ministries, Inc.
P.O. Box 80587
Atlanta, GA 30366
(800) 868-9300
(404) 458-9300

Fas-Track Computer Programs
7030C Huntley Rd.
Columbus, OH 43229
(800) 927-3936

Fearon/Janus/Quercus Education
500 Harbor Blvd.
Belmont, CA 94002
(800) 877-4283
Special education materials (Cx,F)

Fearon Teacher Aids
P.O. Box 280
Carthage, IL 62321
(800) 242-7272
Getting Smarter, You Are the Editor, Digging into Literature (A,C,E,F)

Films for Christ
2628-A West Birchwood Circle
Mesa, AZ 85202
(800) 332-2261 orders only
(602) 894-1300 information
The Genesis Solution video, *The Case for Creation* video, *Origins* video series, and *The Illustrated Origins Answer Book*. Videos are available for rental or purchase. Purchases can be made under one of two options: home-use only viewing versions are much less expensive and are restricted to normal use within the home; church-use licensing is more expensive but covers use with classes of all types at a single church or school. Home-use videos can be licensed for church use by paying the difference in cost at a later date.

Focus on the Family
Colorado Springs, CO 80995
(800) 232-6459 for credit card orders only
(719) 531-5181 for other orders and inquiries
Surviving the Money Jungle, Get a Grip on Your Money, Fatal Addiction (Dx,F)

Charlene Forsythe, RN, MA
735 N. Irwin
Hanford, CA 93230
(209) 582-3936 or
(209) 584-6668
Perceptual-motor consultant/learning disabilities

Foundation For American Christian Education (F.A.C.E.)
P. O. Box 9444
Chesapeake, VA 23321
(804) 488-6601
Information and materials on the Principle Approach. Other sources, such as Lifetime Books and Horne Booke, carry some of the materials published by F.A.C.E.

W.H. Freeman
41 Madison Avenue
New York, NY 10010
(212) 576-9400
Mathematics: A Human Endeavor, Elementary Algebra (both available from Growing Without Schooling), *Geometry, For All Practical Purposes*

Frey Scientific
P.O. Box 8101
Mansfield, OH 44901-8101
(800) 225-FREY
(419) 589-1522 FAX

From Sea to Shining Sea
See Baker Book House.
Or order directly from Peter Marshall (under Marshall). (B,C,D,E)

GCT, Inc.
314-350 Weinacker Ave.
P.O. Box 6448
Mobile, AL 36660-0448
(800) 476-8711
The Gifted Child Today Catalog

Gallaudet Bookstore Catalog
800 Florida Avenue N.E.
Washington, DC 20002
(202) 651-5380

Thomas Geale Publications, Inc.
Alphabetically listed under Thomas

GED Testing Service
American Council on Education
One Dupont Circle, Suite 20-B
Washington, D.C. 20036-1163
(202) 939-9490

General Science Service Co.
221 N.W. 2nd St.
Elbow Lake, MN 56531
(218) 685-4846
Blister Microscope and supplies

Gesell Institute
Child development books by Ilg, Ames, and others: *The Child from Five to Ten*, See Harper and Row; *Your Ten to Fourteen Year Old*, See Dell; *Your One Year Old,...Two Year Old,...etc.* through *Your Seven Year Old*, See Dell.

Globe Book Company
P.O. Box 2649
Columbus, OH 43216
(800) 848-9500
Newspaper Workshop, The Writer's Program, Writing Sense, Chemistry Workshop,

Physics Workshop, Writing for Life, and source for Arco publications (C)

God's World Publications
P. O. Box 2330
Asheville, NC 28802-2330
(800) 951-5437
(704) 253-1556 FAX
Weekly newspapers plus a news magazine

Good Year Books
1900 East Lake Avenue
Glenview, IL 60025
The Complete Science Fair Handbook

Grammar Songs - Learning with Music
See Audio Memory Publishing.

Great Christian Books
P.O. Box 8000
229 S. Bridge St.
Eltkon, MD 21922-8000
(410) 392-0800 for orders
(410) 392-9890 for inquiries
(410) 392-3103 FAX

Greek Programmed Primer
Published by Presbyterian and Reformed Publishing.
Order from Trivium Pursuit or Great Christian Books.

Growing Without Schooling (Holt Associates)
2269 Massachusetts Ave.
Cambridge, MA 02140
(617) 864-3100
Newsletter and bookstore (mail order). They will take phone orders using MasterCard or Visa. (Non-sectarian.)

A Guide to American Christian Education for the Home and School, The Principle Approach
See American Christian History Institute.

Hammond, Inc.
515 Valley St.
Maplewood, NJ 07040
Map skills workbooks, Bible atlas, "history through maps" series plus teachers guides (Cx,Fx)

Harcourt Brace Jovanovich, Inc.
Order from Holt, Rinehart and Winston
Harcourt Brace Jovanovich, Inc. acquired Holt, Rinehart and Winston in 1986. Holt, Rinehart and Winston will specialize in the materials for secondary schools, while HBJ will specialize in elementary level resources. The imprint on upper level HBJ books will change with future printings. Titles published originally by HBJ: *Essentials in Mathematics, Warriner's English Grammar and Composition, Warriner's High School Handbook, Speech for Effective Communication*, foreign language texts, vocabulary workbooks for high school, *Harbrace College Handbook*. (Cx)

Harper and Row Publishers, Inc.
10 E. 53rd St.
New York, NY 10022
The Child from Five to Ten, available through secular bookstores (C)

HarperCollins/Scott Foresman
HarperCollins, Elementary/High School Division
1900 East Lake Ave.
Glenview, IL 60025
(800) 554-4411
The Biology Coloring Book (F), Conceptual Physics, Intermediate Algebra for College Students
To order the algebra text and answer key at school prices, or answer key to *Conceptual Physics*, we must supply evidence that we are either a school or part of a school, or else have a credentialed teacher or school order for us. (Cx)

HarperCollins Publishers
Order Department
1000 Keystone Industrial Park
Scranton, PA 18512-4621
(800) 242-7737
(800) 822-4090 FAX
Modern Times. Available through secular bookstores. (Cx)

Harvest House Publishers
1075 Arrowsmith
Eugene, OR 97402
Christian Charm (A,F), Man in Demand (A,F), Gods of the New Age, The Islamic Invasion, America: The Sorcerer's New Apprentice, and Jim Burns' Bible study series—available from some Christian bookstores. A free catalog from the publisher describes all of Jim Burns' books in depth. (B,C,Dx,E)

D.C. Heath and Company
125 Spring Street
Lexington, MA 02173
(800) 235-3565
for Canada:
100 Adelaide Street West, Suite 1600
Toronto, Ontario, M5H1S9
(416) 362-6483
Contemporary Business Mathematics, Developmental Mathematics (college level text by Novak, 1989 edition) (Cx)

Ethel Herr
731 Lakefair Drive
Sunnyvale, CA 94089
(408) 734-4707
An Introduction to Christian Writing

Hewitt Educational Resources/Hewitt Research Foundation
P.O. Box 9
Washougal, WA 98671
(800) 348-1750
(206) 835-8708
(206) 835-8697 FAX
School service, and source for learning materials: *Winston Grammar, Studying Poetry*, Saxon math, and other books

History of Art
See Prentice-Hall, Order Dept.
Cost is over $50. Check used bookstores for older editions or choose *History of Art for Young People* by the same author (Abrams). (C)

Holt, Rinehart and Winston/Harcourt Brace Jovanovich
National Customer Service Center
6277 Sea Harbor Dr.
Orlando, FL 32821-9989
(800) 225-5425 orders
(800) 544-6678 customer relations
(407) 826-5070 in Florida
Harcourt Brace Jovanovich, Inc. acquired Holt, Rinehart and Winston in 1986. Holt, Rinehart and Winston will specialize in the materials for secondary schools, while HBJ will specialize in elementary level resources. The imprint on upper level HBJ books will change with future printings. Holt titles include *Elements of Writing*. HBJ titles are listed above under Harcourt Brace Jovanovich. (C)

Home Education Center
487 Myatt Drive
Madison, TN 37115
(800) 788-0840 orders only
(615) 860-4060 store number or information
Mail order and walk-in stores, middleman for used curriculum, and testing service.

Home Education Magazine
P.O. Box 1083
Tonasket, WA 98855

The Home School Books and Supplies
3131 Smokey Point Drive
Arlington, WA 98223
(206) 659-6188
(206) 658-1558 FAX
Store, phone, FAX, and mail order.

Home School Legal Defense Association (HSLDA)
Box 159
Paeonian Springs, VA 22129
or 17333 Pickwick Dr.
Purcellville, VA 22132
(703) 338-5600
Constitutional Law (B), *Where Do I Draw the Line?* (B), information on home education, diplomas, and legal protection

Home School Supply House
P.O. Box 170
Harbor Springs, MI 49740
(800) 772-3129
(616) 526-8000

Home School: Taking the First Step
Mountain Meadow Press
P.O. Box 1170
Wrangell, AK 99929
(907) 874-2565
Send your name and address plus a $.29 stamp for catalog. (A,B,C,D,F)

Homespun Tapes, Ltd.
Box 694, Dept. CHE
Woodstock, NY 12498
(800) 338-2737
(914) 679-7832
(914) 246-5282 FAX

The Horne Booke
953 Gardner Avenue
Ventura, CA 93004
(805) 647-3907
Source for Mott Media's *Classic Curriculum, Stansbury's Elementary Catechism on the Constitution*, Principle Approach materials, books and tapes on America's Christian History, and children's classics

Houghton Mifflin Publishers
One Beacon Street
Boston, MA 02108
Send for catalog which lists phone numbers for regional offices (no central ordering number). Specify which book you are interested in, so that they send you the proper catalog.
Secular publisher. *Kitchen Science, Cultural Literacy* (E), foreign language and math texts. Distributor of Riverside materials (E). (C,D)

Houghton Mifflin Trade Ordering Dept.
Wayside Rd.
Burlington, MA 01803
(800) 225-3362
Peterson's Field Guides (Cx,Dx)

Houston Baptist University
R. Philip Kimrey, Director, Office of Admissions
7502 Fondren Road
Houston, TX 77074-3298
(800) 969-3210
(713) 995-3210

How to Identify Your Child's Learning Problems and What to Do About Them
Pioneer Productions
P.O. Box 3997
Prescott, AZ 86302
(602) 772-7195
(A,F)

How to Lie with Statistics
See W.W. Norton and Company (under Norton).

Linda Howe
4187 Bernardo Court
Chino, CA 91710
(714) 628-9441
Learning disabilities/perceptual-motor consultant

The Impossible Child (A Guide for Caring Teachers and Parents/In School At Home)
The Practical Allergy Research Foundation
P.O. Box 60
Buffalo, NY 14223-0060
(F and Bluestocking Press)

Institute for Creation Research
10946 Woodside Avenue North
Santee, CA 92071
(619) 448-0900
Museum and materials to help us learn about and teach science from a creationist viewpoint

Institute in Basic Life Principles
Box 1
Oakbrook, IL 60522-3001
(708) 323-7073
Seminars, curriculum for home schooling under the Advanced Training Institute of America, other reading materials

International Bible Society
P.O. Box 35700
Colorado Springs, CO 80935-3570
(800) 524-1588
(719) 488-9200 Colorado residents

International Linguistics Corporation
3505 East Red Bridge
Kansas City, MO 64137
(816) 765-8855
The Learnables

International Society for General Semantics
P.O. Box 728
Concord, CA 94522
(510) 798-0311
How to Write Clearly, also available through Bluestocking Press

Inter-Varsity Christian Fellowship of the U.S.A.
P.O. Box 7895
Madison, WI 53707-7895
(800) 828-2100
The Search (video), also available from Films for Christ.

InterVarsity Press.
P.O. Box 1400
Downers Grove, IL 60515
(708) 964-5700
(708) 964-1251 FAX
Know Why You Believe. Available from Christian bookstores. (B)

Intrepid Books
P.O. Box 1295
Colfax, CA 95713
(916) 346-2781
America's Christian History: Christian Self-Government series of studies based upon the Principle Approach. (A,Cx,D and Horne Booke)

An Introduction to an Academic Vocabulary: Word Clusters from Latin, Greek, and German
Imprimis Books
P.O. Box 2931 Reston, VA 22090
(703) 759-7214

An Introduction to Christian Writing
Published by Tyndale House Publishers. Order from Ethel Herr (under Herr).

ISHA Enterprises, Inc.
5503 E. Beck Lane
Scottsdale, AZ 85254
Easy Grammar, Daily Grams, and *Easy Writing.* Send SASE for free brochure. (A,B,C,D,E,F)

JL Enterprise
c/o Cary Gibson
440 Old Airport Rd.
Auburn, CA 95603
Complete Homeschool Planner (B)

Jeremiah Films
P.O. Box 1710
Hemet, CA 92546
(800) 828-2290 from outside CA
(800) 633-0869 from CA
Gods of the New Age, The Evolution Conspiracy, The Pagan Invasion and other videos. (B)

Jeremy P. Tarcher, Inc.
5858 Wilshire Blvd., #200
Los Angeles, CA 90036
(213) 935-9980
Drawing on the Right Side of the Brain, Drawing with Children, In Their Own Way (available from Bluestocking Press). Available from secular bookstores. (D,E)

JIST Works, Inc.
720 North Park Ave.
Indianapolis, IN 46202-3431

Josh Jr. Christian Book Club
P.O. Box 2903
Fort Worth, TX 76113
(800) 888-9641

Key Curriculumm Press
P.O. Box 2304
Berkeley, CA 94702
(800) 338-7638
Key To... math series (C and Activity Resources), *Discovering Geometry.* (A,F)
All prepaid orders to the publisher are exempt from shipping charges.

Keyboard Enterprises
5200 Heil, #32
Huntington Beach, CA 92649
(714) 840-8004
The Basics of Algebra on Video Tape

Kids for the World: A Guidebook to Children's Mission Resources
See United States Center for World Mission.

Kid's Stuff
Joshua Harris
P.O. Box 2250
Gresham, OR 97030
Just Enough Stationery

KidsArt
P.O. Box 274
Mt. Shasta, CA 96067
(916) 926-5076
Art activities in newsletter format, plus free catalogs of gift and art items.

Alfred A. Knopf
Alphabetically listed under Alfred. Knopf books are ordered through Random House.

Know Why You Believe
See Inter Varsity Press.
Available from Christian bookstores. (B)

Konos Character Curriculum
P.O. Box 1534
Richardson, TX 75083
(214) 669-8337
(214) 699-7922 FAX
Unit study volumes plus *Creativity Unit.* (F)

L'Abri Fellowship Foundation
1465 N.E. 12th Ave.
Rochester, MN 55906
(507) 282-3292

Landmark Edition, Inc.
P.O. Box 4469
Kansas City, MO 64127
(816) 241-4919
Written and Illustrated by... (D)

Laugh and Learn
R.D. 1, Box 2232
Lafayette, NJ 07848
(201) 579-5421
Laugh with Math

Learning Patterns and Temperament Styles
Manas Systems
P. O. Box 5153
Fullerton, CA 92635
(714) 870-4355
(A,D,E, and Bluestocking Press)

Learning Potentials Publishers, Inc.
230 West Main St.
Lewisville, TX 75057
(214) 221-2564
Developing Your Child for Success (A)

Learning Services
P.O. Box 10636
1203 Willamette St.
Eugene, OR 97440-2636
(800) 877-WEST
(800) 877-EAST
(503) 484-7499 FAX
Educational software and multi-media products

Legacy Communications
P.O. Box 680365
Franklin, TN 37068 (B)

LEGO Dacta, mail order product information:
Attention: Sarah McDonald
555 Taylor Road
Enfield, CT 06083
(800) 527-8339
Ask for free brochure on the educational Technic sets. You may also request a list of LEGO dealers in your area. Educational Technic sets are available from Nasco and Teacher's Laboratory.

Liberty University
School of Lifelong Learning
3765 Candlers Mountain
Lynchburg, VA 24506
(800) 466-5000
(804) 522-4700

Library and Educational Services
8784 Valley View Dr.
P.O. Box 146
Berrien Springs, MI 49103
(616) 471-1400

Lifetime Books and Gifts
3900 Chalet Suzanne Dr.
Lake Wales, FL 33853
(813) 676-6311

The Light and the Glory
See Baker Book House.
Order directly from Peter Marshall (address under Marshall) or purchase at Christian bookstores. Study guides are available from Shekinah Curriculum Cellar. (B,C,D,E)

Lion Publishing
Order from David C. Cook/Chariot Family Publishing.
Bible Mapbook (D,F), *A Book of Beliefs* (B,C,E)

Little Brown and Company
200 West St.
Waltham, MA 02154
(800) 343-9204
(800) 759-0190
Source for Warner Books titles—*The Synonym Finder* (E) and *Smart But Feeling Dumb*

Vic Lockman
Box 1916
Ramona, CA 92065
Biblical Economics in Comics; Big Book of Cartooning; Reading and Understanding the Bible; Water...Water... Everywhere!; Money, Banking, and Usury (A,B,C,D)

Logos
Christian Mission Center
University of Mary Hardin-Baylor
Belton, TX 76513
(800) 44L-OGOS
Spanish language course. Send for free brochure. A self-addressed, stamped envelope is appreciated.

Longman Publishing
10 Bank St.
White Plains, NY 10606
(914) 993-5000 for information
Ecce Romani, Preparatory Latin, The Phenomenon of Language, Composition Handbook. (F) Longman Publishing will provide information about any of their books, however, orders must be placed with Addison-Wesley.

Love, Dating and Sex: What Teens Want to Know
Mailbox Club Books
404 Eager Road
Valdosta, GA 31602
Also available on audio cassettes. Books also available from Audio-Memory.

M/L International Marketing
P.O. Box 152537
Tampa, FL 33684-2537
(813) 933-7065
Basic Library of the World's Greatest Music (D)

Macmillan/McGraw-Hill—Glencoe Division
P.O. Box 543
Blacklick, OH 43004-0543
(800) 334-7344
Trade and Technical Education Catalog and books.(F)

Macmillan/McGraw-Hill—School Division
220 East Danieldale Rd.
DeSoto, TX 75115
(800) 442-9685
Basic Goals in Spelling (also sold by many teacher supply stores), Macmillan *English* program. Teacher's editions must be ordered on school letterhead or the order must be accompanied by an affidavit or other proof that the order is from a school. This address is for Macmillan and McGraw-Hill school books for grades K-8. (Cx,F)

Mantle Ministries
Richard "Little Bear" Wheeler
140 Grand Oak Dr.
San Antonio, TX 78232
(512) 490-BEAR (D and Horne Booke)

Mapping the World by Heart
Tom Snyder Productions
80 Coolidge Hill Rd.
Watertown, MA 02172
(800) 342-0236
(617) 876-0033 FAX

Peter Marshall
36 Nickerson Rd.
Orleans, MA 02653
(508) 255-7705
The Light and the Glory, From Sea to Shining Sea

Master Book Publishers
Box 1606
El Cajon, CA 92022
(800) 999-3777
Creation-science books for adults and children, including *Origins: Creation or Evolution*. (A,B,C,D,E)

Math Teachers Press
5100 Gamble Dr., Ste. 398
Minneapolis, MN 55416
(800) 852-2435
(612) 545-6535
Moving with Math program. Tell them you are a home educator when you write or call so that you are given the correct ordering information and prices.

Mathematics, A Human Endeavor
W.H. Freeman (See Freeman.)
Available from Growing Without Schooling

Maupin House Publishing
P.O. Box 90148
Gainesville, FL 32607
(904) 336-9290
Caught'ya

Mayflower Institute
P.O. Box 4673
Thousand Oaks, CA 91359
(805) 499-2044
Marshall Foster presents seminars on topics related to America's Christian history. Audio and video cassettes are also available of some of these. The Institute publishes *The American Covenant: The Untold Story* and sells this and other titles. (A,Cx)

McDougal, Littell, and Co.
P.O. Box 8000
St. Charles, IL 60174
(800) 225-3809
Writing: Process to Product and *English* series. When ordering directly from the publisher, teacher's editions must be ordered on school letterhead or the order must be accompanied by an affidavit or other proof that the order is from a school. This is not necessary when ordering from home school suppliers. (C-some items)

McGuffey Academy and McGuffey Testing Service
2213 Spur
Grapevine, TX 76051
(817) 481-7008
Correspondence course and testing service

Meet the Classics
See Toys To Grow On.

MEMLOK Bible Memory System
Drake Mariani
420 E. Montwood Avenue
La Habra, CA 90631
(800) 373-1947 from outside CA
(714) 738-0949 from CA
Send SASE for free brochure. (A,B,D,F)

Merrill Publishing Company
Order Merrill titles from Macmillan/McGraw-Hill—Glencoe Division.
Algebra Essentials, Informal Geometry, Advanced Mathematical Concepts, Pre-Calculus Mathematics, Applications of Mathematics (Use ISBN numbers listed within each review.) (C-some items)

Dr. Stephen Meyer/A Child's Life
732 N. Diamond Bar Blvd., Suite 126
Diamond Bar, CA 91765
(714) 861-7150

Micro Star
1945 Camino Vida Roble, Ste. A
Carlsbad, CA 92008
(800) 444-1343
Public domain software for IBM compatible machines

Modern Curriculum Press
13900 Prospect Rd.
Cleveland, OH 44316
(800) 321-3106
Spelling Workout (A,E), *The Writing Program*. (C,F)

Modern Signs Press, Inc.
P.O. Box 1181
Los Alamitos, CA 90720
(310) 596-8548 regular phone or TDD for hearing impaired (same number)
(310) 795-6614 FAX

Modern Talking Picture Service
5000 Park Street North
St. Petersburg, FL 33709
(800) 243-MTPS
(813) 546-0681 FAX
Request free catalog for either elementary or secondary level.

Moody Press
c/o Moody Bible Institute
820 North LaSalle Drive
Chicago, IL 60610
(312) 329-2101
(312) 329-2144 FAX
Seven Men Who Rule the World from the Grave, The Coming Economic Earthquake, Surviving the 90's Economy. (B,C,D)

The Moore Foundation
Dr. Raymond and Dorothy Moore
Box 1
Camas, WA 98607
They have all of Dr. Raymond and Dorothy Moore's books (F), the *Moore-McGuffey Readers* (A,F), other teaching resources, and *The Moore Report International*. They also have Moore Foundation Curriculum Programs for all grade levels.

Mortensen Math
V.J. Mortensen Company
P.O. Box 98
Hayden Lake, ID 83835
(208) 667-1580
Write or call for location of local distributors.

Mott Media
1000 East Huron
Milford, MI 48381
(800) 421-6645
Sower series biographies (A,F), *Original Mott McGuffey Readers* (F), *Harvey's Grammar* (B,C,D,E and Horne Booke)

Moving with Math
See Math Teachers Press.

Mulberry Books
4807 W. 62nd Terrace
Mission, KS 66205
The Great Adventure: A Life-Time Reading Plan for the Great Works of the Western World—send a SASE for information.

Multnomah Press
10209 S.E. Division Street
Portland, OR 97266
(800) 929-0910
Operation World (A,B)

Nadeau Reading Clinics (Dr. Ray Nadeau)
17215 Studebaker Rd., #215
Cerritos, CA 90701-2538
(800) 462-READ

Nasco
901 Janesville Ave.
Fort Atkinson, WI 53538
Send for free catalogs for math, science,
arts/crafts, and home economics. They offer
the greatest selection of supplemental materials at good prices.

Dr. Ronald Nash
Reformed Theological Seminary
P.O. Box 945120
Maitland, FL 32794
*The Christian Parent and Student Guide to
Choosing a College*

National Center for Constitutional Studies
P.O. Box 841
West Jordan, UT 84084
(800) 388-4512
*The Making of America: The Substance and
Meaning of the Constitution, The Real
Thomas Jefferson, The Real Benjamin
Franklin, The Real George Washington,*
and *Soldiers, Statesmen, and Heroes.* (C)

National Gallery of Art
Washington, DC 20565
Extension service programs offer a free library of audio-visual art materials. Send for
free *Extension Programs Catalog.* They
also sell art prints at very low prices. A separate catalog of art prints is also free.

National Geographic Society
Washington, DC 20036
Special books for science, *World Magazine,*
and *Global Pursuit* game

National Homeschool Association
P.O. Box 290
Hartland, MI 48353-0290
(313) 632-5208

**National Homeschool Computer Bulletin
Board (NHBB)**
5285 Straub Road
College Station, TX 77845
(409) 690-0848 voice line
(409) 690-HOME BBS line

National Home Study Council
1601 18th St. N.W.
Washington, DC 20009

**National Public-policy Resource Theme-
packets**
1733 Lancaster Rd.
Manheim, PA 17545
(717) 295-2647

National Textbook Company
A Division of NTC Publishing Group
4255 W. Touhy Ave.
Lincolnwood, IL 60646-1975
(800) 323-4900
(708) 679-2494 FAX
foreign language catalog (F), materials for
debate, speech, drama, and journalism (C-
some items)

National Writing Institute
7946 Wright Road
Niles, MI 49120
(616) 684-5375
Writing Strands and *Reading Strands.* (A,B)

Nature's Workshop
22777 State Rd. 119
Goshen, IN 46526
(219) 534-2245

NavPress
P.O. Box 35002
Colorado Springs, CO 80935
(800) 366-7788
(719) 260-7223 FAX
Well-Versed Kids (B,D,E). Available from
Christian bookstores.

Thomas Nelson Publishers
Alphabetically listed under Thomas.

NeuroEducational Associates, Inc.
511 Tilton Rd., Suite 406
Mainland Professional Plaza
Northfield, NJ 08225
(800) 688-4138
(609) 646-2221
Visual Vocabulary

New Society Publishers
4527 Springfield Ave.
Philadelphia, PA 19143
Dumbing Us Down (D). Also available
from Growing Without Schooling/Holt Associates.

None of the Above
Available from Growing Without Schooling

**North American Cambridge Classics Pro-
jects (NACCP) Resource Center**
P.O. Box 932
Amherst, MA 01004-0932
(413) 256-3564
Answer keys and supplements to *Cambridge Latin* course.

North Dakota Division of Independent Study
State University Station
1510 12th Ave. N.
Box 5036
Fargo, ND 58105
(701) 239-7282
(701) 239-7288 FAX

W.W. Norton and Company
500 Fifth Avenue
New York, NY 10110
How to Lie with Statistics, Norton Literary
Anthologies

Nystrom Atlases
3333 Elston Ave.
Chicago, IL 60618
(800) 621-8086
(312) 463-1144
Maps, globes, atlases, science charts, models, and educational programs

**Ohio University Course Credit by Examina-
tion**
Tupper Hall, Ohio University
Athens, OH 45701

O. T. Studios
John Schweikert
8803 Santa Fe Springs Rd.
Whittier, CA 90606
(310) 693-8173
Offers tapes of home schooling events.
Write for list.

Paradigm
P.O. Box 45161
Boise, ID 83711
(208) 343-3790
Samuel Blumenfeld's books: *NEA: Trojan
Horse in American Education, Is Public Ed-
ucation Necessary?,* and *The New
Illiterates,* plus *The Blumenfeld Oral Read-
ing Assessment Test.* (B,C,D)

Parakletos
202 S. Alamo, Suite A
Marshall, TX 75670
(800) 473-9082
Greek Tools and *Hebrew Tools*

Pelican Publishing Company
P.O. Box 189
Gretna, LA 70054
(800) 843-1724
How To Plan Your Life, Men and Marriage
(B)

Perfection Learning
1000 North Second Ave.
Logan, IA 51546-1099
(800) 831-4190
*Vocabulary Wordshop, Vocabu-Lit,
Wordpak*

Peter Bedrick Books
2112 Broadway, #318
New York, NY 10023
(212) 496-0751
Roman Mythology, ISBN 0911745-56-4

Peterson's
P.O. Box 2123
Princeton, NJ 08543
(800) 338-3282
(609) 243-9150 FAX
*Peterson's Handbook for College Admis-
sions* and other college oriented books

Phoenix Learning Resources
468 Park Avenue South
New York, NY 10016
(800) 221-1274
(212) 684-5910 in New York
Special education materials (F)

A Positive Approach magazine
P.O. Box 910
Millville, NJ 08332
(609) 451-4777
(609) 451-6678 FAX

Praise Hymn, Inc.
P.O. Box 1080
Taylors, SC 29687
God Made Music series

Precept Ministries
P.O. Box 182218
Chattanooga, TN 37422
(615) 892-6814
Line Upon Line, Precept Upon Precept

Prentice-Hall School Division
P.O. Box 2649
Columbus, OH 43216
(800) 848-9500
Jenney Latin Program (C)

Prentice-Hall, Order Department
200 Old Tappan Rd.
Old Tappan, NJ 07675
(800) 223-1360
History of Art (C)

Preparing for Adolescence
See Regal Books.
Available at Christian bookstores. Cassette tape versions are available, published by Gospel Light, a division of Regal. Accompanying *Growth Guide Workbook* and *Growthpack* (book, workbook, and 8 tapes) are also available. (B,C,E,F-book and workbook only)

Preparing Your Children for Courtship and Marriage, From Toddlers to Teens
Hope Chapel Christian Fellowship
P.O. Box 1401
Fair Oaks, CA 95628
(916) 967-4673
Tape set is very reasonably priced at only $26 plus there is a money back guarantee on all but $3 for shipping charges.

A Prescriptive Spelling Program
See Barnell Loft Publications. (C,E).

Pro Series Bible Curriculum
Positive Action for Christ
P.O. Box 1948
Rocky Mount, NC 27802-1948
(800) 688-3008

Professor Phonics Gives Sound Advice and Sound Track To Reading
See S.U.A.

Professor Weissman's Software
Professor Martin Weissman
246 Crafton Ave.
Staten Island, NY 10314
(718) 698-5219, 8 A.M.-10 P.M. eastern time, Sun.-Thurs.
Algebra software. Send any sort of documentation showing that you are a home educator and receive a discount price of $20 per disk (regular price $30 per disk.) A full

working copy of *Algebra 1*, version 1.4 (titled *Algebrax*) is available for $5 from Professor Weissman.

Psychological Seduction: The Failure of Modern Psychology
See Thomas Nelson Publishers (under Thomas).
Available at Christian bookstores.

Public Brand Software
P.O. Box 51315
Indianapolis, IN 46251
(800) 426-DISK from all states except Indiana
(317) 856-7571
Shareware and public domain software for IBM and compatible machines.

Rainbow Re-Source Center
P.O. Box 491
Kewanee, IL 61443
Send $2.50 for current newsletter (which includes inventory list) or $12 a year (6 issues).

Random House
400 Hahn Rd.
Westminster, MD 21157
(800) 733-3000 orders
(800) 726-0600 customer line
(800) 659-2436 FAX or (301) 848-2436 FAX
The Question is College, ISBN# 081291698-0 (also available from Growing Without Schooling/Holt Associates), *20/20 Is Not Enough*, ISBN# 044921991-7. (C,F)

Reflective Educational Perspectives
M. Pelullo-Willis and V. Kindle-Hodson
1451 E. Main St. #100
Ventura, CA 93001
(805) 648-1739

Regal Books
2300 Knoll Drive
Ventura, CA 93003
The Barna Report, Preparing for Adolescence (F), *What the Bible Is All About for Young Explorers* (A). (B,Cx)

Research and Education Foundation
Robert Morey
P.O. Box 141455
Austin, TX 78714

Resources for the Gifted
P.O. Box 15050
Phoenix, AZ 85060
(602) 840-9770

The Riverside Publishing Co.
School texts sold through Houghton Mifflin. Call (800) 323-9540 or write to Hougton Mifflin at the address listed for them for referral to an area office.
Riverside Spelling Program (C,E)

Rod and Staff Publishers
P.O. Box 3, Hwy. 172
Crockett, KY 41413-0003

See "Major Publishers" for a detailed description. (C-some items,F)

Roddy Publications.
P.O. Box 700
Penn Valley, CA 95946
(916) 432-1235
Writing a Short Story: A Creative Curriculum for 4th, 5th and 6th Grade Students

Rummy Roots Card Game
Eternal Hearts
13021 N.E. 100th St.
Kirkland, WA 98033
(206) 243-2559
available from Back Home Industries plus (A,C,D)

S.U.A.
Sister Monica Foltzer
1339 E. McMillan
Cincinnati, OH 45206
Professor Phonics
(A,C,D,E,H)

SAT testing
See College Board ATP.

Saxon Math Series
Saxon Publishers
1320 West Lindsey
Norman, OK 73069
(800) 284-7019
(405) 329-7071
send orders to: Thompson's Book Depository
P.O. Box 60160
Oklahoma City, OK 73146
(A,B,C,D,E,F)

School at Home: Teach Your Own Child
ICER Press
P.O. Box 877
Claremont, CA 91711
(714) 596-3928

Schoolmasters Science
Box 1941
745 State Circle
Ann Arbor, MI 48106
(800) 521-2832

Science Projects, Inc.
P.O. Box 833
Cedar Hill, TX 75104
(800) 742-7805
The Science Projects Store, the Discovery Scope™, and *Affirmative Guides*

Scott, Foresman
1900 East Lake Ave.
Glenview, IL 60025
(800) 554-4411
Speech: Principles and Practice ISBN# 067327046-7

Scripture Memory Fellowship International
Box 411551
St. Louis, MO 63141
(314) 569-0244
Scripture memory programs

Seton Home Study School
1350 Progress Drive
Front Royal, VA 22630
(703) 636-9990
Send for free information packet.

Dale Seymour Publications
Alphabetically listed under Dale

The Shareware Source
Box 925
Greenville, SC 29602

Shekinah Curriculum Cellar
967 Junipero
Costa Mesa, CA 92626
(714) 751-7767
Send $1 for catalog.

Sign Language for Everyone
Bill Rice Ranch
627 Bill Rice Ranch Rd.
Murfreesboro, TN 37129
(615) 893-2767
The book is published by Thomas Nelson
Publishers and can also be obtained through
them.

Simon and Schuster
200 Old Tappan Road
Old Tappan, NJ 07675
(800) 223-2336 orders
(800) 223-2348 customer service
Amateur Naturalists Handbook, ISBN
0130237213 (also available from Growing
Without Schooling/Holt Associates), *Mark
Kistler's Draw Squad,* ISBN 0-671-65694-
5, *The Timetables of History,* softbound
ISBN 0-671-74271-X $20 (also available
from Bluestocking Press). Books also available from secular bookstores. (C,D,F)

Skills Bank Corporation
15 Governor's Court
Baltimore, MD 21207
(800) 42-TUTOR for demo disk (currently
available only in MS-DOS format), fact kit
(includes detailed description), or orders
(410) 265-8874 FAX
Skills Bank Home Tutor program. Send for
free demo disk and fact kit.

South-Western Publishing Co.
13800 Seniac Dr., Suite 100
Dallas, TX 75234
(214) 241-8541
Geometry for Decision Making (C)

Speedy Spanish
36107 S.E. Squaw Mountain Road
Estacada, OR 97023
Speedy Spanish (F) and *Christian Ethics for
YOUth*

Stackpole Books
P.O. Box 1831
Cameron and Kelker Streets
Harrisburg, PA 17105
(717) 234-5041
(717) 234-1359 FAX

*The Book of Forest and Thicket, Suburban
Nature Guide, Discover Nature at the Seashore* (C)

Steck-Vaughn
P.O. Box 26015
Austin, TX 78755
(800) 531-5015
(800) 252-9317 in Texas
*Critical Thinking, Reading, and Reasoning
Skills; Critical Thinking for Adults; Steck-
Vaughn GED* (F), or *Steck-Vaughn Com-
plete GED Preparation* (F);*"Living in
America"* American history and govern-
ment series. (C)

**Stone & Associates Educational Software
Publishing**
7910 Ivanhoe Ave., Suite 319
LaJolla, CA 92037
(619) 459-9173
Algebra Plus, 1 and 2

**Student Missionary Union of Biola Univer-
sity**
13800 Biola Avenue
La Mirada, CA 90639

**A Student's Guide to College Admissions:
Everything Your Guidance Counselor has
No Time to Tell You**
See Facts on File.

Summit Christian Academy
P.O. Box 802041
Dallas, TX 75380
(800) 362-9180

Summit Ministries
P.O. Box 207
Manitou Springs, CO 80829
(719) 685-9103
Understanding the Times book (B) and cur-
riculum

Surrey Books
230 East Ohio St., Suite 120
Chicago, IL 60611
(800) 326-4430
The Teenage Entrepreneur's Guide. Also
available from Bluestocking Press.

Survival Mathematics
See Barron's.
Available from Growing Without School-
ing and secular bookstores. (C,E)

Sycamore Tree
2179 Meyer Place
Costa Mesa, CA 92627
(714) 650-4466 for information
(800) 779-6750 orders only by Visa,
MasterCard or Fax
(714) 642-6750 for orders only by Visa,
MasterCard or Fax
School service, plus source for learning materials. Send $3 for catalog which includes
$3 certificate redeemable on your order. If
you mention *Christian Home Educators'
Curriculum Manual,* they will send the catalog to you at no charge.

The Synonym Finder
See Warner Books.
Also available from Barnes and Noble and
Shekinah.

T & D Christian Sales
P.O. Box 4140
Cleveland, TN 37320
(800) 423-9595
(615) 476-8571 local

Jeremy P. Tarcher, Inc.
Alphabetically listed under Jeremy

Teacher Designed Products
P.O. Box 1013
Hayden Lake, ID 83835
Send $1 for brochure and ordering informa-
tion. ($1 is credited towards your order on
the order form you receive.) A special price
(big savings!) is available to home educators, so mention *Christian Home
Educators' Curriculum Manual* when you
write.

Teacher's Laboratory
P.O. Box 6480
Brattleboro, VT 05302
(802) 254-3457
Send for free catalog of primarily science
material. They carry *Conceptual Physics,
Lego Simple Machine and Robotic* sets, bal-
ances, and more.

**Teaching and Learning America's Christian
History: The Principle Approach**
See Foundation for American Christian Ed-
ucation.

The Teaching Home
P.O. Box 20219
Portland, OR 97220-0219

Teen Missions International, Inc.
885 East Hall Road
Merrit Island, FL 32953

The Teenage Liberation Handbook
Lowry House Publishers
P.O. Box 1014
Eugene, OR 97440-1014
(503) 686-2315
also available from Growing Without
Schooling/Holt Associates

Telemart
8804 North 23rd Ave.
Phoenix, AZ 85021
(800) 426-6659 for orders
(602) 944-0402 for other information
Very low prices on general computer software for IBM compatibles. They will special order items that they do not normally
carry at no extra charge. (Need title and
manufacturer or distributor names for special orders.)

Ten Speed Press
P.O. Box 7123
Berkeley, CA 94707
College Degrees by Mail by John Bear,
Ph.D. (C) Also available from Growing
Without Schooling/Holt Associates.

Thomas Edison State College
101 West State St.
Trenton, NJ 08608-1176

Thomas Geale Publications, Inc.
P.O. Box 370540
902 Harte Street
Montara, CA 94037
(800) 554-5457
(415) 728-5219
Just Think and *Stretch Think* (C,E)

Thomas Nelson Publishers
P.O. Box 141000
Nashville, TN 37214-1000
*Psychological Seduction, Sign Language
for Everyone, The Shaping of a Christian
Family, Evidence That Demands a Verdict*
(B,C,D)

Timberdoodle
E. 1610 Spencer Lk.Rd.
Shelton, WA 98584
(206) 426-0672

Time Minder
Marilyn Rockett
P.O. Box 6544
Waldorf, MD 20603-6544
For inquiries about the Time Minder, future
products, or seminar information, contact
Marilyn at the above address. Order books
from Alpha Omega, Great Christian Books,
Lifetime Books, or Bob Jones University
Press.

Timetables of History
See Simon and Schuster
This book is published by the Touchstone
Books Division. (C,D)

TOPS Learning Systems
10970 S. Mulino Rd.
Canby, OR 97013
TOPS Task Cards or *Worksheet Modules*

Toys To Grow On
P.O. Box 17
Long Beach, CA 90801
(800) 874-4242
Meet the Classics (order number MC1837)

Tretter Violins
13651 Hope St.
Garden Grove, CA 92643
(714) 534-6228

Trivium Pursuit
R.R. 2, Box 169
New Boston, IL 61272
(309) 537-3641 (call noon to 8 p.m. central
time)
*A Greek Alphabetarion, Greek Pro-
grammed Primer* (B), and other foreign lan-

guage materials and thinking skills resources.

Troll Books
Troll Associates
100 Corporate Dr.
Mahwah, NJ 07430
(800) 526-5289
(201) 529-5807 FAX (A,C)

20/20 is Not Enough
Published by Alfred A. Knopf, distributed
by Random House. See Random House for
ordering address or check your library. (C)

Tyndale House Publishers
P.O. Box 80
Wheaton, IL 60189
(800) 323-9400
(708) 668-8300
(708) 669-8905 FAX
Basic Bible Studies (E), Charlotte Mason's
*The Home Schooling Series, The Hidden
Art of Homemaking, Life Application Bible
for Students.* (B,C,D,F)

Understanding Writing
Bradrick Family Enterprises
P.O. Box 2240
Port Orchard, WA 98366
Multiple copy discounts available.
(A,C,D,E)

United States Center for World Mission
Childrens Mission Resource Center
1605 Elizabeth Street
Pasadena, CA 91104
(818) 398-2233, Mon.- Wed.
Kids for the World

**University of Alabama, College of Continu-
ing Studies**
Independent Study Division
Box 870388
Tuscaloosa, AL 35487-0388
(205) 348-7642

University of California
Independent Study Department
2223 Fulton St.
Berkeley, CA 94720
(510) 642-4124 college information
(510) 642-8238 high school information
High school and college correspondence
courses, plus *The Independent Study Catalog.* Address information requests for *The
Independent Study Catalog* to Dept. B, Center for Media and Independent Learning,
University of California Extension, at the
above address.

University of Missouri
Center for Independent Study
136 Clark Hall
Columbia, MO 65211
(314) 882-2491

**University of Nebraska-Lincoln, Division of
Continuing Studies**
Department of Independent Study
269 Nebraska Center for Continuing Education
Lincoln, NE 68583-0900
(402) 472-1926
(402) 472-1901 FAX

University of the State of New York
Regents College
1450 Western Avenue
Albany, NY 12203-3524

University Prints
P.O. Box 485
21 East St.
Winchester, MA 01890
Send for the free "Price List and Introduction" or send $3 for their very extensive
246-page catalog.

Unlocking the Mysteries of Creation
Creation Resource Foundation
P.O. Box 570
El Dorado, CA 95623
(916) 626-4447
(A,B,C,D,E,F)

VGM Career Horizons
A Division of NCT Publishing Group
4255 West Touhy Ave.
Lincolnwood, IL 60646-1975

Van Nostrand Reinhold Company
115 Fifth Avenue
New York, NY 10003
Botany Illustrated

Victor Books
A Division of Scripture Press Publications,
Inc.
1825 College Ave.
Wheaton, IL 60187
*When Skeptics Ask, When Critics Ask, Part-
Time Jobs for Full-Time Mothers, Investing
for the Future.* (B,Dx)

Video Tutor
2109 Herbertsville Rd.
Point Pleasant, NJ 08742
(800) 445-8334

Vis-Ed/Visual Education Association
P.O. Box 1666
581 W. Leffel Lane
Springfield, OH 45501
(800) 543-5947
Foreign language aids

Vision Development Center
Steven R. Shapiro
6218 S. Lewis, Suite 110
Tulsa, OK 74138
(800) 766-5187 toll free
(918) 742-0072
The Learning Connection (A) and *Stepping
Stones Kit.* (also sold by Alpha Omega)

W.W. Norton and Company
Listed under Norton

Wadsworth, Inc.
School Division
10 Davis Drive
Belmont, CA 94002
(800) 831-6996
Mathematics: Its Power and Utility. Call or
write for free Mathematics catalog.

Wallbuilders
P.O. Box 397
Aledo, TX 76008
(817) 441-6044
America's Godly Heritage

**Dr. Stanley Walters/Center for Children
and Parents**
900 West 17th St., Suite F
Santa Ana, CA 92706
(714) 543-1212

Warner Books
Order from Little Brown and Company.
The Synonym Finder (E)—available from
Barnes and Noble at discounted price,
Smart But Feeling Dumb (library call num-
ber 616.8553).

**Warriner's English Composition and Gram-
mar**
See Harcourt Brace Jovanovich. (C)

Western Baptist College
5000 Deer Park Dr. S.E.
Salem, OR 97301-9392
(800) 845-3005
(503) 375-7005

Wff N'Proof Games
1490-GH South Blvd.
Ann Arbor, MI 48104
Logic, math, propaganda games—junior
high to adult levels (B)

What the Bible is All About
See Regal Books.
Available from Christian bookstores.
(B,D,E)

William B. Eerdmans Publishing Company
255 Jefferson Avenue S.E.
Grand Rapids, MI 49503
*A History of Christianity in the United
States and Canada*

William Carey Library
P.O. Box 40129
Pasadena, CA 91114

(818) 798-0819
*Perspectives on the World Christian Move-
ment*

Windows to Learning
8822 Calmada Avenue
Whittier, CA 90605
(310) 693-3268

Window Tree Learning Project
Rudi and Ingrid Krause
R.R. 1, Site 24, Comp. 36
Winfield, B.C.
V0H 2C0, Canada
(604) 766-0568
Canadian educational resources and ser-
vices.

Winning
See CBN Educational Products. (C,F)

Winston Grammar Kit
See Educators Publishing Service. (A,C,E)

Wolgemuth and Hyatt
See Word Incorporated.
Wolgemuth and Hyatt have gone out of
business. Their titles are available through
Word Incorporated until they are sold out.
Some of the titles will become Word publications, while others will be available from
other publishers. Since all of this has happened as I am finishing this update, I might
still indicate Wolgemuth Hyatt as publisher
on some books. Contact Word for further information. There is usually a significant
delay between the time a publisher decides
to print a book and the time it becomes
available, so some of these titles might have
a period of unavailability.
Former Wolgemuth and Hyatt titles reviewed in this book: *Choosing a College,
Dating with Integrity, The Fine Art of
Mentoring, God and Government, Extra
Cash for Kids, 30 Days to Understanding
Church History, Music Education in the
Christian Home, What Are Your Kids Reading?* (B,D)

Word, Incorporated
P.O. Box 2518
Waco, TX 76702
(817) 772-4200
*Children at Risk, Dating With Integrity,
Don't Check Your Brains at the Door, The
Fine Art of Mentoring, Music Education in
the Christian Home (A), The New Millen-

*ium, The New World Order, 30 Days to Un-
derstanding Church History, What Are
Your Kids Reading?* Word now publishes
some titles which were formerly published
by Wolgemuth and Hyatt. They will provide information about where we can get
other Wolgemuth titles that they will not be
publishing themselves. (B,C,D,E)

Wordsmith
Rt.1, Box 135
Weaubleau, MO 65774
(417) 282-5824

The Write Source
Box 460
Burlington, WI 53105
(800) 331-0994
Basic English Revisited and other related
books. (A,E)

**Writing a Short Story: A Creative Curricu-
lum for 4th, 5th and 6th Grade Students**
See Roddy Publications.

Wycliffe Bible Translators
mailing address:
P.O. 2727
Huntington Beach, CA 92647
location: 19891 Beach Blvd.
Huntington Beach, CA
(714) 969-4600
Information and films on other countries
from missions perspective. (F)

You Can Trust the Communists
Published by CACC, Long Beach, CA.
Available from Shekinah Curriculum Cellar.

Young America's Foundation
110 Elden St.
Herndon, VA 22070
(703) 318-9608
The Myth of the Robber Barons.

Youth With A Mission
P.O. Box 55309
Seattle, WA 98155
(206) 363-9844

**Zondervan Publishing House/Academie
Books**
5300 Patterson S.E.
Grand Rapids, MI 49530
(800) 727-1309
From Jerusalem to Irian Jaya (B,C)

Appendix B

GED - Titles of State Credentials and Minimum Age Requirements

(The following information is quoted—including punctuation and grammatical errors—from the *Examiner's Manual For The Tests Of General Educational Development*, published by The General Educational Development Testing Service of the American Council on Education, One Dupont Circle, Washington, D.C. 20036-1163. The author's notations are placed within brackets [ ], although those same brackets are occasionally used by the GED Manual.)

Information is current to the best of my knowledge as of Spring, 1992. However, GED requirements, particularly those relating to age, are changing quite often. Check with your state department of education or the GED Testing Service for any changes and also to verify the accuracy of the information relating to your state.

Alabama

Title: State Certificate of High School Equivalency

18, Applicant may not be enrolled in regular secondary day school. Applicants 17 years of age may take the test if he/she has been out of school for 12 consecutive months. This must be verified on an E-2 Form or by official school records.

Alaska

Title: State of Alaska High School Diploma

Applicants 18 and under are eligible if they have not graduated from a secondary education program, present a withdrawal slip and a parental permission slip.

Applicants may be tested at discretion of Chief Examiners of testing centers with respect to the applications of persons with extenuating or extreme personal circumstances. These include, but are not necessarily limited to, the following: (1) voluntary induction into the Armed Forces; (2) an illness of long-range duration; (3) pregnancy; (4) sole support of family; (5) untenable situation at home which requires the person to leave school to earn a livelihood; and (6) a request from an institution, school, other agency or program certifying that the test is a prerequisite to employment, admission or participation in a program.

Arizona

Title: Arizona High School Certificate of Equivalency

The applicant must be at least eighteen (18) years of age and have not received a high school diploma or high school equivalency certificate. Individuals between sixteen (16) year and eighteen (18) years of age may be tested providing the applicant:

a. present to the Examiner a signed statement (notarized) of consent to take the test, from a parent or legal guardian.

b. present verification, by letter, from the last elementary/secondary school the applicant attended, certifying that the applicant has not been attending school for six (6) consecutive months preceding application for testing.

Arkansas

Title: Arkansas High School Equivalency Diploma

Must be 18 years of age and not enrolled in a high school. (Excluding the special exceptions, see below.)

Special: A person seventeen (17) years of age may be approved for testing provided he/she meets all three (3) of the following criteria:

a. Has been out of school six (6) months or a former member of a senior class which has graduated;

b. Can provide an endorsement of a school (public, private, parochial, or Arkansas home school as per Act 42 of 1985, as amended 1987) official verifying the students last date of attendance;

c. Can provide written consent of (1) parent, legal guardian or other approving adult, or (2) proof of marriage.

OR

A person seventeen (17) years of age may be approved for testing provided he/she can show proof of successful completion of the official GED Practice Test and has the approval of the State Administrator for GED Testing. (In extenuating circumstances approval may be granted after consultation with school authorities, parents, legal guardians, other approving adults, or other persons the State Administrator for GED Testing deems necessary).

OR

A person sixteen (16) years of age may be approved for testing if an extreme circumstance exists, i.e., a court order or a verifiable hardship. To be considered under this exception, a completed application must be submitted to the state administrator for GED testing, who will be responsible to select a review panel of not less than one (1) member from each division. The panel will review and approve or disapprove the application. The review panel will be assembled on a "as needed" basis and will meet on the first Thursday of the first month of each quarter. Applications must be received not later than seven (7) days before a scheduled meeting.

An oral presentation must be made to the panel by a representative of the referring school or court.

The following criteria must be followed when making application for a 16 year old to take the GED test.

1. Can provide justification for making application.

2. Can provide written recommendation from a public, private, parochial, home school or court. Recommendations must be signed by the chief school representative (i.e., superintendent, director, etc.) or court.

3. Can provide an indication of ability to pass the GED test by passing the Official GED Practice Test with a minimum score of 45 on each part of the test.

4. Can provide recommendation of the adult education official administering the Official GED Practice Test.

5. Can provide a statement as to the impact on applicant if approval is not granted.

6. Can provide written consent of parent, legal guardian, or court.

California

Title: State of California High School Equivalency Certificate

Applicants may not be enrolled in regular or continuation high schools.

EXCEPTION:

I. Students 18 years of age or older may test whether or not they are enrolled in school.

II. Students within 60 days of their 18th birthday may test whether or not they are enrolled in school.

Candidates must be 18 years of age.

EXCEPTION: 17-year-olds may test if they meet any one of the following criteria:

I. Applicants must be within 60 days of their 18th birthday (regardless of their school enrollment status).

II. Applicants must be within 60 days of when their class would have graduated had they stayed in school.

III. Applicants have been out of school 60 days and present a written request on official letterhead from the military, a prospective employer, or a postsecondary institution.

[Under Requirements for Issuance of Certificate]

Those who take the tests at seventeen...will not receive their certificate until their 18th birthday; they will receive a letter of intent stating that the certificate is being held pending the candidates' 18th birthday.

[California also offers the California High School Proficiency Examination for teens between the ages of 16 and 18. The minimum age is either 16 or completion of the sophomore year of high school.]

Colorado

Title: High School Equivalency Certificate

The current *GED Examiner's Manual* reads: "17. Seventeen year old candidates must be withdrawn from a regular secondary school program." [However, a new law was signed in April of 1992, lowering the age to 16.]

Connecticut

Title: State High School Diploma

19, or former member of class which has graduated.

Delaware

Title: Delaware State Board of Education Endorsement

18. Applicant cannot be enrolled in regular secondary day school, and the applicant's high school class must have graduated.

Applicants 17 years of age are eligible if they have withdrawn from school and acquired a waiver. A waiver can be requested if they present the following: (1) evidence of completion of a program of instruction provided by such agencies as Job Corps and Postal Service Academy, or an apprenticeship program of similar training certified by the director of the program and presented to the GED Administrator with a request that the applicant be tested; and (2) a written request from the individual certifying that he/she must establish high school equivalency on the basis of GED

Test scores for job opportunities, college or university entrance or enlistment of the applicant into a branch of the Armed Forces.

District of Columbia

Title: High School Equivalency Certificate

Applicant must be 18 years of age or be at least 16 years of age. There are no restrictions on persons 18 years of age or older. Persons 16 or 17 years of age must meet one of the following criteria: (1) the applicant has been out of a formal classroom situation for a period of not less than six (6) months prior to submitting an application. The applicant must also have been enrolled in an adult GED preparatory course for a period of not less than six months; or (2) the applicant was a member of a high school class which has already graduated.

Florida

Title: State of Florida High School Diploma

Any candidate shall be at least 18 years of age on the date of the examination, except that in extraordinary circumstances as provided for in rules of the school board of the district in which the candidate resides or attends school, said candidate may take the examination after reaching the age of 16.

Georgia

Title: High School Equivalency Certificate

(1) An applicant shall be 18 years of age or older, not enrolled in school, and the high school class of which the applicant was last a member shall have graduated; or (2) An applicant shall be under age 18, out of school with a "Special Need" approved by the State GED Administrator; or under age 18 with proof of full time enrollment in a regionally accredited college or university, or on active duty in the Armed Forces, or enrolled in a federally funded job training program, or under Court Order.

Hawaii

Title: Department of Education High School Diploma

17, if approved by parents and school officials.

Idaho

Title: Idaho High School Equivalency Certificate

19. Applicants who are age 17 or 18 are eligible for testing for induction into the Armed Forces upon request of a recruiting official who states that applicant meets all military requirements for induction except for achieving satisfactory scores on the GED Test. The recruiting official must also submit to the Chief Examiner of an Official GED Testing Center a letter from applicant's parent or guardian granting permission, and a statement from the high school principal that applicant has left school. Applicants 18 years of age may be tested at the request of employers or college admission officials.

[Under Requirements for Issuance of Certificate]

A one semester course in American government that includes the U.S. Constitution and principles of state and local government is required. This requirement may be met by resident study in high school or college, or by correspondence study from an accredited education institution or military institute.

Illinois

Title: High School Equivalency Certificate

The following adults may apply to the Regional superintendent of Schools provided they meet one of the following criteria: (1) applicants who are 18 years of age or older, maintained residence in the State of Illinois and are not high school graduates, but whose high school class has graduated; (2) a member of the Armed Forces of the United States on active duty, who is 17 years of age or older and who is stationed in Illinois or is a legal resident of Illinois; (3) a ward of the Department of Corrections who is 17 years of age or older or an inmate confined in any branch of the Illinois State Penitentiary or in a county correctional facility who is 17 years of age or older; (4) a female who is 17 years of age or older who is unable to attend school because she is either pregnant or the mother of one or more children; (5) a male 17 years of age or older who is unable to attend school because he is a father of one or more children; or (6) a person who is successfully completing an alternative education program under Section 2-3.81 of The School Code of Illinois.

Any applicant who cannot qualify as stated above, and who has been out of school for at least one year, may be administered the GED Test upon written request of the director of a program who certifies to the Chief Examiner of an Official GED Testing Center that the applicant has completed a program of instruction provided by such agencies as the Job Corps, the Postal Service Academy or apprenticeship training program, an employer or program director for purposes of entry into apprenticeship programs, another State Department of Education in order to meet regulations established by the Department of Education, a post high school educational institution for purposes of admission, the Department of Registration and Education for licensing purposes, or the Armed Forces for induction purposes. If the applicant meets all of the Illinois standards, said applicant shall be issued the Illinois High School Equivalency Certificate upon reaching the age of 18.

Other: Applicant must pass state examination on American patriotism and principles of representative government as enunciated in the American Declaration of Independence, the U.S. Constitution, the Constitution of the State of Illinois, and the proper use and display of the American flag. After the Regional Superintendent of Schools has determined that the requirements for minimum age, residence, and minimum test scores have been met, the state examination will be authorized.

Indiana

Title: High School Equivalency Certificate

18 years old and out of high school for one year; or 17 and within 90 days of release from a state correctional institution; or 17 and have successfully completed a program of study with the Job Corps; or 17 and a resident of a child caring institution.

Iowa

Title: High School Equivalency Diploma

Every applicant must (1) have attained the age of 18 years, be a non-high school graduate, and not currently enrolled in a secondary school (an applicant is not eligible for the diploma until after the class in which the applicant was enrolled has graduated); or (2) be minimally a 16 year old resident of State of Iowa Training Schools, the Iowa Juvenile Home, or formally placed by an Iowa court under the supervision of a juvenile probation office and having completed a structured high school completion program be appropriately referred to an Official GED Testing Center by a probation office, state training school or juvenile home official.

The GED Test may be administered to persons 17 years of age who need the test for enlistment in the Armed Services, employment, admission to a college, university, or training program, or license for an occupation. Adequate written verification or documentation is required for applicants meeting these conditions.

Kansas

Title: Kansas State High School Diploma

18, and class of which applicant was a member must have graduated. (Active-duty military personnel may receive diploma at age 17.)

Applicants who are 16-18 and whose high school class has not graduated must be wards of the court or state, or be totally self-supporting, and/or with dependents. Applicants 17 years of age applying for induction into the Armed Forces are admitted to testing provided that a recruiting official requests the testing and states that applicant meets all military requirements for induction except for GED Test scores, and provided a letter of permission from applicant's parent or guardian and a letter from principal of applicant's school stating that applicant has left school are furnished.

Kentucky

Title: High School Equivalency Certificate

17; applicant who has been out of a formal classroom situation for a period of one year, or whose high school class (the class of which he/she was or would have been a member) has graduated.

Louisiana

Title: State of Louisiana High School Diploma for some service personnel and veterans; State High School Equivalency Diploma for other adults.

17, or under if married.

Maine

Title: High School Equivalency Diploma

18, and applicant must not have been in attendance at a public or private school approved by the State Department of Education.

Potential candidates that are the age of 17 may be considered for possible exception if they meet the following: (1) Are 17 years of age and have: a documented immediate need; and written approval from the local Superintendent or his designee; Take the pre-GED exam, or enroll in a GED preparation class.

Maryland

Title: Maryland High School Diploma

16. If under age 19, applicant must have been withdrawn from a regular full-time public or private school program for at least three months.

Massachusetts

Title: Massachusetts State High School Equivalency Certificate

19 with no qualifications; however, in order to register and be tested at 16, 17, or 18, a registrant must provide a letter from their last school of attendance attesting that they have officially withdrawn from school and specifying the date that the registrant's class will graduate (otherwise defined as 12 years from the first grade). "Adjucated youth" may be tested on the order of the court, even if they are still enrolled in school.

Michigan

Title: State High School Equivalency Certificate

18, and class of which applicant would have been a member must have graduated.

Applicants for induction into the U.S. Armed Forces who are age 17 may be admitted to testing, provided a written request is made by the recruiting office of any branch of the Armed Forces stating that applicant has met all military requirements for induction except for GED Test scores, and provided request is accompanied by letter or written statement signed by the local school official stating that the individual has left school and that it would probably be in the best interest of the person to be admitted to testing and, also, a letter of permission for induction from the applicant's parent or guardian is furnished. Individuals who are at least 17 years of age and have been out of a regular school program for one calendar year may also be tested.

[Under Requirements for Issuance of Certificate]

Previous high school enrollment: The local high school may require a year or more of previous high school enrollment in addition to attaining the minimum test scores on the GED Test.

Minnesota

Title: Secondary School Equivalency Certificate

19. Under certain circumstances, minimum age requirement may be waived on basis of supportive evidence of special need provided for this purpose. Age waivers are issued only by the Minnesota Department of Education.

Applicants 17-18 years old may be administered the test provided they have been out of the formal classroom situation for at least one year, or the high school class of which they were a member has graduated, or at the written request of one of the following: (1) an employer indicating employment if individual obtains minimum or above test scores; (2) a college, or junior college, university or vocational technical college who will consider accepting applicant for enrollment or financial aid on the basis of GED test scores; (3) an Armed Forces recruiting official who requires high school equivalency as a prerequisite for enlistment purposes; (4) a recognized rehabilitative or ABE agency who must indicate that achieving the GED is a part of the individual's written educational plan.

Mississippi

Title: High School Equivalency Diploma

17. Applicant must have been out of school six months before testing or class of which applicant was a member has graduated. (Waiver of school status may be granted by State GED Administrator, with approval from school official, for employment, further education or training, military service, or alternative programs.)

Missouri

Title: Certificate of High School Equivalence

18; 17 and out of school at least six months from last day of school attendance; 16-17 and (1) have written permission of an authorized school official, head principal or superintendent where attending or last attended school; or (2) have written permission of the juvenile judge if under the court's jurisdiction; or (3) a hardship case such as being head of a household, incarcerated in an institution, etc.

Montana

Title: High School Equivalency Certificate

18. Eighteen-year-olds must provide the Official GED Testing Center with one of the following: (1) letter of approval to take GED test from principal of high school in which presently enrolled; or (2) documentation from principal or superintendent that applicant has been out of school one full semester.

Persons 17 years of age may receive a waiver of the minimum age requirement provided documentation of the following stipulations is presented to the Official GED Test Center upon application [Before testing, all 17-year-old applications and letters of documentation must be submitted by the official GED Test Center to the State GED Administrator for review and approval]:

1.) Letter of verification from superintendent or principal of last school attended documenting applicant has been out of classroom at least one year, or that applicant's high school class has been graduated;

2.) In addition, documentation of one of the following conditions is required:

   A) A written request is made by one of the following on the applicant's behalf and presented to the Official GED Testing Center:

     1a) an employer who requires high school equivalency for job opportunities;

     2b) a college or university official who will consider accepting an applicant on the basis of GED Test scores;

     3c) a recruiting official for an applicant wishing to enter a branch of the Armed Forces for which high school equivalency is a prerequisite.

   B) Applicant has completed a program of instruction provided by such agencies as the Job Corps, Postal Service Academy, or other similar training programs, and a certificate of completion is provided by the director of the program to an Official GED Testing Center.

Nebraska

Title: State of Nebraska Department of Education High School Diploma

18, and the class of which applicant was a member at the time of withdrawal from school has graduated, or the class in which he was enrolled at the time of withdrawal from school has been graduated for at least one year.

Method of Applying - Test Application Procedures:

a. Persons age 18 and older: Submit the following to an official GED Testing center:

   (1) a completed and notarized NDE Form #12-003, available from the Nebraska Department of Education or official GED Testing centers.

   (2) supporting documents required by the GED Testing center.

(3) evidence that 60 days have passed since withdrawal from a secondary school or a waiver of the 60 day period by the school last attended.

b. Persons under 18 years of age: Submit the following to the GED Administrator, Nebraska Department of Education:

(1) a completed and notarized NDE Form #12-003, available from the Nebraska Department of Education or official GED Testing centers;

(2) a letter in the applicant's own handwriting stating the circumstances of withdrawal from the regular school program and the reason(s) for wanting to write the examination;

(3) a copy of the applicant's transcript from the last high school attended, indicating the official date of withdrawal and graduation date of class from which withdrawal took place. Birth date must appear on transcript; otherwise, a copy of the birth certificate must be submitted;

(4) evidence that 60 days have passed since withdrawal from a secondary school or a waiver of the 60 day period by the school last attended.

(5) a notarized letter of permission from his/her parents. The letter of permission should specify the following: (a) reason(s) for the applicant's withdrawal from the regular school program; (b) the identity of the school official who served as counsel previous to termination from the school program; (c) reason(s) of the applicant for writing the examination; (d) agreement of the parent(s) to interview with the state's GED Administrator if requested; (e) expressed permission for the applicant to write the GED Test; and (f) the address and telephone number of parent(s).

Nevada

Title: Certificate of High School Equivalency

Any person who is 17 years of age or older, who has not graduated from a high school and who is not currently enrolled for full-time attendance as a high school student is eligible to take the tests to determine his general educational development.

New Hampshire

Title: Certificate of High School Equivalency

18 and out of school. However, if under 18 and applicant's class has graduated, he/she may take the Test, having submitted written proof from the last school attended, of the graduation date of his/her class. If under 18 and class has not graduated, applicant must receive permission from the GED Administrator of the GED testing Program. Applicant must submit: (a) a written request stating his/her date of birth, reason for taking the Test, and where he/she plans on being tested; (b) an official statement from either the superintendent, principal or guidance counselor, of the last school attended, giving the date the applicant officially withdrew from school, and who considers it to be in the best interests of the applicant to take the Test; and (c) also, where applicable, a written request from any one of the following: a college, university or postsecondary school which requires a high school equivalency certificate, an employer of an applicant whose job is contingent on a high school equivalency certificate, or a recruiting official of the Armed Forces.

New Jersey

Title: High School Diploma

18, and applicant must be out of school. Exceptions may be made for out-of-school applicants who are 16 and 17 years of age. A Certification of Non-Enrollment in School form signed by the applicant, parent or guardian, and superintendent or principal of the applicant's public high school district of residence verifies that the applicant has been counseled on in-school options and is not longer on the school rolls. The applicant must pass the "Official GED Practice Test" at an adult education program. If the applicant passes the practice test a Referral to GED Test form will be issued by the adult education administrator. This allows the applicant to take the GED test at a testing center.

New Mexico

Title: New Mexico High School Diploma

For those under 21 years of age, high school class in which they were last enrolled must have graduated.

The GED Test may be taken by persons who have not graduated from high school or received a high school credential and are 18 years of age or older. In some cases, applicants 17 years old may be permitted to take the GED Test with special written approval by the local school superintendent or his authorized representative, the parent or legal guardian, and the Chief Examiner. Juveniles confined to a correctional institution may take the GED Test at a minimum age of 15 1/2 years with special written approval signed by the institution superintendent, the parent or legal guardian, and the Chief Examiner.

New York

Title: New York State High School Equivalency Diploma

19 on or before examination date with the following exceptions:

i) Applicants 17-18 are eligible to test and to receive a diploma if they have not been regularly enrolled in a full time high school program of instruction for one full year or were members of a high school class which has already graduated.

ii) Applicants 16-18 are eligible to test and receive a diploma if they have been enrolled in an approved alternative high school equivalency preparation program and have been recommended for testing by the instructor.

Applicants who do not meet eligibility requirements for a diploma as stated in [the above two exceptions]... may be admitted to the examination if GED Test scores are needed for (1) admission to an institution of postsecondary education for which high school graduation is the normal prerequisite, or (2) enlistment in the Armed Forces. Applications must be accompanied by a letter from a postsecondary admissions officer or a United States Armed Forces recruiter stating that the applicant will be admitted/inducted upon presentation of satisfactory GED test scores. A score report will be forwarded to the applicant but a diploma will not be awarded until such time as the person becomes qualified.

North Carolina

Title: High School Diploma Equivalency

Individuals 16-17 years of age who are not enrolled in a high school may be considered to have special needs and admitted to testing provided: (1) that the minor applicant has left the school no less than six months prior to the date that application for testing is made (however, all or any part of the six-month waiting period may be waived by the chief administrative school officer of the public or private school unit in which the applicant resides); (2) that the application of the minor applicant is supported by a notarized petition of the minor's parents, legal guardian, or other person or agency having legal custody and control of such minor applicant; the petition certifies the place of residence and date of birth of the minor, the parental or other appropriate legal relationship of the petitioner to the minor applicant, and the date on which minor applicant withdrew from school. Also any person 16, or 17 years of age meeting one of the following conditions may be admitted to testing: (a) incarcerated in a correctional institution, correctional youth center, training school for adjudicated youth, or similar institution; (b) a patient or resident of a state-operated hospital or alcoholic rehabilitation center; (c) enrolled in or have completed a program of instruction provided by the Job Corps or other such agency, or an apprenticeship training program; (d) a member of the United Stated Armed Forces; or (e) an emancipated minor.

[Under Requirements for Issuance of Diploma}

All persons shall have officially dropped out of school prior to applying to take the GED Test.

North Dakota

Title: North Dakota High School Equivalency Certificate
18, and class has graduated.

Applicants between age 17 and 18 may receive approval for testing by establishing an urgent need for early testing, such as (1) entrance into military service; (2) postsecondary vocational programs; (3) postsecondary academic programs; and (4) employment denied.

Ohio

Title: Certificate of High School Equivalence
19 years old. The minimum age can be waived for 16 to 18 year olds when (1) an applicant has written permission to test from a parent, guardian, or court official and the school superintendent or designee from the district where applicant last attended school or presently resides; or (2) applicant is eighteen years of age and his/her class has graduated (attach a transcript to the application); or (3) applicant who has been sworn into active military service in one of the Armed Forces (attach a letter indicati[ng] the date of the swearing-in ceremony) is submitted with the application to the Ohio Department of Education. [Incorrect grammar in (3) is quoted from the publication of the Dept. of Education, but it is the letter rather than the applicant which must be submitted.]

Oklahoma

Title: Certificate of High School Equivalency
18, persons 17 years of age may take the test with a signed, notarized agreement between the parent, guardian, or custodian and the administrator of the school district in which that person resides that it is to the best interest of that person to take the test at that time. A Letter of Intent will be issued to successful 17 and 18 year old candidates. Upon reaching the age of 18 and when the class of which they were a member graduates from high school, a high school equivalency certificate will be issued.

Oregon

Title: Certificate of General Educational Development
18. Person 16 or 17 must receive age waiver authorization before taking the Test from the school most recently attended and from the parents.

Pennsylvania

Title: Commonwealth Secondary School Diploma
18. Candidates under age 18, qualifying for the diploma under [the exceptions] below, will be issued a letter attesting to the successful completion of the examination and stating that the diploma will be issued when he or she reaches age 18.

Applicants 16-17 years of age may take the Test at the written request of (1) an employer for the applicant who must establish high school equivalency for job opportunities; (2) a college or university official who will consider acceptance of the applicant on the basis of GED Test scores; (3) a recruiting official for persons who wish to enter a branch of the Armed Force for which high school equivalency is a prerequisite; or (4) the director of a state institution for residents, patients, or inmates, no earlier than 90 days before anticipated release or discharge from the institution.

Rhode Island

Title: High School Equivalency Diploma
At least 18 years of age and not enrolled in secondary school, or if under 18, the class in which the applicant was last enrolled has graduated.

Persons not meeting the age requirements...above, may be permitted to take the tests under one of the following conditions: (a) Is 17 years of age, not enrolled in secondary school and the class to which s/he was last assigned in high school has graduated, or: (b) Is 17 years of age, not enrolled in secondary school, and has received special permission to test from the Chief Examiner of the test center to which application is made or (c) Is 16 years of age, not enrolled in secondary school for at least six months and has received permission to test from the Commissioner of Education. The high school equivalency diploma will not be issued until all eligibility requirements have been fulfilled.

South Carolina

Title: High School Equivalency Diploma
Applicant must be 17 years of age or older and not enrolled in high school. Persons 17 or 18 years of age shall submit a letter from the principal of the last school attended or the district superintendent over said school. The letter shall verify the candidate's date of birth and the last date of attendance at the school. In the event that the last school attended was outside South Carolina, persons 17 or 18 years of age may submit a letter from an adult education coordinator or director verifying the candidate's date of birth and last date of attendance in school. Verification of the adult education coordinator or director in this instance shall be based upon inspection of transcript records. Verification letters shall be forwarded to the Chief Examiner, GED Testing Services Unit, State Department of Education, 706 Rutledge Building, Columbia, South Carolina, 29201.

Special needs exception for 16-year-old juvenile offenders under the jurisdiction of the South Carolina Department of Youth Services may be allowed under certain State Board of Education Regulations. Contact Chief Examiner, GED Testing Services Unit, State Department of Education.

South Dakota

Title: High School Equivalency Certificate

18, provided applicants are out of school at least six months from last day of school attendance and the class of which they were a member has graduated from high school. (Proof of class graduation and date of termination of high school membership must be furnished by applicants under 19 years of age.)

Requirements for testing:

a. Individual has not been enrolled in a regular high school program six (6) months prior to making application for testing. Regular high school program does not include Special Education Schools approved by GED program.

b. Individual has not graduated from high school or received a high school equivalency certificate.

c. Individual must meet state residence requirements [above].

d. Individual must be 18 years old. Individual 17 years of age may be tested at the discretion of the State Administrator when extenuating circumstances are factors. These factors include but are not necessarily limited to the following;

-Voluntary induction into the Armed Forces;
-School dropouts who are enrolled in anti-poverty pro grams or correctional programs under the supervi sion of the State Board of Charities and Corrections;
-Sole support of family;
-Married or head of household.

The applicant must provide a written recommendation from a local high school principal or guidance counselor where applicant resides with written request from one of the following:

-A prospective employer of applicant who must establish high school equivalency for job opportunities;
-A college, university, or vocational-technical school official who will consider accepting applicant on the basis of GED test scores;
-A recruiting official for a person who wishes to enter the Armed Forces, provided applicant meets all other requirements including submitting a letter of parental permission for entrance;
-The director of a program who certifies to the Chief Examiner of an official GED testing center that the applicants have successfully completed a formal program of instruction provided by such agencies as Adult Basic Education, Job Corps and Correctional Institutions.

Tennessee

Title: Equivalency High School Diploma

The applicant shall not be less than 18 years of age, unless an exception has been granted to a 17-year-old.

Equivalency diploma will be issued only to persons who have legally withdrawn from school prior to graduation and have passed the GED Test.

Texas

Title: Certificate of High School Equivalency

18. A 17-year-old is eligible with parental or guardian consent and 16-year-olds recommended by a public agency that has supervision or custody of the person under a court order.

Must be officially withdrawn from school and must not have received a high school diploma from an accredited high school in the United States.

Utah

Title: Certificate of General Educational Development Eligibility of GED Testing:

a. Age 18 if the high school class of which the applicant would have regularly been a member has graduated; or

b. Age 17 if the high school class of which the applicant would have regularly been a member has not graduated, and the GED Testing Center is provided the following:

1) a letter from the school district within which the applicant resides indicating the applicant is not regularly enrolled in school;

2) a letter from the applicant's parent or guardian authorizing the test; and

3) a letter from an employer or educational institution indicating its acceptance of the applicant upon passing the GED Test.

Vermont

Title: Vermont Secondary School Equivalency Certificate

16. Applicants, ages 16 and 17 must have written permission by their parent or legal guardian to take the test.

Virginia

[Home school regulations might allow earlier testing than is specified here.]

Title: Commonwealth of Virginia General Educational Development Certificate

18. Under special circumstances which are considered by local school authorities to be justifiable, the age limit may be lowered. Applicants below 18 years of age shall provide one of the following: (1) a letter from an official of the regular day school last attended stating that the applicant has been legally withdrawn from school for a period of one year; (2) a letter from an official of the regular day school last attended stating that the applicant has been legally withdrawn from school for period of six months; and, a letter from a director of a high school review program stating that the applicant has successfully completed the program; (3) a letter from an employer, a recruiting officer of the Armed Forces, or an admissions officer of an institution of higher learning or postsecondary training institution stating the applicant meets all requirements for employment or admissions with exception of a General Educational Development Certificate; and, a letter from an official of the regular day school last attended recommending the applicant be tested.

Washington

Title: Certificate of Educational Competence
Minimum age for testing:

a. Any person 19 years of age and over and has not graduated from high school, or

b. Any person between the ages of 15 and 18 who has not graduated from high school and who has been adjudged by a school district to have a substantial and warranted reason for leaving the regular high school program in accordance with WAC 180-96-005 through 180-96-075.

c. Any student in a certified Educational Clinic upon completion of an individual student program in accordance with the provisions of chapter 392-185.

West Virginia

Title: State High School Equivalent Diploma

Individuals who are 18 years of age and have been out of the formal high school classroom situation for a period of six months before making application or whose high school class of which he/she was a member has been graduated, may be admitted to testing.

Individuals who are 17 years of age and have been out of a formal high school classroom situation for a period of one year before making application or whose high school class of which he/she was a member has been graduated, may be admitted to testing under the following conditions:

a. Written verification from the principal of the last school attended stating the exact date of withdrawal from school. This letter must be sent directly to the testing site prior to any formal application for testing and,

b. At the written request of an employer for an applicant who must establish high school equivalency for job opportunities or,

c. At the written request of a college or university official who will consider accepting applicant on the basis of GED test scores or,

d. Written verification of a student being enrolled in such programs as New Careers, Job Corps, Neighborhood Youth Corps, and other federal programs upon successful completion of their training certified in writing by the program administrator (this does not include classes in preparation for the General Education Development Test) or,

e. Seventeen (17) year old applicants for induction into the All-Volunteer Armed Forces of the United States may be admitted to take the GED tests provided:

1) the Chief Examiner of an Official GED Center receives a request from the recruiting officer for each applicant to take the GED tests. This request should be in the form of a letter from the applicant and stating in his/her request that the applicant meets all of the military requirements for induction except for achieving the appropriate scores on the GED Tests, and

2) the recruiting officer submits to the Chief Examiner a copy of a letter from the applicant's parents or guardian granting him/her permission to enter the Armed Forces.

Wisconsin

Title: State of Wisconsin High School Equivalency Diploma or Certificate of General Educational Development

18 years and 6 months or class from which applicant would have entered 9th grade has graduated from high school. Exception to age requirement will allow 17-year-old incarcerated youths to take GED tests, but certificate or di-

ploma will not be issued until they meet the age eligibility requirements.

Counseling Requirement

Wisconsin requires all persons, prior to applying for the Certificate of General Educational Development or High School Equivalency Diploma to complete a counseling session or sessions provided by an educational services officer, a high school, VTAE district, community-based organization, college, university, psychologist licensed by the department or the department of regulation and licensing, or a school counselor licensed by the department. The sessions shall include all of the following:

1. Assessment of the person's reading level and career interests and aptitudes.

2. Discussion of the options available to the individual regarding completion of high school, the High School Equivalency Diploma, and the Certificate of General Educational Development, and the requirements, expectations, benefits, and limitations of each option.

3. Development of a plan for completion of one of the options discussed, and subsequent activities necessary to work toward an identified goal, career or occupation.

[Following this is a section entitled "Five options for earning a High School Equivalency Diploma." Option one discusses health and citizenship requirements. Option two allows those who have completed at least 22 high school credits to obtain an equivalency diploma. Option three allows students to obtain an equivalency diploma after completing specified numbers of units of post-secondary work. Option four allows for consideration of foreign diplomas. Option five speaks in vague terms of other programs approved by the state superintendent.]

Wyoming

Title: High School Equivalency Certificate

18, provided the high school class of which applicant was a member has graduated.

Applicants 17 years of age may apply for a waiver if they are withdrawn from a regular secondary school program and ONE OF THE FOLLOWING CONDITIONS EXISTS: (1) an employer requests the equivalency for job opportunities; or (2) a college or university official requests the equivalency for consideration for admittance; or (3) an Armed Forces recruiting official requests the equivalency as a prerequisite for entering some branch of the service....Applicants who do not meet one or more of the above criteria may request that an exception be granted by the State Superintendent of Public Instruction on the basis of extraordinary circumstances. Requests are to be sent to GED office for referral and approval by the State Superintendent of Public Instruction.

Information on American territories and Canadian provinces is also included in the *Examiner's Manual*.

Appendix C

MOST COMMONLY MISSPELLED WORDS

ability
absence
absolutely
abundance
accept
acceptance
accessible
accident
accidentally
accommodate
accompany
accomplish
accordance
account
accurate
ache
achievement
acknowledge
acknowledg-
  ment
acquaintance
acquire
across
actual
additional
address
adolescent
advertisement
advertising
advice
advise
aerial
aeronautics
affect
affectionate
again
against
aggravate
agreement
agriculture
alcohol
allowance
all right
already
although
altogether
always
amateur
American
among
amount
amusement
analysis
analyze
ancient

angle
anniversary
announce
annual
answer
anticipate
anxious
anything
apologize
apparatus
apparently
appeal
appearance
appetite
application
appoint
appreciate
approach
appropriate
approval
arctic
argument
arithmetic
arrangement
article
artificial
ascend
ascertain
assignment
assistance
association
assume
assurance
athletic
attach
attack
attempt
attendance
attention
attitude
attorney
attractive
audience
authority
automobile
autumn
auxiliary
available
average
aviation
awful
awkward
bachelor
baggage
balance

balloon
ballot
bandage
banquet
bargain
barrel
basement
basis
beautiful
beauty
become
beggar
beginning
behavior
being
belief
believe
believing
beneficial
benefited
between
bicycle
biscuit
blizzard
bought
boundary
breadth
breakfast
breathe
brief
brilliant
Britain
broad
broccoli
brought
bruise
budget
built
bulletin
bureau
burglar
bury
business
cabin
cafeteria
caffeine
calendar
camouflage
campaign
cancel
candidate
canoe
capacity
captain
career

carriage
cashier
category
caught
caution
celebration
cemetery
century
certain
certificate
changeable
character
chauffeur
chief
chimney
chocolate
choose
Christian
circular
civilization
climate
climb
clothes
coach
collar
college
column
coming
commence
commercial
commission
committee
communicate
community
comparative
compel
competent
competition
complain
complement
complexion
compliment
conceive
concerning
concert
concession
conclude
concrete
condemn
condition
conference
confidence
congratulate
conscience
conscientious

consequence	disagreeable	exceed	gratitude
considerably	disappear	excellent	grease
consistent	disappoint	except	grief
constitution	disapprove	excite	grievous
continually	disastrous	executive	grocery
continue	discipline	exercise	guarantee
control	discover	exhibition	guard
controversy	discuss	exhilarate	guardian
convenience	disease	existence	guerrilla
convince	distinguish	exorbitant	guess
co-operate	distribute	expect	guidance
cordial	divide	expedition	guide
corporation	divine	expensive	guilty
correspon-	division	experience	gymnasium
dence	doctor	explain	half
cough	does	explanation	hammer
could	doesn't	expression	handkerchief
country	done	exquisite	handle
courage	don't	extension	handsome
courteous	doubt	extinct	happen
courtesy	duly	extremely	happiness
cousin	duplicate	familiar	harbor
criticism	during	famous	hastily
cruel	dyeing	fascinate	having
curiosity	dying	fashion	height
curtain	early	fatigue	heretofore
custom	earnest	faucet	hesitate
customary	easy	favorite	history
cylinder	economical	feature	hoarse
daily	economy	February	holiday
deceive	ecstasy	federal	honor
decided	effect	fertile	horrible
decision	efficiency	field	hospital
declaration	eighth	fierce	humorous
decorate	either	fiery	hungry
defense	elaborate	finally	hymn
definite	electricity	financially	idea
definitely	elephant	flier	ignorance
definition	elevator	flight	illustrate
delicious	eligible	foreign	imagine
depot	embarrass	fortunate	imitation
descend	emergency	forty	immediately
describe	emphasize	fountain	immense
description	employment	fourth	immortal
desert	encourage	freight	impatient
deserve	endeavor	friend	importance
design	engineer	fundamental	impossible
desirable	English	garage	improvement
desirous	enormous	gasoline	incidentally
desperate	enough	gauge	inconvenience
dessert	entertain	generally	independent
determine	enthusiastic	generous	individual
develop	entrance	genius	industrial
development	envelope	genuine	industrious
diamond	environment	geography	inferior
dictionary	equipment	glorious	ingenious
difference	equipped	government	ingenuous
different	especially	governor	inimitable
difficulty	essential	gracious	innocence
diphtheria	establish	graduation	innocent
diploma	evidence	grammar	instance
director	exaggerated	grateful	instead

institute	magnificent	perhaps	schedule
insurance	maintain	permanent	science
intelligence	maintenance	perseverance	scissors
interesting	majority	personal	secretary
interfere	making	personnel	seize
interrupt	management	persuade	separate
interview	maneuver	physician	sergeant
intimate	manufacture	planned	several
invalid	marriage	pleasant	sheriff
investigate	material	pneumonia	shining
invitation	mathematics	possession	shoes
invoice	mayor	practically	siege
irresistible	meant	precede	silhouette
irrigate	measure	precedence	similar
island	medicine	precious	since
issue	medium,	preference	sincerely
janitor	merit	prejudice	skiing
jealous	message	prevalent	solemn
jewelry	metal	principal	sophomore
journal	mileage	principle	specific
journey	minimum	prisoner	specimen
judgment	minute	privilege	speech
juicy	mirror	probably	sphere
justice	mischief	procedure	stationary
kitchen	mischievous	proceed	stationery
knowledge	miserable	professor	straight
label	misery	pronunciation	studying
laboratory	missionary	psychology	succeed
laid	misspell	pursue	success
language	moisture	questionnaire	sufficient
laugh	monument	quiet	sugar
laundry	mortgage	quite	superintendent
lawyer	murmur	raise	suppose
league	musician	ready	sure
lecture	naive	realize	surely
legal	naturally	really	surprise
legislature	necessary	receipt	syrup
leisure	necessity	receive	tariff
length	nickel	received	technique
lettuce	niece	recognition	telegram
liability	nineteen	recognize	temperament
liable	ninety	recommend	temperature
library	noticeable	reference	temporary
lieutenant	nuisance	referred	terrible
license	occasion	relieve	territory
lightning	occurred	religious	theater
likely	occurrence	remember	therefore
liquid	often	repetition	they're
liquor	omitted	representative	thief
listen	once	respectfully	thorough
literary	opinion	restaurant	thoroughly
literature	opportunity	rheumatism	though
living	opposite	rhythm	tired
loneliness	original	ridiculous	tobacco
loose	paid	sacrifice	together
lose	pamphlet	sacrilegious	tongue
losing	paragraph	said	tonight
lovable	parallel	salary	touch
lovely	paralyze	sandwich	tragedy
luncheon	parliament	satisfactory	train
machine	pastime	Saturday	treasurer
magazine	peculiar	says	tried

tries	usually	visitor	wholly
truly	vacation	voice	whom
Tuesday	vaccinate	volume	whose
tuition	valuable	waive	width
typical	variety	wander	wield
unanimous	various	warrant	worst
university	vegetable	weather	wouldn't
unnecessary	velocity	Wednesday	writing
until	vengeance	weird	written
upon	vicinity	where	yacht
upper	view	whether	yesterday
usable	villain	which	yield
useful	visible	whole	

Index

Course of Study

Student _____ School Year _____

Subject	Texts or materials	Source
Bible		
Math		
Language: Composition/Grammar		
Literature		
Vocabulary/Spelling		
Science		
History/Government/ Economics		
Fine Arts		
Foreign Language		
Physical Education		
Electives		

Master Schedule

Name _____ School Year _____

Time	Monday	Tuesday	Wednesday	Thursday	Friday

Alternate Choices:

_____

_____

_____

Assignments

Name _____ Week of _____

Subject	Monday	Tuesday	Wednesday	Thursday	Friday

Alternate Choices:

_____

_____

_____

Chart C

DATE OF APPLICATION		
MONTH	DAY	YEAR

APPLICATION FOR EMPLOYMENT

ALL APPLICANTS WILL RECEIVE CONSIDERATION FOR EMPLOYMENT WITHOUT REGARD
TO RACE, COLOR, RELIGION, SEX, AGE, MARITAL STATUS, NATIONAL ORIGIN, OR HANDICAP.

PLEASE PRINT IN INK

NAME Last First Middle	OTHER OR FORMER NAME	SOCIAL SECURITY NO.

PRESENT ADDRESS Street City State Zip Code	HOW LONG?	Area Code TELEPHONE Number

POSITION OBJECTIVE

Position Desired:
- ☐ Sales
- ☐ Cashier
- ☐ Receiver
- ☐ Delivery Driver
- ☐ P-Time Stockperson
- ☐ Main Warehouse
- ☐ Main Office
- ☐ Other _____

Work Classification Desired

	Yes	No
Full Time?	☐ Yes	☐ No
Part Time?	☐ Yes	☐ No
Seasonal?	☐ Yes	☐ No

Can You Work

	Yes	No
Evenings?	☐ Yes	☐ No
Sat & Sundays?	☐ Yes	☐ No
Six Days/Week?	☐ Yes	☐ No

DEPARTMENT DESIRED:

	Retail	Trades	School	Hobby	None
BACKGROUND EXPERIENCE					
☐ Lumber Yard	☐	☐	☐	☐	☐
☐ Paint/Home Decor	☐	☐	☐	☐	☐
☐ Hardware	☐	☐	☐	☐	☐
☐ Plumbing & Electric	☐	☐	☐	☐	☐
☐ Garden	☐	☐	☐	☐	☐
☐ Cashier	☐	☐	☐	☐	☐

Wage Desired: $ _____ Per Hour	Date Available To Start Work	Method of Transportation to Work	Driver's License No./or State I.D.

GENERAL INFORMATION

HAVE YOU EVER BEEN CONVICTED OF ANYTHING OTHER THAN A MINOR TRAFFIC OFFENSE?   If "YES" or "I DON'T KNOW," give dates and circumstances:

☐ No   ☐ Yes   ☐ I Don't Know

IF HIRED, CAN YOU FURNISH:

Proof of Age?   ☐ No ☐ Yes

Proof of Citizenship, Permanent Residency or Authorization to Work?   ☐ No ☐ Yes

DO YOU HAVE ANY
RELATIVES ☐
FRIENDS ☐

EMPLOYED BY   **XYZ Company**
_____
FULL NAME   STORE LOCATION

HAVE YOU PREVIOUSLY BEEN EMPLOYED BY **XYZ Company**   YES ☐ NO ☐

HAVE YOU EVER BEEN INVOLUNTARILY DISCHARGED OR FIRED?   YES ☐ NO ☐

IF SO PLEASE EXPLAIN THE CIRCUMSTANCES:

DATES EMPLOYED
From: _____ / ____ /19
To: _____ / ____ /19

ARE YOU CURRENTLY INVOLVED IN THE OPERATIONS OF ANY OTHER BUSINESS?   ☐ No   ☐ Yes — Give Circumstances:

U.S. MILITARY SERVICE		HAVE YOU EVER BEEN REFUSED FIDELITY BOND?
Branch of Service	Dates of Active Service	☐ No ☐ Yes
	From To	

EMPLOYMENT EXPERIENCE
List the last three positions you held of three months or longer duration, including military service or significant volunteer experience. List the most recent first.

COMPANY NAME	STREET ADDRESS City State Zip Code	DATES OF EMPLOYMENT — Month & Year From To
FINAL POSITION	NAME OF SUPERVISOR YOUR Wage Per Hour	Description of Duties
REASON FOR LEAVING:		

COMPANY NAME	STREET ADDRESS City State Zip Code	DATES OF EMPLOYMENT — Month & Year From To
FINAL POSITION	NAME OF SUPERVISOR YOUR Wage Per Hour	Description of Duties
REASON FOR LEAVING:		

COMPANY NAME	STREET ADDRESS City State Zip Code	DATES OF EMPLOYMENT — Month & Year From To
FINAL POSITION	NAME OF SUPERVISOR YOUR Wage Per Hour	Description of Duties
REASON FOR LEAVING:		

D

PERIODS OF UNEMPLOYMENT

List all periods of unemployment (in excess of 30 days duration) that occurred within the span of employment experience listed above.
Do not include periods in school.

FROM: Month Year	TO: Month Year	REASON:

EXPERIENCE

Are there any other experiences, skills, or qualifications which you feel would especially fit you for work with the Company?

_____

_____

_____

EDUCATIONAL BACKGROUND

	NAME OF SCHOOL	STREET ADDRESS City State	MAJOR SUBJECT	Highest Level Attained
HIGH SCHOOL Last Attended				
COLLEGE				
TRADE SCHOOL				

HEALTH

Do you have any condition, illness, or disability, either temporary or permanent, which may affect your ability to do the work in the position applied for?

☐ No   ☐ Yes — Specify: _____

If required by the job, can you or are you willing to lift? (circle one)   LBS.   10   25   50   75   100

Do you have any family, business, health, or social obligations that would prevent you from: Working Consistently:

Yes ☐   No ☐   Working Overtime: Yes ☐   No ☐

If yes, to any of the above, explain _____

_____

I hereby certify that the information provided herein is accurate to the best of my knowledge and subject to verification by   **XYZ Company**
Inc. I authorize the schools, person, previous employers and other organizations named in this form to provide   **XYZ Company**   (its authorized employees, agents, or representatives) with any relevant information that may be required to arrive at a future employment decision, and hereby release any such schools, persons, employers and organizations from any and all liability which they might otherwise incur as a result. I understand that any misrepresentation or omission of a material fact on my application constitutes justification for separation from
XYZ Company   employment.

Criminal conviction records will be reviewed, but will not necessarily bar employment.

I understand that this employment application and any other company documents are not contracts of employment and that any individual who is hired may voluntarily leave employment upon proper notice; or may be terminated by the company with or without notice, and with or without cause. I understand that any written or oral statements to the contrary are hereby expressly disavowed and should not be relied upon by any prospective or existing employee.

Date _____ Applicant's Signature _____

POST EMPLOYMENT — (FOR OFFICE USE ONLY)

PLACEMENT DATA — TO BE COMPLETED BY HIRING OFFICER

SEX	AGE	BIRTHDATE Month Day Year	BIRTHPLACE	CITIZENSHIP—Type	Country

RACE	SELF-IDENTITY Handicapped ☐ Yes ☐ No	Vietnam Vet ☐ Yes ☐ No	Disabled Vet. ☐ Yes ☐ No	SPOUSE'S	First Name	Birthdate	OTHER SOURCE(S) OF INCOME

EMERGENCY NOTIFICATION	Name	Relationship	Street	City	State	Zip Code	Telephone Number

OFFICE/DEPT. NAME	POSITION	TITLE

SALARY $	REASON FOR EMPLOYMENT: ☐ Addition to Force ☐ Replacement	STATUS: ☐ Full Time ☐ Part Time

Reporting Date _____ Authorized Signature _____

E

CHRISTIAN HIGH SCHOOL RECORD

Name of School   Date of Entry
Name of Student   Graduation Date
Parent or Guardian   Credits Earned
Address   Grade Point Average
Phone: (   )   Test Results:
Place of Birth   _____
Date of Birth   _____
Previous School   _____
Church

Class	Semester/Year	Grade	Grade Points	Credits

<u>Outside Credits</u>

Subject	Place	Date

<u>Credits Sent to</u>

Place		Date

<u>Honors or Awards</u>

<u>Grade Points (Credits)</u>

Grade		Grade Points
A - Superior	95-100	4
B - Above average	85-94	3
C - Average	75-84	2
D - Below Average	70-74	1
F - Failure	below 70	0

Signature_____
Date_____

F

HIGH SCHOOL PLANNING CHART
COLLEGE PREPARATORY

Use this chart to plan the program for a college bound student. In the columns marked 9th, 10th, 11th, and 12th, mark in the year in which you plan to cover that subject. Although not specifically included in the chart, critical thinking skills and personal development are neceessary.

Subject	9TH	10TH	11TH	12TH	COMMENTS
BIBLE					4 years suggested
ENGLISH					4 years recommended - emphasize writing skills
MATHEMATICS Algebra Geometry Advanced Math					Algebra and geometry are generally required. Advanced math is recommended. Taking a course in 12th grade will keep you in training for college math.
SOCIAL SCIENCES U.s. History World History American Government Economics					3 years are required. Full year courses of U.S. and World history, one year combination of government and economics.
SCIENCE Biology Chemistry Physics Geology, Oceanography, or other					Biology and chemistry usually required. Should include lab work.
FOREIGN LANGUAGE					Some colleges require 2 years of the same language.
DRIVER'S EDUCATION					Recommended for all students
PHYSICAL EDUCATION					2 years required
FINE ARTS Art, Music, Drama, Dance					In spite of varying requirements, plan on 1 year of fine arts. (California allows the substitution of foreign language for fine arts.)
ELECTIVES Typing Computer Home Economics Woodshop					A computer class is highly recommended. Typing skills are almost a necessity.

CHART G

HIGH SCHOOL PLANNING CHART
GENERAL EDUCATION

Use this chart to plan your high school program for a non-college bound student. In the columns marked 9th, 10th, 11th, and 12th, mark in the years in which you expect to cover that subject. Included are subjects covered in public schools.

SUBJECTS	9TH	10TH	11TH	12TH	COMMENTS
BIBLE					4 years suggested
ENGLISH					3 years required - emphasize writing skills
MATHEMATICS					2 years required - can be consumer or survival math, pre-algebra, algebra, geometry.
SCIENCE 　　Life science 　　Physical science					2 years required - labs are optional
SOCIAL SCIENCE 　　World History 　　U.s. History 　　American 　　Government/Civics 　　Economics					3 years required - full year courses of U.S. and World histories plus 1 semenster each of govenment and economics.
FOREIGN LANGUAGE or FINE 　　ARTS 　　Art, Music, Drama					1 year of either is required
PHYSICAL EDUCATION					2 years required
DRIVER'S EDUCATION					strongly recommended
ELECTIVES 　　Typing 　　Computers 　　Auto Mechanics 　　Woodshop 　　Electronics 　　Home Economics					seek out future job-interest-related work experience. Investigate apprenticeships.

CHART H

DAILY ACTIVITY LOG - INDEPENDENT STUDY

NAME _____ WEEK OF: _____ 19____

SUBJECT	ACTIVITIES
BIBLE	
MATH	
SCIENCE	
GRAMMAR	
VOCABULARY/SPELLING	
LITERATURE	
COMPOSITION	
HISTORY/GEOGRAPHY CIVICS/ECONOMICS CURRENT EVENTS	
FOREIGN LANGUAGE	
PHYSICAL EDUCATION	
FINE ARTS	
ELECTIVES	
WORK EXPERIENCE	

CHART I